PREFACE

Welcome to Abaco! Great Abaco Island and its cays form one of the largest bodies of sem... It is a perfect cruising ground for small boats—power or sail—from 14 to over 50 feet. Harbours ... the water is shallow, it is almost always possible to anchor. Miles of secluded beaches can be found ... offer excellent restaurants, marinas, and other services. The people of Abaco are friendly and help... their best to make your visit a pleasant one. Enjoy the beautiful waters, beaches, and people of Abaco, but please remember to respect the privacy of the Abaconians as well as the fragile physical environment in order to save both for future generations.

This is the twenty-fourth annual edition of this cruising guide; it covers from Walker's Cay in the north to Hole-in-the-Wall and Sandy Point in the south. We have continued the process of updating and improving our charts. We regularly re-survey various volatile areas, and check places where readers have reported problems. *Chelsea*, our hydrographic research boat, is equipped with an on-board computer system built by Jeff Dodge linked to a Garmin 545S. We use Garmin, Fugawi, and Coastal Explorer software, our own digital charts, and our own proprietary hydrographic data system.

This year we have updated seventeen of our charts and added three new ones. We have added a "symbol" (light yellow area along coastline) to designate beaches on many of our medium to large scale charts; this should assist in visually identifying land masses and therefore should make visual navigation easier. We believe our charts are the best available for Abaco, and we have worked hard to make this cruising guide as easy to use as possible. We hope its method of organization helps you to pilot your way through Abaco efficiently and safely, and that you will be able to locate needed information quickly. In general, the book is organized in a clockwise fashion, beginning in Florida with the "Approaches to Abaco" chart, moving east to Grand Bahama Island, then to Walker's Cay in northwest Abaco and moving down the Abaco chain of cays to the southeast, to Hole-in-the-Wall, to North Eleuthera and then back toward Florida with Bimini.

Our system of waypoints and courselines optimizes the advantages of using GPS for navigation, making cruising the Abaco islands and cays easier than ever before. The waypoints and course lines have been carefully placed to keep boats in water 6' MLW or deeper—except in a few cases where course lines cross areas about 5' MLW. These are clearly marked on the charts. Thousands of boats have used our waypoint system successfully. It makes transit of areas safer and more secure, especially when visibility is limited by rain or a course directly toward the sun. All should remember that GPS is a navigational aid—it is not a substitute for watching where you are going with a sharp eye. If you are uncertain of where you are, stop the boat and clarify before continuing. Use of our system certainly does not preclude exploration and gunkholing—two of the joys and rewards of cruising in Abaco.

We have had a lot of help in collecting information for this edition of *The Cruising Guide to Abaco, Bahamas*. We thank all those who have made suggestions for improvements as well as those who have pointed out our mistakes. We especially thank Mr. Jeremie Saunders of the Department of Marine Resources, who provided information regarding the new Marine Preserves at Noname and Crab Cays. Finally, we again express special appreciation to the Lands and Surveys Department of the Government of The Bahamas, and the National Oceanic and Atmospheric Administration of the United States Government.

This book is published by White Sound Press, a small family-owned publishing company. Our website is **www.wspress.com**. We invite you to visit it. The site includes a secure ordering system for all of our publications and links to several weather sites.

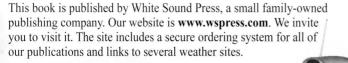

Important Note Regarding Charts

Despite the fact that we have been diligent and used the latest available technology to make our charts accurate, our survey was not uniform—some areas received more attention than others. Therefore, the accuracy of the charts varies somewhat. This, combined with shifting sand bars, and possible errors made in transcribing the data, make it necessary for us to remind all users that the prudent navigator will never rely solely on only one source of information. The author and publisher disclaim all liability for any errors or omissions. The author and publisher disclaim all warranties, expressed or implied, as to the quality, merchantability or fitness of this book and its charts for any particular purpose. There is no substitute for a sharp lookout on any boat to avoid possible hazards and dangers. All depths are given in feet at Mean Lower Low Water (MLLW).

Because Mean Lower Low Water is the average of lower low tides, all should be aware that the water will be more shallow on spring low tides (full moon and new moon) than the charts indicate. Tide times and heights calculated by the United States National Ocean Survey can be found in the tide tables on pages 201-204. All course headings are given in magnetic, but true north is up on all charts. The charts and waypoints are all based on WGS84 map datum, and users should be certain their receivers are set accordingly. The termination of selective availability by the United States government and the advent of WAAS (Wide Area Augmentation System) has made GPS more accurate and more reliable, but all navigators should remember to trust their eyes and not over-rely on any single source of information or aide to navigation.

Duchess of Hope Town, Steve Marinak's Bertram 31 off Tilloo Cay, 6 July 2012. Photo by Steve Dodge.

Table of Contents

Grand Cays
34-35

122

Hope Town

163-170

Dive Charts

Tahiti Beach, Elbow Cay, and Tilloo Cut, 7 July 2012

Additional copies of this cruising guide may be ordered from White Sound Press, 379 Wild Orange Drive, New Smyrna Beach, Florida 32168 USA. Phone: 386 423-7880 Fax: 386 423-7557. All our publications may be ordered on the web at www.wspress.com. E-Mail: orders@wspress.com.

ISBN 978 0932265913

Front Cover: Two Boats at Guana Cay reef with the NW tip of Guana Cay, 30 June, 2012. Photo by Steve Dodge.

Abaco Portfolio

A head at Fowl Cay Reef on a quiet day with 7 boats and 11 snorkelers on this head and 2 more on another head behind it. The crystal clear water allows shadows of the boats on the bottom in about 15-20' water. See the Snorkeling/Diving chart of this reef on page 169. Photo by Steve Dodge, 30 June 2012.

Two Boats anchored near the edge of the reef and bank at Fowl Cay Reef; photo taken from the SE. The deeper ocean water is a deep blue. Note the seven boats at the smaller round head in the background. These are shown in the photo on the facing page taken from the N. Beyond them lies Scotland Cay and Great Guana Cay. See the Snorkeling/Diving chart of Fowl Cay Reef on page 169 Photo by Steve Dodge, 30 June2012. Snorkeling/Diving chart of this reef on page 169. Photo by Steve Dodge, 30 June 2012.

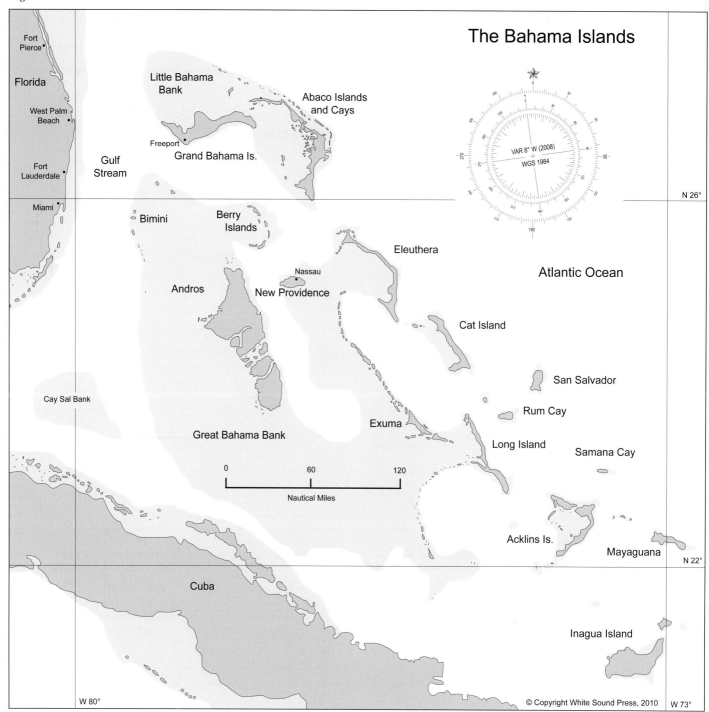

The Bahama Islands

VAR 8° W (2008)
WGS 1984

Florida

Fort Pierce

West Palm Beach

Fort Lauderdale

Miami

Gulf Stream

Little Bahama Bank

Freeport

Grand Bahama Is.

Abaco Islands and Cays

Bimini

Berry Islands

Nassau

New Providence

Andros

Eleuthera

Atlantic Ocean

N 26°

Cat Island

San Salvador

Rum Cay

Cay Sal Bank

Great Bahama Bank

Exuma

Long Island

Samana Cay

0   60   120

Nautical Miles

Acklins Is.

Mayaguana

N 22°

Cuba

Inagua Island

W 80°

© Copyright White Sound Press, 2010

W 73°

ABACO AND THE BAHAMAS

The Bahama Islands are located east and southeast of South Florida and stretch about 550 miles toward Cuba and Hispaniola. They consist of 29 islands, 661 cays and 2387 rocks, according to an official count made for Governor Rawson W. Rawson's report in 1864. We do not know if anyone has tried to count since then. Most of the Bahamian islands are located on banks—very unique geologic structures which rise thousands of feet from the deep ocean floor and have only 10-40 feet of water over their flat tops. They are huge underwater plateaus with higher areas which protrude above the ocean's surface to form the islands. The principal banks are Little Bahama Bank in the northwest Bahamas, and Great Bahama Bank in the central Bahamas.

The population of the islands is about 330,000. Almost 69% of the people live in Nassau, the capital, located on New Providence Island. Freeport, located on Grand Bahama Island, is the second largest city in the country and Marsh Harbour, Abaco, is the third largest. Most Bahamians are of West African descent; the 15% of the population which is white descend from emigrants from Bermuda during the 1600s, and British Loyalists who left the United States shortly after independence, many of whom settled in Abaco. Beginning during the late twentieth century and extending to the present, a significant number of Haitians have migrated to The Bahamas. The islands were a British colony until 1973; since then they have been an independent member of the British Commonwealth with a parliamentary democratic system of government. Abaco is located at the northern end of the island chain. According to Gov. Rawson, Abaco includes 2 islands, 82 cays and 208 rocks. The population is probably about 15,000.

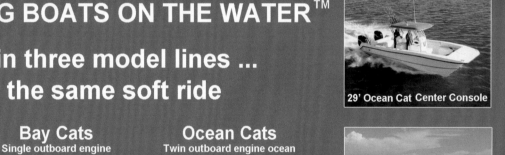

MORE ON THE HORIZON

GARMIN MARINE 2012.

All kinds of mariners, saltwater and fresh, have come to expect more with Garmin marine products. More power. More performance. More value. Satisfying their expectations is what helped us become the industry leader in color touchscreen chartplotters. It's why we made sure our new GSD 24 and GSD 26 digital network sounders set the highest performance standards for noise suppression and clarity. Why we brought full-featured autopilot technology to sailboats and powerboats. And the GDL 40 that delivers low-cost on-demand graphical weather information. In fact, our entire marine lineup from HD and xHD radars; to integrated VHF communications and satellite weather solutions; to our growing array of NMEA 2000® instruments and networking options; plus, our Garmin echo™ series fishfinders with exclusive Garmin HD-ID™ tracking technology; every product innovation is designed to meet or exceed customer expectations. And that's just what's available right now. Wait 'til you see what we have just beyond the horizon.

NAVIGATION IN ABACO

The Global Positioning System (GPS) is clearly the most significant improvement in navigation made during the twentieth century. It is truly amazing that a handheld electronic device costing $100-$200 can tell you where you are, where you wish to go, and how long it will take you to get there. No boat should go to the Bahamas without a GPS receiver. The advent of differential GPS a few years ago made it more accurate for those who purchased differential beacon receivers. The end of selective availability (the intentional de-grading of the signal by the United States Department of Defense) in May 2000 has made GPS more accurate for all users. The Wide Area Augmentation System (WAAS) receivers, which became available in 2001 at very reasonable prices, regularly provide accuracy within 10-20'.

This cruising guide maximizes the advantages of GPS and the benefits it can provide. We offer a system of waypoints rather than random waypoints outside each harbour. We have refined the system over the years; we hope you find it practical and enjoyable. Except where noted, the continuous courselines connecting the waypoints are at least 6' deep at Mean Low Water (MLW) and free of obstructions (please note that **discontinuous courselines are for small boats** and generally carry only about 3' MLW). See pages 201-203 for tide tables for Abaco during 2013 (and page 204 for a tide table for Dec., 2012).

While GPS is a wonderful navigational aide, the prudent mariner will not over-rely on it or any other single aide to navigation. Eyeball navigation and the use of the magnetic compass can confirm the information provided by GPS and vice versa. Cruisers visiting the Bahamas will quickly learn to know the approximate depth of the water on the basis of water color—which ranges from dark blue for deep ocean water, to medium blues, teals and greens in 10-25' over sand, to pale blues and greens in shallow water over sand (4'-10') and white in 1'-3'. Coral heads are brown, as are rocky bars—both should be avoided. It is important to learn how to determine water depth based on colour because there is no better navigational device than your eyes, but some persons have greater color sensitivity than others and read the depth better than others. No one can do it going into the sun, in the middle of a rain squall, or at dusk, or at night. All mariners should try to maximize the advantages of all available aides to navigation.

To best utilize our GPS system set your GPS datum to WGS 1984, utilize routes rather than "go to," pay close attention to cross track error by utilizing the appropriate screen (or "page") on your receiver, be aware that older non-WAAS receivers are not as accurate as a WAAS unit, and use your eyes and your compass to confirm or question what your GPS tells you. If you are unsure of where you are, stop and figure it out before proceeding.

The depth of the water can be determined by colour. This generally requires good sunlight. Photo taken at Tahiti Beach, Elbow Cay, summer 2001.

Complex sand banks can be built by strong tidal current flows through openings between cays (called cuts or passages in Abaco and often inlets in the US) along the edge of the bank. These areas are usually volatile because storms combined with strong current flows can move tons of sand in just a few hours. This is the cut between Top Cay and Jacks Cay in the Carter Cays area. A single boat has found a private and serene anchorage here. Photo by Steve Dodge, 27 May 2011

WEATHER & WEATHER REPORTS

Abaco is within the trade wind belt, so most of its weather is the result of the prevailing easterly winds. In the winter they tend to be easterly or northeasterly, and in the summer easterly or southeasterly. Winter winds are usually a few knots stronger than the summer winds, which average 5-10 knots.

This easterly pattern is disturbed in the winter by outbreaks of cool continental air from the United States. These cold fronts are preceded by wind from the southwest. When the front passes, the wind shifts to the west or northwest and often blows hard (20-25 knots is common). Most cool fronts are dry, and the temperature dips to about 58 degrees. The wind eventually clocks to the northeast after the frontal passage; this process sometimes takes a couple of hours—more often a couple of days.

In the summer the usual 5-10 knot southeast breeze is sometimes disturbed by afternoon thunderstorms which build over the land mass of Great Abaco Island during the day. These storms sometimes meander against the prevailing southeast breeze and move from Abaco out to the cays. They have plenty of lightning and thunder, and lots of water, but the high winds are usually short-lived. The summer weather pattern may also be disturbed by a low pressure trough in the prevailing easterlies. These bring higher winds, overcast skies, and showers. If the winds in a trough (sometimes also called a wave) begin circular movement and reach 33 knots, the trough becomes a tropical storm. If the winds reach 64 knots, it becomes a hurricane. Hurricane season throughout the tropics extends from 1 June to 1 December.

There are a number of excellent weather forecasts available in the Abacos. The cruiser's net on channel 68 at 0815 features an excellent weather report and prediction based on data collected from several sources. Gulf Stream crossing predictions are also provided. Silbert Mills of Radio Abaco (FM 93.5) gives a complete report at 0700, 0800 and again as part of the evening news at 1800. In addition, Bahamian AM radio weather reports can be heard on ZNS Nassau (1540 kHz) at 0735 and 0755 (summary) and ZNS Freeport (810 kHz). The NOAA Wx forecasts can sometimes be heard on VHF Wx channels 1, 2, or 3 if a good antenna is available. These are continuous and give Florida coastal reports and prognoses. Also, some cruisers regularly share their information and knowledge regarding the weather; listen on VHF 16 for announcements regarding the working channel which will be used.

Weather information is available almost 24 hours a day for those with short wave radios. The Waterway Radio and Cruising Club gives a report each day at 0745 on 7.268 MHz. This includes the Bahamas, SW North Atlantic, the Florida coast, and the Gulf of Mexico. All are welcome to listen, and hams with general class licenses or higher may join in if they have their Bahamas reciprocal licenses. For more frequent reports listen to NMN, WLO, or WOM; schedules are as follows:

NMN - Coast Guard, Portsmouth, Virginia				
Time (UTC)*	4426	6501	8764	13089	17314
0400, 0530, 1000	x	x	x		
1130, 1600	x	x	x		
1730				x	x
2200, 2330		x	x	x	

WLO - Mobile, Alabama				
Eastern Time	4369	8806	13152	17362	22804
0100, 0700, 1300, and 1900	x	x	x	x	x

*UTC is Coordinated Universal Time. Eastern Standard Time is 5 hours behind UTC and Eastern Daylight Time is 4 hours behind UTC.

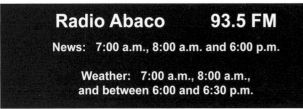

Radio Abaco   93.5 FM

News: 7:00 a.m., 8:00 a.m. and 6:00 p.m.

Weather: 7:00 a.m., 8:00 a.m., and between 6:00 and 6:30 p.m.

Thunderstorm over northern Abaco on 18 June 2001. During the summer months the heat buildup from the sunlight on the land causes moist air to warm and rise. As it rises it is cooled by the lower termperature air aloft. When it cools its volume is reduced, and with that, its capacity to hold moisture. Clouds form and rain occurs. June is usually the wettest month of the year in Abaco, with most of the rain coming from afternoon thunderstorms such as the one shown here. This photo was taken by an astronaut from an altitude of 202 nautical miles. "Image courtesy of Earth Sciences and Image Analysis Laboratory, NASA Johnson Space Center."

A large portion of The Bahamas on 23 April 2009. A cool front had moved through the northern and central Bahamas and clear dry air provides an excellent view of the banks and islands. The cloud cover in the southeastern portion of the photo is forward of the front. Photo courtesy of National Aeronautics and Space Administration.

WEATHER SITES ON THE WEB AND CROSSING THE GULF STREAM
by Harry Weldon

When planning a crossing of the Gulf Stream in a small boat, wind speed and direction are probably the most important factors in deciding when to cross. I look for 10-15 or less and no northerly component in the wind. The Web can be an excellent source of information; the following are a few of the sites I use for gathering information useful in planning a crossing:

http://www.barometerbob.com Provides detailed weather reports on the Cruiser's Net each morning (VHF68, 8:15 am), and posts the reports and predictions on this web site. Provides specific reports for crossing the Gulf Stream, and for boats going south or north from Abaco.

http://www.hpc.ncep.noaa.gov/ (Hydrometeorological Prediction Center) This is a good site for a broad overview of weather patterns showing fronts and spacing of isobars. What you really want to find is a nice fat high-pressure dome sitting right on top of the Northern Bahamas and Florida with isobars spaced wide apart. This is fairly common in the summer months. With all of the prediction models, I look for consistency in the prediction as it moves from the three or four day to the 24-hour prediction. This doesn't happen all that often but when it does you can sometimes find a window in an otherwise lousy bit of weather.

http://adds.aviationweather.noaa.gov/winds/ I look at this site several times a day even when I'm not crossing. Here you will find current surface wind conditions and predictions to about 48 hours out. The 0 to 12-hour forecast are updated every three hours, the rest are updated twice a day at 0 and 1200 UTC.

http://ruc.noaa.gov/pig.cgi?13km_oper

Link to the Rapid Update Cycle (RUC) website. Lots of information here with forecast out 18 or 24 hours. Can cross check the surface winds with ADDS.

http://www.ndbc.noaa.gov/station_page.php?station=lkwf1 Reports conditions at Lake Worth, Florida.

http://www.ndbc.noaa.gov/station_page.php?station=SPGF1 Reports conditions at Settlement Point, Grand Bahama.

http://www.ndbc.noaa.gov/data/Forecasts/FZUS52.KMFL.html The NOAA text forecast. While not always the most reliable, this is a good check of the others.

http://radar.weather.gov/radar.php?product=N0Z&rid=amx&loop=yes Radar which shows precipitation out to the East side of Great Abaco Island.

http://www.wunderground.com/weatherstation/WXDailyHistory.asp?ID=IABACOEL1 White Sound, Elbow Cay (Rocky Bay) daily / monthly / yearly weather graphs. Another use for this link and the following one is to keep tabs on BEC outages. Flat line data normally means that power / internet is down at the site location.

http://www.rockybay.com/weather/ Links to a multitude of weather sites. For the best satellite view of Abaco use the above link and choose "FLORIDA NEXSAT" — the actual link is much too long to print or type.

On all of the weather sites, be sure to look at the date/time stamp and reload often.

Safe crossing.

* Hotlinks to these sites are available on the White Sound Press website (www.wspress.com) and on www.rockybay.com.
** Additional information concerning crossing the Gulf Stream can be found in the article on page 23.

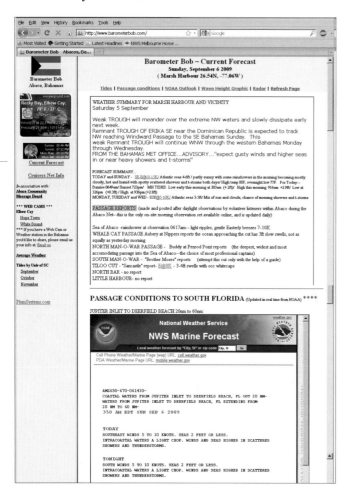

Selected portions of the home page at www.barometerbob.com for 6 September 2009 show the comprehensive weather information which is posted on this page on a daily basis. There are links to webcams at White Sound and Hope Town on Elbow Cay. A text version of the forecast, which is broadcast on the Cruiser's Net at 0815 each morning, is posted on the site each morning. Also, the Cruiser's Net is recorded each morning and is available on the Internet (after about 9:30 am) at www.abacoinet.com. Click on Audio Services and then Cruiser's Net.

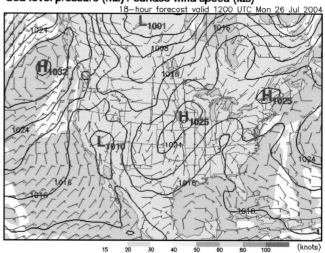

Three day wind forecasts at various altitudes are available at http://adds.aviationweather.noaa.gov/winds/. Intended for use by aviators, the surface wind map will be of greatest interest to mariners. The symbols are called "wind barbs." The plain end of the line shows the direction of flow. The "barbs" at the other end of the line indicate wind strength, Short barbs represent 5 knots and long barbs represent 10 knots, so the symbol ↘ indicates SE wind (flowing to the NW) of 15 knots.

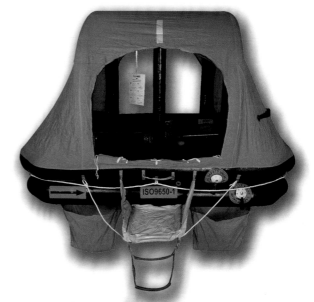

RADAR AND SATELLITE WEATHER

The availability of up to date weather information has made boating safer.   The widespread availability of internet access has made checking weather while planning your trip possible, even while in the islands. For most, this will be adequate.

For those who want real time weather information on board there are two principal options—on board radar and XM weather (WXWorx). On board radar has historically been extremely expensive, but new add-on digital radar which connect to a gps chartplotter display have become quite reasonable.   Garmin offers GMR 18 and GMR 18HD 18" radomes for $1000 and $1200 retail prices respectively.   The least expensive currently available head unit is the GPSMap 720S with a SRP of $1600.

XM weather broadcasts radar images from National Weather Service radar systems via satellite to surface receivers as a commercial service. An advantage is that the user gets the "big picture" available from the Weather Service's high powered doppler radar systems. The disadvantages are that the local picture for the vessel's location will be in smaller scale, and there are subscriber fees for the service. Garmin offers the GXM 51 XM weather receiver for $600. It will interface with a wide array of garmin's GPSMap products, including the $400 Gpsmap 421. WXWorx makes a hardware receiver which will connect to a computer by usb, serial, or ethernet for $830.00. Software is not included. The Least expensive bundle with software, antenna and receiver with usb interface lists for $1,182.   Subscriptions for XM Weather range from $10 - $50 / mo depending upon the service level desired.

Sirius from Atlantic Beach, Florida, anchored at Tilloo Cay for the night on 17 July 2008. Photo by Steve Dodge.

OBSERVATIONS RE: PASSAGES BETWEEN THE SEA OF ABACO AND THE ATLANTIC OCEAN

All passages between the Sea of Abaco and the Atlantic Ocean are at times impassable due to breaking seas. This condition is locally known as a "rage sea." These are not always the result of high winds; they may also be caused by ocean swells generated by far-away Atlantic storms. Some passages may be better than others in certain wind conditions. For example, Jane and Newell Garfield once reported that North Bar Channel, which is used by the mailboat and generally considered to be one of the best and safest passages, was not passable during several days. A rage sea was the result of a strong northeaster. But the passage at Little Harbour, just four miles to the south, was viable because of some protection provided by a protruding reef. The best passage on any particular day depends on wind direction and strength, on the orientation of the passage, and on tidal current—it is almost always much better to transit the passages on a rising tide with current flowing from the Atlantic Ocean to the Sea of Abaco. One should note that Little Harbour, North Bar Channel, and Tilloo Cut generally face east, whereas all passages north of Tilloo Cut generally face northeast.

Also, everyone should be aware that there is another way of getting from Eleuthera or Exuma or Nassau into Abaco Sound. Tom and Sue Dickes were holed up at Eleuthera waiting to get to Abaco with a strong northeaster which they knew would make entering the Sea of Abaco treacherous. Instead of waiting, they sailed around the west side of Abaco, around Little Abaco Island, and around Crab Cay. It added some miles, but the sailing was good and they avoided negotiating a breaking or near breaking inlet. They arrived at Green Turtle Cay while some boats were still waiting for a break in the weather to leave Spanish Wells.

Tilloo Cut on a typical summer day, and Tilloo Cut on 17 September 2003. The rage seas were caused by the passage of hurricane Isabel a couple of hundred miles offshore. Reports on conditions in the passages between the Atlantic Ocean and the Sea of Abaco are given on the Cruisers Net (0815/VHF 68) each morning.

photo by Justin Noice

ANCHORING, ANCHOR LIGHTS, AND POWER CABLES

The Bahamas functions under International Rules of the Road (rather than the U. S. Inland Rules), and under these rules there is no such thing as a "designated anchorage." All boats are therefore required by law to show a 32-point anchor light visible for 2 miles from sundown to sunup. However, even the most casual observer will soon notice that there are many boats moored or anchored on a long-term storage basis in many of Abaco's harbours which show no anchor light, so it has become common practice to anchor in harbours without showing a light. It is very important that this practice, which is still illegal, not be extended to areas outside harbours. No one should conclude that because there is an anchor in a certain place on a chart, that the spot is a designated anchorage. Remember, there are no designated anchorages in the Bahamas. All boats anchoring outside of harbours must show an anchor light. To do otherwise is to foolishly risk damage and injury to one's own boat and crew, to endanger the property and lives of others, and to break the law.

Also, when anchoring outside of harbours try to avoid the most direct access routes to those harbours as well as the high voltage electrical cables. Check the large scale harbour charts for approximate locations.

If you should accidentally snag a power line with your anchor, you will probably not be able to raise the anchor, and therefore you will not be certain of what you have snagged. But if it is in or near the power cable area, assume you have snagged a cable, and do not try to free it. The power cables carry 13,200 volts. Attempts to raise the anchor may well result in a disastrous electrical shock or in severing the power cable which supplies electricity to hundreds of people, or in both. The best thing to do is to buoy the rode, leave it there, and call Bahamas Electricity Corporation at 367-2740. They will arrange for the return of your anchor to you.

Sometimes one anchor is enough, and sometimes it is best to use two. One is almost always adequate for daytime anchoring, or for anchoring in protected areas in settled weather. If the passage of a cool front is expected before morning, it is usually best to set a second anchor off to the west or northwest about 90° from the first (the wind often blows SW before a frontal passage). When anchoring in an area of strong tidal flows, the boat will lie to the current rather than the wind, and the current will reverse direction 180° about every six hours. This reversal could result in pulling the anchor out backwards, and it may not reset easily. In this situation a Bahamian Moor is desirable. Two anchors are set—one "upstream" and one "downstream"—with the boat inbetween. Both anchors are secured at the bow, allowing the boat to swing to current and wind.

LEGAL ENTRY - CUSTOMS AND IMMIGRATION

Boats entering the Bahamas are required to clear customs and immigration as soon as it is practical by going to a Port of Entry. If the first landfall is not a Port of Entry, going ashore is not allowed, and the vessel should proceed to a Port of Entry. The yellow quarantine flag (a yellow rectangle) should be flown to indicate that the boat has not yet cleared. Convenient Ports of Entry for boats traveling from the United States to Abaco include: West End and Port Lucaya on Grand Bahama, Bimini, Nassau, and Walker's Cay, Spanish Cay, Green Turtle Cay, Treasure Cay and Marsh Harbour in Abaco. Clearance must be first priority—before re-fueling, lunch or shopping. Only the captain is allowed to leave the boat until the paperwork is completed. Required documents include the boat's registration certificate and passports for all United States citizens on board. Citizens of other countries may need to apply for a visa in advance of entry and should check with an appropriate Bahamian embassy before departure for the Bahamas. Import permits are required for pets; they are available for $10. (call to verify current amount) from the Director of Agriculture, P. O. N-3704, Nassau, Bahamas (242 325-7502). Firearms must be accompanied by a valid permit, and must be kept under lock and key while in the Bahamas. The fee schedule was revised beginning in July 2003 and is now a flat $150 (cash only) for a twelve-month cruising permit, fishing permit and departure taxes (paid in advance) for up to four persons for boats up to 35 feet. The fee for boats over 35' is $300. The fee for tenders over 18' is $150. One exit and re-entry is permitted within 90 days of the original entry without payment of a second fee. Several forms must be completed; the officials are usually pleased to be helpful in this regard. After clearing, foreign boats should fly the Bahamian courtesy flag (ensign) from the starboard spreader or nearest equivalent.

FISHING AND DIVING REGULATIONS

1. Foreign vessels must obtain a sportfishing permit. These are now provided when foreign vessels clear into The Bahamas and the cost is included in the flat fee. Foreign fishermen may fish from a Bahamian rental boat without a permit; the boat rather than a fisherman receives the permit. Each vessel shall have no more than six (6) rods/reels in use at one time unless the operator is in possession of a permit authorizing the use of more rods/reels.

2. Use of any spear or net (other than landing net) must be endorsed in writing on a fishing permit. Spear guns of any type are illegal in the Bahamas. Pole spears and Hawaiian slings used while free diving are legal, but only with the proper permit. It is illegal to spear within 200 yards of any shore. No underwater air supply may be used while spearing fish.

3. Pelican Cays Land and Sea National Park (Sandy Cay Reef) and Fowl Cay Preserve are restricted areas. No spearing, fishing or shelling of any kind is permitted within the boundaries of either of these parks.

Boat Bag Limits and Closed Seasons:
Billfish- Must be released (some exceptions for tournaments)
Migratory Fish (King, Dolphin, Tuna, Wahoo)- Boat limit- 18
Dermersal fish (Groupers, Snappers, etc.)- Boat limit- 20 fish or 60 lbs.; no Grouper or Rockfish under 3 lbs.; three month closed season for Nassau Grouper 1 Dec-28/29 Feb.
Crawfish- Boat limit- 10; at least 3 5/8" carapace or 6" tail; no females with eggs (red berries under tail) may be taken; Season closed 1 April - 31 July.
Conch- Boat limit- 6; adults only (well-formed flared lip).
Turtle- prohibited
Live coral, Sea Fans, Starfish - prohibited

Note: All cruisers should be aware that the Government of The Bahamas is very serious about enforcing its fishing and diving regulations, and that stiff penalties may be imposed for simple possession of out-of-season, undersized, or prohibited items, even if they were purchased from Bahamian fishermen. Visitors may legally purchase fish from Bahamians, but should have documented receipts and invoices to clarify the origin of any fish above their bag limit. Closed season for grouper may be adjusted as more is learned about the Grouper's reproductive cycle.

VHF RADIO TIPS AND COURTESY

Channel 16 is a calling channel only; switch to a working channel after establishing contact. Wait for a quiet space before trying to establish contact. Channel 68 is now also used as a calling channel in Abaco for cruisers, with channel 16 reserved for making contact with local marinas and restaurants, and for emergencies. Do not give the USA call—it is time consuming and unnecessary. Simply give the call name of the party you wish to contact, repeat it, then give your call name. Example: Falusi, Falusi, Sand Dollar.

Wait a second after pressing the microphone button before speaking so your first word(s) will not be cut off; give the electrons a chance. Some VHF radios require that the "SELECT" button be pressed before the radio can be switched to another channel.

Do not use the following channels for non-emergency conversations; they are reserved for the following specified purposes:
06- local taxis
16- Emergencies/local businesses/calling channel
22A- BASRA (Bahamas Air Sea Rescue) / Coast Guard
65- Dolphin research
66- Port operations
68- Cruising boat calling channel
70- Digital selective calling
71- Fishing tournaments (February - July)
72- Hope Town Fire Rescue (working channel only; call on 16)
78- Abaco Regatta (4-12 July only)
80- Marsh Harbour Emergency Services (medical, fire, police)

If you are confronted by an emergency which threatens you or your vessel with grave and immediate danger, call **Mayday on channel 16**. Do not use Mayday unless you or your vessel are threatened with grave and immediate danger, and you wish to request immediate assistance. Call Mayday 3 times, give the name of your vessel and its position as accurately as possible, state the problem and the number of people on board, and describe the boat. Then repeat the entire message, and then allow time for a response. If there is no response, say everything over again. **Do not transfer to channel 22A until you are told to do so**. If you hear a Mayday call, listen. Write the information. Do not broadcast unless it is determined that you are in the best position to render assistance. If you are unable to provide assistance and no one else has acknowledged the Mayday, you must relay the Mayday by announcing Mayday Relay 3 times and repeating the information. **Please remember to broadcast your Mayday on 16, not on 22A; the latter is a working channel only and is not monitored 24 hours a day.** Also, be aware that the U.S. Coast Guard cannot hear broadcasts from Abaco on VHF; Bahamas Air Sea Rescue (BASRA), a volunteer organization, executes search and rescue in Abaco.

If you are confronted by a situation which jeapardizes the safety of a person or your vessel which is not life-threatening, call a Pan-Pan (pronounced pahn-pahn) rather than a Mayday on channel 16. Use the same general procedure outlined above for the Mayday, repeating Pan-Pan three times, giving the name of your vessel and its position, and explain the problem.

If you have called either a Mayday or a Pan-Pan and then find that you no longer require assistance, announce the cancellation several times on channel 16 so that search and rescue or assistance efforts can be cancelled.

Remember that your vessel's VHF radio is your most valuable source of assistance in any emergency. Ensure that **every** member of your crew knows how to use it and how to call for help. It should always be in good operating condition.

CELL PHONES

The Bahamas Telecommunications Company Ltd. (BTC) introduced GSM cell phone service in Abaco during fall 2006. GSM (Global System for Mobile Communications) is the most popular standard for mobile phones in the world—it is in use in more than 200 countries. This will make it easier for visitors from the United States to use their GSM phones in Abaco.

Those who visit for short periods carrying their GSM phones from the US (AT&T and T-Mobile are GSM) will find that automatic roaming is much more likely to work than in the past. Our Florida-based AT&T phones work immediately. The rate is $1.50/minute.

Visitors who stay in The Bahamas for extended periods are now able to establish accounts with BTC and acquire a BTC SIM card to insert in their US GSM phone. The SIM (Subscriber Identity Module) card enables them to utilize the BTC system directly rather than through roaming. SIM cards can be purchased at Caribbean Mobile Distributors or Island Care Wireless in Marsh Harbour at very reasonable prices.

BTC lists both pre-paid and post-paid (standard monthly billed service) on their website. As of September 2012 their pre-paid price was: $0.33/min peak (7am-7pm); $0.15/min off-peak (7pm-7am); and $0.20/min weekend. Calls to the US were historically $0.50/min but are not currently published. We think they are the same, but of course all rates are subject to change. BTC has recently added data plans for prepaid wireless: 1 day for $3., 7 days for $10. and 30 days for $30. Visit www.btcbahamas.com for current prepaid rates and information on standard monthly cell-phone service.

Unfortunately, even if you have your own GSM Telephone, the transition to the BTC SIM may not be without difficulty. You must ensure that your handset is not "provider" or "subsidy" locked. The easiest way to test this is to try a SIM card from a competing provider. If your phone is locked and you have an account in good standing and have had it for more than 3 months—AT&T should provide you with the unlock code for your phone. Other providers may do the same. Obtaining the unlock code for my AT&T handset took just over 3 weeks. It is possible to purchase unlocked phones in the US or Marsh Harbour, and some businesses in Marsh Harbour can unlock locked cell phones.

EPIRBs and SPOT

Crossing the Gulf Stream in a small boat is a lot different than cruising a few miles up the Intracoastal for lunch and a swim. Help is not readily available in the middle of the stream; on several of our crossings we did not see a single other vessel. Engines and other equipment should be thoroughly checked before departure to avoid breakdowns—belts, hoses, battery cables, etc. should all be in top notch condition. All through-hull fittings and their hoses and clamps should be in sound condition. Life preservers should be readily available to all on board, and a ditch bag should be prepared and be accessible. If a dinghy or life raft is carried, there should be a plan for deployment in an emergency, and in the unlikely event that the vessel sinks, calling for help will be very important.

If there is time before leaving the vessel, call 'May Day" on the VHF radio on channel 16; if there is no time, call on the portable VHF which should be in the ditch bag. Know your position so you can tell potential rescuers where to find you. Nearby vessels may respond and be your best chance for timely assistance, and the Coast Guard monitors channel 16 with large antennas and powerful receivers on the Florida coast.

406 EPIRBs broadcast distress signals which include your latitude, longitude, and boat identification to a constellation of satellites which relay the data to a central clearing office which verifies it and then dispatches rescuers. 406 EPIRBS are readily available at most marine stores.

Another device which can summon assistance is the SPOT by Globalstar. This pocket size device has an SOS button which, when pressed, sends a message to a different constellation of satellites which is then relayed to the Coast Guard. A very interesting feature of the SPOT is that in normal operation it is programmed to send your position every ten to twenty minutes to its constellation of satellites and that position is then relayed to the FindMeSpot website which your family and friends can use to monitor your progress on Google Maps.

We carry both a 406 EPIRB and a SPOT when we cross the Gulf Stream; we think it is the prudent thing to do and recommend that all who cross the stream consider carrying these emergency devices. We all hope, of course, that none of us will ever have to use them to signal distress.

BASRA and TowBoatUS

The Bahamas Air-Sea Rescue Association (BASRA) has provided emergency rescue service in the Bahamas for over 50 years. It is not a branch of the Bahamian government; it is funded by member dues and contributions. Its Abaco base is Hope Town. BASRA can be called directly on VHF, or they respond to May-Day calls. The organization is dedicated to saving lives, not salvaging or towing boats. BASRA should be called only when lives are in danger. Situations of less significance will be handed off to others who may be willing to provide help.

During the past few years TowBoat US had a base in Marsh Harbour and provided towing services to members and non-members in Abaco. Unfortunately, that service is no longer available. Vessels needing a tow will have to find a local Abaconian willing and able to help. Rainbow Rentals in Marsh Harbour has experience towing and may be able to assist, or find someone else who can assist; contact information is VHF 16 "Rainbow Rentals" or phone 242 367-4602.

Support the Bahamas Air-Sea Rescue Association.

You are not required to take an active part in BASRA.

Send $40.00 for one year's membership dues to:

BASRA ABACO
Hope Town, Abaco
Bahamas

A turtle at Albury's Sail Shop on Man-O-War Cay getting a free lunch from Richard Albury, husband to Mrs. Annie Albury. This turtle knows when Mr. Richard arrives at the dock daily when returning home from work. Photo by Steve Dodge, 10 March, 2012.

Clear water, puffy clouds and light wind for boats anchored off Green Turtle Cay, 21 May 2012. Photo by Steve Dodge.

WIRELESS INTERNET IN ABACO

Wifi in Abaco has gone from occasional to common, if not ubiquitous in settled areas. The two dominant providers in Abaco are Out Island Internet (OII) and Bahamas WiMax. Both providers have free trial options as well as captive portals for subscription or activation of a free trial. A captive portal means that the wireless provider automatically redirects all web page requests (i.e.- yahoo, google, etc.) to their own sign up / trial page. This means that by the time you're making the decision on whether to pay for the service, you've generally gotten past the hardest part of the connection—sending and recieving data from the provider's system.

For those who want to increase their chances of being able to pick up wifi, there are numerous options for high gain antenna systems. Two of the most popular are radiolabs and ubiquity networks. Radiolabs (www.radiolabs.com) specializes in usb connected systems and are a bit easier to manage for technical amateurs. Ubiquity networks (www.ubnt.com) supply mainly ethernet bridges and are more suited for fixed or semi-fixed installations. It's best to contact the provider you expect to use for up to date advice on device compatibility. That said, many people report perfectly acceptable connection performance with the built in wireless antenna on their laptops or tablets.

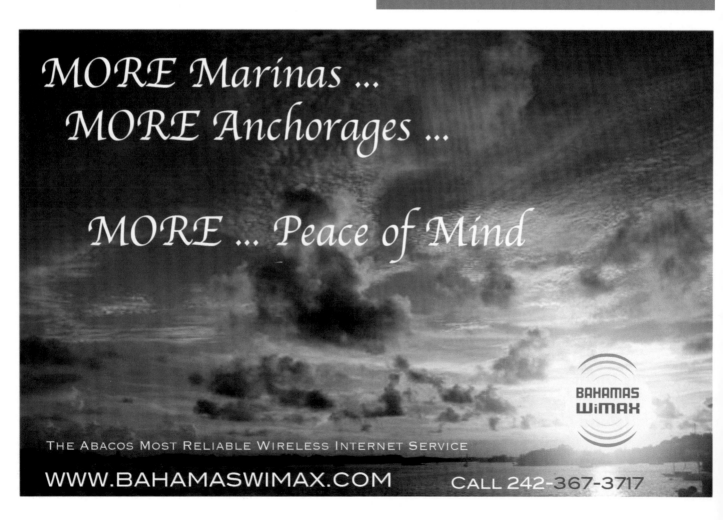

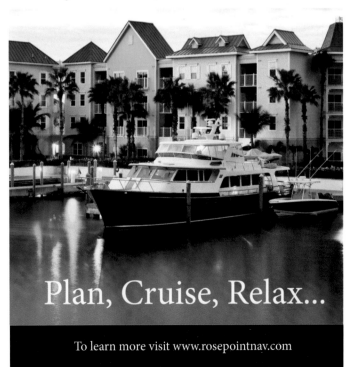

APPROACHES TO ABACO
Mercator Projection

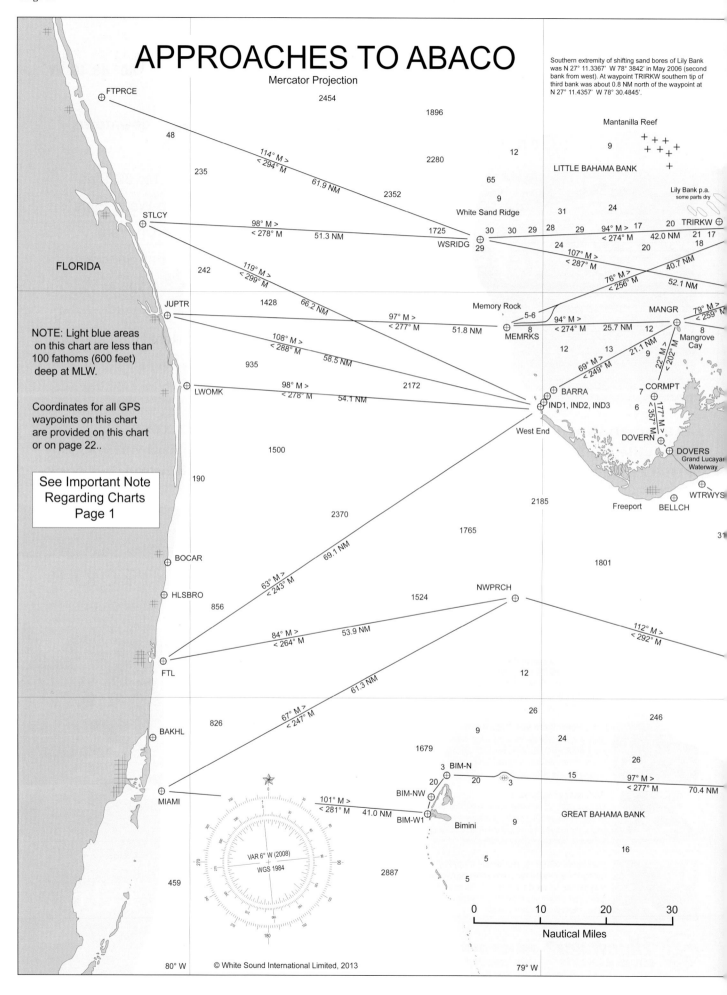

Southern extremity of shifting sand bores of Lily Bank was N 27° 11.3367' W 78° 3842' in May 2006 (second bank from west). At waypoint TRIRKW southern tip of third bank was about 0.8 NM north of the waypoint at N 27° 11.4357' W 78° 30.4845'.

FTPRCE

2454

1896

Mantanilla Reef

9

48

2280

12

LITTLE BAHAMA BANK

235

114° M >
< 294° M

61.9 NM

2352

65

9

Lily Bank p.a.
some parts dry

White Sand Ridge

31   24

STLCY

98° M >
< 278° M

51.3 NM

1725

30   30   29   28   29   94° M >   17   20   TRIRKW
< 274° M   42.0 NM   21 17

WSRIDG
29

24   20   18

FLORIDA

242

119° M >
< 299° M

107° M >
< 287° M

40.7 NM

76° M >
< 256° M

52.1 NM

NOTE: Light blue areas on this chart are less than 100 fathoms (600 feet) deep at MLW.

JUPTR

1428   66.2 NM

97° M >
< 277° M

51.8 NM

Memory Rock

5-6

94° M >
< 274° M   25.7 NM

MANGR

79° M >
< 259° M

MEMRKS   8   12   8

Mangrove Cay

108° M >
< 288° M

58.5 NM

935

12   13   21.1 NM   9

69° M >
< 249° M

22° M >
< 202° M

CORMPT

7

177° M >
< 357° M

Coordinates for all GPS waypoints on this chart are provided on this chart or on page 22..

LWOMK

98° M >
< 278° M

54.1 NM

2172

BARRA

IND1, IND2, IND3

6

West End

DOVERN

DOVERS
Grand Lucayan Waterway

See Important Note Regarding Charts Page 1

1500

190

2370

69.1 NM

2185

Freeport   BELLCH

WTRWYS

BOCAR

63° M >
< 243° M

1765

1801

31

HLSBRO

856

1524

NWPRCH

112° M >
< 292° M

84° M >
< 264° M   53.9 NM

FTL

12

61.3 NM

26

BAKHL   826

67° M >
< 247° M

246

9

24

26

1679

3   BIM-N

20   20   3   15   97° M >
< 277° M   70.4 NM

MIAMI

101° M >
< 281° M   41.0 NM

BIM-NW

BIM-W1

Bimini

9

GREAT BAHAMA BANK

459

VAR 6° W (2008)
WGS 1984

2887

5

5

16

0   10   20   30

Nautical Miles

80° W

79° W

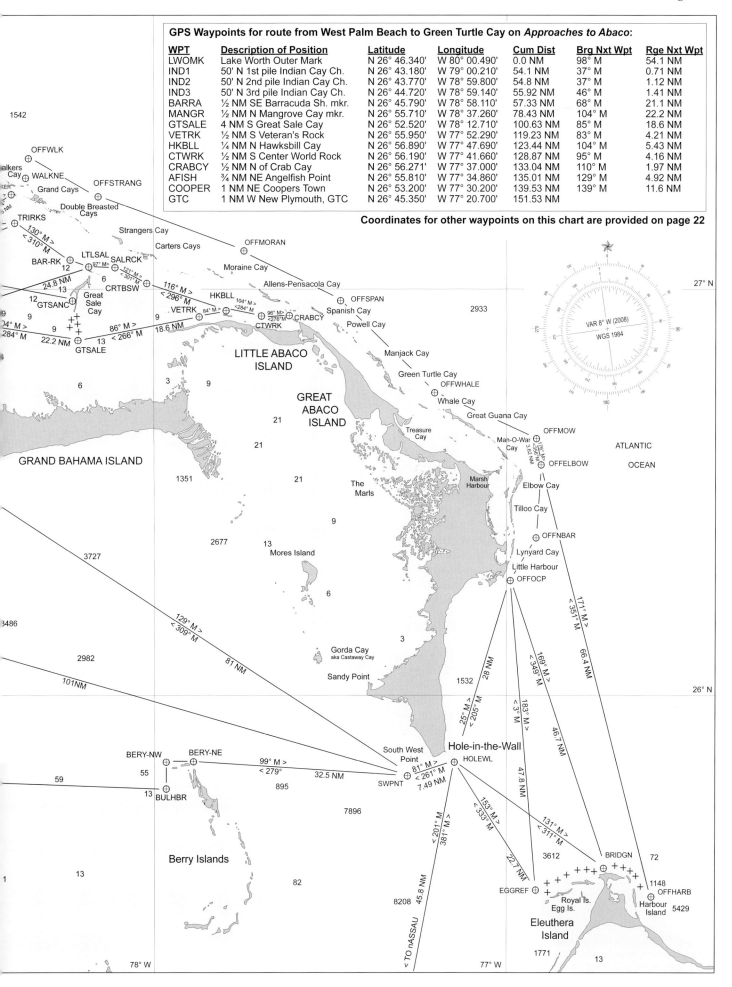

GPS Waypoints for route from West Palm Beach to Green Turtle Cay on *Approaches to Abaco*:

WPT	Description of Position	Latitude	Longitude	Cum Dist	Brg Nxt Wpt	Rge Nxt Wpt
LWOMK	Lake Worth Outer Mark	N 26° 46.340'	W 80° 00.490'	0.0 NM	98° M	54.1 NM
IND1	50' N 1st pile Indian Cay Ch.	N 26° 43.180'	W 79° 00.210'	54.1 NM	37° M	0.71 NM
IND2	50' N 2nd pile Indian Cay Ch.	N 26° 43.770'	W 78° 59.800'	54.8 NM	37° M	1.12 NM
IND3	50' N 3rd pile Indian Cay Ch.	N 26° 44.720'	W 78° 59.140'	55.92 NM	46° M	1.41 NM
BARRA	½ NM SE Barracuda Sh. mkr.	N 26° 45.790'	W 78° 58.110'	57.33 NM	68° M	21.1 NM
MANGR	½ NM N Mangrove Cay mkr.	N 26° 55.710'	W 78° 37.260'	78.43 NM	104° M	22.2 NM
GTSALE	4 NM S Great Sale Cay	N 26° 52.520'	W 78° 12.710'	100.63 NM	85° M	18.6 NM
VETRK	½ NM S Veteran's Rock	N 26° 55.950'	W 77° 52.290'	119.23 NM	83° M	4.21 NM
HKBLL	¼ NM N Hawksbill Cay	N 26° 56.890'	W 77° 47.690'	123.44 NM	104° M	5.43 NM
CTWRK	½ NM S Center World Rock	N 26° 56.190'	W 77° 41.660'	128.87 NM	95° M	4.16 NM
CRABCY	½ NM N of Crab Cay	N 26° 56.271'	W 77° 37.000'	133.04 NM	110° M	1.97 NM
AFISH	¾ NM NE Angelfish Point	N 26° 55.810'	W 77° 34.860'	135.01 NM	129° M	4.92 NM
COOPER	1 NM NE Coopers Town	N 26° 53.200'	W 77° 30.200'	139.53 NM	139° M	11.6 NM
GTC	1 NM W New Plymouth, GTC	N 26° 45.350'	W 77° 20.700'	151.53 NM		

Coordinates for other waypoints on this chart are provided on page 22

APPROACHES TO ABACO

The route from West Palm Beach to Abaco via Indian Cay Channel is all over 6' except for Indian Cay Channel itself, which carries about 5½' MLW. See the large scale chart on page 26. Boats drawing more need tide help. Planning the passage through Indian Cay Channel for 1-2 hours before high tide will provide 6½-7' on neap tides and 7½-8' on springs. Another alternative is to go north of Sandy Cay or either side of Memory Rock. The suggested course from MEMRKS to MANGR carries more than 6' MLW, but the straight-line course from MEMRKS to TRIRKS is very close to or over a 5-6' shoal which is 1-2 NM ENE of MEMRKS. If your draft is more than about 4', we suggest a course of 94° M (head for MANGR) until about 4 NM east of MEMRKS before turning to port to head for TRIRKS. White Sand Ridge is another deep water route, and is especially useful for boats departing from St. Lucie Inlet or Ft. Pierce and going to Walker's Cay. Note that we now show a route to Walker's Cay from waypoint TRIRKW; the route is north of Triangle Rocks and south of Lily Bank.

The routes north and south of Great Sale Cay both carry well over 6'; the northern route, which comes closer to visible landmarks, is 1.59 nautical miles longer. The Grand Lucayan Waterway carries 6-7' MLW, but the channel approaching it through Dover Sound at its northern end carries only about 3' MLW. Also, a bridge over the waterway limits passage to vessels under 27½' high at MHW. See the large scale chart on page 28.

Boats entering the Sea of Abaco through North Man-O-War Channel or South Man-O-War Channel should go offshore to OFFMOW (and OFFELBOW if approaching from the south) before heading for the openings. From either OFFMOW or OFFELBOW one may go to the waypoints located "east, east" of the channels (SMOWEE and NMOWEE) and then approach the "east" waypoints for the channels (SMOWE and NMOWE). These courses will keep boats off the many dangerous reefs in the area. All boats should use them unless very familiar with the area. It is very important to stay east of Elbow Reef, which extends eastward from Hope Town. **More boats ground on this reef than any other in Abaco—please be wary of this reef and go to OFFELBOW when passing Elbow Cay and Reef.** For more detail and for waypoints and coordinates not on this small scale chart, please see the charts on pages 86 and 94. Boats leaving Abaco via these channels and heading south should use these same waypoints. Note that we now show an offshore route from Walker's Cay to Little Harbour which keeps boats well off Abaco's barrier reef.

The best entrances to the Sea of Abaco for those coming from Eleuthera are North Bar Channel (see page146 and 144) and North Man-O-War Channel (see page 86 and paragraph above). The waypoints at the Eleuthera end of the suggested courses provide access to Spanish Wells and Harbour Island. The waypoint BRIDGN is at the north end of the Bridge Point opening in Devil's Backbone Reef. Local knowledge and good visibility are required for this passage the first time.

Island Queen heading west back to Florida after nine months in Abaco on the route north of Grand Bahama, 20 July 2011. Photo by Steve Dodge.

Other GPS Waypoints on Approaches to Abaco (pp. 20-21):

WPT	Description of Position	Latitude	Longitude
SEBAST	E Sebastian Inlet (not shown)	N 27° 51.674'	W 80° 26.450'
FTPRCE	E Ft. Pierce inlet	N 27° 28.680'	W 80° 15.180'
STLCY	Outer mark St. Lucy inlet	N 27° 10.000'	W 80° 08.000'
JUPTR	1 NM E Jupiter inlet	N 26° 56.605'	W 80° 03.877'
BOCAR	E Boca Raton inlet	N 26° 20.061'	W 80° 03.940'
HLSBRO	½ NM SE Hillsboro Inlet	N 26° 15.116'	W 80° 04.420'
FTL	FtL outer mark	N 26° 05.400'	W 80° 04.700'
BAKHL	½ NM E Baker's Haulover inlet	N 25° 54.011'	W 80° 06.625'
MIAMI	S Govt. Cut Outer Mark	N 25° 45.950'	W 80° 05.000'
LTLSAL	½ NM NW Little Sale Cay	N 27° 03.274'	W 78° 10.809'
SALRCK	¾ NM N Sale Cay Rocks	N 27° 03.229'	W 78° 06.552'
CRTBSW	¾ NM SW of Carters Bank	N 27° 00.994'	W 78° 01.049'
WSRIDG	33 NM NNW West End	N 27° 08.000'	W 79° 10.500'
MEMRKS	2 NM S Memory Rock	N 26° 55.000'	W 79° 06.000'
GTSANC*	Great Sale Cay anchorage	N 26° 58.581'	W 78° 13.149'
TRIRKS	SE Triangle Rocks	N 27° 09.750'	W 78° 23.500'
TRIRKW	4 NM W Triangle Rocks	N 27° 10.638'	W 78° 30.045'
WALKER	S of Walker's Cay Markers	N 27° 14.077'	W 78° 24.145'
SWPNT*	3 NM WSW South West Point	N 25° 48.000'	W 77° 17.000'
OFFOCP	1 NM ESE Ocean Point	N 26° 17.079'	W 76° 59.349'
HOLEWL*	2 NM SE Hole-in-the-Wall	N 25° 50.000'	W 77° 09.000'
NWPRCH	West end NW Prov. Channel	N 26° 15.000'	W 79° 05.000'

Waypoints for off shore route from Walker's Cay to Little Harbour:

WALKNE	2 NM ENE Walker's Cay	N 27° 16.289'	W 78° 21.598'
OFFWLK	4.2 NM NE Walker's Cay	N 27° 19.100'	W 78° 21.200'
OFFSTRANG	6.8 NM NW Strangers Cay	N 27° 13.500'	W 78° 09.337'
OFFMORAN	3.3 NM NNE Moraine Cay	N 27° 05.635'	W 77° 44.700'
OFFSPAN	3.5 NM NE Spanish Cay	N 26° 58.340'	W 77° 28.400'
OFFMANJ	3.3 NM N north tip Manjack	N 26° 53.730'	W 77° 22.940'
OFFWHALE	2.8 NM NE Whale Cay	N 26° 44.772'	W 77° 12.430'
OFFMOW	5.0 NM NE MOW Cay	N 26° 37.820'	W 76° 55.000'
OFFELBOW	3.6 NM NE Hope Twn hbr	N 26° 34.270'	W 76° 54.250'
OFFNBAR	3.6 NM E North Bar Channel	N 26° 23.410'	W 76° 55.000'
OFFLHB	1.4 NM SSE Little Hrbr Bar	N 26° 18.971'	W 76° 58.858'

Grand Bahama Island:

CORMPT	Pole 2.5 NM NW Cormorant Pt.	N 26° 44.540'	W 78° 40.800'
DOVERN	Pole north end Dover Sound	N 26° 38.280'	W 78° 39.650'
DOVERS	south end Dover Sound	N 26° 36.800'	W 78° 38.470'
WTRWYS	Buoy S. end Grd. Luc. Wtrwy.	N 26° 31.670'	W 78° 33.270'
BELLCH	200' S buoy off Bell Channel	N 26° 29.826'	W 78° 37.791'

Eleuthera:

BRIDGN**	N end Bridge Pt. reef opening	N 25° 34.298'	W 76° 43.344'
EGGREF	0.8 NM west of Egg Reef	N 25° 31.102'	W 76° 55.031'
OFFMAN	2 NM NE Man Island	N 25° 33.500'	W 76° 36.500'
OFFHARB	3.0 NM NE Harbour Mouth	N 25° 30.000'	W 76° 35.000'

Nassau:

NASSAU	north Nassau Hbr. entrance	N 25° 05.447'	W 77° 21.340'

Bimini:

BIM-N*	1/3 NM N of North Rock	N 25° 48.250'	W 79° 15.500'
BIM-NW	1.0 NM NW North Bimini	N 25° 45.000'	W 79° 18.450'
BIM-W1	entrance dredged channel	N 25° 42.630'	W 79° 18.450'

Berry Islands:

BULHBR	5.0 NM WNW Bullocks Hbr	N 25° 46.000'	W 77° 57.500'
BERY-NW	1.2 NM NW Little Stirrup Cay	N 25° 50.000'	W 77° 57.500'
BERY-NE	1 NM NE entrance Grt. Hbr.	N 25° 50.000'	W 77° 53.000'

* Waypoints designated by an asterisk were acquired from reliable sources, but have not been personally checked on-site by the author.

**This waypoint is at the north end of the Bridge Point opening in Devil's Backbone Reef. Local knowledge and good visibility are required for this passage the first time.

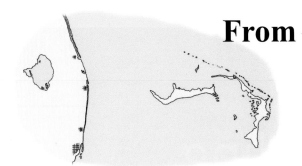

From Florida to Abaco --
Crossing the Gulf Stream

by Marcel Albury and Steve Dodge

The crossing from Florida to Abaco is about 135 nautical miles—55 miles across the Florida Straits from West Palm Beach to West End, Grand Bahama Island, and then 80 miles across Little Bahama Bank from West End to Crab Cay, where one enters into Abaco Sound, sometimes called the Sea of Abaco. It is another 15 nautical miles to Green Turtle Cay, and then another 20 to Marsh Harbour. A planing powerboat can make the trip in one day; a sailboat generally requires 3 to 5 or more days. There are good overnight anchorages or dockage at West End (Old Bahama Bay Marina), Great Sale Cay, Fox Town, Spanish Cay (Spanish Cay Marina), Powell Cay/Cooperstown, and, of course, Green Turtle Cay.

The most challenging part of the trip is crossing the Florida Straits. The Gulf Stream flows northward through the Straits at a speed of about 3 knots. It is about 20-25 miles wide, and is usually located in the center of the Straits. If the wind blows hard (15 or more knots) from the north—against the current—the equivalent of a tide rip 25 miles wide is created, with short, steep, treacherous waves. This condition often exists during the winter months after the passage of cold fronts, and makes the Gulf Stream almost impassable for small boats. Add to this the navigation problem created by the current sweeping one's vessel to the north when the destination is east and, of course, the usual challenges of any 50-mile open ocean crossing, and it should be clear that the trip across the Florida Straits must be taken seriously. But it is not difficult, and most anyone with some open water experience can do it successfully if they follow the general rules of good seamanship, and pay attention to certain special aspects of this crossing.

The single most important factor affecting the comfort and safety of crossing the Gulf Stream is the weather. One should make certain that there will be adequate time to cross before any bad weather moves in. Marcel Albury, who crossed the Gulf Stream well over 100 times, drove over to the beach to look at the ocean before leaving. He did this even if the weather report was good: "If you see elephants out there on the horizon, forget it. It should look nice and flat. I realize that what you can see is not all that you are going to run into, but it gives you a pretty good idea. The weather report, along with what I can see—the two of these things together—is what makes me decide. And then I leave within about 2 hours. It takes about 6 hours to cross, and I know the weather will be good for that long, so I leave right away."

The boat and the boat's equipment should be in good condition with all standard Coast Guard equipment including life jackets, flares, etc. Fuel should be ample, which like an airplane, should be about 50% more than what you need for the trip. It may be necessary to reduce speed because of sea conditions, making the boat less efficient and the extra fuel essential. The most important extra piece of equipment is a VHF radio, which should be in good operating condition. Some boats carry a portable or a spare. The safety of the crossing can be greatly enhanced by traveling with another boat. Then if problems develop, help is close at hand. Crossing alone in a small open boat—a runabout—is not recommended. Larger boats may cross alone, but Marcel Albury did not recommend single-handed crossings, unless it is an emergency: "I have done it, but you get different as you get older. There are just too many things that can go wrong with me, or it, or that, or them, or what have you. I want somebody else; I just like company. I might twist my ankle and not be able to get up. When one thing happens, it causes something else to happen; it always seems to snowball. It's not in the best interest of anyone to cross the Gulf Stream single-handed."

Notify someone that you are making the crossing and arrange to call them after arrival. The Coast Guard can serve in this way, but it is probably better to call a relative or friend who will be more immediately concerned if you do not telephone on schedule indicating your arrival.

Do not depart from any point north of Ft. Pierce, because you will be fighting the current of the Gulf Stream. Embarkation from West Palm Beach puts the current on the beam, and departure from Fort Lauderdale gives the boat a boost getting to the north with the current helping. The Gulf Stream flows at about 3 knots, but you are not in it all the time as you are crossing. I figure 2 knots drift and usually that works out about right. So, if you figure the crossing to West End will take 6 hours, set your course for a spot 12 nautical miles south of West End. You should be able to see the condominiums at West Palm Beach for 20-30 miles, and you will pick up West End when still about 8 miles west of it, so you will only be out of sight of land for about 25 miles.

The landfall is an easy one—before you see the land you should be able to see the water tower at West End from about 8 miles out. If you make a little too much to the north, then you would probably see Sandy Cay, which lies about 6 miles north of West End and has a very high clump of casuarinas (Florida or Australian Pines) visible for about ten miles. So you've got two good landfalls. You can hardly be so far one way or the other that you're not going to pick up either Sandy Cay or the water tower at West End. You can see the tower if you are 6-8 miles south, and you can see Sandy Cay if you are 6-8 miles north, so you have a broad area there. Its not like going back to the states, when you can't miss it, but if you get within this 18-20 mile area, you will see one or the other landfall. If you go too far south, you will realize it because you are not in the shallow water of the bank, so if you turn and head north you will find Grand Bahama Island and Freeport. So, you probably are not going to miss land.

Memory Rock, which is about 8 miles north of Sandy Cay, is a fairly small rock and is therefore difficult to distinguish from a distance. You can enter on to Little Bahama Bank on either side of it. It is almost on a straight-line course to Sale Cay from West Palm Beach, but most small boats will need to re-fuel—they will not be able to make the additional 100 miles to Green Turtle Cay without re-fueling at West End. Other possible re-fueling stops are at Fox Town and Spanish Cay.

Finally, all boats entering The Bahamas are required to clear Customs and Immigration at a Port of Entry as soon as possible after arriving in Bahamian waters. This can be done at West End, Freeport, Walker's Cay, Spanish Cay, Green Turtle Cay, or Marsh Harbour.

Note: Marcel Albury passed away in 2005. He is missed.

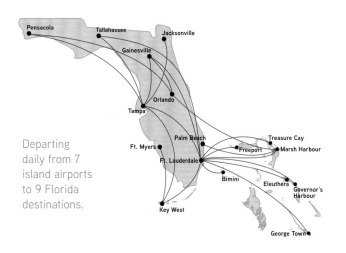

Grand Bahama Section

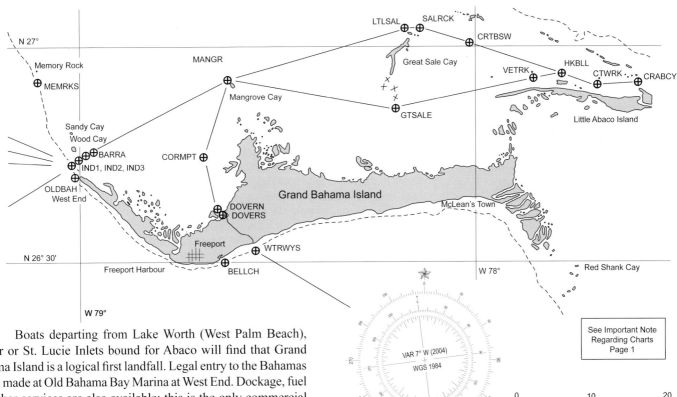

Boats departing from Lake Worth (West Palm Beach), Jupiter or St. Lucie Inlets bound for Abaco will find that Grand Bahama Island is a logical first landfall. Legal entry to the Bahamas can be made at Old Bahama Bay Marina at West End. Dockage, fuel and other services are also available; this is the only commercial marina on the north side of Grand Bahama Island.

The island is about sixty nautical miles long and six nautical miles wide. Its northern coast is very shallow and not approachable in cruising boats for much of its length. Those transiting the area can find some protection at Mangrove Cay (see chart p. 27) or Great Sale Cay (see chart p. 29). . The Grand Lucayan Waterway bisects the island about 20 nautical miles east of West End (see the chart in this section on page 28).

The southern coast is close to the edge of Little Bahama Bank. A barrier reef parallels the coast for much of its length a short distance offshore, and just beyond that there is a steep drop-off to deep ocean water at the edge of the bank. Freeport, the Bahamas' second largest city, is located close to the southern coast, but Freeport harbour is primarily commercial and does not cater to cruising boats. There are several harbours with marinas east of Freeport Harbour. Closest is the Xanadu Beach Marina and Resort. Just beyond that is the Running Mon Marina, then the Ocean Reef Yacht Club, and then Bell Channel, site of the Lucayan Marina and Port Lucaya. See the chart on page 28 of this section for more information.

There is a land and sea park at Peterson Cay, 1¼ miles east of the southern entrance to the Grand Lucayan Waterway. Further east is McLean's Town. Refer to DMA chart #26320.

The redevelopment of West End will be of interest to many cruising in or transiting this area. The old Jack Tar Marina became Old Bahama Bay Marina during the late 1990s. New docks and new buildings regularly appeared. A "beachfront cottage hotel" east of the marina and several private residences on the canal-front lots were built. In early 2007 the Ginn Company assumed management control of Old Bahama Bay. Ginn, a US-based development company, planned to build a huge $4.9B resort complex southeast of Old Bahama Bay. Bobby Ginn, who once compared himself (somewhat favorably) to Louis XIV of France, defaulted on a construction

loan payment in June 2008. Credit Suisse and other stakeholders argued over the spoils. Much of the infrastructure for the grandiose new development is completed, but further construction is stalled. The marina is open and fuel as well as customs and immigration services are available. The restaurant/bar at the marina was closed in August 2012, but the beach bar and grill, a short walk away, was open. It was said that the property owners (homes and condos) assumed management of the complex on 1 August 2012. It is hoped that local control by stakeholders will result in improvement of the property and the services it provides to cruisers.

GPS Waypoints for Grand Bahama Section (generally from west to east):

WPT	Description	Latitude	Longitude
MEMRKS	2 NM S Memory Rock	N 26° 55.000'	W 79° 06.000'
IND1	50' N 1st pile Indian Cay Ch.	N 26° 43.180'	W 79° 00.210'
IND2	50' N 2nd pile Indian Cay Ch.	N 26° 43.770'	W 78° 59.800'
IND3	50' N 3rd pile Indian Cay Ch.	N 26° 44.720'	W 78° 59.140'
BARRA	½ NM SE Barracuda Sh. mkr.	N 26° 45.790'	W 78° 58.110'
OLDBAH	500' W ent. Old Bah Bay Mar.	N 26° 42.256'	W 78° 59.818'
MANGR	1/2 NM N Mangrove Cay mkr.	N 26° 55.710'	W 78° 37.260'
CORMPT	pole 2½ NM NW Cormorant Pt.	N 26° 44.540'	W 78° 40.800'
DOVERN	pole north end Dover Sound	N 26° 38.280'	W 78° 39.650'
DOVERS	south end Dover Sound	N 26° 36.800'	W 78° 38.470'
WTRWYS	buoy S. end Grd. Luc. Wtrwy.	N 26° 31.670'	W 78° 33.270'
BELLCH	200' S buoy off Bell Channel	N 26° 29.826'	W 78° 37.791'
GTSALE	4 NM S Great Sale Cay	N 26° 52.520'	W 78° 12.710'
LTLSAL	1/2 NM NW Little Sale Cay	N 27° 03.274'	W 78° 10.809'
SALRCK	3/4 NM N Sale Cay Rocks	N 27° 03.229'	W 78° 06.552'
CRTBSW	3/4 NM SW of Carters Bank	N 27° 00.994'	W 78° 01.049'
VETRK	1/2 NM S Veteran's Rock	N 26° 55.950'	W 77° 52.290'
HKBLL	1/4 NM N Hawksbill Cay	N 26° 56.890'	W 77° 47.690'
CTWRK	1/2 NM S Center World Rock	N 26° 56.190'	W 77° 41.660'
CRABCY	½ NM N of Crab Cay	N 26° 56.271'	W 77° 37.000'

Indian Cay Channel and West End, Grand Bahama Island

VAR 7° W (2004)
WGS 1984

N 26° 48'

2

Sandy Cay

3-4

N 26° 47'

The water tower at West End and the tall stand of casuarinas on Sandy Cay six miles to the north can be seen for about 8 miles. These are the first landmarks one will see when approaching West End. The entire area between Sandy Cay and West End is fairly shallow and strewn with rocky bars and reefs, but Indian Cay Channel, which now carries about 6' MLW (8-9' at high tide), is a viable route through the area. Boats drawing more than 5½' will need tide help or should go about 4 NM north of Sandy Cay. Indian Cay Channel is supposed to be marked with three pilings, but no pilings have been in place since 2006. There is a light on a small steel tower on Indian Cay Rock. **The light is not a marker for the deepest water; the pilings are ... or were**. The pilings marked the south side of the "channel," and the waypoints IND1, IND2 and IND3 were positioned in the middle of the channel about 50' north of the piling locations. So, until new pilings are installed, use the waypoints (and your eyes) to transit this area in the deepest water. The Barracuda Shoal marker, located northeast of Indian Cay Channel, is mounted on the shoal itself and should be given about a ¼ NM berth; go SE of it. Entrance to Old Bahama Bay Marina is from the west. The channel is wide and deep (15-17'). Entry is straightforward except for a breakwater extending across the channel after you are inside. Leave it to port. Proceed eastward around the breakwater, and when you cannot go further east, turn to starboard to enter the main marina basin. See page 25 for waypoint coordinates.

For continuation see pages 20-21

One of the pile markers at Indian Cay Channel is clearly visible in the foreground; the Indian Cay light can be seen behind it and off to the right, and beyond that is the northern shoreline of the west end of Grand Bahama Island. The water tower is to the left of center, almost shielded from view by trees. Unfortunately, all the pile markers have been missing since 2006.

For continuation see pages 20-21

to MANGR >
21.1 NM

9   9   9

9

Barracuda Shoal Marker
Fl 4 Sec
2½

68° M >
< 248° M

N 26° 46'

BARRA   8   8   5   Church Bank

9   7   8

46° M > < 226° M 1.41 NM   8   8   4   3

7   4

N 26° 45'

2

5½   5½   8   4   See Important Note
Regarding Charts
Page 1

8   IND3
5

pile (missing since 1997)

8   5½

37° M > < 217° M 1.12 NM   8

1

59   Wood Cay

N 26° 42.5'   10

N 26° 44'
110   73   4   16   3½

to STLUCY
66.2 NM

119° M >
< 299° M   69   7   8   17   4

to JUPITR
58.5 NM   7   IND2   22   13   9   11   8
108° M >   pile (missing since 2005)   21   2   9   6
< 288° M   90   4½   34

to LWOMK   60   15   17   FlR   17   17   12
54.1 NM   98° M >   11   IND1   4½   FlR   16   11
< 278° M   30   15   pile (missing since 2006)   OLDBAH   14   10
N 26° 43'   Indian Cay Rock   fuel
33   25   Fl 6 sec 40 ft 8 M   < to LWOMK

103   35   28   19   Indian Cay
63° M >   30
< 243° M   100   48   28

to LWOMK   40   29   10
54.5 NM   99° M >   48   8   Old Bahama
180   189   < 279° M   48   Bay Marina

N 26° 42'   187   OLDBAH

to FTL   186   West End
69.1 NM   Ant.
Fl 4 sec 44Ft 6M   Fl R over Fl R
215'   Water
Tower

Entrance to Old Bahama Bay Marina

W 79° 02'   W 79° 01'   W 79° 00'   W 78° 59'   W 78° 58'   W 78° 57'

Entrance to Old Bahama Bay

Approach from the west. After entering between the breakwaters, move to the starboard side to avoid the spur breakwater, the end of which is marked with a white sign in the above photo. After passing it and the branch canal which goes to the south, turn to starboard to enter the marina basin. The fuel dock is on on the starboard side as you enter.

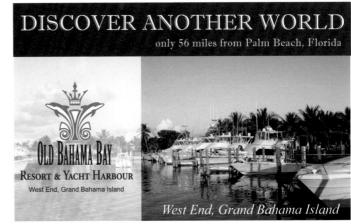
MANGROVE CAY

Mangrove Cay is located about halfway bewtween West End / Memory Rock and Great Sale Cay, and therefore is a conveninent anchorage for some boats transiting the area. It can provide good protection from the SW and W, and from the NE and E, marginal protection from SE winds, and little protection from NW winds. The cay is appropriately named—it consists of mangroves with some other trees on slightly higher land in the center of the cay, and a single palm tree at the north end. The flashing white light is mounted on a tall pole; unfortunately it is unreliable. The waypoint MANGR is located on the principal east/west routes and is located about 0.6 NM north of the pole.

Sailboat anchored at Mangrove Cay,. Photo taken several years ago before Palm tree grew at the northern end. Photo by Steve Dodge.

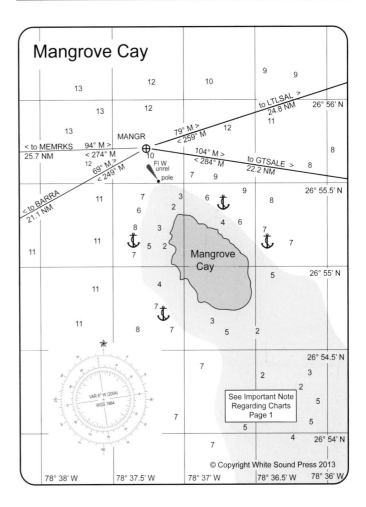

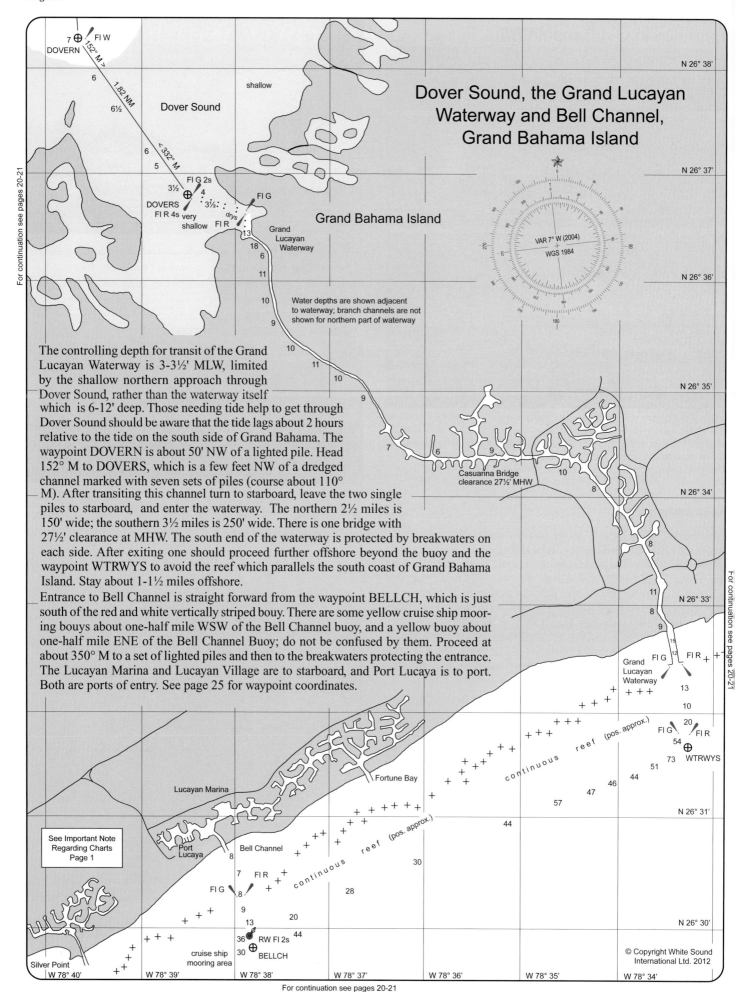

Dover Sound, the Grand Lucayan Waterway and Bell Channel, Grand Bahama Island

Grand Bahama Island

Dover Sound

Water depths are shown adjacent to waterway; branch channels are not shown for northern part of waterway

The controlling depth for transit of the Grand Lucayan Waterway is 3-3½' MLW, limited by the shallow northern approach through Dover Sound, rather than the waterway itself which is 6-12' deep. Those needing tide help to get through Dover Sound should be aware that the tide lags about 2 hours relative to the tide on the south side of Grand Bahama. The waypoint DOVERN is about 50' NW of a lighted pile. Head 152° M to DOVERS, which is a few feet NW of a dredged channel marked with seven sets of piles (course about 110° M). After transiting this channel turn to starboard, leave the two single piles to starboard, and enter the waterway. The northern 2½ miles is 150' wide; the southern 3½ miles is 250' wide. There is one bridge with 27½' clearance at MHW. The south end of the waterway is protected by breakwaters on each side. After exiting one should proceed further offshore beyond the buoy and the waypoint WTRWYS to avoid the reef which parallels the south coast of Grand Bahama Island. Stay about 1-1½ miles offshore.

Entrance to Bell Channel is straight forward from the waypoint BELLCH, which is just south of the red and white vertically striped bouy. There are some yellow cruise ship mooring bouys about one-half mile WSW of the Bell Channel buoy, and a yellow buoy about one-half mile ENE of the Bell Channel Buoy; do not be confused by them. Proceed at about 350° M to a set of lighted piles and then to the breakwaters protecting the entrance. The Lucayan Marina and Lucayan Village are to starboard, and Port Lucaya is to port. Both are ports of entry. See page 25 for waypoint coordinates.

VAR 7° W (2004)
WGS 1984

Casuarina Bridge
clearance 27½' MHW

Grand Lucayan Waterway

Grand Lucayan Waterway

WTRWYS

continuous reef (pos. approx.)

Fortune Bay

Lucayan Marina

continuous reef (pos. approx.)

See Important Note Regarding Charts Page 1

Port Lucaya

Bell Channel

continuous reef (pos. approx.)

RW Fl 2s

cruise ship mooring area

BELLCH

Silver Point

DOVERN

DOVERS
Fl R 4s

very shallow

Fl G 2s

Fl R

drys

Fl G

GREAT SALE CAY

Great Sale Cay provides coveniently located anchorages roughly half-way between the western edge of Little Bahama Bank and Green Turtle Cay. The cay is generally low lying with mangroves, but there is some elevation at the northern end. Anchorages can be found in the bight on the western side which is generally known as Northwest Harbour. The holding is best in sand at and around the waypoint GTSANC; further north in the harbour the bottom is mud, but, of course, there is more protection. The anchorage along the northwestern shore of the cay is good for southeast winds, and the anchorage on the east side of the cay is good for northwest winds. The shoals extending from the southern point stretch for about 3 NM. It is possible ro carry up to 6' MLW between them, but it should only be attempted in settled weather with good visibility on a rising tide. The waypoint GTSALE is on the suggested east-west route south of Great Sale Cay and is located about 4 NM south of the southern point (see the chart on page 30). At the northern end of the cay rocky shoals extend north to Little Sale Cay and the Sale Cay Rocks. Vessels transiting the area should use the waypoint LTSAL. Great Sale Cay is not particularly pretty; its greatest asset is its location on the route between Florida and Abaco.

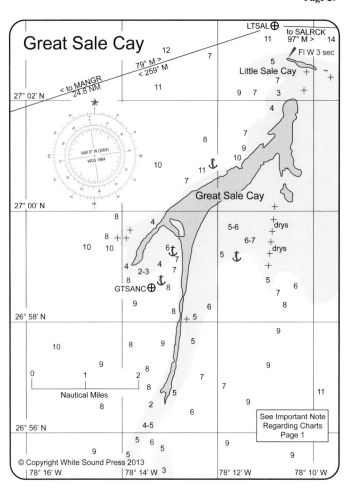

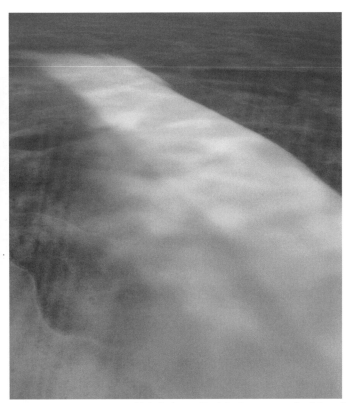

Fish muds are common on Little Bahama Bank in the area north of Grand Bahama Island. This one was photographed from the air in July, 2002. When approaching them in a boat they often appear, at first, to be a shoal area, but homogenous colour and sometimes fuzzy edges give them away as fish muds rather than shoals. There are several theories regarding their cause; the most common being schools of bottom feeding fish.

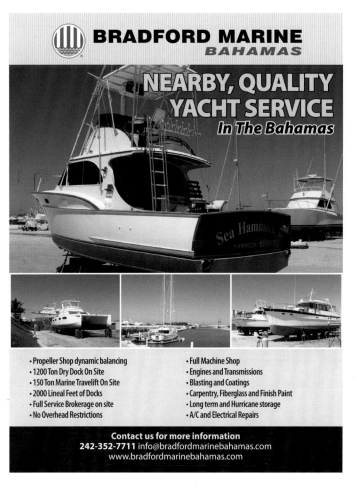

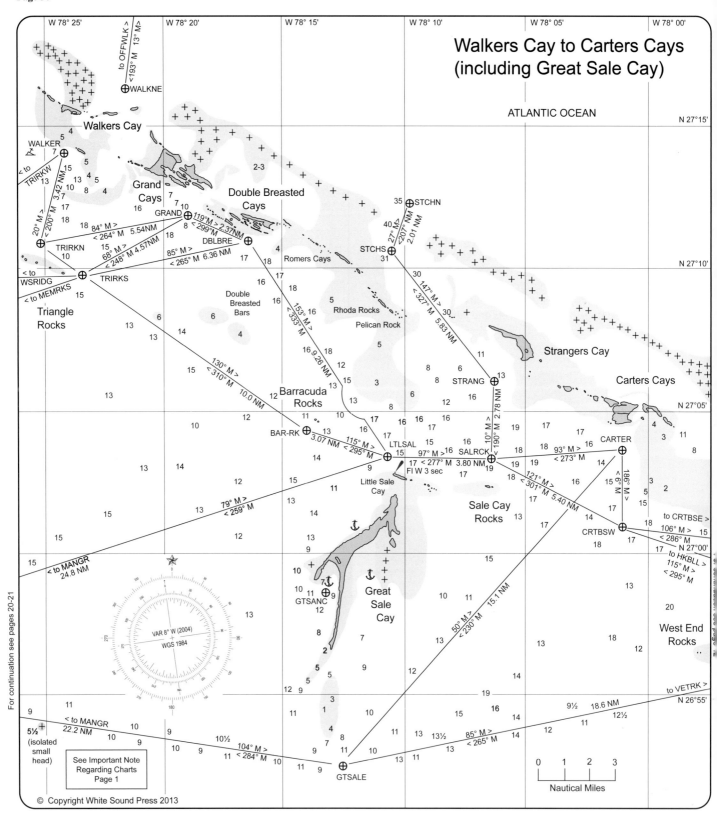

Walkers Cay to Carters Cays
(including Great Sale Cay)

ATLANTIC OCEAN

GPS Waypoints for *Walker's Cay to Carters Cays* (generally from north to south):

WPT	Description of Position	Latitude	Longitude	WPT	Description of Position	Latitude	Longitude
OFFWLK	4.2 NM NE Walker's Cay	N 27° 19.100'	W 78° 21.200'	CRTBSW	Southwest of Carter Bank	N 27° 00.994'	W 78° 01.049'
WALKNE	2.0 NM ENE Walker's Cay	N 27° 16.289'	W 78° 21.598'	GRAND	South of Grand Cays	N 27° 11.884'	W 78° 18.970'
WALKER	South of Walker's Cay markers	N 27° 14.077'	W 78° 24.145'	DBLBRE	South of Double Breasted Cays	N 27° 11.000'	W 78° 16.500'
TRIRKN	Northeast of Triangle Rocks	N 27° 10.766'	W 78° 25.056'	STCHN	N end Stranger Cay Channel	N 27° 12.400'	W 78° 09.770'
TRIRKW	4 NM W Triangle Rocks	N 27° 10.638'	W 78° 30.045'	STCHS	S end Stranger Cay Channel	N 27° 10.500'	W 78° 10.500'
TRIRKS	Southeast of Triangle Rocks	N 27° 09.750'	W 78° 23.500'	STRANG	1¾ NM S of W tip Stranger Cay	N 27° 06.000'	W 78° 06.350'
BAR-RK	Southwest of Barracuda Rocks	N 27° 04.258'	W 78° 14.071'	CARTER	2 NM SW of Carters Cays	N 27° 03.528'	W 78° 01.087'
LTLSAL	Northwest of Little Sale Cay	N 27° 03.274'	W 78° 10.809'	GTSALE	4 NM south of Great Sale Cay	N 26° 52.520'	W 78° 12.710'
SALRCK	¾ NM North of Sale Cay Rocks	N 27° 03.229'	W 78° 06.552'	GTSANC*	Great Sale Cay anchorage	N 26° 58.581'	W 78° 13.149'

WALKER'S CAY TO CARTERS CAYS
(including Great Sale Cay)

All vessels operating in the area SW of Walker's Cay should note the abandoned drill rig located approximately 2 NM SW of Walker's Cay. It is indicated on the chart.

Boats drawing 4' or more and transiting the area from Walker's Cay to Carters Cays must take care to avoid the shoal between Walker's and Grand Cays, the Double Breasted Bars which are about 5 NM S of Double Breasted Cays, and the large shoal extending from the Rhoda Rocks and Pelican Rock. GPS waypoints are shown on the chart for this route. It extends generally S from Walker's Cay to Triangle Rocks, then SE to Barracuda Rocks, ESE to Little Sale Cay, and then E to Carters Cays. This route is not the shortest distance between Walker's and Carters, but it is clear of obstacles and carries over 6' MLW (except for the final approach to Walker's over the bank there, which carries about 3-3½' MLW). Waypoints for this route are listed below the chart.

Possible overnight anchorages along the way (within about 5 NM) include Grand Cays, Double Breasted Cays, Strangers Cay and Great Sale Cay. Grand Cays is the next anchorage to the SE. Grand Cays has a settlement with restaurants and stores, and fuel service is available. Beaches on the east side of the cays are beautiful, and bone-fishing is good in the entire area. See the chart on page 34 for more detail.

Double Breasted Cays is a beautiful collection of small cays and rocks. An anchorage offering protection from the west, north, and east is available near the NW end of the archipelago. See the chart on page 36 for more detail.

Strangers Cay has a settled weather anchorage near its NW tip. See the chart on page 38 for more detail.

Great Sale Cay has a bight on its west side which offers good protection from west, north, and east winds, but is open to the south. It is a favorite overnight stop for boats making the Abaco-Florida passage. The approach to it is straightforward—the only obstacle is a shoal extending westward from Great Sale Cay. Give it a wide berth. Another possible anchorage is just east of the cay—but this offers protection only from the west and north, being exposed to the east and south.

Note that the old Elephant Rock route between Walker's Cay and Grand Cays has silted in and now carries only about 2-3' MLW. A new route further off Burying Piece Rocks carries over 6' MLW. See the Grand Cays chart on page 34.

Double Breasted Cays can be approached directly from the waypoint GRAND or from the SW tip of Big Grand Cay on the Atlantic side. See pages 34-36 for larger scale charts and a detailed description.

From the waypoint DBLBRE note that a straight courseline to LTLSAL, the waypoint north of Little Sale Cay, passes near the edge of the bank extending south from the Rhoda Rocks and Pelican Rock. Watch cross track error carefully here, or just alter course to the west to make certain that you avoid the edge of the bank.

There is a deep and wide channel from the Sea of Abaco to the Atlantic Ocean NW of Strangers Cay. See page 38 for more details.

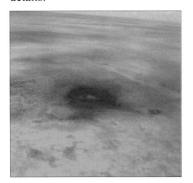

This blue hole is located on the shoal extending from the southern tip of Great Sale Cay. Blue holes are located in the shallow waters (or on the land areas) of the Bahama Banks. They are connected to deep ocean waters through a tunnel or tunnels cut through the limestone base of the banks by rainwater during the ice ages when sea level was several hundred feet lower than it is today.

The anchorage at Carters Cays from the south. Photo 27 May 2011 by Steve Dodge.

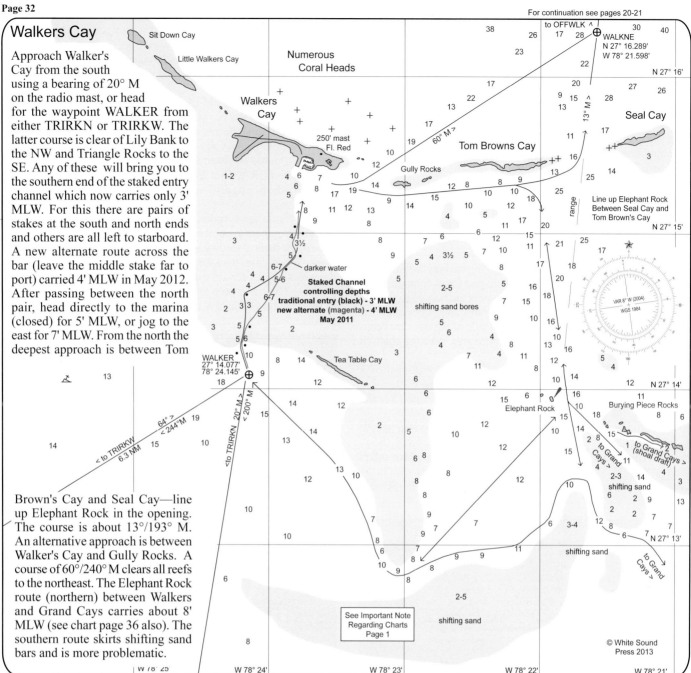

Walkers Cay

Approach Walker's Cay from the south using a bearing of 20° M on the radio mast, or head for the waypoint WALKER from either TRIRKN or TRIRKW. The latter course is clear of Lily Bank to the NW and Triangle Rocks to the SE. Any of these will bring you to the southern end of the staked entry channel which now carries only 3' MLW. For this there are pairs of stakes at the south and north ends and others are all left to starboard. A new alternate route across the bar (leave the middle stake far to port) carried 4' MLW in May 2012. After passing between the north pair, head directly to the marina (closed) for 5' MLW, or jog to the east for 7' MLW. From the north the deepest approach is between Tom

Brown's Cay and Seal Cay—line up Elephant Rock in the opening. The course is about 13°/193° M. An alternative approach is between Walker's Cay and Gully Rocks. A course of 60°/240° M clears all reefs to the northeast. The Elephant Rock route (northern) between Walkers and Grand Cays carries about 8' MLW (see chart page 36 also). The southern route skirts shifting sand bars and is more problematic.

Sit Down Cay

Little Walkers Cay

Numerous Coral Heads

Walkers Cay

250' mast Fl. Red

Gully Rocks

Tom Browns Cay

Seal Cay

Line up Elephant Rock Between Seal Cay and Tom Brown's Cay

range

to OFFWLK ^
WALKNE
N 27° 16.289'
W 78° 21.598'

N 27° 16'

N 27° 15'

Staked Channel
controlling depths
traditional entry (black) - 3' MLW
new alternate (magenta) - 4' MLW
May 2011

darker water

shifting sand bores

VAR 8° W (2004)
WGS 1984

WALKER
27° 14.077'
78° 24.145'

Tea Table Cay

Elephant Rock

Burying Piece Rocks

to Grand Cays >
to Grand Cays > (shoal draft)

to Grand Cays >

to TRIRKW 6.3 NM

to TRIRKN

shifting sand

shifting sand

N 27° 14'

N 27° 13'

See Important Note Regarding Charts Page 1

shifting sand

shifting sand

© White Sound Press 2013

For continuation see page 30

The serpentine staked route through the sand bank southwest of Walker's Cay has silted in during the past couple of years. The traditional entry route now carries only 3' MLW. An alternative route marked above (coloured magenta) carried 4' MLW in May 2012. The aerial photo above (taken 26 July 2010) clearly shows the sand which has shifted into the tradtitional route southwest of the middle pile. The piles marking the channel have been enhanced on the photo for better identification. The photo should make the chart easier to understand and vice verse. The turns appear to be sharper on the photo because it was taken at a low angle whereas the chart is a true bird's eye view. It is likely that the sand on this bank will continue to shift position, so mariners should exercise caution when crossing this bar. Photo by Steve Dodge.

Staked Channel
controlling depths
traditional entry (black) - 3' MLW
new alternate (magenta) - 4' MLW
May 2011

WALKER'S CAY

Walker's Cay Marina and Hotel is closed. Deteriorating concrete pilings and docks, complicated by damage from the hurricanes of September 2004, resulted in shutting down all commercial operations on the cay. There have been many rumors about buyers and interesting stories about the sellers as well as buyers, but years have passed and nothing has happened on the cay other than continuing deterioration. Walker's continues to be a port of entry with Customs and Immigration available even though the marina and hotel are closed. Walker's is a convenient place to clear for boats coming from St. Lucie or Ft. Pierce Inlets. The route for the crossing is almost a straight line from St. Lucie Inlet (STLCY) to White Sand Ridge (WSRIDG) to Triangle Rocks (TRIRKW) to WALKER (see the chart on pages 20-21). The airport has remained open and continues to service the community at Grand Cays with flights to Freeport, Grand Bahama Island. It is assumed this will continue.

Chelsea, the author's hydrographic research boat, at Walker's Cay in June 2000.

Fuel, dockage and restaurants are all available for cruisers at Grand Cays just 4 NM southeast of Walkers. Of course, the anchorage in the lee of the cay is still available, and the fishing and the diving are still excellent (see the diving/snorkeling chart of Walker's Cay area on page 166).

A small drill rig has been abandoned and wrecked approximately 2 NM SW of Walkers Cay and approximately 1 NM W of the WALKER waypoint. It is easily visible during the daytime. Coordinates are N 27° 14.050' W 78° 25.498'. See the chart on the facing page.

Walkers Cay Marina from the south. This photo was taken when the marina was still open on 11 July 2002.

The Elephant Rock route between Walker's Cay and Grand Cays from the south (27 May, 2011). This area has been very volatile since hurricane Floyd in 1999; the best channel has changed each year. The old route lying close to Burying Piece Rock (shown on chart but not on the photo) only carries about 3' MLW now and is good for outboards only without tide help. A new route running NW-SE carries over 6' MLW; it is marked on the photo above and also shown on the chart. You should be able to see the deeper water based on water colour. Note that there is a second and wider deep water route southwest of the one marked on this photo and the chart. The turns appear to be sharper on the photo because it was taken at a low angle whereas the chart is a true bird's eye view.

Grand Cays

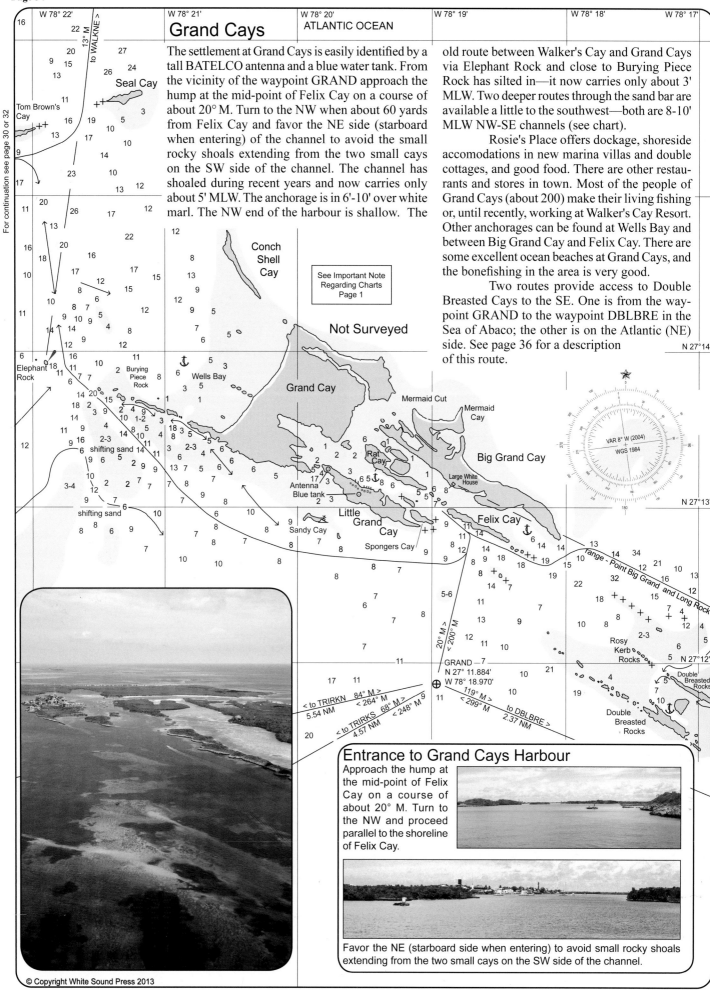

ATLANTIC OCEAN

The settlement at Grand Cays is easily identified by a tall BATELCO antenna and a blue water tank. From the vicinity of the waypoint GRAND approach the hump at the mid-point of Felix Cay on a course of about 20° M. Turn to the NW when about 60 yards from Felix Cay and favor the NE side (starboard when entering) of the channel to avoid the small rocky shoals extending from the two small cays on the SW side of the channel. The channel has shoaled during recent years and now carries only about 5' MLW. The anchorage is in 6'-10' over white marl. The NW end of the harbour is shallow. The old route between Walker's Cay and Grand Cays via Elephant Rock and close to Burying Piece Rock has silted in—it now carries only about 3' MLW. Two deeper routes through the sand bar are available a little to the southwest—both are 8-10' MLW NW-SE channels (see chart).

Rosie's Place offers dockage, shoreside accomodations in new marina villas and double cottages, and good food. There are other restaurants and stores in town. Most of the people of Grand Cays (about 200) make their living fishing or, until recently, working at Walker's Cay Resort. Other anchorages can be found at Wells Bay and between Big Grand Cay and Felix Cay. There are some excellent ocean beaches at Grand Cays, and the bonefishing in the area is very good.

Two routes provide access to Double Breasted Cays to the SE. One is from the waypoint GRAND to the waypoint DBLBRE in the Sea of Abaco; the other is on the Atlantic (NE) side. See page 36 for a description of this route.

See Important Note Regarding Charts Page 1

Entrance to Grand Cays Harbour

Approach the hump at the mid-point of Felix Cay on a course of about 20° M. Turn to the NW and proceed parallel to the shoreline of Felix Cay.

Favor the NE (starboard side when entering) to avoid small rocky shoals extending from the two small cays on the SW side of the channel.

Rosie's Place

• Overnight Dockage •
Water and Electricity

• Fuel Dock •
Gasoline and Diesel

• Air Conditioned Marina Villas and Cottages •
• Good Bahamian Food •

Grand Cays • Abaco • Bahamas
VHF 68 "Rosie's Place"
voice: 242 353-1200   fax 242 353-1202
www.rosiesplace.com rosie@rosiesplace.com

Grand Cays from the SE with Walkers Cay in the background and suggested courseline for entry to Grand Cays anchorage. Note also two boats in the anchorage at Wells Bay at the NE end of Grand Cay. Photo by Steve Dodge, 27 May 2011.

Double Breasted Cays

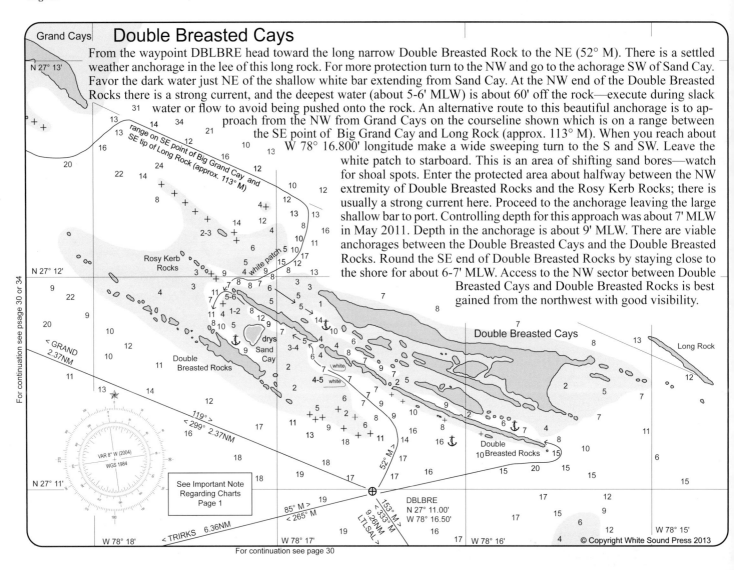

From the waypoint DBLBRE head toward the long narrow Double Breasted Rock to the NE (52° M). There is a settled weather anchorage in the lee of this long rock. For more protection turn to the NW and go to the achorage SW of Sand Cay. Favor the dark water just NE of the shallow white bar extending from Sand Cay. At the NW end of the Double Breasted Rocks there is a strong current, and the deepest water (about 5-6' MLW) is about 60' off the rock—execute during slack water or flow to avoid being pushed onto the rock. An alternative route to this beautiful anchorage is to approach from the NW from Grand Cays on the courseline shown which is on a range between the SE point of Big Grand Cay and Long Rock (approx. 113° M). When you reach about W 78° 16.800' longitude make a wide sweeping turn to the S and SW. Leave the white patch to starboard. This is an area of shifting sand bores—watch for shoal spots. Enter the protected area about halfway between the NW extremity of Double Breasted Rocks and the Rosy Kerb Rocks; there is usually a strong current here. Proceed to the anchorage leaving the large shallow bar to port. Controlling depth for this approach was about 7' MLW in May 2011. Depth in the anchorage is about 9' MLW. There are viable anchorages between the Double Breasted Cays and the Double Breasted Rocks. Round the SE end of Double Breasted Rocks by staying close to the shore for about 6-7' MLW. Access to the NW sector between Double Breasted Cays and Double Breasted Rocks is best gained from the northwest with good visibility.

See Important Note Regarding Charts Page 1

For continuation see page 30

Narrow Passage Between NW end of Double Breasted Rocks and NW end Sand Cay Sand Bar

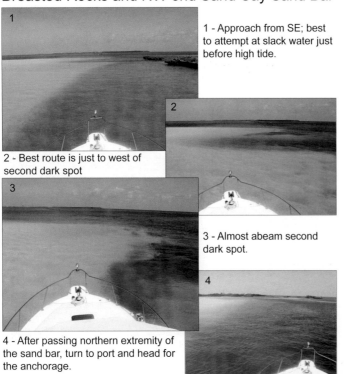

1 - Approach from SE; best to attempt at slack water just before high tide.

2 - Best route is just to west of second dark spot

3 - Almost abeam second dark spot.

4 - After passing northern extremity of the sand bar, turn to port and head for the anchorage.

Four sailboats in the anchorage northeast of Double Breasted Rocks at Double Breasted Cays.

Sand Cay anchorage a Double Breasted Cays from the WNW

Double Breasted Cays from the south, 27 May 2011
Photo by Steve Dodge

Double Breasted Cays from the northwest, 26 July 2010
Photo by Steve Dodge

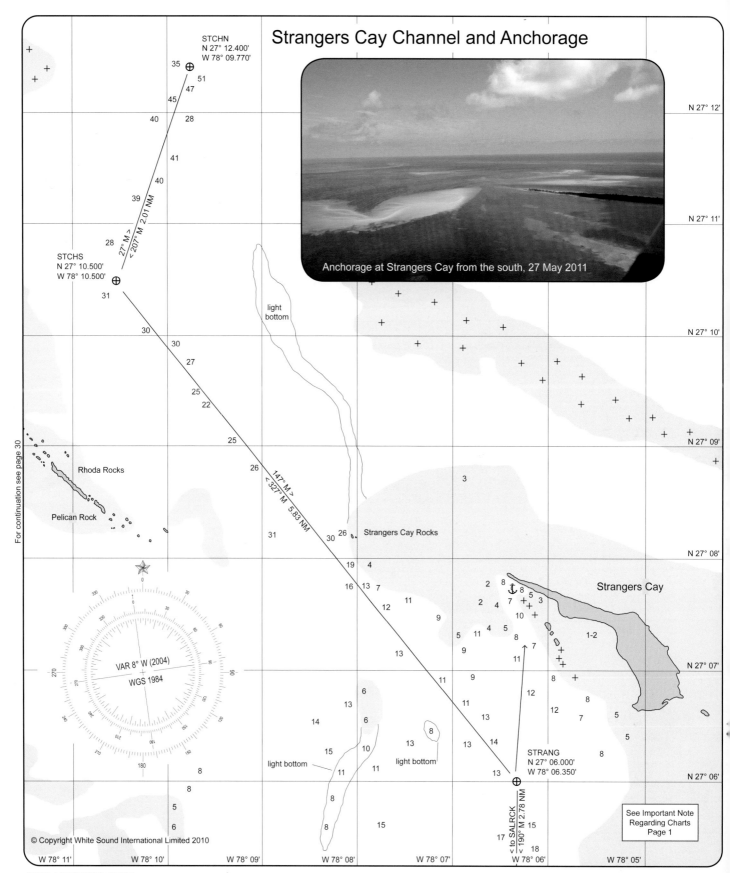

Strangers Cay Channel and Anchorage

STCHN
N 27° 12.400'
W 78° 09.770'

Anchorage at Strangers Cay from the south, 27 May 2011

STCHS
N 27° 10.500'
W 78° 10.500'

STRANG
N 27° 06.000'
W 78° 06.350'

27° M >
< 207° M 2.01 NM

147° M >
< 327° M 5.83 NM

< 190° M 2.78 NM
< to SALRCK

Rhoda Rocks

Pelican Rock

light bottom

Strangers Cay Rocks

Strangers Cay

light bottom

light bottom

VAR 8° W (2004)

WGS 1984

For continuation see page 30

See Important Note
Regarding Charts
Page 1

© Copyright White Sound International Limited 2010

STRANGERS CAY

Strangers Channel is a deep and wide route between the Sea of Abaco and the Atlantic Ocean. It is not frequently used because Strangers Cay has no development and only a marginal anchorage. The channel is remote from Bahamian communities, secure anchorages and marinas. The waypoints and routes should keep one in deep water, but please remember to keep a sharp lookout for stray coral heads (we looked, but found none close to the routes).

The anchorage at Strangers can be approached from the waypoint STRANG. The shoal water on both sides should be clearly visible. The anchorage is in 8' MLW, but it is small and completely exposed to winds from SSE to NW. Use it as a daytime anchorage, or stay overnight in settled weather. There are some nice beaches on the NE side of the cay, but the anchorage presents only a rocky shoreline.

Carters Cays

Proceed from the waypoint CART-ER toward the marker on Gully Cay (a radar reflector on an aluminum pipe) on a course of about 39° M. The approach had a controlling depth of 4½' MLW when last surveyed on 22 May 2008. When about 50' off Gully Cay turn to port and head roughly NW until clear of the end of Gully Cay. Anchor between Gully Cay and Big Carters Cay to avoid the swift current which runs in the main part of Carters Cay Harbour. The anchorage area is not large, and shoals rapidly as you go east. An alternative entrance across the bar on the SW side of the "harbour" carries only about 2-3' MLW and is less desirable because of stronger current flows and shifting sand. Big Carters Cay has some temporary houses on the SW point which are inhabited during the crawfishing season, and it has the remnants of a US missile tracking station. A small hurricane hole called Hogstye Harbour is located between Old Yankee Cay and Top Cay. The entrance carries 3' MLW; there is 13' inside.

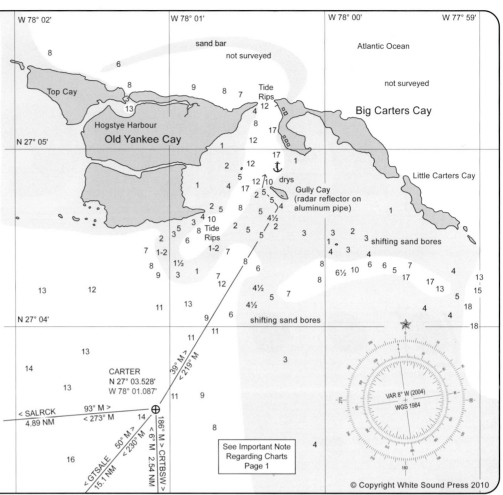

For continuation see page 30 or page 42

The anchorage at Carters Cays from north. Old Yankee Cay is on the right, with Big Carters Cay on the left, and Gully Cay, which has a range for the best entrance, center back. Photo by Steve Dodge, 27 May 2011.

Carters Cays from the SSE with boats in the anchorage. Gully Cay is in the foreground, Big Carters Cay on the right, the east tip of Old Yankee Cay on the left, and the Atlantic Ocean in the back. By anchoring on the extreme east side of the cut, the boats have avoided the strongest current in the center.

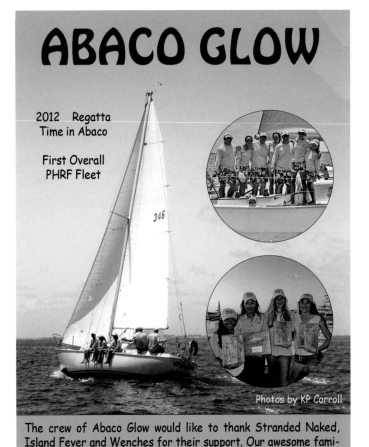

Regatta Time in Abaco is a sailboat race series hosted by five different towns in Abaco in early July of each year. The races are open to cruising sailboats as well as go fast racing boats. The first race is off Green Turtle Cay on or about 4 July; it is followed by races at Great Guana Cay, Man-O-War Cay, Hope Town and Marsh Harbour. There are parties at each town and lay days inbetween race days. Bobb Henderson and his wife Patrica sponsor a kick-off "Cheeseburger in Paradise" picnic at Fiddle Cay (just NW of Green Turtle Cay) each year—usually on or about 3 July. Andy Burke of *Abaco Glow* is an enthusiastic participant in the regatta.

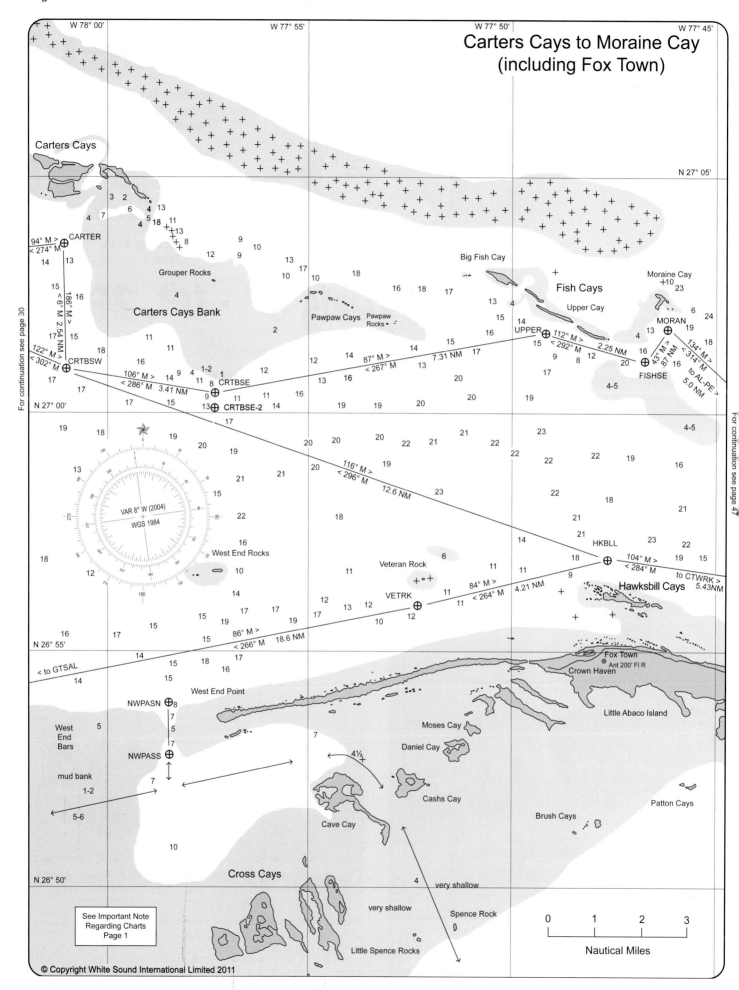

Carters Cays to Moraine Cay
(including Fox Town)

W 78° 00' W 77° 55' W 77° 50' W 77° 45'

N 27° 05'

Carters Cays

Big Fish Cay

Moraine Cay
+10   23

Fish Cays

3 2
6
7   4 13
4
5 18   11
4   +13
+ 8
9
12   9 10

CARTER
94° M >
< 274° M

14   13

Grouper Rocks

Upper Cay

MORAN
19

6   24

4 13

18

186° M >
< 6° M 2.54 NM

15   16
17   15

Carters Cays Bank

4

Pawpaw Cays   Pawpaw
Rocks

13

4

15

16

14

UPPER   112° M >
< 292° M   2.25 NM

16
87° M 13   20

43 M >
87° M 16

134° M >
< 314° M
to AL-PE >
5.0 NM

FISHSE
4-5

122° M >
< 302° M

CRTBSW

18

11

11

16   1-2 1

12

14   87° M >
< 267° M   7.31 NM

17

15
9   8

112
20

17

106° M >
< 286° M 3.41 NM

14   9
11

CRTBSE

12

13

20

N 27° 00'

17

17

15

9
13

11
CRTBSE-2 14

16

19

19

20

4-5

19

18

19

20

20

20

22

21

22

23

4-5

13

20

21

22

22

22

16

VAR 8° W (2004)
+
WGS 1984

15

21

21

116° M >
< 296° M   12.6 NM

19

23

22

18

21

18

14

22

22

16

18

West End Rocks

16

6

21

22   HKBLL
18

23

21

18

22

104° M >
< 284° M
to CTWRK >
5.43NM

19   15

10

Veteran Rock

11   11

14

18

9

Hawksbill Cays

12

11

84° M >
< 264° M   4.21 NM

11

13 12
12

VETRK
12

11

10

15

19
17   13   12

17

16

15

19

15

86° M >
< 266° M   18.6 NM

N 26° 55'

14

15   18   17

< to GTSAL

14

15

16

15

West End Point

Fox Town
Ant 200' Fl R

Crown Haven

Little Abaco Island

NWPASN 8
7
5

West
End
Bars

5

7

Moses Cay

7

Daniel Cay

NWPASS

7

4½

Cashs Cay

Patton Cays

mud bank

1-2

Brush Cays

5-6

Cave Cay

10

N 26° 50'

Cross Cays

4   very shallow

very shallow   Spence Rock

Little Spence Rocks

For continuation see page 30

For continuation see page 47

See Important Note
Regarding Charts
Page 1

0   1   2   3

Nautical Miles

CARTERS CAYS TO MORAINE CAY (including Fox Town)

Boats transiting this area from Carters Cays to Moraine Cay or beyond must avoid the Carters Cays Bank and also the shoals stretching southeast from the Fish Cays. Waypoints for a suggested route are shown on the chart, and coordinates are printed below.

The preferred route from the Carters Cays to the Fish Cays requires a detour to the south around the Carters Cay Bank, which extends about 7 nautical miles ESE from the Carters Cays. There are several islets and rocks along its northern edge—the Pawpaw Rocks, the Pawpaw Cays, and Grouper Rocks. It is possible to go on the Atlantic side of the bank, but access to Carters Cays is more difficult from this side because of the shifting sand bank south of Big and Little Carters Cays, so the Sea of Abaco route is generally better. Please note that the waypoint CRTBSE is only about .25 NM from the edge of Carters Cays Bank. During the past ten years several cruisers have reported that Carters Bank has expanded and moved closer to the waypoint. We do check this waypoint and the bank each year, and we have found that the edge of the bank has **not** moved south. The edge of the bank is shallower than it used to be—it now consists of a series of ridges which are only about 1'-2' deep at MLW (a couple of years ago it was 3' MLW). The waypoint CRTBSE is a good waypoint located over 1500' away from the edge of the bank, but because it has led to some discomfort, we have added waypoint CRTBSE-2 to the chart. It is located about .6 NM south of the tip of the bank. Those who wish to stay a little further from Carters Bank should substitute CRTBSE-2 for CRTBSE. Anchorages can be found at the Fish Cays (for more detail see p. 44) and Moraine Cay (see page 46).

Boats transiting the southern portion of the chart are also provided with GPS waypoints. The suggested route passes south of Veteran Rock and West End Rocks, and north of the Hawksbill Cays. West End Rocks are generally plainly seen, but Veteran Rock is low-lying and difficult to see—we passed it several times going back and forth from Abaco to Florida before we saw it. Pay close attention and keep a sharp lookout when near it.

Along this route the only reasonable stop is Fox Town, which is on Little Abaco Island south of the Hawksbill Cays. See the large scale chart on page 45. Go west around the outermost rocks extending from Hawksbill Cays and proceed SE toward Fox Town. Avoid taking the western "short cut" when approaching or leaving Fox Town from the west because of several submerged rocks and heads in this area. Fuel, groceries and restaurants are all available at Fox Town. Anchor off or tie up at Fox Town Shell. It is also possible to anchor just south of the Hawksbill Cays and dinghy over to Fox Town. This provides better protection from the north.

Note that approximate course lines are provided for the Cave Cay/Spence Rock route to the Bight of Abaco. Give West End Point a 4.5 mile berth (off chart to west) to round West End Bars, then head for the northern tip of Cave Cay. Keep a sharp lookout and negotiate on a rising tide if you draw more than 4½'; controlling depth for this part of the route is about 5-6' MLW. A shorter route from the north to the south side of Little Abaco Island was recently found a little less than one nautical mile west of West End Point. Called the NW Pass, it carries 5' MLW over a hard rock and coral bottom. The course is true north and south (7°M/187°M). Waypoints are provided for it; attention should be given to cross track error. The route around the east side of Cave Cay and south to Spence Rock and the deeper waters of the Bight of Abaco will carry only about 4' MLW.

GPS waypoints for *Carters Cays to Moraine Cay*:

WPT	Description of Position	Latitude	Longitude
Northern route, west to east:			
CARTER	1 NM SSW Carters Cays	N 27° 03.528'	W 78° 01.087'
CRTBSW	SW Carters Bank	N 27° 00.994'	W 78° 01.049'
CRTBSE	SE corner of Carters Bank	N 27° 00.440'	W 77° 57.277'
CRTBSE-2	.6 NM S of SE corner Crts Bk	N 27° 00.080'	W 77° 57.277'
UPPER	¼ NM S Upper Cay	N 27° 01.683'	W 77° 49.210'
FISHSE	1 NM SE Fish Cays	N 27° 01.085'	W 77° 46.779'
MORAN	½ NM S Moraine Cay	N 27° 01.781'	W 77° 46.201'

Southern route, west to east (This is a portion of route from Florida to Abaco; for the entire route see page 17):

VETRK	½ NM S Veteran Rock	N 26° 55.950'	W 77° 52.290'
HKBLL	¼ NM N Hawksbill Cays	N 26° 56.890'	W 77° 47.690'

NW Pass waypoints:

NWPASN	N end NW Pass	N 26° 53.900'	W 77° 58.150'
NWPASS	S end NW Pass	N 26° 52.830'	W 77° 58.150'

Veteran Rock is difficult to see from the surface. It lies about halfway between Hawksbill Cays and West End Rocks, both of which are easily seen. It is located about .5 NM north of waypoint VETRK. The waypoint is located here to minimize cross track error in this area. This photo taken from the NE in July 2007 shows the western extension of Little Abaco Island in the background.

Cave Cay and Cashs Cay from the south with western extension of Little Abaco Island in the background. The route to the back side of Abaco is between these two cays; it carries about 4- 4 ½' MLW. See the chart on the facing page.

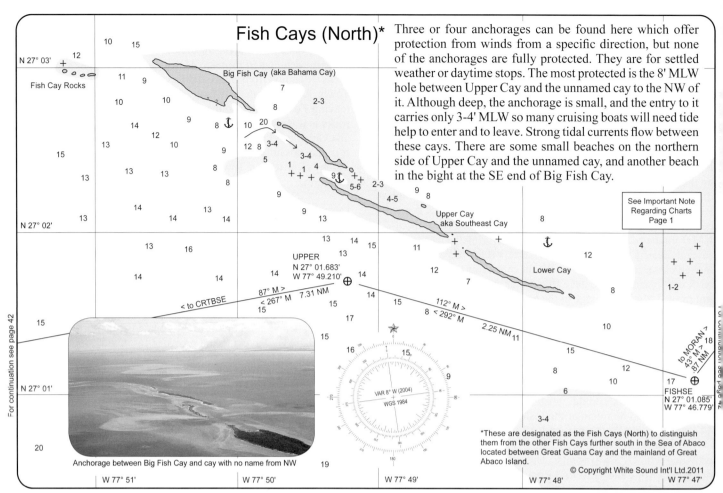

Fish Cays (North)*

Three or four anchorages can be found here which offer protection from winds from a specific direction, but none of the anchorages are fully protected. They are for settled weather or daytime stops. The most protected is the 8' MLW hole between Upper Cay and the unnamed cay to the NW of it. Although deep, the anchorage is small, and the entry to it carries only 3-4' MLW so many cruising boats will need tide help to enter and to leave. Strong tidal currents flow between these cays. There are some small beaches on the northern side of Upper Cay and the unnamed cay, and another beach in the bight at the SE end of Big Fish Cay.

See Important Note Regarding Charts Page 1

N 27° 03'
Fish Cay Rocks
Big Fish Cay (aka Bahama Cay)

UPPER
N 27° 01.683'
W 77° 49.210'

Upper Cay
aka Southeast Cay

Lower Cay

< to CRTBSE
87° M >
< 267° M 7.31 NM

112° M >
< 292° M
2.25 NM

to MORAN >
43° M >
.87 NM

FISHSE
N 27° 01.085'
W 77° 46.779'

VAR 8° W (2004)
WGS 1984

For continuation see page 42

Anchorage between Big Fish Cay and cay with no name from NW

N 27° 02'
N 27° 01'

W 77° 51'
W 77° 50'
W 77° 49'
W 77° 48'
W 77° 47'

*These are designated as the Fish Cays (North) to distinguish them from the other Fish Cays further south in the Sea of Abaco located between Great Guana Cay and the mainland of Great Abaco Island.

Crown Haven on Little Abaco Island with Foxtown and Hawksbill Cay in the background. Photo by Steve Dodge, 27 May 2011.

Hawksbill Cays and Fox Town

W77° 49' to CRTBSW
W 77° 48'
W 77° 47'
W 77° 46'

N 26° 57'

115° M
295° M
18

CTWRK >

HKBLL
N 26° 56.89'
W 77° 47.69'

84° M >
< 264° M   4.21 NM

< to VETRK

tire on pole

Hawksbill Cays

bares at MLW

bares at MLW

VAR 8° W (2004)
WGS 1984

7½

#4 stake
#3 #2 #1   stake

stake

3½

pole

Gov't Dock

Fox Town

Ant 200' Fl R

Parker Fuel

Fox Town Shell

Scherlin Bootle Highway

Little Abaco Island

N 26° 55'

For continuation see page 42

From the waypoint HKBLL proceed WSW in a sweeping turn to port, leaving the outermost rocks extending from the Hawksbill Cays (one of which is marked with a tire on a pole) a berth of about 150 yards. Round up into the anchorage and anchor in about 6' water over grass. Or proceed SE toward Fox Town staying far enough west to avoid the rocky bar, parts of which bare at MLW. Fuel (gas and diesel) is usually available in Fox Town. There is an outer line of four small brush covered rocks lying about 1/4 mile off Fox Town (numbered 1-4 from east to west on chart). Go between #1 and #2 to go to the public dock. To get to Fox Town Shell round rock #1. To go to Parker Fuel go east of #4. Controlling depth for these is about 3-4' MLW, with Fox Town Shell a little deeper than Parker Fuel. Fox Town Shell can be contacted at 365-2046 or VHF 16 if in range. Local pilots will usually offer services if you wait outside the four rocks.

See Important Note Regarding Charts Page 1

© Copyright White Sound Int'l Ltd. 2010

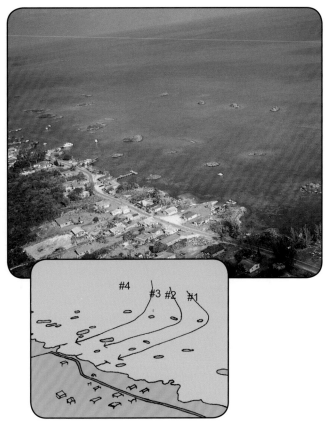

#4 #3 #2 #1

Fox Town

Moraine Cay

Proceed directly toward the mid-point of the beach on Moraine Cay from the waypoint MORAN and enter the anchorage in about 7-8' MLW. Anchor in about 6-7' MLW over grass. This reef protected anchorage offers protection from west, north, and east winds, but is fully exposed to the south. Moraine Cay is a delightful daytime or (good weather) overnight stop. The beach is just a few feet from the anchorage, and the reef to the east is pristine and beautiful. The island is private, and a residence has been built there by the owner. The reef, which breaks in almost all weather, offers protection but does not impede the view to the east, and the vistas from this anchorage give one the feeling of being anchored on the edge of civilization. Reports indicate thc cay is for sale.

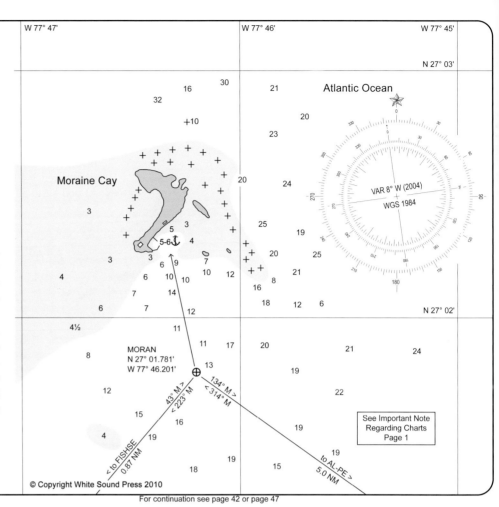

For continuation see page 42 or page 47

Moraine Cay from the SSW 11 July 2002.

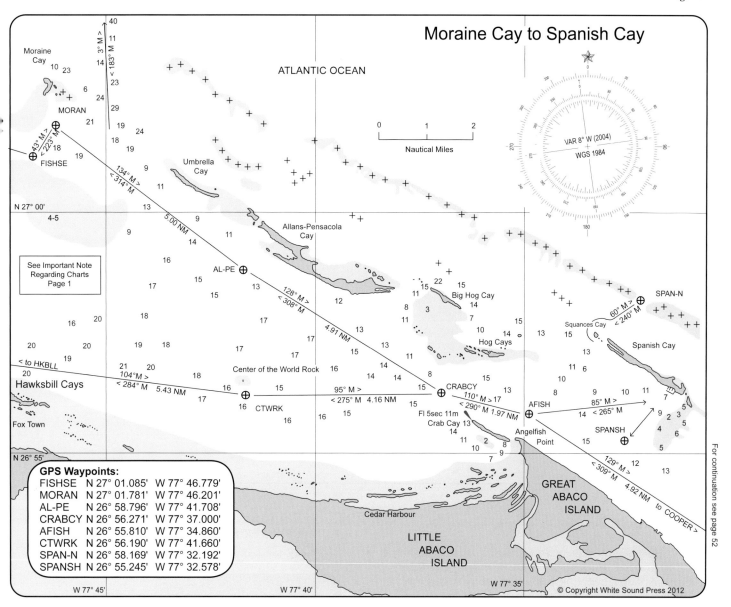

Moraine Cay to Spanish Cay

GPS Waypoints:
FISHSE	N 27° 01.085'	W 77° 46.779'
MORAN	N 27° 01.781'	W 77° 46.201'
AL-PE	N 26° 58.796'	W 77° 41.708'
CRABCY	N 26° 56.271'	W 77° 37.000'
AFISH	N 26° 55.810'	W 77° 34.860'
CTWRK	N 26° 56.190'	W 77° 41.660'
SPAN-N	N 26° 58.169'	W 77° 32.192'
SPANSH	N 26° 55.245'	W 77° 32.578'

© Copyright White Sound Press 2012

For continuation see page 52

MORAINE CAY TO SPANISH CAY

Boats transiting this area need to avoid three shoal areas: the first is a very large area which extends southeastward from the area of the Fish Cays, which are off the chart west of Moraine Cay, and stretches to the south of Moraine Cay, the second surrounds the Hog Cays, and the third lies south of the southeast point of Spanish Cay. Also, the north coastline of Little Abaco Island is shoal and sprinkled with small, low islets. One should stay a mile or two off shore. Fox Town is the only settlement on Little Abaco Island which has an anchorage for boats drawing over 1-2'. Center of the World Rock, lying about two miles north of Little Abaco Island, is about halfway between Crab Cay and Foxtown. It is marked with a white post.

Moraine Cay is a beautiful reef anchorage exposed from the southeast to southwest, but offering good protection in other winds. It has a beautiful beach and the reef offers excellent snorkeling. See the chart on page 46.

Allans-Pensacola has an abandoned missile tracking station, some nice beaches, and a good harbour at its northwest end. See the chart on page 48.

The Hog Cays are a group of small cays and rocks on a shallow bank, but there is deep water and a reasonable anchorage off the southwest corner of the southeasternmost cay. The very small

harbour on the north side of this same cay has shoaled in recent years and is no longer useable by boats larger than outboards.

There is an anchorage protected from the east and south located southwest of Crab Cay. Round the northern end of the cay and go either side of a shoal area (2-5' MLW) running roughly parallel to Crab Cay. Anchor in 8' MLW just SW of the SE end of Crab Cay. There are no beaches and no development in this area, but plenty of small islets and shallow water for dinghy exploration.

Spanish Cay has a large full service marina with a well-stocked store, resort accomodations ashore, restaurant, bar, pool, beautiful beaches, an airstrip and friendly service. See page 50 for more detailed information about Spanish Cay.

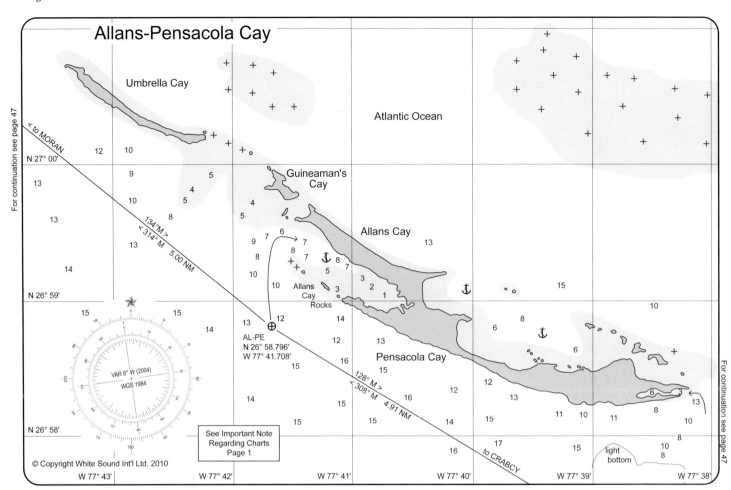

Allans-Pensacola Cay

Umbrella Cay

For continuation see page 47

< to MORAN

N 27° 00'

134° M >
< 314° M   5.00 NM

Guineaman's Cay

Atlantic Ocean

Allans Cay

N 26° 59'

VAR 8° W (2004)
WGS 1984

Allans Cay Rocks

AL-PE
N 26° 58.796'
W 77° 41.708'

Pensacola Cay

128° M >
< 308° M   4.91 NM

N 26° 58'

© Copyright White Sound Int'l Ltd. 2010

See Important Note Regarding Charts Page 1

to CRABCY

light bottom

For continuation see page 47

W 77° 43'   W 77° 42'   W 77° 41'   W 77° 40'   W 77° 39'   W 77° 38'

Allans-Pensacola Cay

To enter the principal anchorage at Allans-Pensacola Cay proceed to the north from waypoint AL-PE toward Guineaman's Cay. Leave the northwesternmost Allans Cay Rock about 75 yards to starboard to avoid the submerged rocks and bar extending from it, and then turn to starboard into the harbour favouring the northeast side. Anchor in 7-8' over grass and sand which is over marl. The holding ground is not the best. Allans-Pensacola's popularity is based on the easy access and good protection in all winds except W and NW. For winds in this sector, shelter can be found on the Atlantic Ocean side of the cay (see anchorages indicated on chart), but these will be exposed and unsafe if or when the NW wind clocks to the N and NE as it usually does during the winter months.

Within the past few decades Allans Cay and Pensacola Cay were two separate cays. They were joined as the result of a hurricane, and now seem to be permanently a single cay—Allans-Pensacola. The ruins of a United States missile tracking station can be found on the isthmus at the head of the harbour, which is also the site of the best beach on the island. There is a "signing tree" on the ocean beach northeast of the anchorage, where cruisers have left signed momentos of their visit here.

There is complete protection in the very small mangrove-lined hurricane hole at the east end of the cay. Controlling depth in the small creek is about 3' MLW in several places (favour the south side)—there is 6' MLW inside.

Allans-Pensacola Cay

Allans-Pensacola Cay in May 2003.

CRAB CAY / ANGELFISH POINT

The anchorage at Crab Cay / Angelfish Point offers excellent protection for all winds except NW through W. It is a pleasant normally empty anchorage off a pretty beach with low scubby rocks on the western side. Enter on either side of the shoal from the waypoint CRABCY. Off this chart to the south the water narrows and ends at a causeway built to support the road connecting Great Abaco Island to Little Abaco Island. It is generally believed that this causeway has caused environmental damage, and the Bahamian government has announced that it will replace the causeway, which blocks water flow from the Sea of Abaco to the waters west of Great Abaco Island, with a bridge. When this project is completed it is likely that there will be a strong current through this area which may make a Bahamian Moor a necessity.

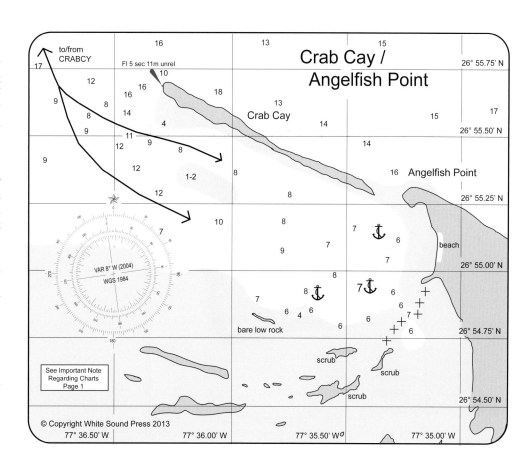

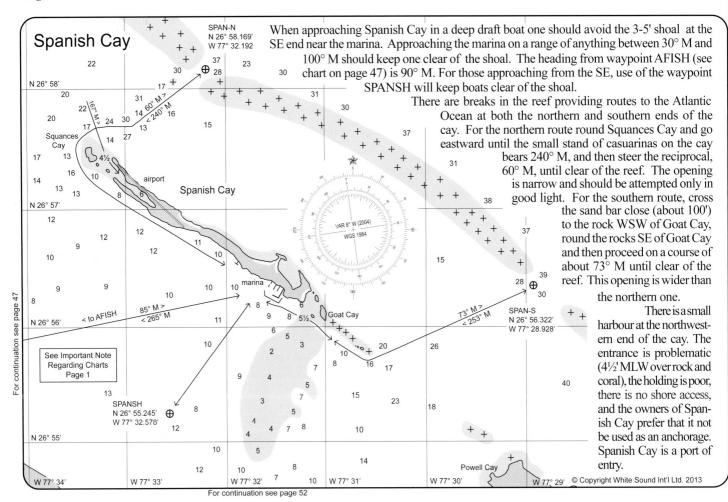

Spanish Cay

When approaching Spanish Cay in a deep draft boat one should avoid the 3-5' shoal at the SE end near the marina. Approaching the marina on a range of anything between 30° M and 100° M should keep one clear of the shoal. The heading from waypoint AFISH (see chart on page 47) is 90° M. For those approaching from the SE, use of the waypoint SPANSH will keep boats clear of the shoal.

There are breaks in the reef providing routes to the Atlantic Ocean at both the northern and southern ends of the cay. For the northern route round Squances Cay and go eastward until the small stand of casuarinas on the cay bears 240° M, and then steer the reciprocal, 60° M, until clear of the reef. The opening is narrow and should be attempted only in good light. For the southern route, cross the sand bar close (about 100') to the rock WSW of Goat Cay, round the rocks SE of Goat Cay and then proceed on a course of about 73° M until clear of the reef. This opening is wider than the northern one.

There is a small harbour at the northwestern end of the cay. The entrance is problematic (4½' MLW over rock and coral), the holding is poor, there is no shore access, and the owners of Spanish Cay prefer that it not be used as an anchorage. Spanish Cay is a port of entry.

© Copyright White Sound Int'l Ltd. 2013

For continuation see page 47

For continuation see page 52

See Important Note Regarding Charts Page 1

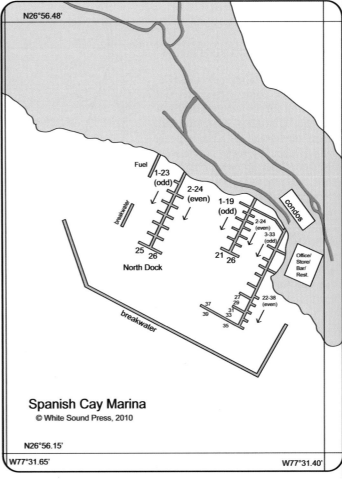

Spanish Cay Marina
© White Sound Press, 2010

N26°56.48'

N26°56.15'

W77°31.65'

W77°31.40'

Fuel
1-23 (odd)
2-24 (even)
1-19 (odd)
2-24 (even)
3-33 (odd)
breakwater
25 26
21 26
North Dock
condos
Office/ Store/ Bar/ Rest.
37 39
27 29 31 33
22-38 (even)
35
breakwater

Spanish Cay

Spanish Cay is a beautiful private resort now open to the boating world. Our facilities include eighty-one new slips with full hook-ups, a new air conditioned bar and a new fresh water pool and jaccuzzi. Come stay in one of our new beachfront rooms on the ocean. Two and four bedroom condo and hotel suites are also available. Rent a golf cart to visit one or all of our three beautiful beaches. You can leave your boat and have your pilot bring you back to paradise on our 5,000 foot runway. Spanish Cay is a port of entry offering Customs and Immigration seven days a week. We now offer both gas and diesel at our new fuel dock located right by the marina. If tennis is your game, we have four courts. Dine at our on-site restaurant or shop in our grocery store and gift shop. Our beautiful sunsets are free.

Marina: Water at low tide: 8½-9 feet • Power: 30; 50; 100; single & 3 phase • Water - Reverse Osmosis • Public Telephone • Accomodation for boats up to 200 feet

Rooms: • 18 Hotel Rooms beachfront or marina view • 5 Condos - two and four bedrooms • 2 Private Homes

Spanish Cay • Abaco, Bahamas
Island: 1-954-213-6195 / 1-242-365-0083
Fax 1-242-365-0453
Florida Office: 1-954-689-9248   Fax: 1-954-689-9249
spanishcay@aol.com • www.spanishcay.com
VHF 16

3006 SW 2nd Avenue, Fort Lauderdale, FL 33315

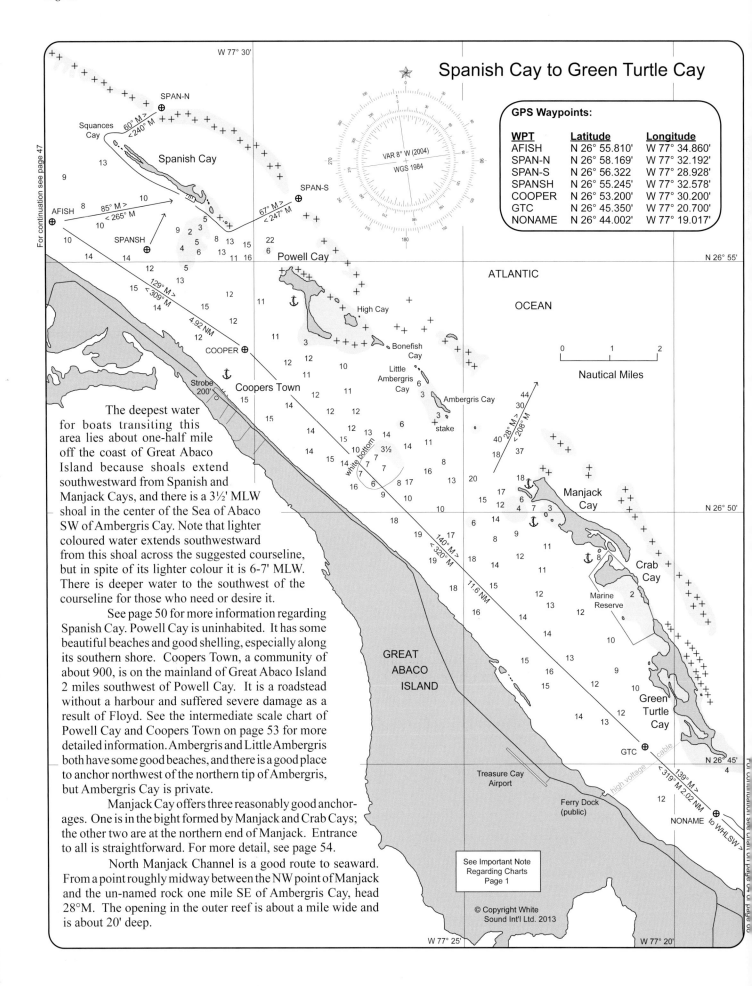

Spanish Cay to Green Turtle Cay

GPS Waypoints:

WPT	Latitude	Longitude
AFISH	N 26° 55.810'	W 77° 34.860'
SPAN-N	N 26° 58.169'	W 77° 32.192'
SPAN-S	N 26° 56.322'	W 77° 28.928'
SPANSH	N 26° 55.245'	W 77° 32.578'
COOPER	N 26° 53.200'	W 77° 30.200'
GTC	N 26° 45.350'	W 77° 20.700'
NONAME	N 26° 44.002'	W 77° 19.017'

VAR 8° W (2004)
WGS 1984

ATLANTIC OCEAN

Nautical Miles

The deepest water for boats transiting this area lies about one-half mile off the coast of Great Abaco Island because shoals extend southwestward from Spanish and Manjack Cays, and there is a 3½' MLW shoal in the center of the Sea of Abaco SW of Ambergris Cay. Note that lighter coloured water extends southwestward from this shoal across the suggested courseline, but in spite of its lighter colour it is 6-7' MLW. There is deeper water to the southwest of the courseline for those who need or desire it.

See page 50 for more information regarding Spanish Cay. Powell Cay is uninhabited. It has some beautiful beaches and good shelling, especially along its southern shore. Coopers Town, a community of about 900, is on the mainland of Great Abaco Island 2 miles southwest of Powell Cay. It is a roadstead without a harbour and suffered severe damage as a result of Floyd. See the intermediate scale chart of Powell Cay and Coopers Town on page 53 for more detailed information. Ambergris and Little Ambergris both have some good beaches, and there is a good place to anchor northwest of the northern tip of Ambergris, but Ambergris Cay is private.

Manjack Cay offers three reasonably good anchorages. One is in the bight formed by Manjack and Crab Cays; the other two are at the northern end of Manjack. Entrance to all is straightforward. For more detail, see page 54.

North Manjack Channel is a good route to seaward. From a point roughly midway between the NW point of Manjack and the un-named rock one mile SE of Ambergris Cay, head 28°M. The opening in the outer reef is about a mile wide and is about 20' deep.

GREAT ABACO ISLAND

Treasure Cay Airport

Ferry Dock (public)

Green Turtle Cay

Crab Cay

Marine Reserve

Manjack Cay

See Important Note Regarding Charts Page 1

For continuation see page 47

Coopers Town and Powell Cay

The map shows positions with depth soundings. Key labels:

- W 77° 31', W 77° 30', W 77° 29', W 77° 28'
- N 26° 55', N 26° 54', N 26° 53', N 26° 52'
- VAR 8° W (2004), WGS 1984
- Powell Cay
- Soldier Cay
- High Cay
- COOPER N 26° 53.200' W 77° 30.200'
- < to AFISH 4.92 NM
- 129° M > < 309° M
- 140° M > < 320° M
- to GTC > 11.6 NM
- Great Abaco Island
- Coopers Town
- Public Dock
- Strobe 200'
- Murray's Service Station
- © Copyright White Sound Int'l Ltd. 2013

For continuation see page 52

The approach to both the Powell Cay anchorage and Coopers Town from the vicinity of waypoint COOPER is straightforward and requires no elaboration. Powell Cay and Coopers Town are a good pair. Powell Cay offers solitude and pristine beauty, Coopers Town offers services and supplies. The Powell Cay anchorage is good for N and E winds, and if it kicks up from the S or W, it is possible to weigh anchor and power over to Coopers Town and drop the hook again. Neither one offers good protection from the NW.

There are excellent beaches on Powell Cay, which also offers good hiking and exploring. There is a path to the top of the bluffs where a fine view of the entire anchorage can be gained.

Coopers Town has grown dramatically during the past thirty years. It is the seat for the Administrator for northern Abaco, and also houses other government offices. A government medical clinic opened a few years ago. All docks in Coopers Town were destroyed by hurricane Floyd in 1999 and again by Frances and Jeanne in 2004. Coopers Town Shell re-opened for business, but call them on VHF 16 to make certain they have fuel. Nearby alternatives are Spanish Cay and Green Turtle Cay. The M and M Restaurant is on the Scherlin Bootle Highway near the south edge of town. There are two grocery stores.

Powell Cay from the north with a few boats in the anchorage. Coopers Town and Great Abaco Island can be seen in the background. Beyond Great Abaco is the Bight of Abaco.

Coopers Town from the southeast.

Manjack and Crab Cays

The large bight formed by Manjack (pronounced Munjack or sometimes Nunjack) and Crab Cays provides a delightful anchorage, though it is not protected from the south through the west. Entry is straightforward. Vessels drawing more than 4' should not go east of Rat Cay. The docks on the NW side of the anchorage are private. The mangrove creek is shallow, but is easily explored by dinghy at high tide. The beach along the northeast side of Manjack is pretty and there is some good diving and snorkeling just offshore. The two anchorages at the NW end of Manjack are both attractive. The northernmost one is open to the northwest and north, and the other is open to the west and southwest. A shallow rocky bar extends NW from the rocks at the SE side of the entrance to the latter, so stay close to the NW side. The dock

Several boats in the anchorage at Manjack and Crab Cays. This photo was taken from the SE. Generally boats drawing more than four feet should not go east of Rat Cay.

on the north side is part of a land development in which there are roads which lead to a very beautiful beach along the north shore of Manjack Cay. There is also a park in a mangrove swamp area and a nature walk. Visitors are welcome.

For continuation see page 52

N 26° 51'

N 26° 50'

N 26° 49'

N 26° 48'

ATLANTIC

OCEAN

scattered heads
(not surveyed)

scattered heads
(not surveyed)

Manjack Rocks

Manjack
Beach

Manjack Cay

Coconut Tree
Bay

Manjack Bluff

SEA

OF

ABACO

Rat Cay

Manjack
Cay

Manjack
Harbour
(shallow)

Crab Cay Bluff

Crab Cay

Fiddle Cay

Crab Cay Marine Reserve

VAR 8° W (2004)
WGS 1984

See Important Note
Regarding Charts
Page 1

© Copyright White Sound Int'l Ltd. 2013

W 77° 24'

W 77° 23'

W 77° 22'

W 77° 21'

For continuation see page 52

The anchorage at Manjack and Crab Cays from the northwest in 2004.

This is the limestone rock bluff near the southwest extremity of Crab Cay, and is typical of the limestone base of the Bahamian islands. The Bahama Banks were built of calcium carbonate over a period of 200 million years; they now tower about 1 1/2 miles above the floor of the sea. The calcium carbonate was extracted from the sea in a variety of ways, including the growth and death of shell fish, the growth of coral reefs, and the creation of oolitic sand. The present islands were built up higher than the rest of the banks when sea level was up to 100' higher than it is today. When the earth cooled and the polar ice caps re-formed, sea level declined leaving the limestone islands. Limestone is a soft rock which has been carved by the waves of the sea at the periphery of the islands and cays, dissolved by rainfall, and weathered by winds.

Green Turtle Cay

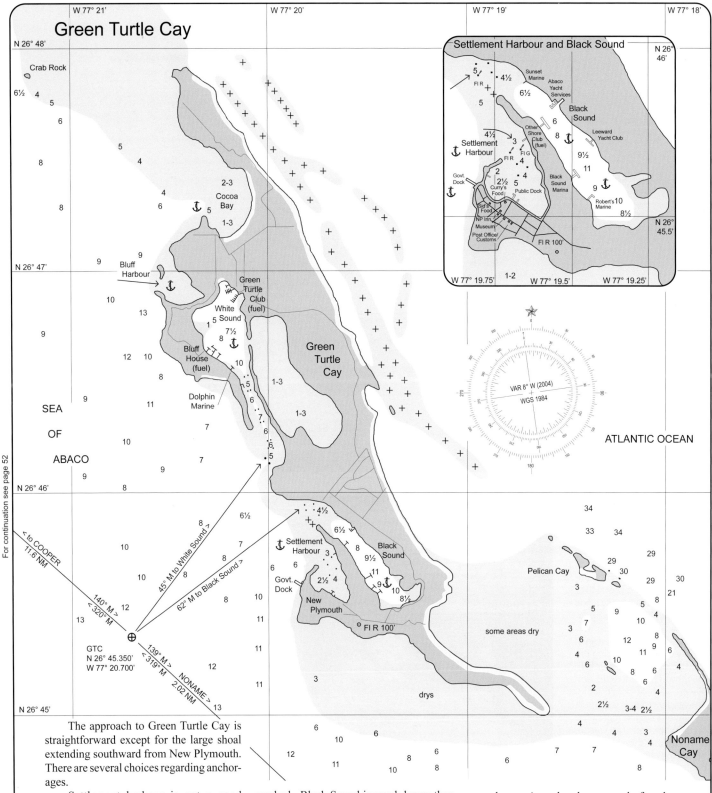

SEA

OF

ABACO

ATLANTIC OCEAN

VAR 8° W (2004)
WGS 1984

Settlement Harbour and Black Sound

The approach to Green Turtle Cay is straightforward except for the large shoal extending southward from New Plymouth. There are several choices regarding anchorages.

Settlement harbour is not a good choice for boats drawing more than about 2'. Although the channel is well-marked and carries about 3', there is very little room inside. When it is possible to rely on easterly winds, boats often anchor in the area off the government dock rather than going into the harbour. This is not a good winter anchorage because it is exposed to the west and northwest.

The entrance to Black Sound carries about 4½-5' MLW. It is narrow but well-marked. Black Sound is much larger than the harbour at New Plymouth, but deep grass often clogs anchors, especially Danforths. Dockage is available at Abaco Yacht Services, Leeward Yacht Club, the Other Shore Club, and Black Sound Marina. Fuel is available at the Other Shore Club on the NW side of Black Sound.

There are two signs at the entrance to the channel to White Sound. The dredged channel is 30' wide and carries about 4½-5' MLW. Stay between the pairs of red and green buoys. A good anchorage can be found in the area between the Bluff House dock and the Green Turtle Club dock. Avoid the 1' MLW rocky shoal just north of the Bluff House docks. Dockage and fuel can be purchased at either place. Quiet anchorages can be found further north at Bluff Harbour and Cocoa Bay, but Bluff Harbour is small and there is no public dinghy dock, and Cocoa Bay is shallow. See marina maps for Green Turtle Club and Bluff House on p. 58.

For continuation see page 52

For continuation see page 64 or 68

Entrance to White Sound, Green Turtle Cay

Approach from the SW. Head to the left of the beach.

Go between the signs.

Turn to the NNW following the green and red buoys.

Continue approx. NNW for about .5 NM and enter the anchorage.

Approaches to Settlement Harbour, New Plymouth, Black Sound, and White Sound, Green Turtle Cay.

Aerial of entrance to White Sound, Green Turtle Cay, 11 July 2002.

Entrance to Black Sound, Green Turtle Cay

Approach from WSW; note that the deep water channel is on the north (port side when entering) side of the opening. A rocky shoal extends across the rest of the opening.

Pilings with red and green arrows mark the channel, which turns to the SE (starboard when entering).

Turn to starboard (marked by pilings with arrows) and enter Black Sound. Abaco Yacht Services is to port, the Other Shore Club and Black Sound Marina to starboard.

NEW PLYMOUTH AND GREEN TURTLE CAY

Green Turtle Cay is a small island with a population of about 450, but it offers visiting yachtsmen exceptional variety with several different anchorages, and an excellent array of restaurants, hotels, marine services, and shopping facilities. Restaurants in New Plymouth include the McIntosh Restaurant and Bakery, the Blue Bee Bar and Restaurant, the Wreckin' Tree Bakery and Restaurant, the Plymouth Rock, and Pineapples Bar and Grill. At White Sound the Green Turtle Club and Bluff House both offer excellent dining. Bluff House has rebult and re-opened its beach bar on the Sea of Abaco—with a complimentary dock (up to 30') and moorings for bar patrons.

There are three hotels—Bluff House and the Green Turtle Club at White Sound, and the New Plymouth Inn in New Plymouth. Leeward Yacht Club has rental accomodations, and there are cottages and houses for rent throughout the island.

Abaco Yacht Services on Black Sound is a complete boat yard with a large Travelift. Marine fuel is available at the Other Shore Club, the Green Turtle Club, and the Bluff House. Abaco Yacht Services is a Yamaha dealer; Roberts Marine and Sunset Marine (both in Black Sound) are Evinrude/Johnson dealers.

There are three grocery stores—Sid's, Lowe's, and Curry's—and two hardware stores—Roberts Hardware and New Plymouth Hardware. There are several gift shops in town.

The Albert Lowe Museum houses artifacts and photographs which tell the story of the history of New Plymouth. It has ship models built by the late Albert Lowe, and paintings by Albert's talented and well-known artist son, New Plymouth native Alton Lowe. Alton's brother Vertrum has ship models he builds on display in his home near Curry's food Store. The Memorial Sculpture Garden features bronze busts of persons who have played important roles in Bahamian history, and a centerpiece sculpture depicting the arrival of loyalists from the United States. The Captain Roland Roberts House Environmental Center features the restored house itself and educational information on the ecology of local coral reefs. Also, there is a gallery with paintings on display in a section of Alton Lowe's hilltop home, which is located east of New Plymouth.

Green Turtle Cay is small enough so that one can cover a good part of the island on foot, but bicycles and golf carts can be rented.

See the business directory on page 198 for a more complete list of businesses and services available at Green Turtle Cay .

Entrance to Black Sound in July 2010. Note that the pilings marking the entry can be seen in this photograph. The large boat yard on the port side soon after entering is Abaco Yacht Services The dock opposite it is the Other Shore Club. Leeward Yacht Club is beyond Abaco Yacht Services on the NE shore; Black Sound Marina is about 0.5 NM from the entrance on the starboard side (SW shore). Sunset Marine is located off the starboard side of the boat exiting Black Sound.

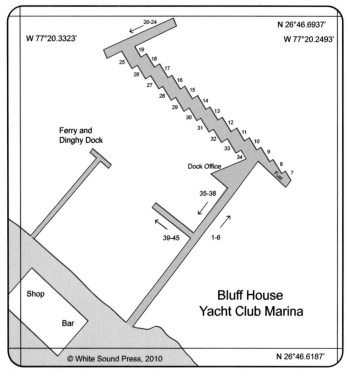

Bluff House
Yacht Club Marina

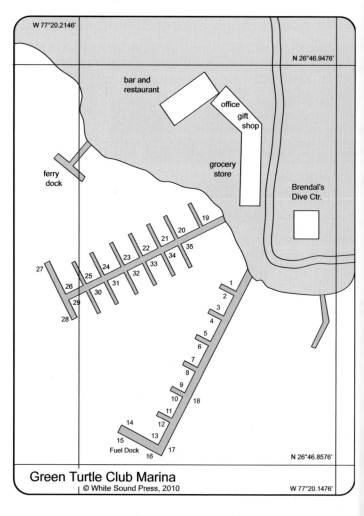

Green Turtle Club Marina
© White Sound Press, 2010

Bluff House

BEACH RESORT & MARINA

Green Turtle Cay
BAHAMAS

Bluff House Beach Resort & Marina has been described as the "most special piece of property in Abaco." Perched on the highest point of Green Turtle Cay, this 12 acre tropical Bahamian paradise stretches from White Sound Harbour to the Sea of Abaco. The new owners are currently creating a "major makeover" on the more than 50-year-old Bluff House while remaining dedicated to retaining its old charm and first class service. See what the new Bluff House has to offer!

Full-Service, 46-Slip Marina accommodating vessels up to 120' as well as six large catamaran slips. Fuel, gas, ice and bait are available from our docks on White Sound. Complimentary cable TV and Wi-Fi. Seven new restrooms, showers and laundry facilities.

Luxurious **Bluff House Hotel Suites** with spectacular views overlooking the Sea of Abaco. All suites have overwater balconies, flat-screen TVs, complimentary Wi-Fi and the Bluff House Private Beach is just steps away from your suite. New **Home Sites** on the Bluff House property are also available.

Our latest addition is the **Tranquil Turtle Beach Bar** located directly on the Sea of Abaco where guests can swim and lounge on our private beach and enjoy island food and tropical drinks on the Patio Deck. Tie up at our dock or dinghy in for the local music, stunning sunsets and unsurpassed hospitality.

The **Jolly Roger Bar & Bistro** serves up delicious breakfasts, lunches and dinners seven days a week. Dine outside on the harbourside deck or inside in our cozy, air-conditioned dining room with great views of the water. Relax in the sun by our fresh water Swimming Pool adjacent to the Jolly Roger.

The **Low Tide Gift Shop** is filled with island goodies, resort wear, stylish tees, hats and jewelry.

Our front desk can arrange golf cart rentals, boat rentals, fishing trips, diving excursions and local information for the best spots to explore on Green Turtle and surrounding cays.

Inquire about our ever popular **Wedding and Honeymoon Packages**.

Bluff House
BEACH RESORT & MARINA
Green Turtle Cay
BAHAMAS

Bluff House Beach Resort & Marina, Green Turtle Cay, Abaco, The Bahamas • GPS: 26°46'37" N 77°20'20" W
Phones: Toll Free (800) 745-4911 • Local (242)365-4247 • Fax (954) 656-1073
Website: www.bluffhouse.com • Email: frontdesk@bluffhouse.com

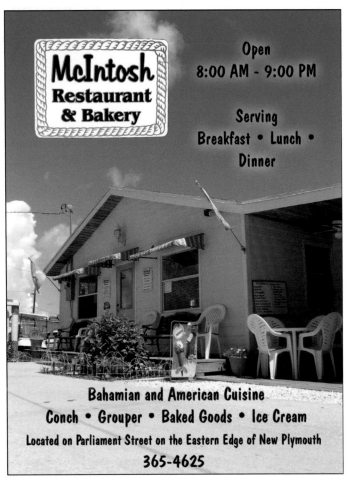

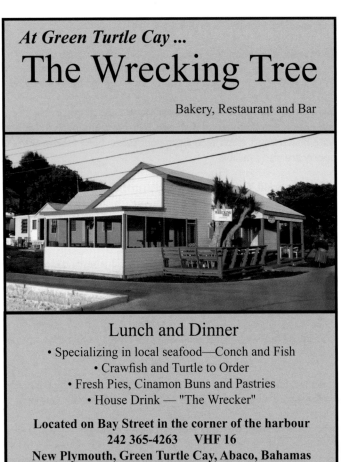

Serving New Plymouth and the entire Green Turtle Cay Area

- Fresh Fruit and Vegetables
- Frozen Meat
- Dry and Canned Goods
- Homemade Breads
- Block Ice and Bait

Wide Selection   Fast Efficient Service

VISA MasterCard

**Located Near Town Dock
New Plymouth, Green Turtle Cay
242 365-4055**

Brendal's Dive Center
Established 1985

Bahamas Tourism Cacique
Award for Tourism's Finest

Platinum Pro Instructor
OVER 5000 STUDENTS TAUGHT

One of the Caribbean's Best 5 Dive
Destinations ... *Frommer's March 2009*

DIVE with The BAHAMAS LEGENDARY
Brendal - over 25 years experience

**242 365-4411 Direct
VHF 16**
White Sound, Green Turtle Cay
Abaco, Bahamas
www.brendal.com
Email: brendal@brendal.com

as featured
on the Discovery and CNN Travel Channel

- P.A.D.I. International Resort
- S.S.I. Teaching Facility
- S.D.I. Training Facility
- Universal Referral Location - NAUI,SSI,NASDS,PDIC, IDEA,YMCA
- Adventure Specialty Trips -Fresh Seafood prepared on the beach with Hand Feed the Sting Rays Day! -Wild Dolphin Encounter Day! -Island Hopping Day!
- Dive "Original Tarpon Dive" Discovered by Brendal
- Reef, Historic Wreck, Catacombs, Mini Walls, Caverns and Night Dives
- Discover Scuba through Assist. Instructor Courses
- Sunset Sailing Cruises
- Glassbottom Reef Tours
- Private Charters
- Kayak Rentals
- NEW Full Service Dive Center and Retail Sales

ON THE WATER — SPECTACULAR SUNSETS!!!
Located at The Other Shore Club • Serving Lunch and Dinner...Open
11:00 am until ... HAPPY HOUR 4-6 - Fresh Conch Salad • Great food and
drinks ... lots of fun things to do ... live music and sunfish races ... friendly
and courteous service ... Please join us!
242 365-4226 • VHF 16
othershoreclub@gmail.com • www.othershoreclub.com

The new dinghy dock located adjacent to the commercial dock on the
Sea of Abaco at the foot of Parliament Street in New Plymouth

NATIVE CREATIONS

Floral and Gift Shop
*Come browse in our friendly shop located in the
heart of New Plymouth on Parliament Street. It is
chock full of silk flowers and locally made gifts,
sterling silver jewelery, including work from Silver
Moon Designs, Abaco Ceramics pieces, Androsia
Products and Fabric, and much more. It would be
our pleasure to serve you.*

**Green Turtle Cay, Abaco, Bahamas
242 365-4206**

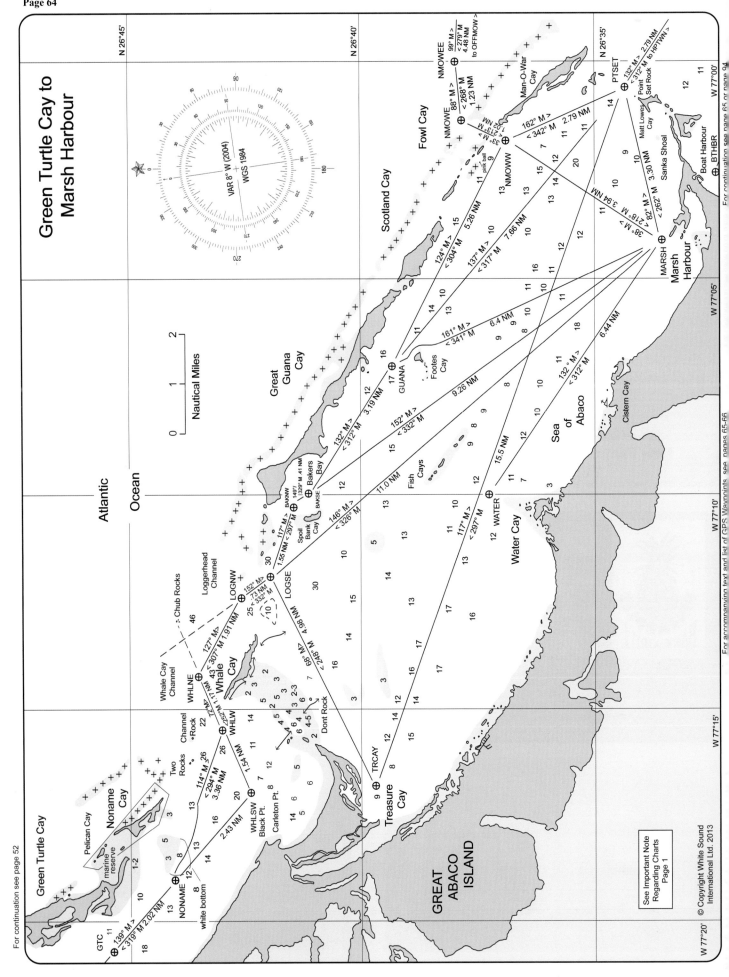

Green Turtle Cay to Marsh Harbour

VAR 8° W (2004)
WGS 1984

Nautical Miles

Atlantic

Ocean

Green Turtle Cay

Pelican Cay

Noname Cay

marine reserve

Two Rocks

Channel Rock

Chub Rocks

Loggerhead Channel

Whale Cay Channel

Whale Cay

Dont Rock

Black Pt.

Carleton Pt.

Great Guana Cay

Scotland Cay

Fowl Cay

Man-O-War Cay

pink ball

Footes Cay

Bakers Bay

Spoil Bank Cay

Fish Cays

Water Cay

Cistem Cay

Sea of Abaco

GREAT ABACO ISLAND

Matt Lowes Point
Set Rock
Sanka Shoal
Boat Harbour

NMOWEE
99° M >
< 279° M
4.48 NM
to OFFMOW >

NMOWE
88° M >
< 268° M
1.23 NM

PTSET
132° M >
< 312° M 2.79 NM
to HPTWN >

BTHBR

NMOWE
33° M >
< 213° M 1.21 NM

NMOWW

162° M > 2.79 NM
< 342° M

14

MARSH
38° M >
< 218° M 3.94 NM
82° M >
< 262° M 3.30 NM

Marsh Harbour

124° M >
< 304° M 5.26 NM

137° M > 7.66 NM
< 317° M

161° M >
< 341° M 6.4 NM

152° M >
< 332° M 9.26 NM

132° M >
< 312° M

15.5 NM

6.44 NM

GUANA

117° M >
< 297° M 3.19 NM

132° M >
< 312° M

117° M >
< 297° M

WATER

BAKNW
149'
BAKSE

146° M >
< 326° M

11.0 NM

LOGNW
152° M >
< 332° M

.73 NM

LOGSE
.10

68° M >
< 248° M 4.98 NM

25

30

WHLNE
127° M >
< 307° M 1.91 NM

43° M >
< 223° M 1.17 NM

72° M >
< 252° M

WHLW

114° M >
< 294° M 3.36 NM

WHLSW
1.54 NM

2.43 NM

TRCAY

Treasure Cay

9

GTC
139° M >
< 319° M 2.02 NM

NONAME

white bottom

18

90

Great Guana Cay

Scotland Cay

For continuation see page 52

For continuation see page 65 or page 94

For accompanying text and list of GPS Waypoints see pages 65-66

See Important Note Regarding Charts Page 1

N 26°45'   N 26°40'   N 26°35'

W 77°20'   W 77°15'   W 77°10'   W 77°05'   W 77°00'

Marsh Harbour to Little Harbour

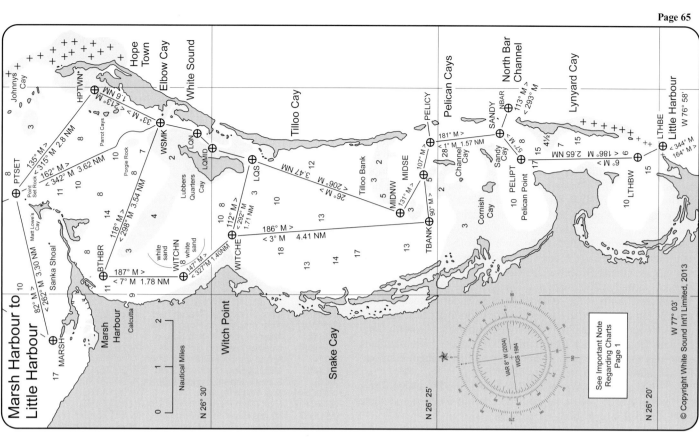

For continuation see page 150

GREEN TURTLE CAY TO MARSH HARBOUR

The area from Green Turtle Cay to Marsh Harbour is probably the most popular cruising area in Abaco—perhaps the most popular in the entire Bahamas. It is about 20 miles long and about 5 miles wide and offers the cruiser incredible variety—snug harbours, beautiful beaches, ocean cruising, quaint villages, good diving, excellent restaurants, good anchorages, fancy marinas, and good shopping. All continuous suggested course lines on the chart carry at least 6' MLW.

Boats drawing more than about 4' must avoid the shallow bank extending the area from Treasure Cay (which is actually located on the mainland of Great Abaco Island) to Whale Cay. The prefered route in moderate weather is outside Whale Cay. The inside routes (shown as discontinuous lines) carry about 3-5' MLW. For more detailed information regarding Whale Cay passage, see pages 68-69.

After re-entering the Sea of Abaco there are shoals extending from Spoil Bank Cay, created when a cruise ship channel was dredged at Baker's Bay at the north end of Great Guana Cay in 1989. There are some additional small shoals between this cay and Treasure Cay. There are no other major obstacles to navigation in the area.

There is a daytime anchorage at No Name Cay, which is uninhabited. Head for a point near the northern end of the cay on a heading of about 40 degrees to avoid the bars extending SE from Green Turtle Cay and W from the SE end of No Name Cay. When about ¼ mile offshore, turn to starboard and anchor off the entrance to the island's lagoon. A shallow rocky bar at the entrance of the lagoon bares at low water—so exploration is by dinghy at half tide or better.

A new marina—Sand Bank Landing—on the mainland of Great Abaco Island north of the Treasure Cay beach is expected to open in 2013 with 16 slips and a fuel dock. It will offer an excellent view of conditions in the Whale Cay Channel. See page 66 for more information.

There is another daytime anchorage to the west of the north tip of Whale Cay, which is also uninhabited. Like the anchorage at No Name Cay, it is exposed from the S to the NW.

Treasure Cay is a resort community. It has a marina, condominiums, privately owned
continued on page 66

The Sea of Abaco narrows at its southern end, but continues to offer great variety for the visitor. Two of Abaco's principal communities—Marsh Harbour and Hope Town—are at the northern perimeter of this area. There are beautiful beaches, Pelican Cays Land and Sea Park, and three viable passages between the Sea of Abaco and the Atlantic Ocean. At its southern perimeter is Little Harbour, home of the art community founded by the late Randolph Johnston and now maintained by his son Pete.

There are several shoals in the area. The largest are Lubbers Bank, which extends about 2½ miles NW of Lubbers Quarters Cay, and Tilloo Bank, which extends 1½ to 2 miles W from Tilloo Cay. Also, most of the area west of Channel, Gorling, Sandy, and Cornish Cays is shallow. All suggested course lines on this chart carry about 6' MLW, with the exception of the course through Lubber's Quarters Channel, which carries about 4½-5', a 5½' bump on the route between White Sound and Boat Harbour, the approach to Hope Town Harbour which has several 5-5½' bumps, and the entrance to Little Harbour, which carries only 3½'.

Boat Harbour is one of the largest and finest marinas in The Bahamas. It offers complete marina services. For more information see pp.118-121.

Hope Town has a fully protected harbour. There are two marinas, one of which has fuel service. For more information, see page 122-133.

White Sound has two restaurants and one full-service marina (including fuel) with easy access to the ocean beach. There is no room to anchor in the dredged channels in White Sound, but there is a fair weather anchorage just outside. For more information, see pages 134-140.

Lubbers Quarters Channel carries about 4½-5' MLW and requires careful piloting to avoid the shallow grassy shoals on each side of the suggested course lines. Tilloo Cut carries about 5½' MLW and is usually a viable passage to the Atlantic Ocean. There are some good fair weather anchorages in the area. For more detail, see pages 140-144.

There is a popular summer anchorage just north of Tilloo Bank and close to Tilloo Cay. Boats drawing more than about 2' need to go
continued on page 66

Green Turtle Cay to Marsh Harbour, continued from page 65

villas and homes, stores, various services, and one of the most beautiful beaches in the world. Transient boats are welcome at the marina, or may pick up a mooring or anchor in the fully protected basin on the way to the marina. For more information, see page 72.

Great Guana Cay also has one of the most beautiful beaches in the world. It is long, wide, and sparsely developed. A favorite anchorage at Guana Cay is Baker's Bay. It was developed as "Treasure Island" for cruise ship visitors, but the "Big Red Boat" stopped visiting in 1993. It is presently being developed by Discovery Land Company as the Baker's Bay Club. The new marina opened in 2009. Great Guana Cay has two more viable anchorages. Settlement harbour offers excellent protection from the prevailing easterlies, but is exposed from the S through the W. Orchid Bay Marina, located on the south side of Settlement Harbour near the entrance, has a breakwater and offers good protection at new docks. Guana Hideaways (marina) in the NW corner of the harbour opened in 2009 with new docks. Fisher's Bay, the harbour immediately north of the settlement, offers better protection from the SW, but is exposed to the NW. A dock for dinghies at the head of this harbour is maintained by Grabbers. A dock on the north shore services Dolphin Beach Resort and Dive Guana which maintains moorings for transients in Fisher's Bay and Settlement Harbour. For more information, see pages 76-83.

The Man-O-War/Marsh Harbour/Hope Town area forms the Hub of Abaco. For a larger scale chart of the area and some more detailed information, see page 94.

The harbour at Man-O-War Cay offers complete protection, and Man-O-War Marina has slips for transients. Complete repair and maintenance services are available from Edwin's Boat Yard, which has a sail loft as well. There are two grocery stores, and several clothing and gift shops. The harbour is a busy place, and it can sometimes be difficult to find swinging room. For more information, see pages 86-92.

Marsh Harbour is the largest protected deep water anchorage in Abaco. It is the third largest city in The Bahamas, and is growing rapidly. It has four banks, numerous restaurants, and a wide variety of stores. For more information see pages 96-121.

Marsh Harbour to Little Harbour, continued from page 65

west of TillooBank. See page 144 for a detailed description of the Middle Passage through Tilloo Bank as well as the entire region of the Pelican Cays Land and Sea Park, where there are moorings for daytime use by small boats (under 25') and a daytime anchorage in Pelican Harbour NW of the reef. North Bar Channel is the best passage to the Atlantic in this area. See pages 144 and 146.

Boats proceeding south to Little Harbour should stay about 1/3 mile off the coast of Great Abaco Island in order to avoid shoals extending W from Lynyard Cay. The entrance to Little Harbour carries only about 3½' MLW, and boats drawing more will need tide help. It is possible to anchor west of Tom Curry's Point in the Bight of Old Robinson or in the lee of the point on which the old lighthouse is located to wait for the tide. For more information, see pages 147-149.

Waypoints: *Marsh Harbour to Little Harbour* (generally north to south):

WPT	Description of Position	Latitude	Longitutde
PTSET	1/4 mile NE Point Set Rock	N 26° 34.370'	W 77° 00.550'
MARSH	Near entrance to Marsh Hrbr	N 26° 33.520'	W 77° 04.110'
HPTWN	Near entrance to Hope Town	N 26° 32.608'	W 76° 58.063'
WSMK	Near entrance White Sound	N 26° 31.130'	W 76° 58.870'
BTHBR	Near entrance to Boat Hrbr	N 26° 32.410'	W 77° 02.550'
LQN	N end Lubbers Quarters Chan	N 26° 30.330'	W 76° 59.110'
LQMID	Mid Lubbers Quarters Chan	N 26° 29.990'	W 76° 59.460'
LQS	S end Lubbers Quarters Chan	N 26° 29.100'	W 76° 59.720'
WITCHN	N of Witch Point	N 26° 30.630'	W 77° 02.550'
WITCHE	E of Witch Point	N 26° 29.550'	W 77° 01.550'
MIDNW	Middle Channel NW end	N 26° 25.830'	W 77° 01.010'
MIDSE	Middle Channel SE end	N 26° 25.280'	W 77° 00.090'
TBANK	SW of end of Tilloo Bank	N 26° 25.160'	W 77° 01.220'
PELICY	SW of the N Pelican Cay	N 26° 25.150'	W 76° 59.290'
SANDY	SE of Sandy Cay	N 26° 23.590'	W 76° 59.090'
NBAR	Atlantic End North Bar Chan	N 26° 23.410'	W 76° 58.470'
PELIPT	NE Pelican Point	N 26° 23.110'	W 76° 59.730'
LTHBW	Abaco Sd. end Little Hrbr Chan	N 26° 20.470'	W 76° 59.660'
LTHBE	Atlantic end Little Hrbr Chan	N 26° 19.900'	W 76° 59.390'

Waypoints: *Green Turtle Cay to Marsh Harbour* (generally north to south):

WPT	Description of Position	Latitude	Longitutde
GTC	1 NM W of Green Turtle Cay	N 26° 45.350'	W 77° 20.700'
NONAME	1 NM WSW Noname Cay	N 26° 44.002'	W 77° 19.017'
WHLSW	Whale Cay Channel SW end	N 26° 42.380'	W 77° 17.000'
WHLW	W of N tip Whale Cay	N 26° 43.009'	W 77° 15.426'
WHLNE	Whale Cay Channel NE end	N 26° 43.510'	W 77° 14.250'
LOGNW	Loggerhead Channel NW end	N 26° 42.560'	W 77° 12.400'
LOGSE	Loggerhead Channel SE end	N 26° 41.960'	W 77° 11.930'
TRCAY	SE of entrance Treasure Cay	N 26° 39.570'	W 77° 16.800'
BAKNW	northwest side Baker's Bay	N 26° 41.430'	W 77° 10.300'
BAKSE	southeast side Baker's Bay	N 26° 41.110'	W 77° 10.020'
GUANA	SW Guana Cay settlement	N 26° 39.310'	W 77° 07.080'
WATER	½ NM N Water Cay	N 26° 37.200'	W 77° 10.000'
NMOWW	Abaco Sd. end NMOW Chan.	N 26° 36.900'	W 77° 01.860'
NMOWE	Atlantic end NMOW Chan.	N 26° 37.820'	W 77° 01.360'
NMOWEE	ENE of NMOW Channel	N 26° 38.000'	W 77° 00.000'
PTSET	¼ mile NE Point Set Rock	N 26° 34.370'	W 77° 00.550'
MARSH	near entrance Marsh Harbour	N 26° 33.520'	W 77° 04.110'
BTHBR	near entrance Boat Harbour	N 26° 32.410'	W 77° 02.550'

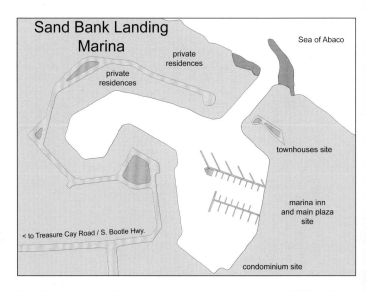

Sand Bank Landing Marina was under construction during 2012 and may be open sometime in 2013. It is located north of the Treasure Cay beach along the shore of Great Abaco Island near the original loyalist settlement in Abaco at Carleton. Its location at the northern end of the Whale Cay passage will make it a strategically useful stop (see charts on pages 68 and 72). The entry and the approach are deep and the marina will have 88 slips and be able to accomodate vessels up to 150'. The first stage of construction is for a fuel dock and 16 slips. It will be the first marina in Abaco with floating docks. A small hotel, restaurant, condominiums, townhouses and private residences are all in the plans for the future; the beautiful beach is there now ... just south of the marina.

A striking overview of a large portion of the principal cruising area in central Abaco, showing from Marsh Harbour and Man-O-War Cay in the south to Manjack and Crab Cays in the north. The shallow bar at Sand Banks between Treasure Cay and Whale Cay is clearly visible. Image courtesy of Earth Sciences and Image Analysis Laboratory, NASA Johnson Space Center, ST5107-E-5400 (http:/eol.jsc.nasa.gov)..

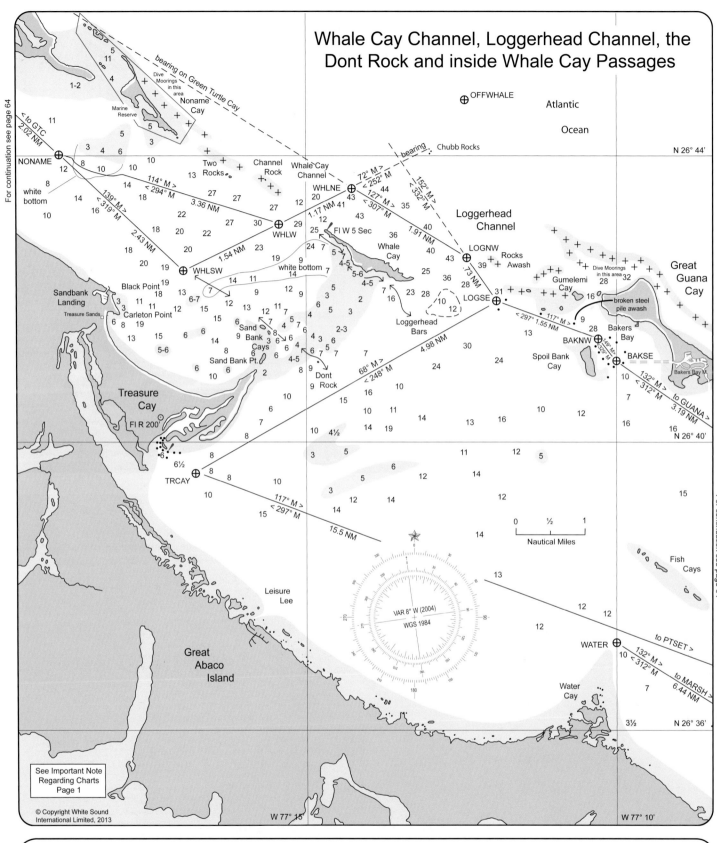

Whale Cay Channel, Loggerhead Channel, the Dont Rock and inside Whale Cay Passages

See Important Note Regarding Charts Page 1

GPS Waypoints fo *Whale Cay Channel, Loggerhead Channel, ..* (along course outside of Whale Cay, generally from north to south):			
NONAME	1 NM WSW No Name Cay	N 26° 44.002'	W 77° 19.017'
WHLSW	Whale Cay Channel SW end (Abaco Sound end)	N 26° 42.380'	W 77° 17.000'
WHLW	west of north tip of Whale Cay	N 26° 43.009'	W 77° 15.426'
WHLNE	Whale Cay Channel NE end (Atlantic Ocean end)	N 26° 43.510'	W 77° 14.250'
LOGNW	Loggerhead Channel NW end (Atlantic Ocean end)	N 26° 42.560'	W 77° 12.400'
LOGSE	Loggerhead Channel SE end (Abaco Sound end)	N 26° 41.960'	W 77° 11.930'
BAKNW	northwest side of Baker's Bay	N 26° 41.430'	W 77° 10.300'
BAKSE	southeast side Baker's Bay	N 26° 41.110'	W 77° 10.020'
TRCAY	southeast of entrance to Treasure Cay	N 26° 39.570'	W 77° 16.800'
WATER	½ NM N Water Cay	N 26° 37.200'	W 77° 10.000'

WHALE CAY CHANNEL, LOGGERHEAD CHANNEL, THE DONT ROCK AND INSIDE WHALE CAY PASSAGES

The Whale Cay area is clearly the most difficult and treacherous part of the Abacos. Certain weather conditions may make it impossible to traverse the area for several days, though at other times transit can be easily accomplished in one hour even in a slow boat.

The difficulties are the result of the fact that a shallow bank extends all the way from Whale Cay to "Treasure Cay" on the mainland of Great Abaco Island, and the passage across it is difficult for vessels drawing more than about 3-4'. This makes it necessary for most cruising boats to pass outside Whale Cay. Although both Loggerhead Channel (southeast of Whale Cay) and the Whale Cay Channel (northwest of Whale Cay) are wide, the Whale Cay Channel, especially, is fairly shallow (about 12') and is susceptible to a rage sea condition (breaking waves all the way across) when ocean swells come from the northeast. This most often occurs during a strong northeaster, but can also be the result of storms hundreds of miles away, which can cause a rage during deceptively sunny and light wind days in Abaco.

The single greatest problem is deciding whether or not the Whale Cay and Loggerhead Channels are passable. Of the two, the Whale Cay Channel is the most critical. Boats contemplating the passage often consult with one another in the morning on the VHF, so it is sometimes possible to get information about conditions just by listening, or by calling "any boat in the Whale Cay area." The single best source is the cruiser's net, which airs each morning at 8:15 am on VHF 68, and almost always reports on conditions at Whale Cay as well as other passages between the Sea of Abaco and the Atlantic Ocean.

If conditions are appropriate for going around Whale Cay, follow the course lines on the chart. Coming from waypoint GTC (about 1 mile west of New Plymouth Harbour), head toward the Sand Bank Cays and Dont Rock on a heading of about 139° M. At the waypoint NONAME you may continue on 139° M to WHLSW and then turn to WHLW, or change course to head for just below the northern tip of Whale Cay on a course of 114° M and go directly to WHLW. This will keep you clear of the shoal extending SW from No Name Cay but rather close to it, so watch your cross track error and alter course to the SW if the water becomes shallow. Note the suggested courseline. This "shortcut" saves .61 NM. When you reach the waypoint WHLW Chubb Rocks (white water) bears 72° M. Turn (or continue) to head for them. This course will take you through Whale Cay Channel approximately halfway between Channel Rock and the NW point of Whale Cay in 12'-14' water. When Green Turtle Cay bears 307° M, you will have reached the next waypoint, WHLNE. Turn to put Green Turtle Cay on your stern

and assume the reciprocal heading, 127°M. You will be heading toward Gumelemi Cay, which will be difficult to distinguish from Great Guana Cay, which lies immediately behind Gumelemi. Hold this course until you are about 1/4-1/3 mile beyond the point at which the SE tip of Whale Cay is abeam (Chubb Rocks should be off the port quarter), and then, at LOGNW, turn to starboard and head in through Loggerhead Channel. Take care not to go too far SE before making this turn—be wary of Rocks Awash! Your heading should be 152°M, and you should be headed toward a point just to the north of the Fish Cays, which appear as 4-5 lumps on the horizon SE of the land mass of Great Abaco Island. Continue to the next turning point, LOGSE, and then change course to 117°M, proceeding through the dredged cruiseship channel (see photo page 71) toward Baker's Bay (waypoint BAKNW) with the spoil bank cays (casuarinas) off the starboard bow. The cruise ship channel is well marked here, with several successive sets of buoys or piles (some are missing). Premier Cruise Lines discontinued use of this channel in 1993, so there should be no cruise ship traffic in the area. GPS waypoints are provided for all turning points on the route around Whale Cay. Use the reciprocal headings when going from SE to NW.

The inside passages are not necessarily viable alternatives to the outside passage on rough days, because high wind or rage conditions usually make the inside passages impassable also. A swell running across the shallow bank with a hard sand bottom makes it as treacherous as the outside route. Neither one of the two inside routes is straightforward because of shifting sand, and they should be negotiated only when visability is good on a rising tide.

The Dont Rock passage, which carried 3½' MLW in 2011, deepened to 4' (actually 4.4') during summer 2012. At high tide it would carry 6-7'. The "bay area" N and E of the Treasure Cay beach has several migrating sand bars and under certain conditions the ocean swells coming through Whale Cay Channel break on these bars, sometimes even in rather calm weather.

The passage along the southwest shoreline of Whale Cay carries about 3' MLW, and therefore 5-6' at high tide. To go from south to north stay about 100 yards off the shore near the division line between the light and the dark water, passing close to the small rocky point, which is southeast of the mid-point of Whale Cay. Give a wider berth to the next point, a sandy one (about 200-250 yards), and then turn back toward Whale Cay to avoid a very shallow bar to the west. Proceed northwestward past the northern tip of Whale Cay, which has a small navigation light on a pole. Watch for shoals, and be prepared to alter course to avoid them. This inside route is generally recommended only for vessels drawing less than 3-4'.

Sand Banks and Whale Cay from the south with small boat approaching shoals and sailboat entering Sea of Abaco through Whale Cay Channel in distance. Part of the channel inside Whale Cay between Whale Cay and Sand Banks is visible in the photo—note the darker blue water close to the Cay.

Dont Rock from the northeast showing the southern edge of Sand Banks. Dont Rock marks the southeastern end of the Dont Rock passage which carried 4.4' MLW during summer 2012 . When there is a rage in Whale Cay or Loggerhead Channels, the inside passages are usually not useable either.

Whale Cay Channel from the West Northwest with Channel Rock in the foreground. The shoal area extending Southwestward from Whale Cay to Treasure Cay on the mainland of Great Abaco Island makes it necessary for most cruising boats to go outside of Whale Cay when transiting the area. Note that the best passage is approximately midway between Channel Rock and the Northwest tip of Whale Cay. The suggested course line for this Channel using the waypoints provided in this cruising guide is in the deepest water, but all should be aware that in a rage sea breakers can extend all the way across the opening. Cruisers can listen to the Cruiser's Net on channel 68 at 8:15 each morning for a report on conditions in the Whale Cay Channel. Photo by Steve Dodge March 2004.

The deep channel inside Loggerhead Channel leading to Baker's Bay was dredged for use by cruiseships in 1989. During the early 1990s, the cruiseship company discontinued visits to the area because entry and egress were not always possible during the winter months when rage seas sometimes made Loggerhead Channel impassable. Some of the large steel pipes driven into the seabed to mark the channel are still in place and can be seen in this photo; others are missing. The channel is viewed here from the west northwest; the anchorage at Baker's Bay and Great Guana Cay can be seen in the background. This photo was taken before the construction of Baker's Bay Marina. Photo by Steve Dodge, March 2004.

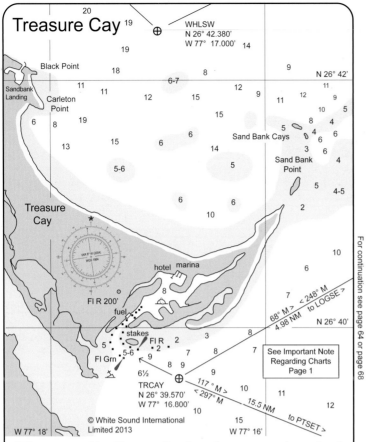

When approaching Treasure Cay from the east or southeast, head for the low part of Great Abaco Island . There is a radio tower near this point. Head NW from the waypoint TRCAY and go between the stakes, making a sweeping turn to starboard, and then proceed NE through the entrance channel. Controlling depth is abour 6' MLW. Dockage is available at the marina (150 slips). Moorings are available in the basin to starboard on the way in, or anchor there. Register for either at the Marina Office. Fuel is available at the fuel dock on the port side of the main entrance channel.

For continuation see page 64 or page 68

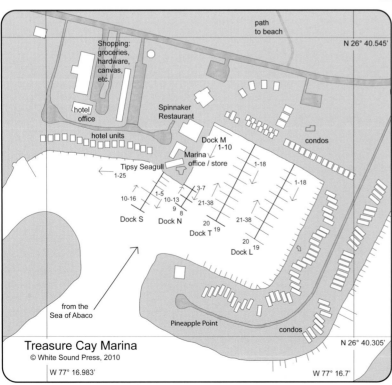

Entrance to Treasure Cay from the southwest.

TREASURE CAY

Treasure Cay started as a hotel/marina development and has grown into a medium-sized vacation community. The main attraction at Treasure Cay is its beach, which is surely one of the loveliest in the world—it extends for about 3 miles in a beautiful semi-circle. There are sailboats and windsurfers for rent. The marina is full service and a marine store has supplies for boats as well as clothing items. There is a grocery store, a doctor's office, a bank, and a hardware store. Abaco Ceramics, located on the entrance road, is a special attraction for shoppers. There are villas, private homes, and condominiums for rent.

The Tipsy Seagull bar at the marina, located adjacent to the swimming pool, offers drinks and snacks. The hotel, which is located west of the marina, has 64 rooms and 32 suites. The Spinnaker Restaurant is conveniently located north of the marina office. Treasure Cay also has an 18-hole golf course and several tennis courts. The new Treasure Sands Club is located near the north end of the beach near Carleton Point (by road just outside the Treasure Cay entrance gate). They serve lunch, dinner, drinks, have a pool, and of course, the beautiful beach. They have 3 moorings for boats to tie up (6' MLW) and provide dinghy service. to the beach.

Walking the beach is pleasant, and those who want a good bit of exercise can walk all the way to the northern end and through the brush to a path leading to the rocky point extending northeast from the beach. This point was named Carleton Point in 1983 in honor of the bicentennial of the arrival of the first loyalist settlers in Abaco. They left New York and the United States because they opposed independence; they travelled to Carleton to found a new British colony which they believed would prosper because it would gain the British trade which the new United States would lose. The settlement lasted only a few years. A plaque cemented in the rocks at Carleton Point commemorates this first settlement in Abaco.

Treasure Sands Club

We offer a delectable fusion of cuisine, music and decadence, creating a utopia for the senses. The Treasure Sands Club is one of the Bahamas most beautiful venues. We are a sophisticated, elegant Beach Club and Restaurant located on the stunning, world famous Treasure Cay Beach... Breathtaking panoramic views, sumptuous luxury, gourmet cuisine accompanied by attentive service. Complimentary dinghy service ashore. Pick up one of our moorings (5-6ft MLT) or anchor off. Open to the public daily from 12pm for lunch and dinner or cocktails by the pool.

242 365-9385
reservations@treasuresandsclub.com
www.treasuresandsclub.com

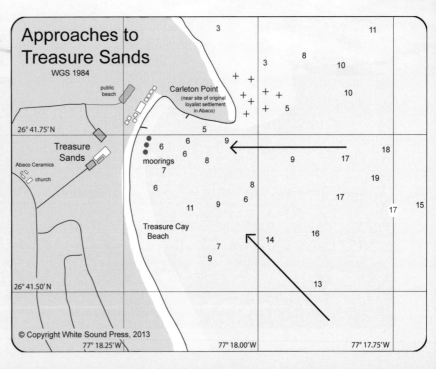

Approaches to Treasure Sands

WGS 1984

Carleton Point
(near site of original loyalist settlement in Abaco)

public beach

26° 41.75' N

Treasure Sands

Abaco Ceramics

church

moorings

Treasure Cay Beach

26° 41.50' N

© Copyright White Sound Press, 2013

77° 18.25' W   77° 18.00' W   77° 17.75' W

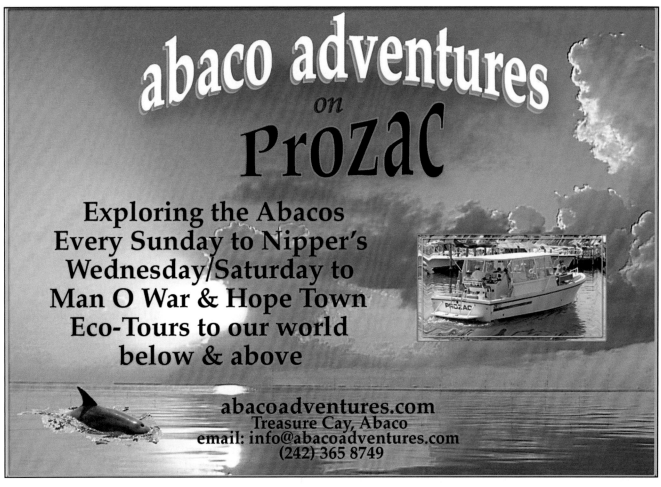

Great Guana Cay

The approaches to Settlement Harbour and to Fisher's Bay west of it are both straightforward and direct. Settlement Harbour is obviously exposed to the south and southwest. The bottom is grass, making it difficult to get a Danforth anchor to hold. Orchid Bay Marina in the SE corner of the harbour a full service marina with 66 slips; a breakwater protects their docks. Guana Hideaways (marina) in the NW corner of the harbour west of the public dock has slips for transients as well as long-term rentals.

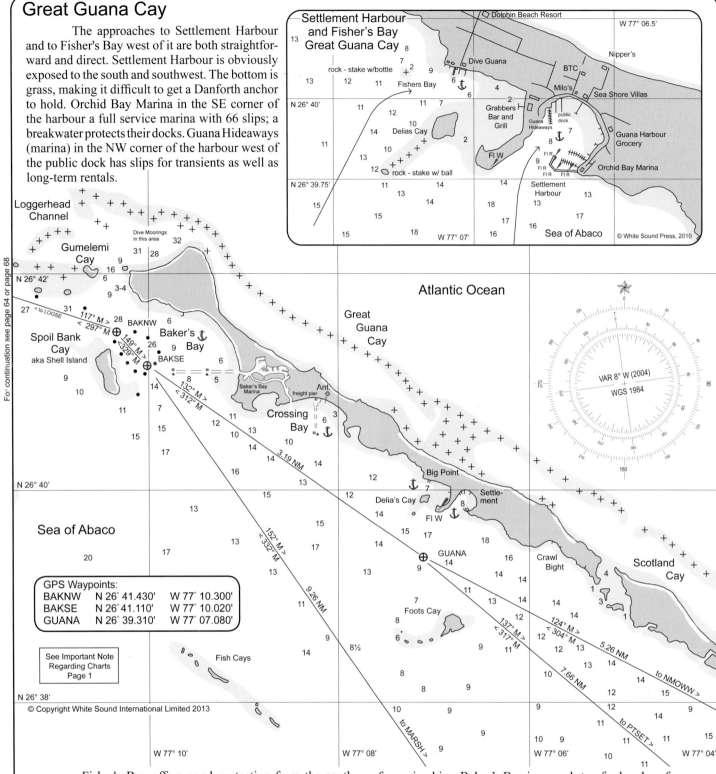

Fisher's Bay offers good protection from the south, but is exposed to the west and northwest. There is a dock (not a marina) at Big Point at the NW corner of the harbour. Moorings for transients in Fisher's Bay (6) as well as in Settlement Harbour (6) are maintained by Dive Guana, which is based at the Big Point dock. There is a submerged rock off Big Point at the north side of the harbour. It is usually marked with a white pipe (missing June, 2012). A shallow rocky bar runs from Delia's Cay southwest to the off-lying rock. All boats should avoid trying to cross the bar and should go to the southwest of the off-lying rock, which is usually marked with a pole with a ball at the top.

The northwestern end of Great Guana Cay is also of interest to cruisers. The cruiseship channel is no longer in use

for cruiseships. Baker's Bay is a good stop for lunch or for overnight. The anchorage is beautiful, and it is very comfortable in the prevailing winds. It does not offer protection from the south through the northwest. The spoil bank cay created by dredging the channel and mooring basin for the cruiseship is said to be a good place for shelling. The new marina at Baker's Bay Club opened in 2009 with a well-marked deep approach channel. Dockage is available and there are two restaurants in the Marina Village. See the marina map on page 81.

Crossing Bay, to the southeast of Baker's Bay, offers only modest protection and is shallow quite far from shore. The concrete pier is a freight dock for the Baker's Bay development.

The settlement at Great Guana Cay is one of the smallest in the central part of Abaco, but it is growing. The 1990 census reported only 95 persons living on the cay; by 2000 the population was 163. The cay's principal asset has long been its beautiful ocean beach, which is one of the widest in Abaco and extends almost the entire 5½ mile length of the island. The beach made Guana a popular stop for cruisers for many years.

During the past two decades Guana has experienced a boom, and several new developments have made the cay even more attractive for visitors. The opening of Nipper's Beach Bar and Grill during summer 1996 brought large numbers of cruisers, tourists, and local residents to the cay. Nipper's is located a short walk from the settlement high on a dune overlooking the beach and the reef, and continues to be Great Guana Cay's most popular destination.

The opening of Orchid Bay Marina in 1999 provided well protected dockage at Guana for the first time. It is also a residential development with lots for sale, and a restaurant opened on the site in 2002. Construction of a new second dock in 2004 expanded the marina to 66 slips.

Guana Hideaways (marina) opened in 2009—with a brand new dock to replace the old Guana Harbour Club dock in the NW corner of the harbour. They have transient slips, but power is not available.

Grabbers Bar and Grill, located on the site of the old Guana Harbour Club is on the peninsula between Settlement Harbour and Fisher's Bay. The hallmark "Guana Grabber" rum drink and strikingly beautiful sunsets make this a choice lunch or dinner stop. There is a dinghy dock on Fisher's Bay and overnight lodging is available in thirteen hotel rooms.

Other facilities in the settlement include the well-stocked Guana Harbour Grocery Store, a small liquor store, and Pirate's Cove at Sea Shore Villas, an open air bar, short-order restaurant, and limited grocery store. Guana Drug Store shares a building with Bambi's Cafe, which specializes in breakfast—both opened in 2011. Also, Island Flavours, a small take-away built on a dock in the harbour, was open during summer, 2011. Ice is available from the liquor store. See page 200 for the Great Guana Cay business directory.

Dolphin Beach Resort, located just northwest of the settlement on the ocean beach includes about 20 rooms/cottages with a pool and a residental development.

If you want to walk, swim, snorkel, or picnic, cross to the ocean side at the settlement, and then walk southeast on the beach to High Rocks, where the reef is just off the beach. It will be obvious when you reach High Rocks.

The NW end of Great Guana Cay—Baker's Bay— has long been a favorite anchorage for cruisers. It was developed as a cruise ship desination in 1989-90; that operation was terminated in 1993. A few years ago the land was sold to developers who are presently building the Baker's Bay Club, an up-scale residential community with a golf course and a marina. These plans were strongly opposed by a segment of the local population and some foreign residents, but the government approved the project and construction began during the summer, 2005. The 158-slip marina, which can accomodate boats to 250', opened to the public in 2009. It is adjacent to the Marina Village, which is patterned after Caribbean port towns of the 1700s and has two restaurants open to the public. The club will eventually include 358 residential units.

Fisher's Bay and Settlement Harbour, Great Guana Cay, viewed from the Northwest. The cruising boats in Fisher's Bay are anchored or are on moorings maintained by Dive Guana. Orchid Bay Marina offers full services and their dock, protected by a breakwater, can be seen on the south side of Settlement Harbour. Since this photo was taken, they have added a second dock located northeast of the dock shown here. Grabbers has a small boat dock along the east side of Fisher's Bay near the center of the beach which can be seen clearly in this photo. There is a public dock in the northwest corner of Settlement Harbour which services local needs as well as visitors, and the new (2009) Guana Hideaways dock with slips available for transients is adjacent to it. This photo was taken by Steve Dodge in March 2004.

Nipper's
Beach Bar and Grill

- Overlooking the most beautiful beach in the Abacos and the world's third largest barrier reef
- Snorkeling 75 yards off the beach
- Featuring Bahamian Home Cooking with a Pig Roast every Sunday
- On the north side of Great Guana Cay at the settlement, Abaco, Bahamas
- Michael and Johnnie Roberts • VHF 16 • 365-5111 • nippers@batelnet.bs

Sleepy Great Guana Cay during the middle 1970s with the mailboat, the *Deborah K*, arriving from Nassau. Photo by Steve Dodge.

Church of God at Great Guana Cay during evening service in middle 1970s. The preacher said, "De Lord, who put the sun in the sky... De Lord, who put the fish in the sea, he loves ya brother, he loves ya." Drawing by Laurie Jones, from Steve Dodge, *Abaco: The History of an Out Island and its Cays*.

Nippers Beach Bar and Grill shortly after opening during summer 1996. Photo by Steve Dodge.

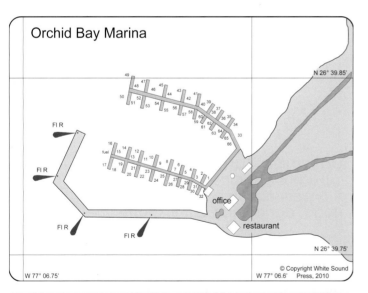

Orchid Bay Marina

N 26° 39.85'

FI R
FI R
fuel
FI R
FI R
office
restaurant
N 26° 39.75'

W 77° 06.75'
W 77° 06.6'

© Copyright White Sound Press, 2010

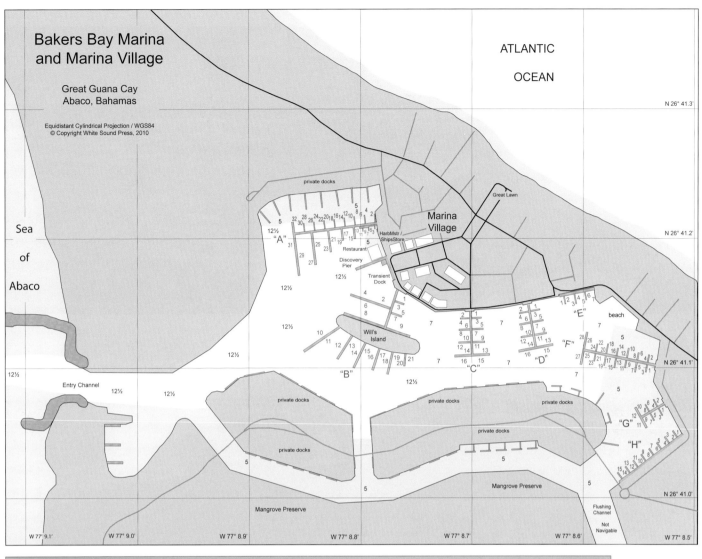

Bakers Bay Marina and Marina Village

Great Guana Cay
Abaco, Bahamas

Equidistant Cylindrical Projection / WGS84
© Copyright White Sound Press, 2010

ATLANTIC

OCEAN

N 26° 41.3'

Sea

of

Abaco

private docks

Marina
Village

Great Lawn

HarbMstr /
ShipsStore

Restaurant

Discovery
Pier

Transient
Dock

Will's
Island

"A"

"B"

"C"

"D"

"E"

"F"

"G"

"H"

beach

Entry Channel

private docks

private docks

private docks

private docks

private docks

private docks

Mangrove Preserve

Mangrove Preserve

Flushing
Channel

Not
Navigable

12½

N 26° 41.2'

N 26° 41.1'

N 26° 41.0'

W 77° 9.1'   W 77° 9.0'   W 77° 8.9'   W 77° 8.8'   W 77° 8.7'   W 77° 8.6'   W 77° 8.5'

Baker's Bay Marina and Marina Village with the Atlantic Ocean beyond from the south. Entrance to the marina basin from the west in photo at right. Photos by Steve Dodge, 30 June 2012.

The Marina at Baker's Bay

Abaco's private mega-yacht luxury port within Baker's Bay Golf & Ocean Club is a state-of-the-art facility with deep water access via Whale Cay Cut. Accommodating vessels up to 250 feet, its unique deep water channel approach from the sea has a final controlling depth of 12.5' MLW. Baker's Bay Golf & Ocean Club is home to a private Tom Fazio Golf Course, a wide variety of real estate offerings and a full-service, environmentally friendly Marina. Adjacent to the marina is a vibrant Marina Village which provides luxury amenities including:

- 24-hour security
- Power (50A 120/240V single phase, 100A 120/240V single phase, 100A 208 3-phase power)
- Food and beverage provisioning, potable water
- Friendly dock attendants to assist with all requests
- Villa and golf cart rentals
- Wireless Internet access

- In-slip sanitary pump-out, solid waste collection
- Boutique featuring Bahamian treasures and the latest in fashion
- Private Atlantic beach access with incredible near shore reefs for snorkeling

- **The Market** – restaurant, café and grocery (breakfast, lunch, dinner): Mon.-Sun.: 8am-11pm; Inspired international cuisine focusing on local seafood
- **The Conch Shack** (all day menu): Mon.-Sun.: Noon-11pm; Tasty lunch and dinner menus, bar foods and daily drink specials — overlooking the beautiful Baker's Bay Marina

Baker's Bay
GOLF & OCEAN CLUB

HARBOUR MASTER TELEPHONE: (242) 365-5802
WWW.BAKERSBAYCLUB.COM

North Man-O-War Channel from the southwest. It is the widest and deepest passage between the Sea of Abaco and the Atlantic Ocean in central Abaco. Note the southeast tip of Fish Hawk Cay and a Fowl Cay Reef on the left, and the northwest tip of Man-O-War Cay with the rock which almost always breaks, as well as a portion of the barrier reef off Man-O-War Cay on the right. See the top photo on the next page, and the charts and descriptions on page 86, and also on pages 20-21 and 22. Abbreviation "p.a." is for "position approximate." Photo by Steve Dodge, 19 March 2010.

South Man-O-War Channel from the west. This passage is narrower than North Man-O-War Channel and entry is not straighforward. Note the southeastern tip of Man-O-War Cay on the left and the barrier reef offshore. The opening is clearly visible. Vessels approaching this channel from the south must use extreme caution to avoid Elbow Reef; it is recommended that all vessels coming from the south go to the waypoint OFFSMOWE before approaching SMOWE. See the bottom photo on the next page and the charts and descriptions on pages 20-21, 22, 86 and 94. Abbreviation "p.a." is for "position approximate." Photo by Steve Dodge, 19 March 2010.

North Man-O-War Channel from the northnorthwest. Fowl Cay reef is in the foreground with the darker blue water of the channel beyond it and Man-O-War Cay beyond that. Abbreviation "p.a." is for "position approximate." Photo by Steve Dodge, 4 February 2008.

South Man-O-War Channel from the eastnortheast with Man-O-War Cay in the background. The opening in the reef is clearly visible, and the darker water is the deepest entry route. Abbreviation "p.a." is for "position approximate." Photo by Steve Dodge 4 February 2008.

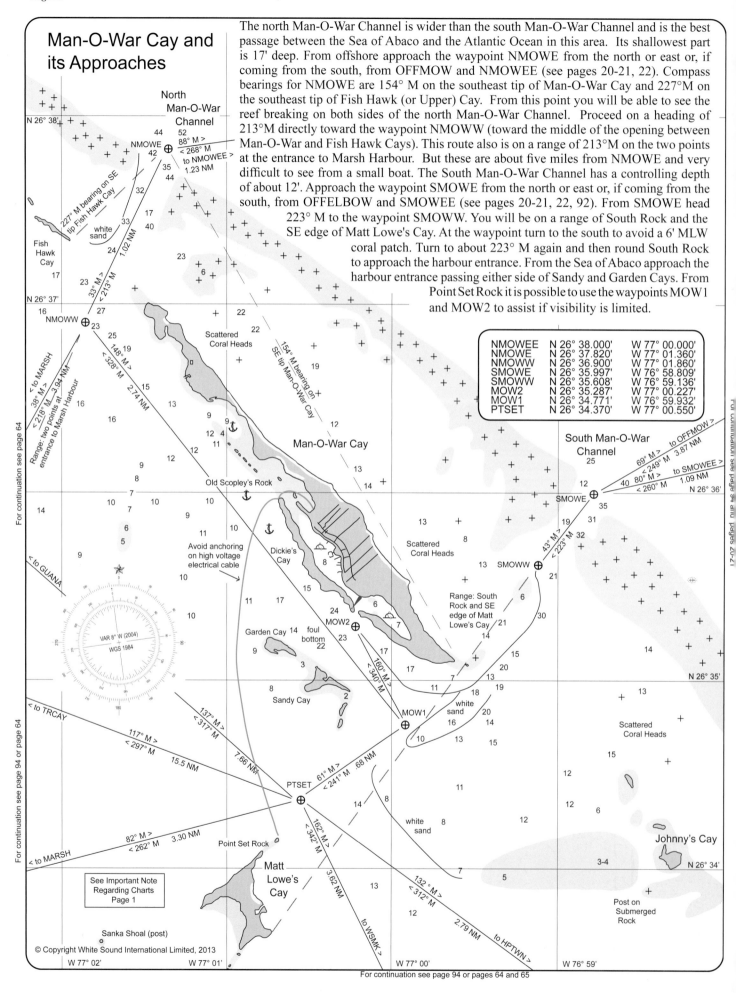

Man-O-War Cay and its Approaches

The north Man-O-War Channel is wider than the south Man-O-War Channel and is the best passage between the Sea of Abaco and the Atlantic Ocean in this area. Its shallowest part is 17' deep. From offshore approach the waypoint NMOWE from the north or east or, if coming from the south, from OFFMOW and NMOWEE (see pages 20-21, 22). Compass bearings for NMOWE are 154° M on the southeast tip of Man-O-War Cay and 227°M on the southeast tip of Fish Hawk (or Upper) Cay. From this point you will be able to see the reef breaking on both sides of the north Man-O-War Channel. Proceed on a heading of 213°M directly toward the waypoint NMOWW (toward the middle of the opening between Man-O-War and Fish Hawk Cays). This route also is on a range of 213°M on the two points at the entrance to Marsh Harbour. But these are about five miles from NMOWE and very difficult to see from a small boat. The South Man-O-War Channel has a controlling depth of about 12'. Approach the waypoint SMOWE from the north or east or, if coming from the south, from OFFELBOW and SMOWEE (see pages 20-21, 22, 92). From SMOWE head 223° M to the waypoint SMOWW. You will be on a range of South Rock and the SE edge of Matt Lowe's Cay. At the waypoint turn to the south to avoid a 6' MLW coral patch. Turn to about 223° M again and then round South Rock to approach the harbour entrance. From the Sea of Abaco approach the harbour entrance passing either side of Sandy and Garden Cays. From Point Set Rock it is possible to use the waypoints MOW1 and MOW2 to assist if visibility is limited.

NMOWEE	N 26° 38.000'	W 77° 00.000'
NMOWE	N 26° 37.820'	W 77° 01.360'
NMOWW	N 26° 36.900'	W 77° 01.860'
SMOWE	N 26° 35.997'	W 76° 58.809'
SMOWW	N 26° 35.608'	W 76° 59.136'
MOW2	N 26° 35.287'	W 77° 00.227'
MOW1	N 26° 34.771'	W 76° 59.932'
PTSET	N 26° 34.370'	W 77° 00.550'

North Man-O-War Channel

NMOWE

227° M bearing on SE tip Fish Hawk Cay

white sand

Fish Hawk Cay

NMOWW

Scattered Coral Heads

154° M bearing on SE tip Man-O-War Cay

Range: two points at entrance to Marsh Harbour

Man-O-War Cay

Old Scopley's Rock

Avoid anchoring on high voltage electrical cable

Dickie's Cay

Scattered Coral Heads

South Man-O-War Channel

SMOWE

SMOWW

Range: South Rock and SE edge of Matt Lowe's Cay

MOW2

Garden Cay

foul bottom

Sandy Cay

MOW1

white sand

Scattered Coral Heads

VAR 8° W (2004)
WGS 1984

PTSET

Johnny's Cay

See Important Note Regarding Charts Page 1

Point Set Rock

Matt Lowe's Cay

Sanka Shoal (post)

Post on Submerged Rock

© Copyright White Sound International Limited, 2013

For continuation see page 64

For continuation see page 94 or page 64

For continuation see pages 94 and pages 20-21

For continuation see page 94 or pages 64 and 65

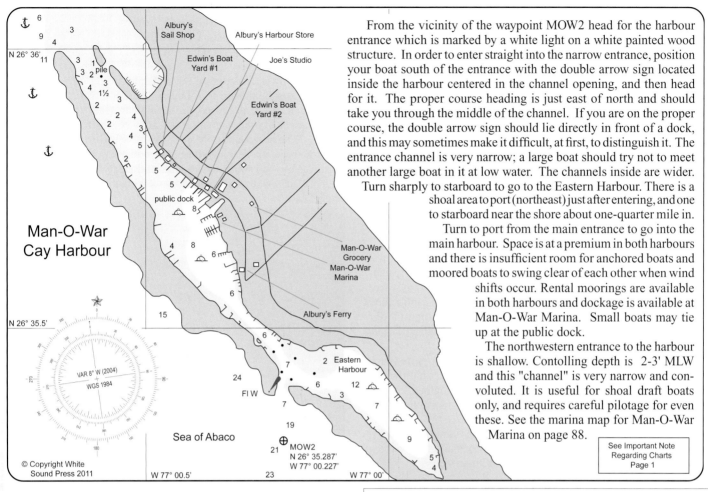

**Man-O-War
Cay Harbour**

Albury's
Sail Shop

Albury's Harbour Store

Edwin's Boat
Yard #1

Joe's Studio

Edwin's Boat
Yard #2

public dock

Man-O-War
Grocery
Man-O-War
Marina

Albury's Ferry

Eastern
Harbour

Fl W

Sea of Abaco

MOW2
N 26° 35.287'
W 77° 00.227'

VAR 8° W (2004)
WGS 1984

N 26° 36'

N 26° 35.5'

© Copyright White
Sound Press 2011

W 77° 00.5'   W 77° 00'

See Important Note
Regarding Charts
Page 1

From the vicinity of the waypoint MOW2 head for the harbour entrance which is marked by a white light on a white painted wood structure. In order to enter straight into the narrow entrance, position your boat south of the entrance with the double arrow sign located inside the harbour centered in the channel opening, and then head for it. The proper course heading is just east of north and should take you through the middle of the channel. If you are on the proper course, the double arrow sign should lie directly in front of a dock, and this may sometimes make it difficult, at first, to distinguish it. The entrance channel is very narrow; a large boat should try not to meet another large boat in it at low water. The channels inside are wider.

Turn sharply to starboard to go to the Eastern Harbour. There is a shoal area to port (northeast) just after entering, and one to starboard near the shore about one-quarter mile in.

Turn to port from the main entrance to go into the main harbour. Space is at a premium in both harbours and there is insufficient room for anchored boats and moored boats to swing clear of each other when wind shifts occur. Rental moorings are available in both harbours and dockage is available at Man-O-War Marina. Small boats may tie up at the public dock.

The northwestern entrance to the harbour is shallow. Contolling depth is 2-3' MLW and this "channel" is very narrow and convoluted. It is useful for shoal draft boats only, and requires careful pilotage for even these. See the marina map for Man-O-War Marina on page 88.

Approach from the south. Line up the piling with the double arrow (points left and right) in the center of the opening.

The opening is narrow; do not meet another large boat here. Note the piling with the double arrow in front of the powerboat at the dock. It should be centered in the opening.

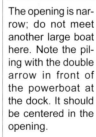

When about 50-60' from the piling with the double arrow, turn to port and proceed toward the main harbour.

MAN-O-WAR CAY

During the early twentieth century the Commissioner, who at that time was based in Hope Town, described Man-O-War Cay as a small island which had a few enterprising men. The same could be said today, though there are undoubtedly more enterprising men (and women). Until recently Man-O-War was the home base for Albury's Ferry. Marcel Albury, who ran it, was one of the most experienced pilots in Abaco. See his article on crossing the Gulf Stream to Abaco on page 23. Man-O-War has been a center for boat building and repair for many years. Edwin's Boat Yard does excellent work and maintains a good stock of marine parts. They actually have two yards—boat yard #1 is near the Sail Shop at the northwest end of town; boat yard #2 is located near the center of town. Albury Brothers Boat Building, located just northwest of Edwin's Boat Yard #2, builds sturdy round bilge deep-V fiberglass outboard boats. These are now also built in Florida for the US market.

Man-O-War Marina is centrally located, and offers full dockage and fuel services, ice and water. The Dock & Dine restaurant overlooks the docks. No alcoholic beverages are sold anywhere on Man-O-War Cay. Two grocery stores supply the island's food needs. Albury's Harbour Grocery is on the water, and Man-O-War Grocery is at the top of the hill back from Man-O-War Marina. Both deliver groceries to all docks at Man-O-War.

Joe's Studio is one of the most unique gift shops in Abaco because Joe Albury's hand-crafted items made of Abaco hardwoods are sold there. Beautiful frame models of Abaco dinghies, candlestick holders, goblets and folding chairs are all available. They also offer jewelry, T-shirts and other gift items.

Emerson's Shop is now operated by his son Andy Albury, who builds beautiful half models as well as the same sturdy rocking chairs his father built in the same shop for many years.

Sally's Seaside Shop sells Androsia batik fabrics (from Andros Island in the Bahamas) and a wide variety of unique locally sewn items. It is located on the lower road on the harbour side.

Another very unique shop—the Sail Shop—is located at the far northwestern edge of the settlement right on the harbour, past Edwin's Boat Yard #1. Durable and colorful canvas duffle bags, sewn on the premises, are available. Hats, jackets, purses and a variety of other canvas goods are also sewn and sold there.

The ocean side of Man-O-War Cay is worth a visit—there are some beautiful beaches alternating with rock outcroppings. The northwestern and southeastern ends of the cay are well developed with private residences. Explore by walking the road, or by bicycle or golf cart.

Basil Sands' boat yard at Man-O-War Cay during the 1950s. Photo courtesy of Dave Gale.

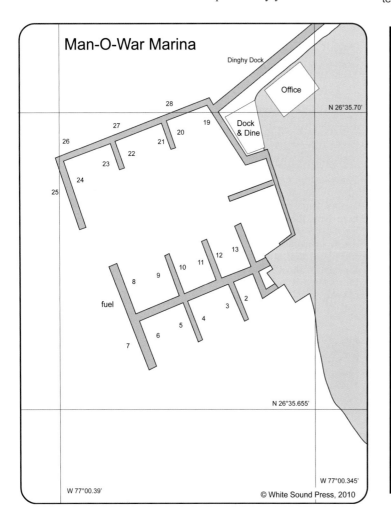

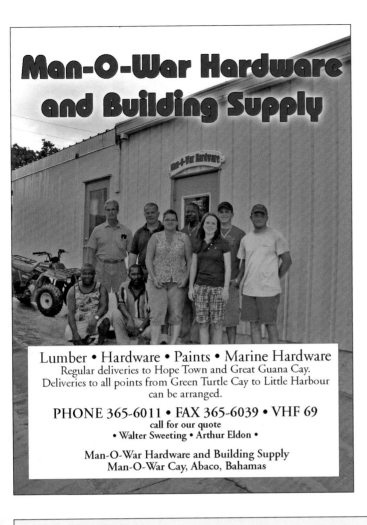

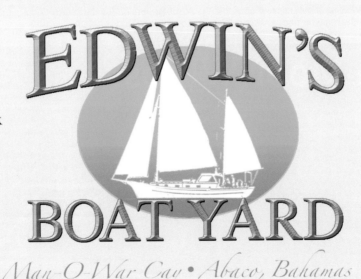

Dickie's Cay and Man-O-War Cay form the main harbour at Man-o-War. Photo by Steve Dodge, 2007.

The Sail Shop is at the extreme left with Edwin's Boatyard #1 (yellow buildings) to its right; Edwin's Boatyard #2 is at the extreme right with Albury Brothers Boats (white building) to its left. Photo by Steve Dodge, 19 March 2010.

Where will they go from here?

Abaco schools provide excellent elementary and secondary education for the children of Abaco. These children were photographed several years ago while on their way to a school in Dundas Town. But elemenatary and secondary education is not enough. To help them do more, support Abaco Pathfinders.

Abaco Pathfinders is a charitable foundation set up with the specific goal of providing scholarships for the young people of Abaco. Funding is provided on a need and merit basis to those desiring a vocational or academic training program. Applications are provided on a non-discriminatory basis. We helped more than a dozen students during 2001-2002, our first year of operation, and have helped about 10 additional students every year since then. Many have completed school and are now working in Abaco or elsewhere.

We need your help through contributions.The more generous you are to this fund, the more kids we can help. Donations from the United States to Abaco Pathfinders will be received by a United States based not for profit corporation and should be tax deductable for the donor.

If you are a local resident of The Bahamas, a winter resident, a frequent visitor or just a passing sailor, this is your chance to do something valuable. Your help will be meaningful.To help, contact:

Abaco Pathfinders, P. O. Box AB20213, Marsh Harbour, Abaco, The Bahamas

Web: www.abacopathfinders.org
Email: administrator@abacopathfinders.org

The Toughest Antifouling System
for Caribbean Waters...

Tin Based
Islands 44 Plus

Self-cleaning
copolymer with
a high load of tin
and copper

Tin Free
Islands 77 Plus

Harder self-polishing
polymer binding system
with biocide technology

...Just Got Tougher!

Introducing

Premium Blister Protection

- Keeps water out!
- Highest build epoxy
- Fewer coats needed

High Build Epoxy Primer
with Microsheet Silicate Technology

- 24-hour window
- Repair & prevention
  of blistering

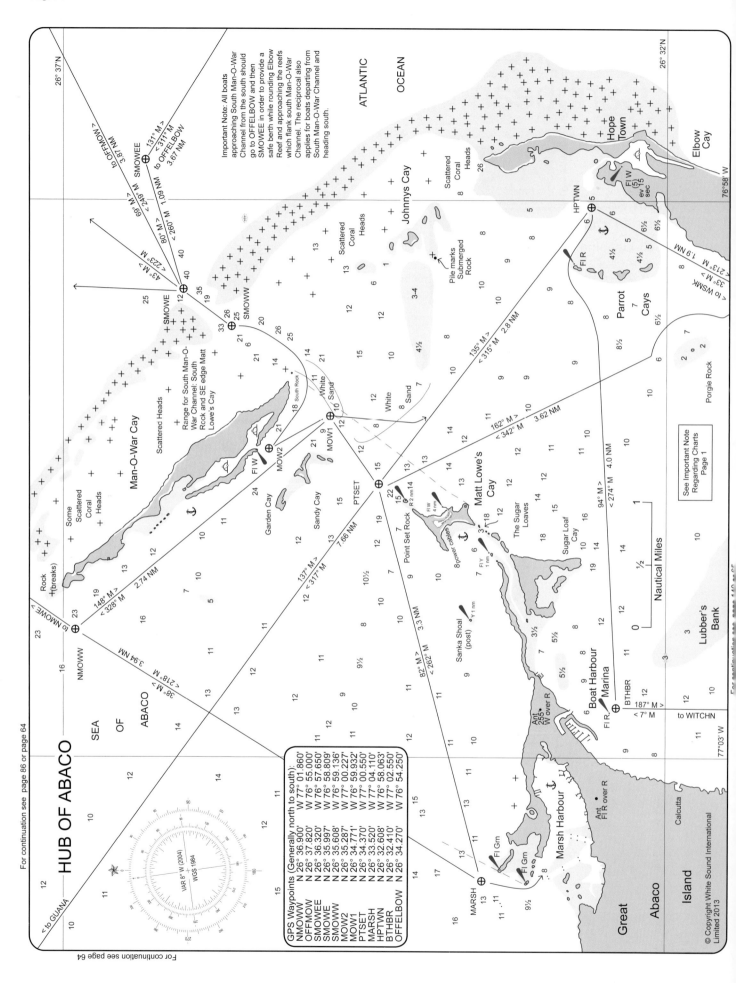

HUB OF ABACO

For continuation see page 86 or page 64

For continuation see page 64

Important Note: All boats approaching South Man-O-War Channel from the south should go to OFFELBOW and then SMOWEE in order to provide a safe berth while rounding Elbow Reef and approaching the reefs which flank south Man-O-War Channel. The reciprocal also applies for boats departing from South Man-O-War Channel and heading south.

ATLANTIC OCEAN

SEA OF ABACO

Man-O-War Cay

Matt Lowe's Cay

The Sugar Loaves

Sugar Loaf Cay

Boat Harbour Marina

Marsh Harbour

Great Abaco Island

Calcutta

Lubber's Bank

Parrot Cays

Porgie Rock

Johnnys Cay

Hope Town

Elbow Cay

Scattered Coral Heads

Garden Cay

Sandy Cay

Point Set Rock

Sanka Shoal (post)

Range for South Man-O-War Channel: South Rock and SE edge Matt Lowe's Cay

See Important Note Regarding Charts Page 1

VAR 8° W (2004)
WGS 1984

GPS Waypoints (Generally north to south):

NMOWW	N 26° 36.900'	W 77° 01.860'
OFFMOW	N 26° 37.820'	W 76° 55.000'
SMOWEE	N 26° 36.320'	W 76° 57.650'
SMOWE	N 26° 35.997'	W 76° 58.809'
SMOWW	N 26° 35.608'	W 76° 59.136'
MOW2	N 26° 35.287'	W 77° 00.227'
MOW1	N 26° 34.771'	W 76° 59.932'
PTSET	N 26° 34.370'	W 77° 00.550'
MARSH	N 26° 33.520'	W 77° 04.110'
HPTWN	N 26° 32.608'	W 76° 58.063'
BTHBR	N 26° 32.410'	W 77° 02.550'
OFFELBOW	N 26° 34.270'	W 76° 54.250'

Nautical Miles

HUB OF ABACO

Most passages in this part of the Sea of Abaco are straight-forward with few unmarked shoals. The shoal extending westward from the small cay south of Johnny's Cay is marked with a pile, as is Sanka Shoal, about ½ mile west of Matt Lowe's Cay. Lubber's Bank is clearly visible. Please see larger scale and harbour charts for Man-O-War Cay (pp. 86-87), Marsh Harbour (p. 96), Boat Harbour (p. 118) and Hope Town (pp. 122-123).

The straight-line route from Hope Town to Man-O-War passes over a 3-4' bank. Boats needing more water should head 306° M from Hope Town toward a point east of Point Set Rock, which lies just NE of Matt Lowe's Cay. When the entrance to Man-O-War bears roughly magnetic north, turn and head for it. This will keep you well west of the bank. The final approach to Man-O-War will take you over a white bank which is, however, 8' deep.

The route from Hope Town to Marsh Harbour is simple. Head 315° M from Hope Town toward Point Set Rock; leave it to port. Then head about 262° M toward Outer Point, leaving Sanka Shoal far to port. The route from Hope Town to Boat Harbour is also straightforward and simple. Leave the Parrot Cays and Lubber's Bank to the south.

The south Man-O-War Channel is a narrow passage from Abaco Sound to the Atlantic Ocean. Its controlling depth is 12 feet. Round South Rock giving it a good berth because of the submerged rock lying about a hundred yards northeast of it. Head seaward on a course of about 45° for about ¾NM to avoid the 6' coral head ½NM northeast of South Rock. Then head north to get on the range of South Rock and the southeast edge of Matt Lowe's Cay. Then head through the channel on that range (course should be about 43°M). This course will take you between the two extensive reefs to the northwest and southeast of this channel. Alternatively, use the waypoints. Enter from the Atlantic heading toward South

Point Set Rock lies off the NE point of Matt Lowe's Cay and is seen here with Hope Town, on Elbow Cay, in the background. The small white shack which housed electrical junction equipment was removed in early 2010. Point Set Rock is the crossroads of the Hub of Abaco; all vessels travelling between Hope Town or Man-O-War and Marsh Harbour pass in the vicinity of Point Set Rock.

Rock and southeast shoreline of Matt Lowe's Cay on a heading of 223° M. See the chart on page 86 for a larger scale view of this route.

The north Man-O-War Channel is wider than the south Man-O-War Channel and is the best passage between the Sea of Abaco and the Atlantic Ocean in this area—it is clearly the preferred passage. Its shallowest point is 17 feet deep. See the chart on page 86 for a detailed description.

Some good snorkeling areas can be found northeast of Johnny's Cay (see snorkeling maps on page 164, 165 and 170). There are some scattered heads between Johnny's Cay and the main reef, so one should not enter the area unless the sun is high so as to make the heads visible beneath the water. Johnny's Cay is private. There are also scattered heads between Man-O-War Cay and the barrier reef. Exercise extreme caution in these areas.

Matt Lowe's Cay has been developed into 17 residential lots with a deep water canal system for private dockage. The electrical distribution hub for the outer cays has been moved to the western point of Matt Lowe's Cay with several high voltage cables buried in the northern third of the anchorage. Cruisers should anchor only in the southern two-thirds of the anchorage west of Matt Lowes Cay.

The anchorage at Matt Lowe's Cay from the northeast with Sugar Loaf Creek and Eastern Shores behind and to the left and Marsh Harbour in the background to the right. The development of this cay has included the laying of high voltage electrical cables in the northern third of the anchorage. Cruisers should anchor only in the southern two-thirds of the anchorage.

For continuation see page 94 or pages 64 and 65

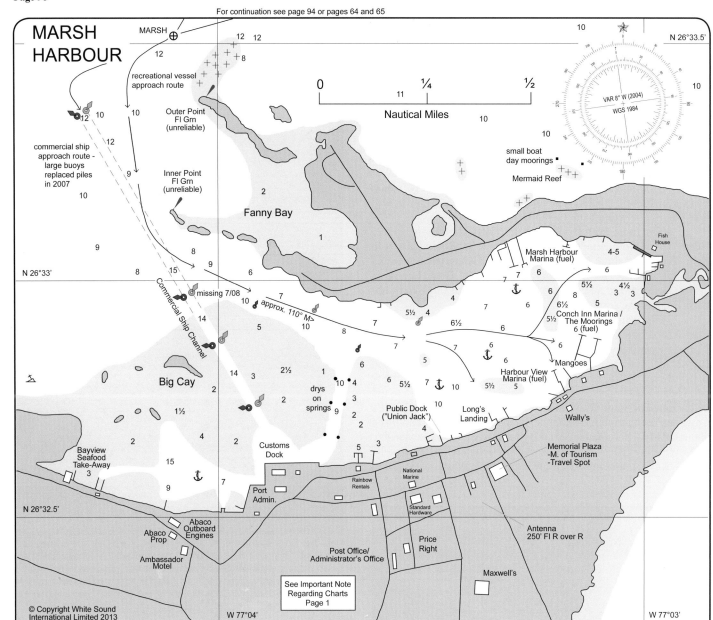

MARSH HARBOUR

MARSH ⊕

recreational vessel approach route

Outer Point Fl Grn (unreliable)

commercial ship approach route - large buoys replaced piles in 2007

Inner Point Fl Grn (unreliable)

Fanny Bay

VAR 8° W (2004)
WGS 1984

small boat day moorings

Mermaid Reef

Fish House

Marsh Harbour Marina (fuel)

Conch Inn Marina / The Moorings (fuel)

Mangoes

Harbour View Marina (fuel)

0   ¼   ½

Nautical Miles

Commercial Ship Channel

missing 7/08

approx. 110° M

Big Cay

drys on springs

Public Dock ("Union Jack")

Long's Landing

Wally's

Bayview Seafood Take-Away

Customs Dock

Memorial Plaza -M. of Tourism -Travel Spot

Rainbow Rentals

National Marine

Port Admin.

Standard Hardware

Abaco Outboard Engines

Abaco Prop

Ambassador Motel

Post Office/ Administrator's Office

Price Right

Antenna 250' Fl R over R

Maxwell's

See Important Note Regarding Charts Page 1

© Copyright White Sound International Limited 2013

W 77°04'   W 77°03'

Though entry to Marsh Harbour is basically simple, there are two possible difficulties. The first is finding it. The landmarks are not very distinctive, and a newcomer to the area may wish to follow a rough compass course toward it until Outer Point can be distinguished. Entry itself is simple and direct. Stay about 200 yards off the outer point and about 50 yards off the inner point, and proceed into the harbour favoring the north shore in order to avoid the large shoal area extending from Big Cay at the western end of the harbour. Even though this is simple enough, there is a potential problem. When the new commercial port facility was built in 2002-2003, a new commercial ship channel was dredged. It is now marked with 4 pair of large red and green lighted steel buoys (it was previously marked with 6 pair of piles). This commerical ship channel has led to some confusion. Some cruisers have decided to enter via this straight channel. When they realize that they are headed toward the new commercial port rather than the anchorage and the marinas, some have turned to port to head for the main part of the harbour and grounded on the 1-3' MLW shoal shown on the chart. We recommend that recreational cruising vessels ignore the commercial channel and the large lighted steel buoys which mark it.

After rounding Inner Point, recreational vessels should head approx. 110° M toward the anchorage. Four small composite lighted red nuns and green cans **sometimes** mark the route and are shown on the chart. These are much smaller than the buoys which mark the commercial channel; see the photos on page 98. The main harbour is mostly 6-8-10' deep. Shoals are clearly marked—two shoals flanking the old (east) channel leading to the commercial port and customs dock, a small shoal area extending from the small point on the north shore, and the two shoals flanking the channel leading to the Fish House, a commercial fishing facility with a retail store, at the east end of the harbour. The holding ground is generally good.

Boats should avoid anchoring within about 100' of the approach lines shown on the chart to allow all vessels easier ingress to and egress from the marinas. Anchoring is not permitted in either of the channels leading to the commercial port.

Those who prefer to tie up to a dock rather than anchoring off will find excellent facilities at the Conch Inn Marina, Harbour View Marina, Mangoes, and Marsh Harbour Marina. See the marina maps on pp. 100 and 101.

MARSH HARBOUR

Marsh Harbour is the largest town in Abaco—in fact it is the third largest in the Bahamas, exceeded in size only by Nassau and Freeport. The population is about 5000, and its many businesses and shops offer visitors the best selection in Abaco of everything from conch fritters and clothing to stereos and automobile parts.

Good restaurants abound—with Mangoes, Curly Tails at the Conch Inn Marina and Snappas just west of Harbour View Marina at the three marinas along Marsh Harbour's "gold coast." Wally's is across the street. The Jib Room, located at Marsh Harbour Marina on the harbour's north side, is well known for its weekly specials. Angler's is located at Boat Harbour Marina. The Golden Grouper and Mother Merle's Fishnet are good modest restaurants offering local cuisine. The Copper Cannon Kitchen at Long's Landing sells fresh fish and some homemade specialties. Jamie's Place is on East Bay Street about one-half mile east of Conch Inn Marina.

There are two supermarkets in Marsh Harbour, both of which are located within a few blocks of each other within walking distance of the Union Jack Dock (named after a restaurant which was located near the dock which burned down more than 30 years ago). See the street

Entrance to Marsh Harbour viewed from the south. Note the commerical ship channel and the new commercial port facility. Recreational vessels should ignore the channel and enter the harbour as shown above and on the chart on the facing page. The buoys have been enhanced on this photo to make them more visible; they are in the correct positions. Note also the smaller composite buoys (2 of the 4 appear in the photograph—look carefully, they are small) marking the suggested recreational vessel entry route. Both of the small boats underway in this photo are in the suggested entry channel.

map of the Marsh Harbour central business district on page 104 for locations. The new Maxwell's opened in August 2010 and is located two blocks south of the old store, which was destroyed by fire in July 2008. It is the largest supermarket not only in Abaco, but in the entire Bahamas. Closer to the waterfront on Stratton Drive, the old Price Right store was combined with Save A Lot and re-opened in July 2011; it offers a good selection of lower priced brands. Abaco Groceries, a warehouse type store located on Don MacKay Blvd. near the airport roundabout has been recently expanded and sells items in small enough quantities to be of interest to cruisers. Convenience stores include the new Harbour General, located on Bay Street just east of Long's Landing, and Bahamas Family Market, located near the traffic light. Long's Landing sells fresh fish and conch. The chart on page 96 and the maps on pp. 104 and 108 show locations of these stores. Most of these stores are open 7 days a week, but hours on Sunday are limited. Maxwell's alone offers excellent choice; combined these stores offer an amazing selection of product at excellent prices — clearly the best in the Out Islands.

The Conch Inn Marina is Marsh Harbour's largest. It has about 75 full-service slips, Curly Tails Restaurant, nine harbourside rooms, a laundry, three boat charter operations (The Moorings, Sunsail and Concept Boat Rentals), the Dive Abaco dive shop and a swimming pool all on the premises. Located nearby are Mangoes and Harbour View Marina. Mangoes' new docks opened during summer 2007, and there is a restaurant and boutique, as well as a swimming pool, on site. Harbour View Marina has a pool and patio deck, two on-site restaurants (Wally's and Snappas) as well as Blue Wave Boat Rentals. Marsh Harbour Marina with its Jib Room Bar and Restaurant is on the harbour's north side with excellent protection from northwest winds in winter cold fronts and good exposure to southeastern summer breezes. Boat Harbour Marina

Continued on page 98

A pair of the new large steel lighted buoys marking the commercial ship entrance channel to the commercial port. These buoys should be ignored by recreational vessels, which should enter Marsh Harbour as shown on the chart and the aerial photographs. If a foreign vessel is clearing in, it should go directly to one of the commercial marinas flying a Q flag, and then phone Bahamian Customs (367-2522 or 367-2524) to arrange for clearance.

A boat entering Marsh Harbour along the northern shoreline of the harbour viewed from the northwest. This boat has corrrectly turned to port out of the commercial ship channel (marked with buoys and not visible on this photo) and is heading approximately 120° M toward Conch Inn Marina. Marsh Harbour Marina can be seen along the northern shoreline, an area known as Pelican Shores. Beyond the mainland, Matt Lowe's Cay is visible on the left and Sugarloaf Cay on the right. The Hope Town lighthouse on Elbow Cay is visible in the distance on the right side of the photo.

Continued from page 97

is in the town of Marsh Harbour, but not the harbour itself—it is located east of Marsh Harbour, directly off the Sea of Abaco. It is the largest and most comprehensive marina development in Marsh Harbour. For further information regarding Boat Harbour, see page 118. Marsh Harbour Boat Yards opened at Calcutta Creek south of Boat Harbour during fall 1999. They have an 85-ton travelling marine hoist and can provide most repair and re-building services. A marine store is located on the premises.

Clothing stores include the boutiques at Mangoes and Wally's, Iggy Biggy, Alexis Fashions, His and Her Jeans, Victor's Department Store, and several others. The selection is very good. Standard Hardware, on Queen Elizabeth Drive completed a major expansion in 2007, and Ace/Abaco Hardware, on Don MacKay Boulevard, both offer broad selections of hardware and appliances. Both also carry some marine supplies, and National Marine on Queen Elizabeth Drive across from Standard Hardware and the marine store at Marsh Harbour Boat Yards all have selections of marine items. Please see the classified business directory for Marsh Harbour to learn the full extent of the goods and services available in this bustling Out Island town. It can be found on pages 194-196. Also see the street maps of Marsh Harbour on pages 104 and 108.

Marsh Harbour is a port of entry for vessels coming to the Bahamas from foreign ports. Customs and immigration are located at the new port facility at the west end of town. This new port is a busy place, with two or more ships from West Palm Beach unload-

One of the four small buoys placed by the Royal Marsh Harbour Yacht Club to mark the entry channel for recreational vessels in Marsh Harbour. Red and green flashing lights were added to these buoys in 2007. **Recreational vessels should not enter via the commercial ship channel, and should not go to the commercial port, even to clear in.**

ing each week, as well as the mail boat which arrives from Nassau early every Wednesday morning. **Recreational vessels should not go to the commercial port; they should go directly to one of the marinas** flying the Q flag, and then call Immigration and Customs to come to clear them. Phone numbers are 367-2522 or 367-2524.

Marsh Harbour is the seat of the Administrator for central Abaco. A new government office building in Dundas Town is expected to open before the end of 2012 and will house the Administrator as well as several ministires and other government offices. See the directory of government offices on page 200 for more detailed information.

Taxicabs are readily available in Marsh Harbour (call on VHF 06), and automobiles, bicycles and minibikes can be rented, making it possible to get around easily. Paved roads make it possible to drive to Treasure Cay or Cooperstown or even Little Abaco Island on a day trip, or south to Cherokee Sound or Sandy Point. See the article "Exploring Abaco by Land: ..." (pp. 184-187).

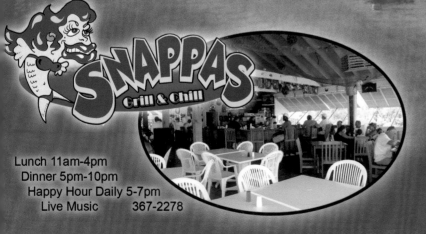

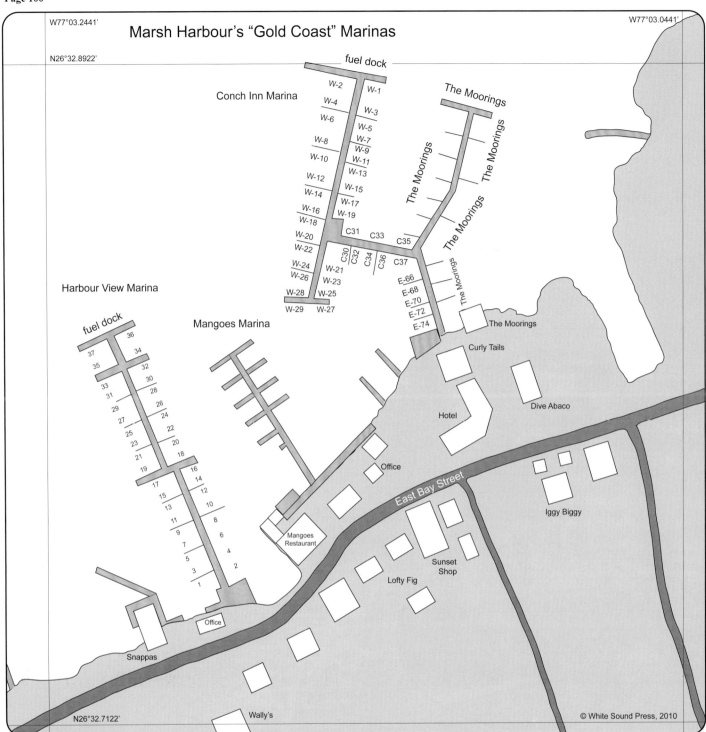

Marsh Harbour's "Gold Coast" Marinas

Marsh Harbour Marina
Yacht Club & Jib Room Restaurant
www.jibroom.com

- FAMILY RUN
- FULL SERVICE MARINA
- FUEL - Gas and Diesel
- WATER
- POWER - 110/220
- NEW SHOWERS
- CATAMARAN SLIPS
- POOL
- ICE
- BAR & RESTAURANT
- CABLE T.V.
- MARINA EXPANDED 2000
- MERMAID REEF
- COURTESY PHONE
- INTERNET AVAILABLE

"BEST COOKOUTS"

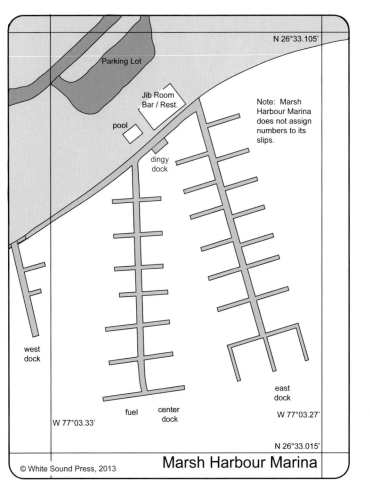

Come to The Marsh Harbour Marina on beautiful Pelican Shores. Convenient to all Marsh Harbour services but in a peaceful setting just steps from Mermaid Reef for swimming and snorkeling. We enjoy the southerly summer breezes and are protected from the nasty winter northerlies. Enjoy a true Bahamian setting with Dancing in our tropical gardens during our world famous Barbecues.
A BOAT/US Cooperating Marina.

Marsh Harbour, Abaco, Bahamas · Phone 242 367-2700 · Fax 242 367-2033 · jibroom@hotmail.com

Parking Lot

N 26°33.105'

Jib Room Bar / Rest.

pool

Note: Marsh Harbour Marina does not assign numbers to its slips.

dingy dock

west dock

fuel / center dock

east dock

W 77°03.33'

W 77°03.27'

N 26°33.015'

© White Sound Press, 2013

Marsh Harbour Marina

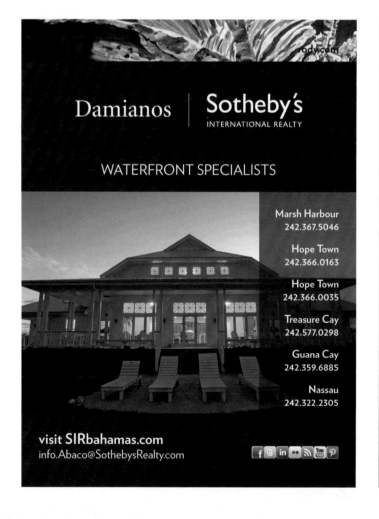

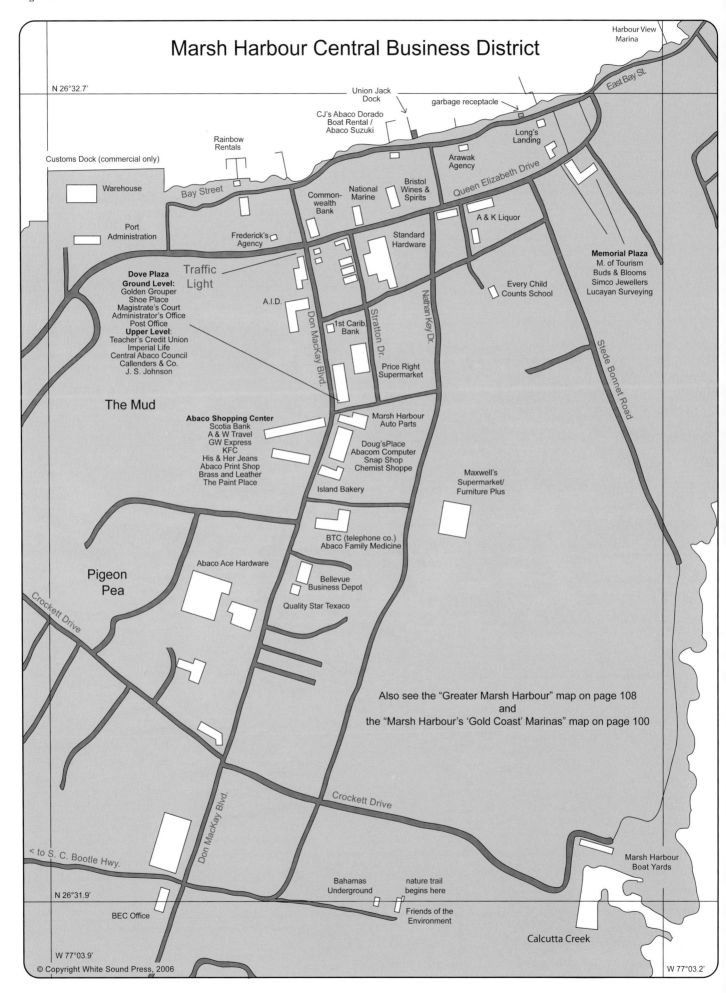

Marsh Harbour Central Business District

Harbour View Marina

N 26°32.7'

Union Jack Dock

garbage receptacle

East Bay St.

CJ's Abaco Dorado Boat Rental / Abaco Suzuki

Long's Landing

Rainbow Rentals

Arawak Agency

Queen Elizabeth Drive

Customs Dock (commercial only)

Bay Street

Bristol Wines & Spirits

Warehouse

Common-wealth Bank

National Marine

A & K Liquor

Port Administration

Frederick's Agency

Standard Hardware

Memorial Plaza
M. of Tourism
Buds & Blooms
Simco Jewellers
Lucayan Surveying

Dove Plaza
Ground Level:
Golden Grouper
Shoe Place
Magistrate's Court
Administrator's Office
Post Office
Upper Level:
Teacher's Credit Union
Imperial Life
Central Abaco Council
Callenders & Co.
J. S. Johnson

Traffic Light

A.I.D.

A.I.D.

Every Child Counts School

Don Mackay Blvd.

1st Carib. Bank

Stratton Dr.

Nathan Key Dr.

Stede Bonnet Road

Price Right Supermarket

The Mud

Abaco Shopping Center
Scotia Bank
A & W Travel
GW Express
KFC
His & Her Jeans
Abaco Print Shop
Brass and Leather
The Paint Place

Marsh Harbour Auto Parts

Doug'sPlace
Abacom Computer
Snap Shop
Chemist Shoppe

Maxwell's Supermarket/ Furniture Plus

Island Bakery

BTC (telephone co.)
Abaco Family Medicine

Abaco Ace Hardware

Pigeon Pea

Bellevue Business Depot

Quality Star Texaco

Crockett Drive

Also see the "Greater Marsh Harbour" map on page 108
and
the "Marsh Harbour's 'Gold Coast' Marinas" map on page 100

Crockett Drive

Don Mackay Blvd.

< to S. C. Bootle Hwy.

Marsh Harbour Boat Yards

N 26°31.9'

BEC Office

Bahamas Underground

nature trail begins here

Friends of the Environment

Calcutta Creek

W 77°03.9'

W 77°03.2'

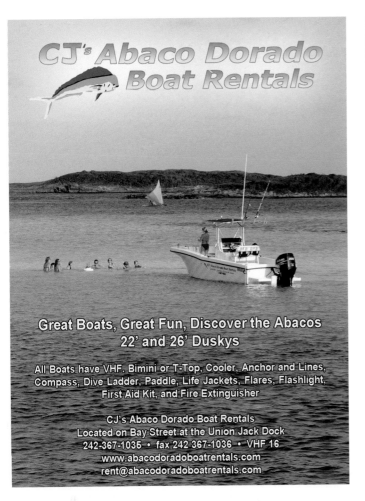
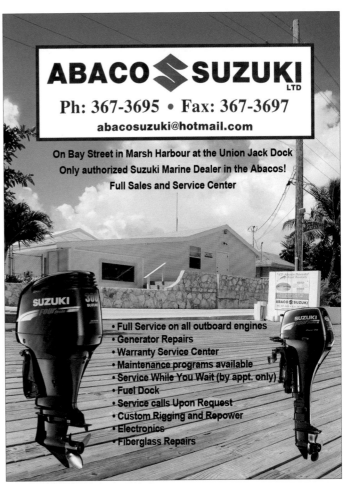
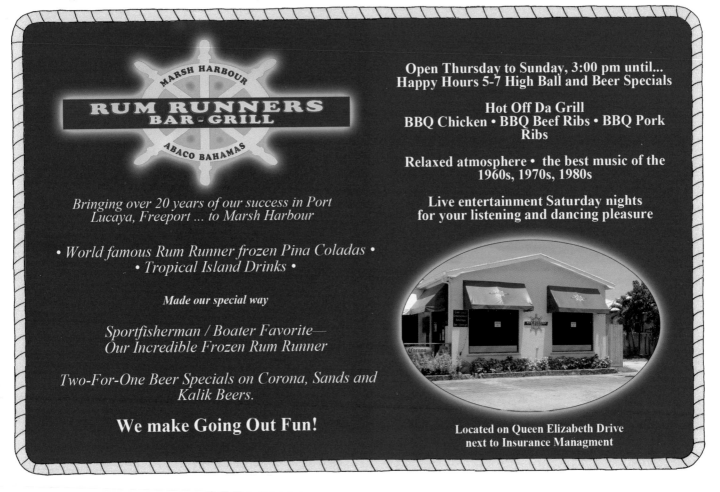

Marsh Harbour from the east with Conch Inn Marina, Harbour View Marina and Mangoes on the left and part of Marsh Harbour Marina, located on the northern side of the harbour know as Pelican Shores), visible on the right. East Bay Street stretches toward the west—to the traffice light and the commerical port of Marsh Harbour. Photo by Steve Dodge, 30 June 2012.

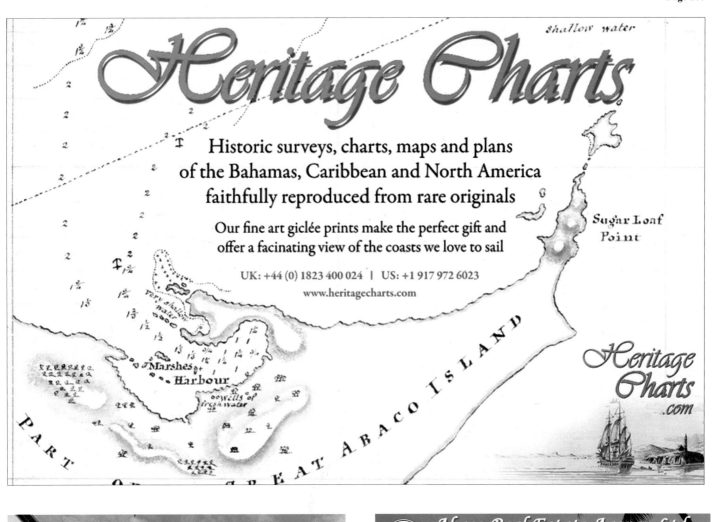

Heritage Charts

Historic surveys, charts, maps and plans
of the Bahamas, Caribbean and North America
faithfully reproduced from rare originals

Our fine art giclée prints make the perfect gift and
offer a facinating view of the coasts we love to sail

UK: +44 (0) 1823 400 024 | US: +1 917 972 6023

www.heritagecharts.com

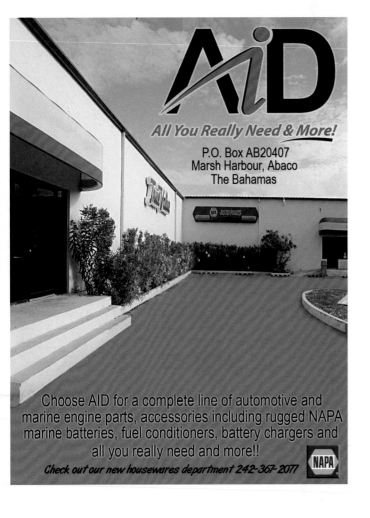
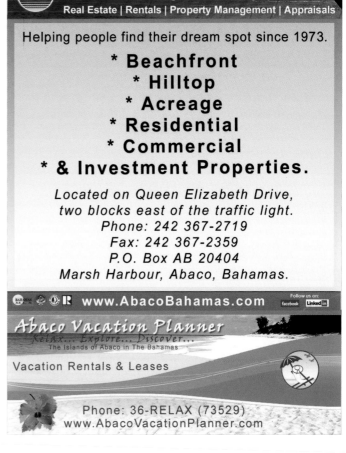

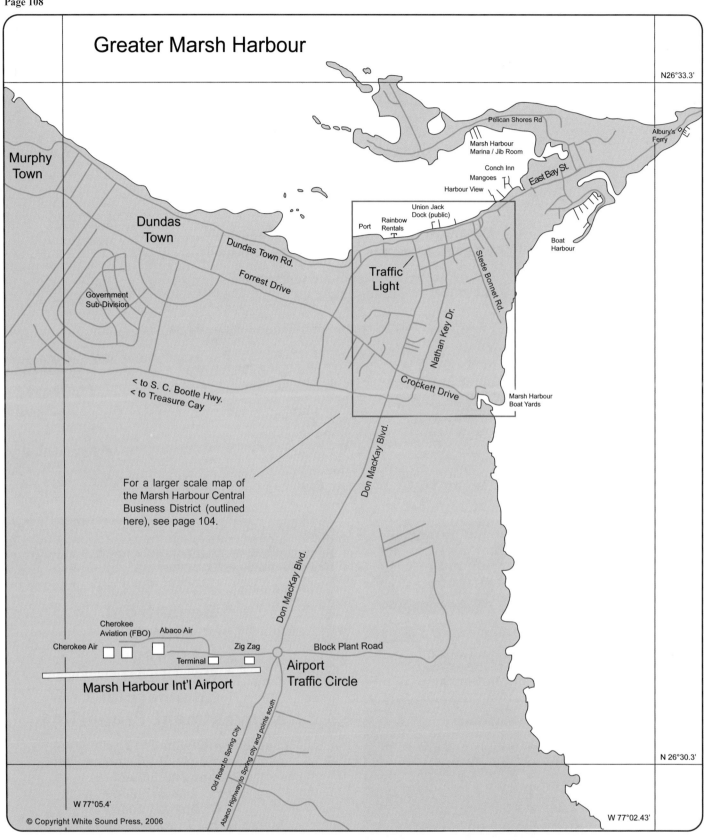

Greater Marsh Harbour

N26°33.3'

Murphy Town

Pelican Shores Rd

Marsh Harbour Marina / Jib Room

Albury's Ferry

Conch Inn

Mangoes

Harbour View

East Bay St.

Dundas Town

Union Jack Dock (public)

Port

Rainbow Rentals

Dundas Town Rd.

Forrest Drive

Boat Harbour

Traffic Light

Stede Bonner Rd.

Nathan Key Dr.

Government Sub-Division

Crockett Drive

Marsh Harbour Boat Yards

< to S. C. Bootle Hwy.
< to Treasure Cay

For a larger scale map of the Marsh Harbour Central Business District (outlined here), see page 104.

Don MacKay Blvd.

Don MacKay Blvd.

Cherokee Aviation (FBO)

Abaco Air

Cherokee Air

Zig Zag

Block Plant Road

Terminal

Airport Traffic Circle

Marsh Harbour Int'l Airport

N 26°30.3'

Old Road to Spring City

Abaco Highway to Spring city and points south

W 77°05.4'

W 77°02.43'

© Copyright White Sound Press, 2006

The commercial port of Marsh Harbour with the *Duke of Topsail* and the *Legend* both in port. Photo taken from the west. 7 July. 2009

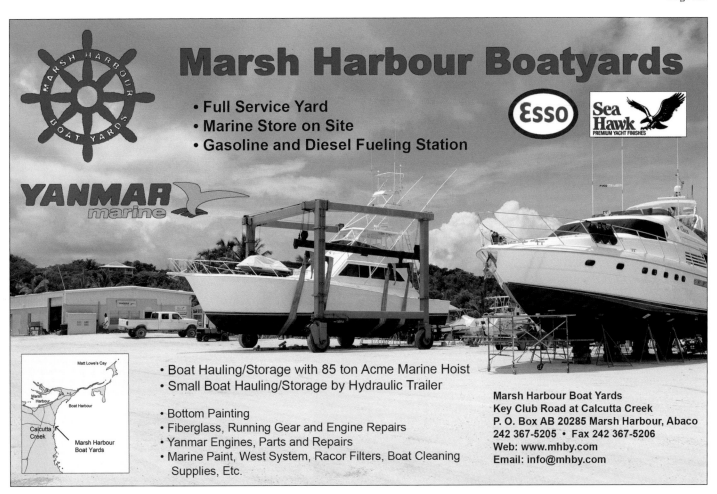

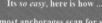

Page 112

Downtown Marsh Harbour from the SE with the two large Standard Hardware buildings in the foreground and Price Right/Save a Lot a block behind them. Don Mackay Boulevard is another block further west with AID clearly visible. The port and the harbour with the Duke of Topsail is beyond. Photo by Steve Dodge, 30 June 2012.

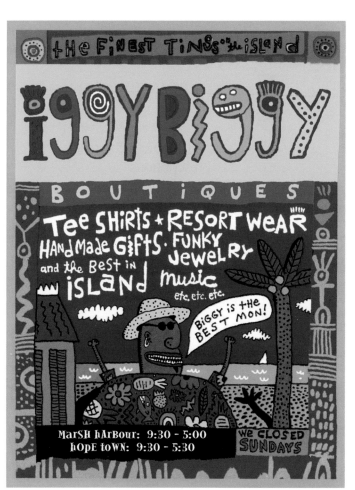
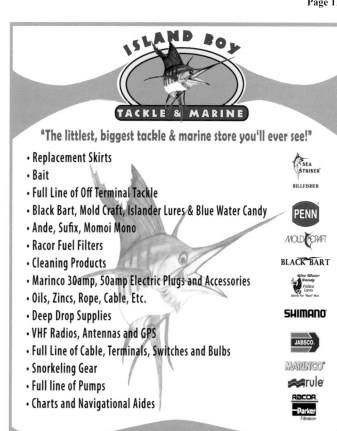

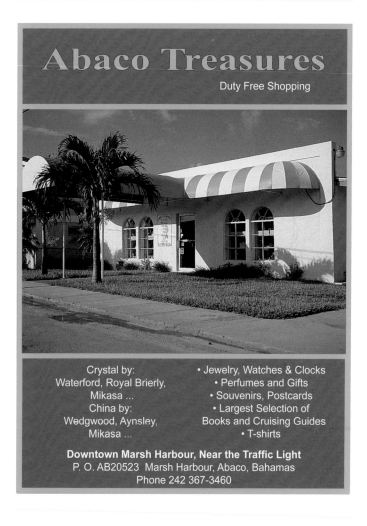

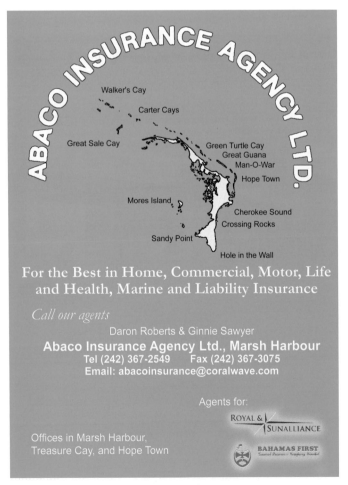
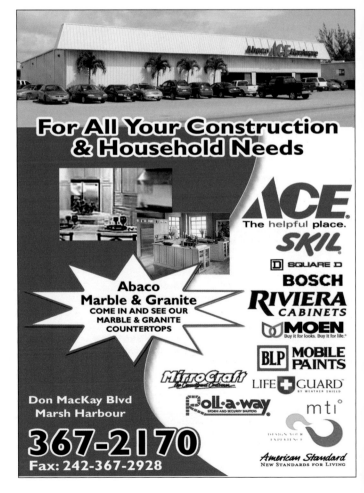

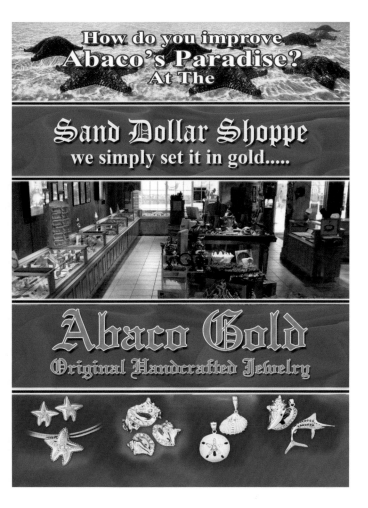
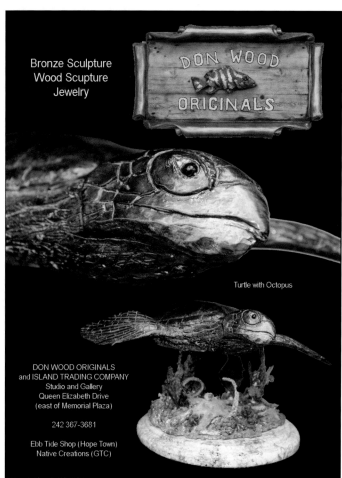
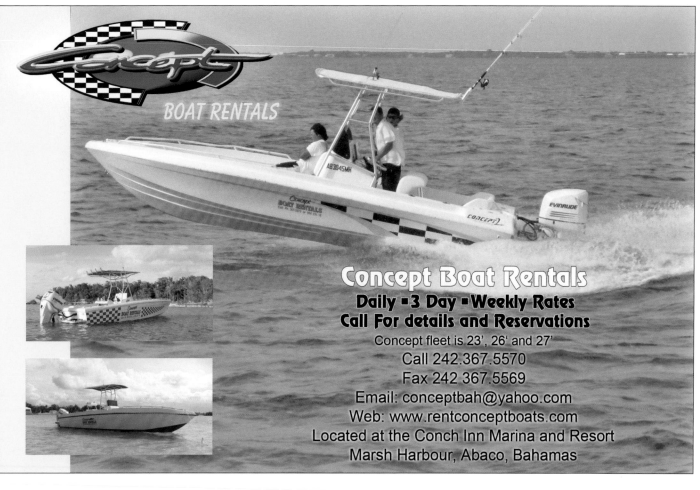

Marsh Harbour from the NE with Mermaid Reef visible just off the sandy beach (see charts pp. 96 and 164). Marsh Harbour Marina on Pelican Shores as well as Conch Inn and Harbour View Marinas on MarshHarbour's "Gold Coast" are all clearly visible. Photo by Steve Dodge, 30 June 2012.

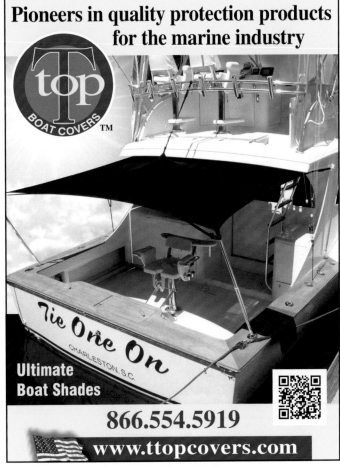

BOAT HARBOUR MARINA

For continuation see page 64   For more detaail see page 94

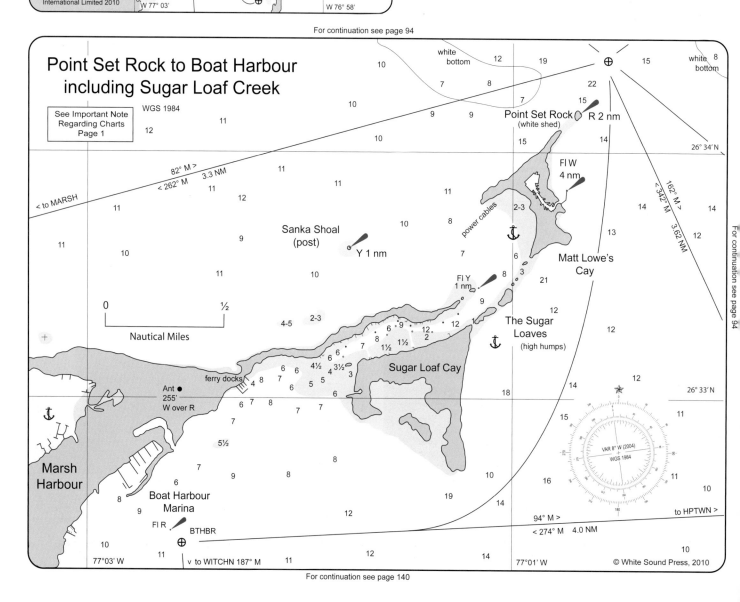

Boat Harbour Marina is conveniently located on the southeast shoreline of Great Abaco Island in the town of Marsh Harbour. Access to Marsh Harbour's business district is very good (about five minutes by car), and access by water to Hope Town, White Sound, Man-O-War Cay, or to the Atlantic Ocean via Tilloo Cut, South Man-O-War Channel or North Man-O-War Channel is easy and direct.

The waypoint BTHBR (N 26° 32.410'; W 77° 02.550') is located about 100 yards SE of the piling with the flashing red light, which is located about 100 yards ESE of the entrance to the marina. Approach the waypoint from the east on a course of 274° M, or from White Sound on a course of 298° M. Approach it from the south from the waypoint WITCHN on a course of 7° M. See intermediate scale charts of the Hub of Abaco (p. 94), the Lubbers Quarters area (p. 140), and Man-O-War Cay and its Approaches (p. 86 for more detail).

Boat Harbour offers gasoline, diesel, and complete marina services, has two bars and restaurants, the Abaco Beach Resort at Boat Harbour, and Sea HorseBoat Rentals on the premises. Marsh Harbour's "Gold Coast" shopping is a short walk away. See the marina map on page 120.

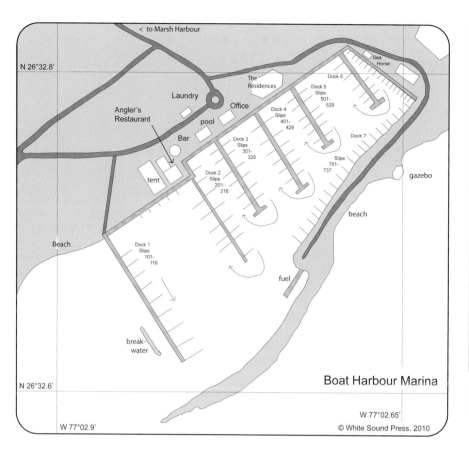

Boat Harbour Marina

Boat Harbour Marina and Abaco Beach Resort from the southwest with Man-O-War Cay in the background. The fuel dock is to starboard after entering.

SUGARLOAF CREEK

Sugarloaf Creek separates Eastern Shores, Marsh Harbour, from Sugarloaf Cay and the Sugar Loaves. The photo upper left shows the creek with Matt Lowes Cay and Man-O-War Cay in the background; it was taken from the southwest. The photo above shows the northeastern end of the creek with the Sugar Loaves and the tip of Sugarloaf Cay, and with Hope Town in the background; it was taken from the west. The photo to the left shows the creek itself and Eastern Shores, Marsh Harbour; It was taken from the eastnortheast. See the chart on page 118. Photos by Steve Dodge, 2008 and 2010.

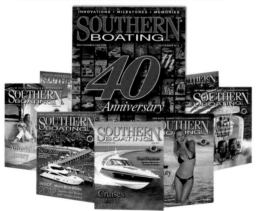

Elbow Cay and its Approaches / Hope Town

For continuation see page 94 or page 65

For a draft of 5-6' MLW from a spot north of the Parrot Cays (or from the waypoint HPTWN), head toward Eagle Rock (yellow house). When the narrow concrete road (which looks like a sidewalk) is straight, turn and head directly toward it (bearing of 149° M), as though you were going to drive onto it. Two white posts with red triangles on the northeast side of the road form a range. At night they have white rope perimeter lighting. The channel is usually marked with red and green balls. Turn to starboard into the center of the opening to the harbour. For a draft of 5½-6' MLW from the same spot north of the Parrot Cays head for the old rock quarry and then turn northeast as indicated on the chart. Proceed into the harbour as explained above. From the south: for a draft of about 5' MLW proceed northeastward toward the waypoint HPTWN until on the appropriate range for Eagle Rock. Then proceed as described above. The entire area between Hope Town and the Parrot Cays has scattered 5-5½' bumps; boats drawing 5' or more should plan to utilize some tide help. See harbour entry photos on page 124.

Hope Town Point

to PTSET

135° M >
< 315° M
2.8 NM

< to BTHBR
4.0 NM
94° M >
< 274° M

FI R
Parrot Cays
high voltage cables

Island Marine

Fl W
Cook's Cove

Anna Cay
(pink house)

HPTWN
5 - 6

Eagle Rock
FI G

5 - 6

FI W (5)
ev 15 sec
old quarries

Hope Town

Frys Mangrove

Elbow Cay

Porgie Rock

162° M >
< 342° M
3.62 NM

33° M >
< 213° M
1.6 NM

Firefly

118° M >
< 298° M
3.54 NM

WSMK
FI W
White Sound

VAR 8° W (2004)
WGS 1984

22° M >
< 202° M

Abaco Inn

Sea Spray Marina

Cruise Abaco base

LQN

Marne's Landing

Lubbers Quarters

49° M >
< 229° M

Dorros Cove

Tahiti Beach

Tilloo Cut

LQMID

Cracker P's
Lubber's Landing

23° M >
< 203° M

TCUT

OFFTCT

< TO WITCHE

112° M >
< 292° M

1.71 NM

LQS

Tilloo Cay

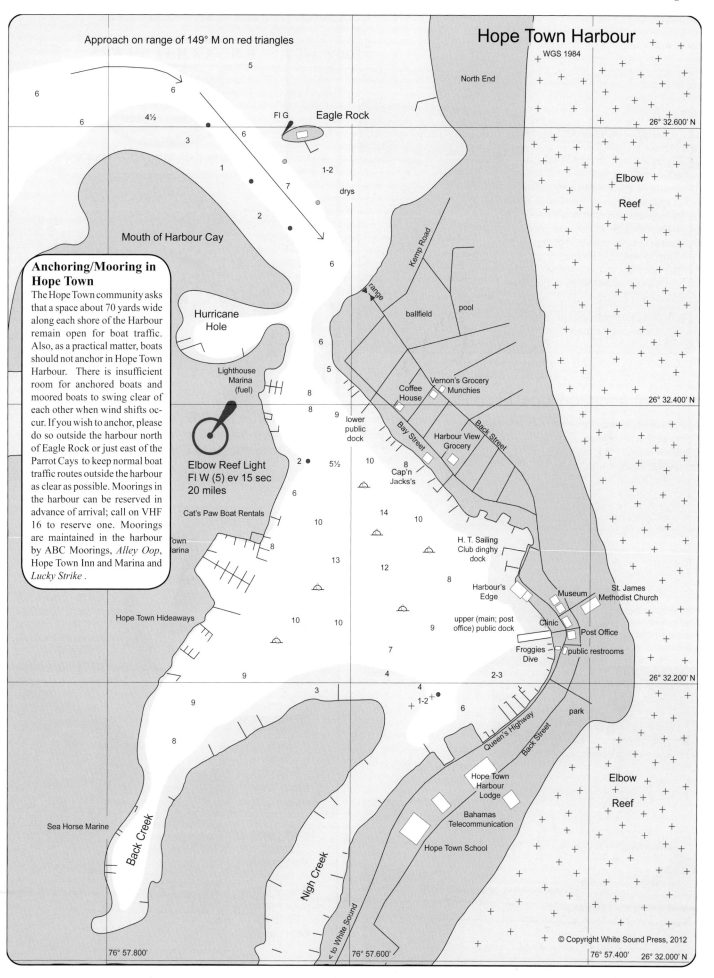

Hope Town Harbour

Approach on range of 149° M on red triangles

WGS 1984

North End

26° 32.600' N

Fl G   Eagle Rock

Elbow

Reef

drys

1-2

Mouth of Harbour Cay

Kemp Road

ballfield   pool

range

Anchoring/Mooring in Hope Town

The Hope Town community asks that a space about 70 yards wide along each shore of the Harbour remain open for boat traffic. Also, as a practical matter, boats should not anchor in Hope Town Harbour. There is insufficient room for anchored boats and moored boats to swing clear of each other when wind shifts occur. If you wish to anchor, please do so outside the harbour north of Eagle Rock or just east of the Parrot Cays to keep normal boat traffic routes outside the harbour as clear as possible. Moorings in the harbour can be reserved in advance of arrival; call on VHF 16 to reserve one. Moorings are maintained in the harbour by ABC Moorings, *Alley Oop*, Hope Town Inn and Marina and *Lucky Strike* .

Hurricane Hole

Lighthouse Marina (fuel)

Coffee House

Vernon's Grocery
Munchies

26° 32.400' N

lower public dock

Bay Street

Back Street

Harbour View Grocery

Elbow Reef Light
Fl W (5) ev 15 sec
20 miles

Cap'n Jacks's

Cat's Paw Boat Rentals

H. T. Sailing Club dinghy dock

Town Marina

Harbour's Edge

Museum

St. James Methodist Church

upper (main; post office) public dock

Clinic

Post Office

Hope Town Hideaways

Froggies Dive

public restrooms

26° 32.200' N

1-2

Queen's Highway

Back Street

park

Sea Horse Marine

Back Creek

Nigh Creek

Hope Town Harbour Lodge

Elbow

Reef

Bahamas Telecommunication

Hope Town School

< to White Sound

76° 57.800'   76° 57.600'   76° 57.400'   26° 32.000' N

Correct entry and exit to and from Hope Town Harbour is clearly shown by three boats. Photo by Steve Dodge, June 2004.

Entrance to Hope Town Harbour

Eagle Rock | green ball (leave to port) | road and range markers for entrance channel | red ball (leave to starboard)

Approach to Hope Town Harbour from the NW showing the road and the range markers for the approach channel.

range markers (white rope light at perimeter of triangles at night)

road

Keep the two red triangular range markers lined up to stay in center of the channel, or proceed as though you were going to go straight onto the road.

Turn to starboard ...

and proceed into the harbour.

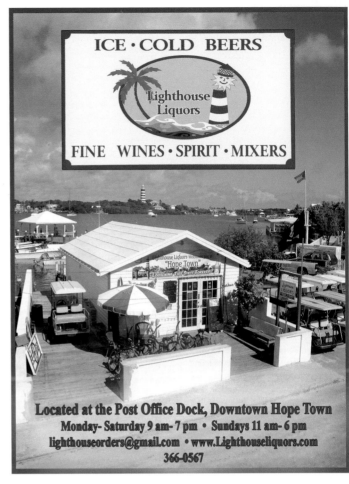

HOPE TOWN

Hope Town is clearly one of the most picturesque settlements in the Bahamas. Its candy-striped lighthouse was built by the British Imperial Lighthouse Service in 1863, and still uses a small kerosene-fueled mantle and a huge rotating glass fresnel lens to send a beam of light which can be seen for up to 20 miles. The town has many charming old houses, some of them beautifully restored. The ocean beach, just to the east, has powdery pink sand and is protected by an extensive offshore reef. Founded by loyalists in c. 1785, the community maintains the Wyannie Malone Historical Museum, which has many interesting artifacts and photographs.

Hope Town provides many services for visitors. There are two grocery stores—Harbour View Grocery and Vernon's Grocery. Vernon's includes the Upper Crust Bakery where pies and bread are baked daily. Vernon's business slogans—"Let Them Eat Key Lime Pie" and "Pies 'R' Us" exemplify his delightful sense of humor. Harbour View Grocery is on the waterfront, and has its own dock. Both stores are well stocked; what one does not have can likely be found at the other.

There are three marinas—all are on the west side of the harbour across from the town. Lighthouse Marina is just inside the entrance and offers fuel, wet and dry storage, and has a well-stocked marine store. Hope Town Inn & Marina has 50 new slips and a new restaurant and pool bar which opened in 2012. Hope Town Hideaways is a small resort with villas, tropical landscaping, 12 slips and a pool; it is now part of Hope Town Inn and Marina.

The Hope Town Harbour Lodge is a resort/restaurant complex, and has recently been completely refurbished. It offers snorkeling just off its ocean beach, a pool bar and fine dining. Other bars and restaurants include Harbour's Edge and Cap'n Jack's, both located in the heart of town north of the main dock (also called the post office dock or the upper public dock). Wine Down Sip Sip on Back Street offers a wide assortment of wines and beer (some on tap) as well as mixed drinks in a relaxed, comfortable, homelike atmosphere with complimentary internet service. The Hope Town Coffee House offers specialty coffees roasted on site as well as baked goods, teas, and internet service. They are located near the lower public dock. Munchies offers take-away food, and has a small eating area on the premises. The Sugar Shack, located across the street and just south of the Post Office dock, offers deli sandwiches as well as ice cream specialties. The Abaco Inn and the Boat House Restaurant (at Sea Spray Marina and Resort), both located at White Sound (3 miles south), serve breakfast, lunch, and dinner. On Da Beach, at Turtle Hill Resort, is located about a mile south of the main dock overlooking a beautiful ocean beach. All offer excellent food and friendly service—and provide the visitor with exceptional variety in a small town.

There are several excellent gift and souvenir shops—the Ebb Tide Shop, Iggy Biggy, El Mercado, and the Da Crazy Crab. The Ebb Tide offers Androsia Batik clothing, and all have a good assortment of other clothing, jewelry, T-shirts, books, and various gift items. Iggy Biggy specializes in art prints, paintings, island clothing, and jewelry. Da Crazy Crab sells a variety of Cuban Cigars as well as hats, bags and gifts. Sun Dried T's, located beneath the Sugar Shack, features silk screened T-shirts printed on Elbow Cay as well as other beach clothing, and rents surfboards and bicycles. Froggies Dive Shop is across the street.

Golf carts are available from Island Cart Rentals (366-0448), JR's Cart Rentals (366-0361), Hope Town Cart Rentals (366-0064), T&N Carts (366-0069) and Elbow Cay Cart Rentals (366-0530). White Sound is a 3-mile ride with Mackey's TakeOut on the way, and Abaco Inn and Sea Spray at White Sound (see pp. 134-138). Tahiti Beach is another 1½ miles. Hope Town Point is a 1-mile ride or walk north of town. Motorized vehicles (including golf carts) are not allowed in town without a permit.

Elbow Reef and Hope Town from ESE with the Parrot Cays, Matt Lowe's and Sugarloaf Cays, and Marsh Harbour in the background. Photo by Steve Dodge, 30 June, 2012.

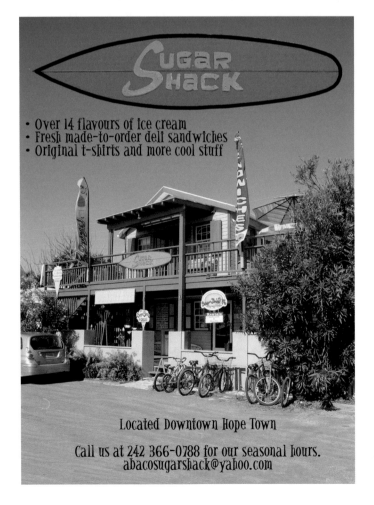

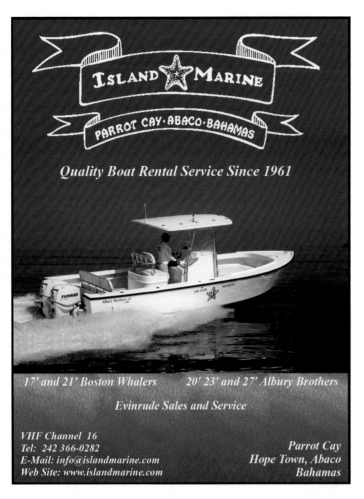

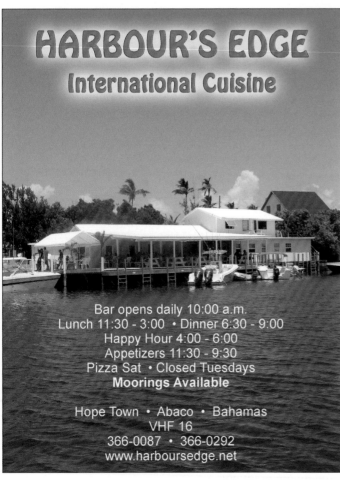

HOPE TOWN
Inn & Marina

We invite you to live like a local at our quaint historic island resort, with 5-star amenities and all the comforts of home.

Hope Town Inn & Marina is a 15-acre private estate bordered by the Sea of Abaco and Hope Town Harbour. Come stay with us at our marina, Hope Town Harbour's newest, featuring brand new docks and first-class pedestals. Our Hideaways at Hope Town offer four 2-bedroom/2-bathroom villas, each with private wrapping verandas, harbour views, personal dock slips, and beautiful garden settings. Choose to relax in one of our newly constructed second story "penthouse style" apartments with private balconies, and undoubtedly the best views of Hope Town Harbour. Don't overlook our charming historic inn, also with private balconies overlooking the beautiful pool and Harbour.

- New restaurant offering Caribbean cuisine and specialty cocktails
- Steps away from famous candy cane-striped lighthouse
- Shower/locker/laundry facilities for marina guests
- Two private pools and jacuzzi
- Poolside massage pavilion
- Private harbourside beach
- Special event designed grounds

Call Today:
242-366-0003
U.S. Phone: 850-588-4855
www.hopetownmarina.com
Email: office@hopetownmarina.com

 Find us on Facebook for weekly updates and specials! www.facebook.com/hopetowninn&marina

The Wyannie Malone Historical Museum

Hope Town was settled by British Loyalists who were seeking safe refuge after the American Revolution. Many of the settlers came from the Carolinas by way of East Florida after that area was turned over to Spain in the Peace of Paris in 1783. The same treaty called for the evacuation of New York by the Loyalists and many moved back to England or into Canada or down to the British Caribbean. The initial settlements were at Carleton, near the current Treasure Cay, and Marsh's Harbour. Marsh Harbour is now the largest community in Abaco and the third largest town in the Bahamas; whereas, the settlement at Carleton has disappeared. By 1785 there were over 1000 refugees in Abaco distributed in five or six settlements. The settlement at Hope Town was founded in 1785, in part, by a widow from South Carolina named Wyannie Malone. Wyannie along with her four children started a dynasty in Hope Town that spread the Malone name through the Bahamas over to Key West and other parts of Florida and outwards from there. Hence the choice of the name of: The Wyannie Malone Historical Museum.

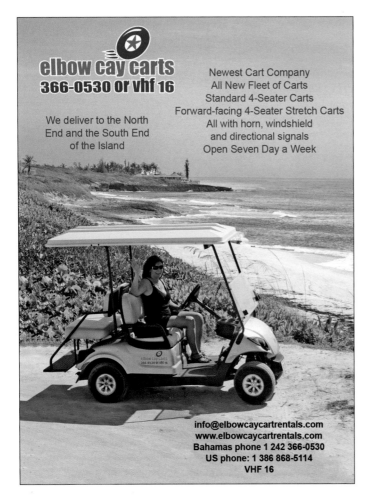
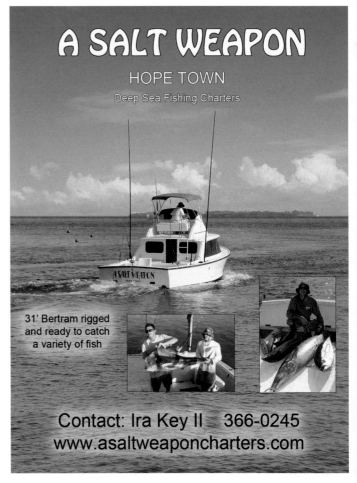

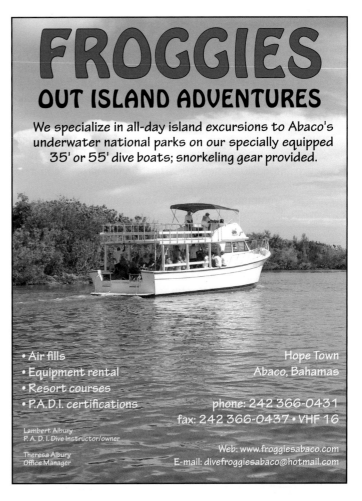

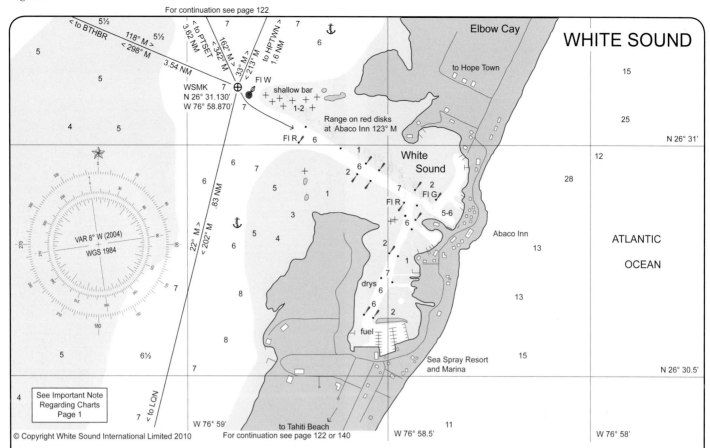

For continuation see page 122

WHITE SOUND

For continuation see page 122 or 140

Boats transiting the area should stay west of the White Sound mark which indicates the channel entrance and also the western end of the White Sound Bar. This rocky bank lies just to the north of the channel and has a depth of only about 1' at MLW, so even small outboard boats should stay west of the mark.

Enter White Sound in the dredged channel which carries about 5-6' at mean low water. It is marked by the White Sound mark (Fl W) at its northwestern end and a range consisting of two large red disks on the Abaco Inn at its southeastern end. Enter on a bearing of 123° M. The range is lit by red lights at night. Most (but not all) of the channel marker pilings are now lit by flashing red and green lights. Pilings are often missing or askew because of errant barge traffic. Proceed directly to the Abaco Inn dock, or turn to starboard and follow the marked channel to Sea Spray Marina and Resort.

Complimentary dockage is available for restaurant and bar patrons at the Abaco Inn. Space is limited, so boats should Mediterranean moor—drop an anchor off the bow, back off, and tie the stern to the dock. Power and water are not available.

The channel to Sea Spray Marina branches off the main channel with about a ninety degree turn to starboard and is marked with stakes with red and green targets. Just after entering the branch channel, there is a rock pile outside the channel off to starboard (exposed only at low water). The channel leads west of a free-standing sand and rock breakwater which protects the fuel dock. Gasoline and diesel fuel are available. Slips are serviced with power and water, and ice, bait, etc. are available. See the marina map on page 137.

Anchoring in the dredged channels of White Sound is prohibited, and vessels drawing more than about 2 feet will be unable to find secure anchorage outside the channels in White Sound. Good anchorages in prevailing easterlies can be found just outside White Sound, both north and south of the entrance. It is a short dinghy ride into either Abaco Inn or Sea Spray Resort and Marina.

WHITE SOUND

White Sound has a residential community of about sixty homes and two small resorts. The Abaco Inn is situated on a narrow strip of land between White Sound and the Atlantic Ocean, and has rooms facing each. It offers informal gourmet dining on open air patios with sensational views of breaking surf to the east and placid White Sound to the west. Its swimming pool is built into a rock outcropping on the ocean side, and its bar is a friendly place.

Sea Spray Marina and Resort has 60 slips with power and water, gasoline and diesel fuel service, a small boutique, and it is located just a couple of hundred yards from an ocean beach. The Boat House Restaurant serves breakfast, lunch, and dinner, and offers both fully air conditioned indoor or pleasant outside dining. There is a freshwater pool and deck overlooking White Sound adjacent to the Garbonzo Bar. Complimentary transportation to and from Hope Town is provided for marina, resort and restaurant guests.

The ocean beaches at White Sound are beautiful; the beach to the north of the Abaco Inn is better for swimming than the one to the south, which has shallow coral and rock. Because there is no offshore reef here, the area offers some of the best surfing in the Bahamas, with at least six good breaks all within half a mile of the Abaco Inn. The walk to Tahiti Beach is about 1½ miles and offers some spectacular views of both White Sound and Tilloo Cut. Hope Town is a 3-mile walk.

The ocean dune at White Sound was severely damaged by hurricane Floyd in September 1999; The recovering dune received additional blows from Francis and Jeanne in 2004 and then again from Irene in 2011. Dune reconstruction has been necessary each time, and reconstruction makes the dune fragile. Visitors are asked to stay off the recovering privately-owned dunes between the Abaco Inn and Sea Spray Resort. Access to the ocean beach is available at Abaco Inn and Sea Spray.

Round red range marks
(red lights at night) on Abaco Inn

North
Channel
Marker
Fl G

South
Channel
Marker
Fl R

WHITE ◯ SOUND

White Sound Mark
(flashing white -visible 2 miles)

The White Sound Channel from the west with the Atlantic Ocean in the background. The Abaco Inn is located at the end of the channel; range markers with round red targets provide an easy way to enter in the middle of the channel. The range is lit at night with red lights and several pairs of pilings are usually lit with flashing red and green lights. A branch channel goes south to Sea Spray Marina.

White Sound Mark and entrance channel showing range marks and channel markers from the WNW.

A grounding like this could ruin your whole day... and more... and the White Sound Bar is one of the most popular places in Abaco to run aground. During the summer season it seems to happen at least once every two weeks. **Happily, avoiding the bar is simple. All boats, outboards included, should go west of the White Sound Mark** which designates the southwestern extremity of the bar as well as the western end of the main White Sound Channel.

Photo was taken from the NE looking SW. The power boat beyond the sailboat is in the channel approaching Abaco Inn (controlling depth 6' MLW), the land in the background is Lubbers Quarters. Photo by Steve Dodge, 8 July 2011.

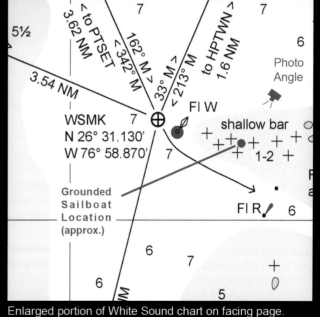

Enlarged portion of White Sound chart on facing page.

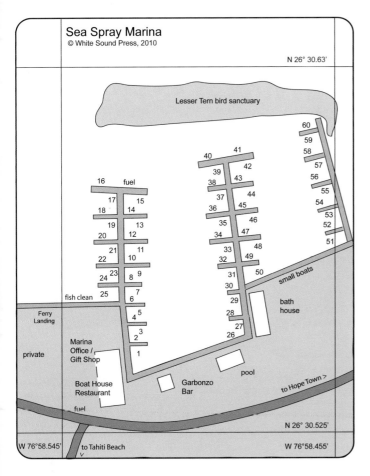

Sea Spray Marina
© White Sound Press, 2010

N 26° 30.63'

Lesser Tern bird sanctuary

Lesser Tern bird sanctuary

16   fuel

fish clean

Ferry Landing

private

Marina Office / Gift Shop

Boat House Restaurant

fuel

Garbonzo Bar

pool

small boats

bath house

to Hope Town >

N 26° 30.525'

W 76°58.545'   to Tahiti Beach   W 76°58.455'

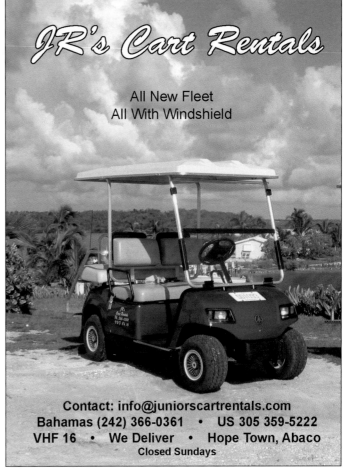

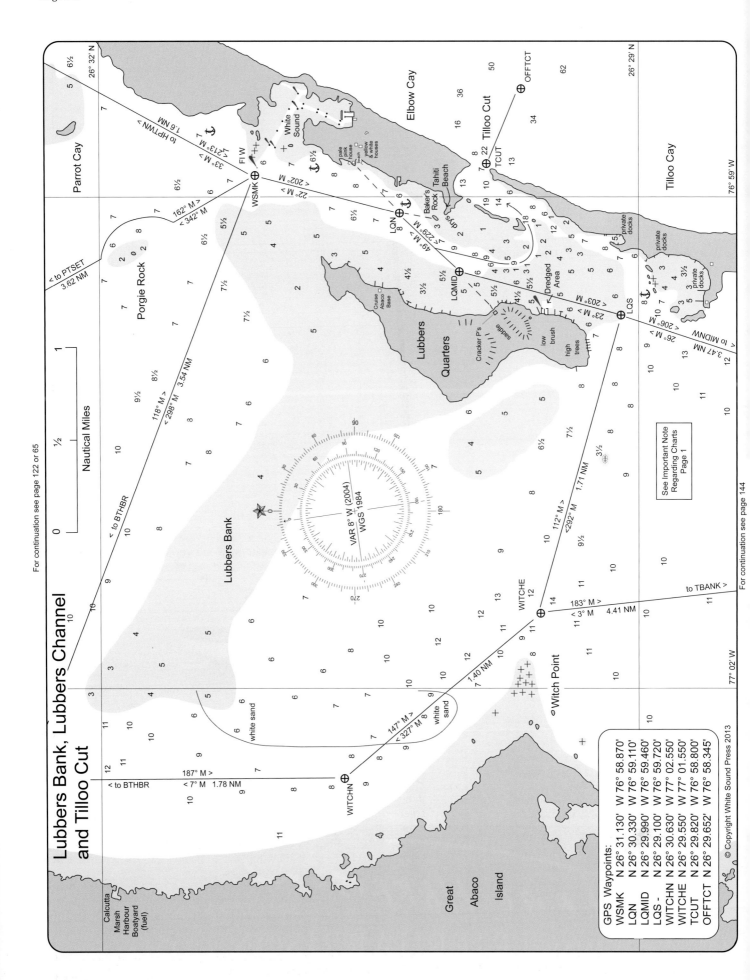

Lubbers Bank, Lubbers Channel and Tilloo Cut

For continuation see page 122 or 65

For continuation see page 144

© Copyright White Sound Press 2013

GPS Waypoints:

WSMK	N 26° 31.130'	W 76° 58.870'
LQN	N 26° 30.330'	W 76° 59.110'
LQMID	N 26° 29.990'	W 76° 59.460'
LQS	N 26° 29.100'	W 76° 59.720'
WITCHN	N 26° 30.630'	W 77° 02.550'
WITCHE	N 26° 29.550'	W 77° 01.550'
TCUT	N 26° 29.820'	W 76° 58.800'
OFFTCT	N 26° 29.652'	W 76° 58.345'

See Important Note Regarding Charts Page 1

Lubbers Channel from the north with Tahiti Beach, the Cooperjack (pronounced Coopyjack) Cays and Tilloo Cay on the left and Lubbers Quarters on the right. Photo by Steve Dodge, 21 June 2006.

LUBBER'S BANK, LUBBER'S CHANNEL, AND TILLOO CUT

Lubber's Quarters and the bank extending northwest of it lie athwart the Sea of Abaco, making it necessary for boats to maneuver through Lubbers Quarters Channel or to go west of the cay and the bank. The channel is shallow and has shoaled during recent years—it is now about 4½-5' MLW—and passage through it is not straightforward. Many cruising boats make the mistake of going directly down the middle of the channel because it looks OK and the outboards sometimes do it successfully. If they draw more than 2-3', and the tide is lower than high, they usually find themselves aground on a bar which is somewhat difficult to see because it is grassy rather than sandy. To carry 4½' MLW through the channel follow the course lines as drawn on the chart. Approaching from the north, go from the White Sound Mark toward Baker's Rock on a heading of 202° M, with the Parrot Cays on your stern. When the large pale pink house located at the north end of the small beach on your port quarter bears 49°, turn to put it on your stern, heading toward the saddle on Lubbers Quarters on the reciprocal heading of 229° M (directly toward Cracker P's dock, which has several flags on it when they are open). Beware of the "false saddle" which results from the high trees and low bush at the southern end of Lubbers. Stay on this course until you are rather close to Lubbers—until the western shoreline of Tavern Cay bears 203° M, then turn and head toward Tavern Cay. If you are in the right place, you will pass over the outer edge of the dredged area at the Abaco Ocean Club's community dock. Continue on this course until you are abeam the southern tip of Lubbers Quarters.

For passage from south to north sail the reciprocals—go toward the channel area heading toward a point between the northern tip of Lubbers Quarters and the Parrot Cays on a heading of 23° M. When the large pale pink house located at the north end of the small beach bears 49° M, turn and head for it. When you reach the point at which your position and Baker's Rock are in range with the Parrot Cays, turn and go toward the Parrot Cays on a heading of 22° M, which will take you to the White Sound Mark.

There is a good route to the ocean through Tilloo Cut. From the north, proceed as though you were going to go through Lubber's Channel, but when about halfway between Baker's Rock and Lubber's Quarter's, turn and head toward the north tip of the curved natural deep channel which has a white sandy bottom and is therefore visible. Your heading should be about 200° M. Then follow the channel around Cooperjack Cay, passing between the cay and a rock to starboard. Proceed to the cut. Go close to the south side of the cut (only about 40 yards off the north tip of Tilloo Cay) and then turn southeast when in the ocean to avoid a shallow bar on which waves often break straight out and northeast of the cut. The depth at the cut itself is 7', but controlling depth is 5-6 feet inside just north of the north end of the natural curved channel.

All should be aware of the wrecked barge located a little more than .5 NM almost due west (magnetic) of the southern extremity of Lubbers Quarters (see the chart for location; coordinates are N 26° 29.173' W 77° 00.602'). It is covered by only 3½' MLW in an area which is generally 8' to 9' MLW. It is definitely a hazard to navigation, but also holds some fish.

There are several pleasant anchorages in this area. Just north of Baker's Rock near Tahiti Beach is a favorite summer anchorage for many boats; others can be found on either side of the entrance to White Sound, and a fourth can be found just north of the small shallow harbour on Tilloo. All of these offer little protection from the northwest.

Cracker P's Bar and Restaurant is located near the middle of the east coast of Lubbers and features fresh grilled foods. There is a nice beach, a good dock, and a play area for children. Those anchoring off are asked to stay well off to avoid fouling electrical cables. Lubbers Landing is a new restaurant located next to Cracker P's. There is good protection along this shoreline when the wind is from the west and northwest.

continued on page 143

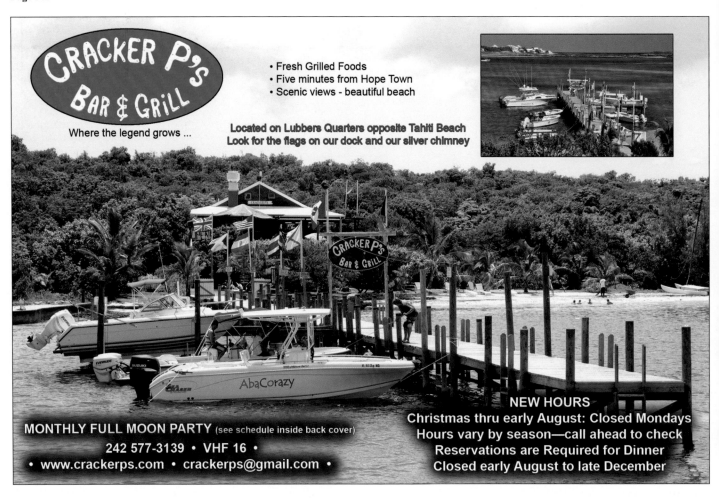

Tilloo Cut from the southwest, July 2005. Photo by Steve Dodge.

continued from page 141

Lubbers Quarters Cay is a developing residential community of over 60 homes. It has grown substantially since being serviced by electricity, telephones and internet about 10 years ago. An old coral path winds its way around the south end in the Abaco Ocean Club subdivision. A small marina in the subdivision is comprised of privately owned boat slips and a small public dock for its homeowners. Throughout the entire cay there is a nice mix of well-spaced homes in peaceful settings owned by Bahamians as well as foreigners.

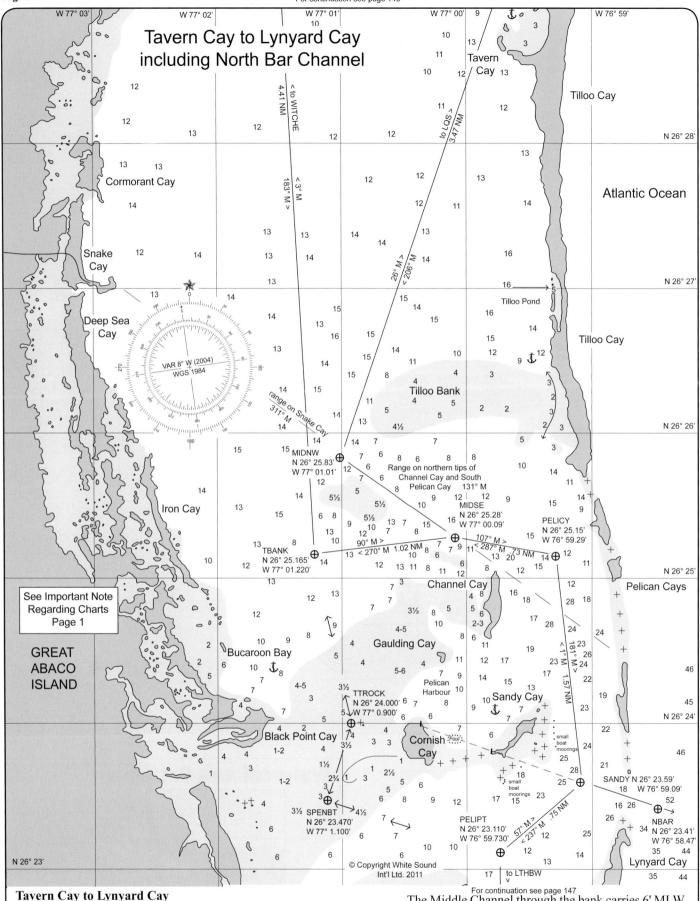

Tavern Cay to Lynyard Cay including North Bar Channel

Tavern Cay to Lynyard Cay

The area south of Tavern Cay down to Tilloo Bank is wide open and averages 12-14' deep. Tilloo Bank is easily seen; go west of it or use the middle channel. The route along the Casuarina-lined beach on Tilloo Cay inside Tilloo Bank is for small outboard boats (drawing 2' or less) and only at half tide or better. Go slowly and look for the deepest water.

The Middle Channel through the bank carries 6' MLW. Go through on a range of the northern tips of Channel Cay and the southernmost Pelican Cay or use the GPS waypoints. Your heading should be 131° M and Snake Cay should be on your stern at 311° M. Or go around the entire bank using the waypoint TBANK.

text continued on next page

For continuation see page 147

The deep water route to the south is east of the the four small cays (Channel, Gaulding, Cornish and Sandy) located in this part of the Sea of Abaco. Give Sandy Cay Reef, which is marked by a high rock near the north end and a low rock near the south end, a wide berth. Snorkeling is excellent on the reef, which is part of the Pelican Cays Land and Sea Park. All fishing is prohibited in the park and no shells or coral may be taken. See the more detailed chart on page 146 for the boundaries of the park. Holding ground off the reef is poor (smooth round rocks covered with about 2" of sand), but there are several small boat moorings (for boats 24' or less) located just east of the reef. Anchoring on the reef is prohibited; it damages the coral. Larger boats should anchor in Pelican Harbour to the west of Sandy Cay and dinghy to the small boat moorings. Holding ground in Pelican Harbour is less than ideal, and there is a swell in the area. This is a daytime anchorage only; Pelican Harbour is not really a harbour. See the separate snorkeling/diving charts on pages 165 and 170 for more detailed information about the reef.

North Bar Channel is one of the best passages from the Sea of Abaco to the Atlantic Ocean, providing about 16-17' of water at its shallowest point. The range for this channel consists of two white concrete posts, one on Sandy Cay and the other on Cornish Cay. When entering on the range, the heading should be 295° M. This course should take you about midway between the north tip of Lynyard Cay and Channel Rock, avoiding the rocky shoal area just off Lynyard Cay.

A shoal draft route (about 2' 9''' MLW) exists west of the four cays. It passes close to Tea Table Rock west of Cornish Cay, and is quite narrow at one point, so GPS waypoints are provided.

Several settled weather or daytime anchorages can be found in appropriate weather on the west side of Tilloo Cay (see page 146) and at Snake Cay (see chart this page). Anchoring in Tilloo Pond is not recommended; it is small and a Bahamian moor is necessary to hold the boat in position if the wind shifts. It can, of course, be used in an emergency, and it offers excellent shelter. The cut leading to the lagoon behind Snake Cay and Deep Sea Cay is deep with excellent protection, but it is also very small and strong tidal currents exist, so if one chooses to be anchored here during a reverse of tidal flow, a Bahamian moor is absolutely necessary.

Iron Cay and Mocking Bird Cay beyond on the right, John Doctor Cay and Deep Sea Cay on the left, with Snake Cay center/left background and Witch Point and Marsh Harbour beyond. Taken from the south July 2007 Compare this photo to the chart to the right. This pristine and serene shallow area can be explored by kayak or dinghy at half tide or higher.

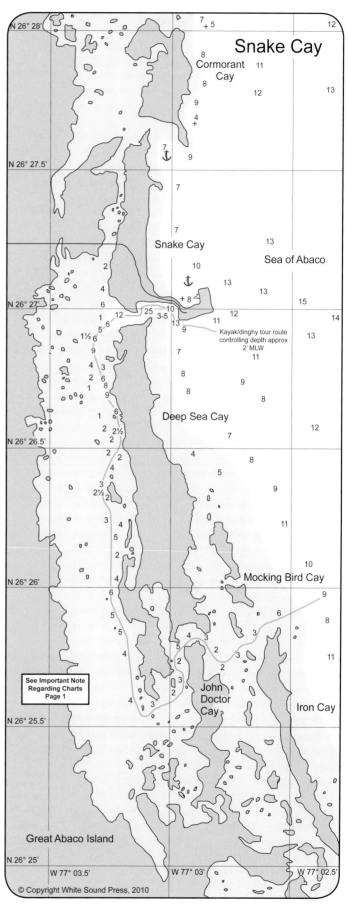

Snake Cay   The cut between Snake Cay and Deep Sea Cay is deep, but very strong tidal flows make it absolutely necessary to use a Bahamian moor if one chooses to anchor there. There are two acceptable anchorages east of Snake Cay. Note the suggested route for a kayak/dinghy tour of the flats recommended for half tide or better.

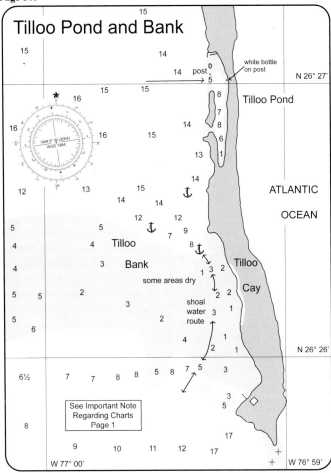

Tilloo Pond and Bank

15

15

15

14

14 post

white bottle on post

N 26° 27'

Tilloo Pond

16

16

16

16

16

VAR 8° W (2004)
WGS 1984

15

15

8

7

8

6

13

14

15

ATLANTIC

OCEAN

12

13

14

14

14

15

14

14

12

12

7

9

5

5

4

4

8

Tilloo

3

Bank

Tilloo

Cay

some areas dry

1

2

5

5

2

2

shoal
water
route

3

3

2

1

5

5

6

2

4

1

4

2

1

8

6½

7

7

8

8

5

8

7

5

3

See Important Note
Regarding Charts
Page 1

3

5

8

17

9

10

11

12

17

W 77° 00'

W 76° 59'

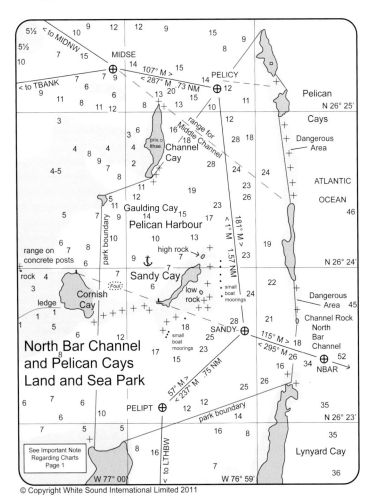

5½ < to MIDNW

10

9

12

12

9

15

9

5½

7

15

MIDSE

14 107° M >

15

8

PELICY

< 287° M > 73 NM

14

9

10

< to TBANK

7

6

9

7

6

13 20

15

Pelican

11

11

8

11 12

8

10

12

N 26° 25'

Cays

3

6

16

Channel

12

28

18

Dangerous
Area

5

4

4

priv. o.
lthse.

Channel
Cay

18

24

24

9

8

28

ATLANTIC

4-5

7

8

19

23

26

OCEAN

11

12

23

46

5

11

Gaulding Cay

15

17

5

7

park boundary

14

Pelican Harbour

19

23

N 26° 24'

range on
concrete posts

6

7

10

13

high rock

6

6

9

o

23

rock 4

7

Sandy Cay

7

small
boat
moorings

22

3

Foul

low
rock

24

Dangerous
Area

45

ledge

Cornish
Cay

6

Channel Rock
North
Bar
Channel

1

5

18

SANDY

21

28

115° M > 18

North Bar Channel
and Pelican Cays
Land and Sea Park

6

12

small
boat
moorings

25

23

< 295° M 26

34

52

NBAR

17

15

16

6

7

6

PELIPT

12

12

26

35

6

10

14

N 26° 23'

7

5

5

16

16

8

35

See Important Note
Regarding Charts
Page 1

8

16

7

Lynyard Cay

W 77° 00'

W 76° 59'

36

The southern sector of the Sea of Abaco from the north. The southern-most Pelican Cay is on the left in the foreground. Moving south from there is North Bar Channel with Channel Rock clearly visible. Boats should be to the south of Channel Rock, between Channel Rock and Lynyard Cay. Little Harbour on the mainland of Great Abaco Island is beyond Lynyard and Winding Bay is visible beyond that. Cointinuing clockwise, another peninsula protruding eastward from Great Abaco is visible. It is the site of the old settlement of Wilson City (1906-1916). In the foreground on the right is Sandy Cay with its reef to the east. Three boats are anchored in the area known as Pelican Harbour, which usually has a surge and is not recommended for overnight, but it is a place where large boats can anchor in order to dinghy to the moorings at the reef, which are limited to boats under 24' LOA. Photo by Steve Dodge, 13 July 2008.

North Bar Channel is one of the best passages between the Atlantic Ocean and the Sea of Abaco. It is 18' deep at MLW and is used by the mailboat. Enter between the northern tip of Lynyard Cay and Channel Rock. The area north of Channel Rock is shallow and should be avoided. The photo above was taken from the west on a calm day during the summer 2004. Channel Rock is on the left side, and the northern tip of Lynyard Cay is on the right. Boats entering North Bar Channel must alter course about .33 NM after entering to avoid Sandy Cay reef. For waypoint coordinates see chart p. 144.

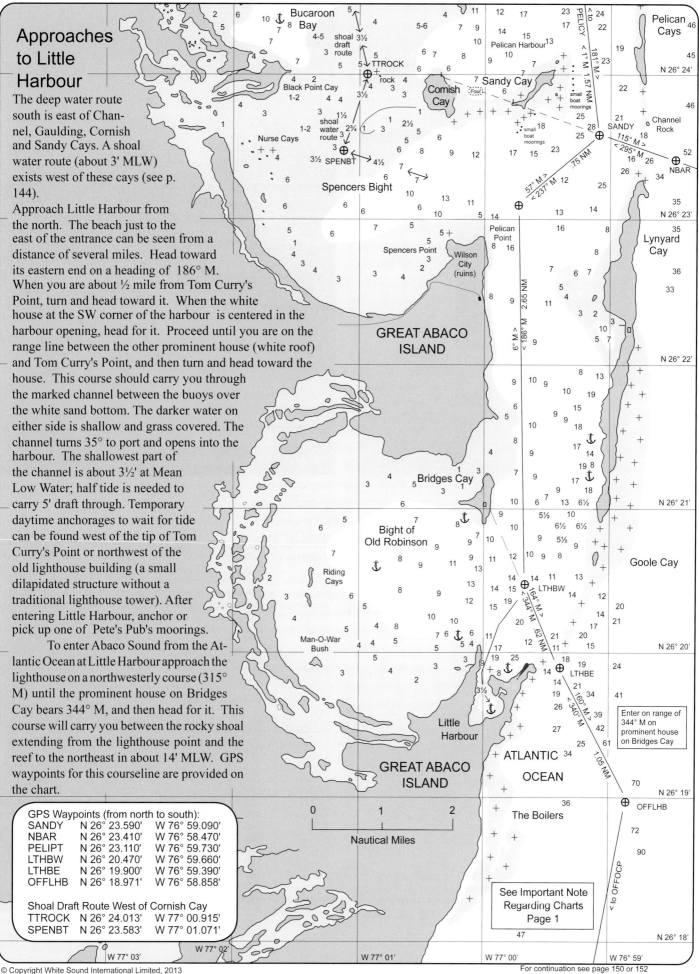

Approaches to Little Harbour

The deep water route south is east of Channel, Gaulding, Cornish and Sandy Cays. A shoal water route (about 3' MLW) exists west of these cays (see p. 144).

Approach Little Harbour from the north. The beach just to the east of the entrance can be seen from a distance of several miles. Head toward its eastern end on a heading of 186° M. When you are about ½ mile from Tom Curry's Point, turn and head toward it. When the white house at the SW corner of the harbour is centered in the harbour opening, head for it. Proceed until you are on the range line between the other prominent house (white roof) and Tom Curry's Point, and then turn and head toward the house. This course should carry you through the marked channel between the buoys over the white sand bottom. The darker water on either side is shallow and grass covered. The channel turns 35° to port and opens into the harbour. The shallowest part of the channel is about 3½' at Mean Low Water; half tide is needed to carry 5' draft through. Temporary daytime anchorages to wait for tide can be found west of the tip of Tom Curry's Point or northwest of the old lighthouse building (a small dilapidated structure without a traditional lighthouse tower). After entering Little Harbour, anchor or pick up one of Pete's Pub's moorings.

To enter Abaco Sound from the Atlantic Ocean at Little Harbour approach the lighthouse on a northwesterly course (315° M) until the prominent house on Bridges Cay bears 344° M, and then head for it. This course will carry you between the rocky shoal extending from the lighthouse point and the reef to the northeast in about 14' MLW. GPS waypoints for this courseline are provided on the chart.

GPS Waypoints (from north to south):

SANDY	N 26° 23.590'	W 76° 59.090'
NBAR	N 26° 23.410'	W 76° 58.470'
PELIPT	N 26° 23.110'	W 76° 59.730'
LTHBW	N 26° 20.470'	W 76° 59.660'
LTHBE	N 26° 19.900'	W 76° 59.390'
OFFLHB	N 26° 18.971'	W 76° 58.858'

Shoal Draft Route West of Cornish Cay

TTROCK	N 26° 24.013'	W 77° 00.915'
SPENBT	N 26° 23.583'	W 77° 01.071'

Enter on range of 344° M on prominent house on Bridges Cay

See Important Note Regarding Charts Page 1

GREAT ABACO ISLAND

Bucaroon Bay

Black Point Cay

Cornish Cay

Sandy Cay

Pelican Harbour

Pelican Cays

Nurse Cays

Spencers Bight

Spencers Point

Wilson City (ruins)

Pelican Point

Lynyard Cay

Channel Rock

Bridges Cay

Bight of Old Robinson

Riding Cays

Goole Cay

Man-O-War Bush

Little Harbour

ATLANTIC OCEAN

The Boilers

0 1 2

Nautical Miles

© Copyright White Sound International Limited, 2013

Entrance to Little Harbour

The opening is between the beach and Tom Curry's Point.

Get on a range with Tom Curry's point on the transom and the group of houses on the bow.

The channel is marked with buoys, and the deepest water is the light green water (approx. 3½' MLW).

Turn about 35° to port and enter the anchorage.

For continuation see page 147 or 65

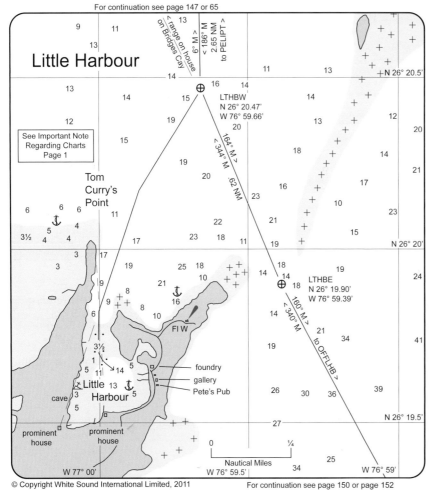

Entrance to Little Harbour from the north. Note that the entry should be made over the white sand bottom. The channel through that area is always marked with buoys. It carries 3½' MLW and up to 7' at the top of the tide.

 For continuation see page 150 or page 152

Little Harbour

Little Harbour is a beautiful, small, fully-protected anchorage. Randolph and Margot Johnston made Little Harbour their home during the middle 1950s, and founded an art colony there. Randolph, who died in late 1992, was an internationally known artist renowned for his lost wax casting in bronze, and his wife Margot worked with ceramics. Their son Pete now runs Pete's Pub and Gallery, and makes life size marine bronzes and jewelry inspired by local motifs. The gallery is open seven days a week from about 11:00 to about 4:00. Foundry tours are available for a nominal fee. Pete's Pub is an open air bar on the beach. It serves hot dogs and hamburgers, fish, ribs, chicken, lobster and bouillabaisse. It is open seven days a week beginning at 11:00 am, serving lunch from noon to 4:00 pm, and dinner from 6:00 to 9:00 with reservations (except Mondays). No other shopping or services are available.

The walk to the lighthouse and the ocean side is well worth it, and the caves on the west side of the harbour in which the Johnstons lived when they first came to Little Harbour, are interesting. The small reef to the east of the entrance is convenient for snorkeling, and the larger open water reef off Lynyard Cay is quite beautiful. The Bight of Old Robinson, to the west, has numerous interesting shallow creeks, some with blue holes.

The anchorage at Lynyard Cay from the NNE..

Bronze dolphin mounted on driftwood by Pete Johnston, Pete's Pub and Gallery, Little Harbour, Abaco, Bahamas.

This almost straight down photo of Little Harbour supplements the chart and clearly shows the passage from the Atlantic Ocean to the Sea of Abaco at Little Harbour as well as the entry to Little Harbour itself. Photo by Steve Dodge, 13 July 2008.

For continuation see page 65 or page 147

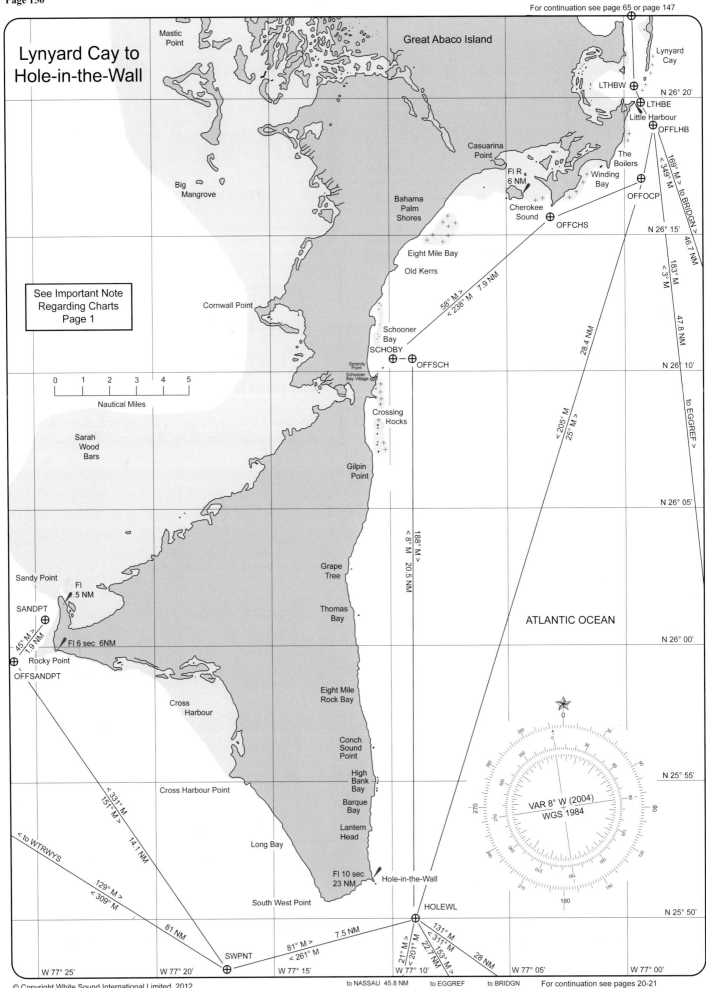

Lynyard Cay to Hole-in-the-Wall

Mastic Point

Great Abaco Island

Lynyard Cay

LTHBW

N 26° 20'

LTHBE

Little Harbour

OFFLHB

Big Mangrove

Casuarina Point

The Boilers

Winding Bay

< 169° M > to BRIDGN >

< 349° M

See Important Note
Regarding Charts
Page 1

Bahama Palm Shores

Fl R 6 NM

Cherokee Sound

OFFOCP

46.7 NM

OFFCHS

N 26° 15'

183° M

< 3° M

Cornwall Point

Eight Mile Bay

Old Kerrs

47.8 NM

58° M >
< 238° M 7.9 NM

to EGGREF

0   1   2   3   4   5

Nautical Miles

Schooner Bay

SCHOBY

OFFSCH

N 26° 10'

Serenity Point

Schooner Bay Village

28.4 NM

Sarah Wood Bars

Crossing Rocks

< 205° M >
25° M >

Gilpin Point

188° M >
< 8° M 20.5 NM

N 26° 05'

Grape Tree

Sandy Point

Fl
.5 NM

Thomas Bay

ATLANTIC OCEAN

N 26° 00'

SANDPT

45° M >
7.9 NM

Fl 6 sec 6NM

Rocky Point

OFFSANDPT

Eight Mile Rock Bay

Cross Harbour

Conch Sound Point

380   0   30

330   30

High Bank Bay

Cross Harbour Point

Barque Bay

N 25° 55'

< 331° M >
151° M >

270   90

Lantern Head

VAR 8° W (2004)
WGS 1984

14.1 NM

Long Bay

180

< to WTRWYS

Fl 10 sec
23 NM

Hole-in-the-Wall

< 129° M >
< 309° M

81 NM

South West Point

HOLEWL

N 25° 50'

SWPNT

81° M >
< 261° M

7.5 NM

2° M >
< 201° M

131° M >
< 311° M

153° M >
227 NM

28 NM

to NASSAU 45.8 NM   to EGGREF   to BRIDGN

For continuation see pages 20-21

Lynyard Cay to Hole-in-the-Wall

North Bar Channel and the opening between Little Harbour and Lynyard Cay are both viable routes between the Sea of Abaco and the Atlantic Ocean. See pages 144 and 146, and page 147 respectively for more information. Once in the ocean, care should be taken to give a wide berth to the Boilers, a reef lying off the coast of Great Abaco Island between Little Harbour and Ocean Point. Use of the waypoints and courselines provided will keep boats well clear of all reefs. Cherokee Sound offers limited protection to the west of Cherokee Point, where there is often a surge, and the route to the small inner anchorage only carries about 3' MLW. For more detail see page 152.

The 27-mile coastline of Great Abaco Island from Cherokee Sound to Hole-in-the-Wall is forbidding and hostile, offering no secure anchorages or protection for boats. A new development offers relief—Schooner Bay Village at the south end of Schooner Bay (about halfway between Little Harbour and Hole-in-the-Wall) has a small harbour with deep water entrance (controlling depth 8' MLW) and a fledgling town. See the chart on page 154.

It is possible to anchor just west of Hole-in-the-Wall to gain protection from the prevailing easterlies, but this anchorage is completely exposed to the S and SW.

Sandy Point, located about 15 NM northwest of Hole-in-the-Wall offers good protection for winds from the east, but the only protection from the west is the other side of a bar which carries only 3' MLW. See the chart on page 156.

Waypoints: Lynyard Cay to Hole-in-the-Wall and beyond

LTHBW	Abaco Sd. end Little Hrbr Ch.	N 26° 20.470'	W 76° 59.660'
LTHBE	Atlantic end Little Hrbr Ch.	N 26° 19.900'	W 76° 59.390'
OFFLHB	1¼ NM SSE Little Harbour	N 26° 18.971'	W 76° 58.858'
OFFOCP	1¼ NM ESE Ocean Point	N 26° 17.079'	W 76° 59.349'
OFFCHS	0.4 NM S Cherokee Point	N 26° 15.663'	W 77° 03.152'
SCHOBY	0.75 NM E Schooner Bay	N 26° 10.500'	W 77° 09.800'
OFFSCH	0.7 NM E SCHOBY	N 26° 10.500'	W 77° 09.000'
HOLEWL	2 NM SE Hole-in-the-Wall	N 25° 50.000'	W 77° 09.000'
SWPNT	3 NM WSW South West Pt.	N 25° 48.000'	W 77° 17.000'
OFFSANDPT	3NM SW Sandy Point	N 25° 59.500'	W 77° 26.000
SANDPT	.75 NM SW Sandy Point	N 26° 1.000'	W 77° 24.650'

Eleuthera:

BRIDGN*	N end Bridge Pt. reef opening	N 25° 34.298'	W 76° 43.344'
EGGREF	0.8 NM west of Egg Reef	N 25° 31.102'	W 76° 55.031'

Nassau:

NASSAU	north Nassau Hbr. entrance	N 25° 05.447'	W 77° 21.340'

Grand Bahama Island:

See pages 20-21 and 25-28

*This waypoint is at the north end of the Bridge Point opening in Devil's Backbone Reef. Local knowledge and good visibility are required for this passage the first time. For charts and waypoints for Eleuthera, see pages 158-159.

Hole-in-the-Wall Lighthouse from the northwest .

Cherokee Sound from the southwest 15 March 2010. Note the shallow reef in the foreground, and the protected deeper area west of Cherokee Point. Winding Bay and even houses at Little Harbour can be seen in the background. The long dock extending from the shore east of the town is visible: the end of it is still in water which is only 1-2' deep at MLW. Boats can fiind some protection by using the channel just east of Duck Cay (controlling depth is 3' MLW). This cannot be seen on this photo, but can be found on the chart of Cherokee Sound on page 152. Photo by Steve Dodge.

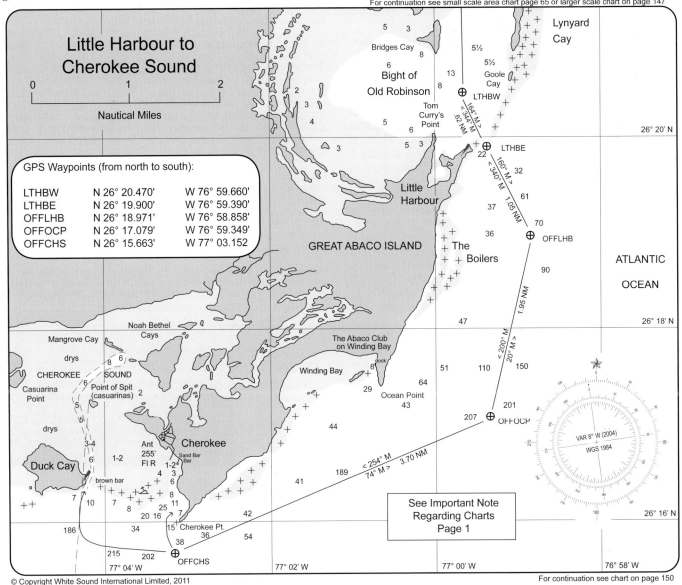

For continuation see chart on page 150

LITTLE HARBOUR TO CHEROKEE SOUND

Vessels proceeding southward from Little Harbour should stay well clear of the Boilers, a breaking reef extending about ½ mile offshore from Great Abaco Island located about 1½ miles south of the Little Harbour channel. The waypoints and suggested course lines shown on the chart keep boats about 1 mile offshore. Cherokee Sound, located 5 miles SW of Little Harbour, is an extensive region of shallow water with a small settlement. Entrance to either one of the two possible anchorages there should be attempted in flat or moderate conditions only as breaking seas extend across both entrances in an easterly blow or when there is a strong surge.

From the waypoint OFFCHS proceed on a heading of about 0° toward the radio antenna located in the settlement. This should keep you well clear of Cherokee Point. Round the point, turning to starboard and head for the beach with the limestone cliff. The anchorage is just west of the beach with 7-11' MLW. This provides good shelter from the prevailing easterlies, but offers little protection from the SW to W, and there is often a surge in this area. Shoal draft vessels may be able to get to the dock which may well be the longest in The Bahamas, but still has only 1-2' MLW at its end. Stay fairly close to shore in order to avoid the reef to port. Proceed slowly toward the dock and look for the deepest water. Plan your visit for a tide which offers sufficient water for departure as well as arrival.

A second anchorage in the center of Cherokee Sound offers better protection, but access is not straightforward, and the anchorage is about a mile away from the settlement. Approach Duck Cay from the south on a range which lines up the lighthouse on Duck Cay with the W shoreline of Point of Spit, which has a stand of casuarinas. When about 100-150 yards off Duck Cay, turn about 20-25° to starboard and pass between Duck Cay and the brown bar to starboard. You should pass over two or three black spots. Then turn gradually to port to assume a course which will leave Point of Spit well to starboard. The shallowest spot is near where you make this turn—it is between a grassy patch (west side) and a sand bar (east side)—and it carries about 3' MLW. The remainder of the route to the anchorage is a narrow dredged channel clearly visible in good light which carries about 5' MLW. The anchorage is about 7' MLW and is just SE of Mangrove Cay and W of Noah Bethel Cays. From this anchorage you can take the dinghy to small boat docks on the creek which borders the NW side of the town.

The settlement at Cherokee Sound is small, but there is a grocery store, a radio-telephone station, and a road which goes to Marsh Harbour. Cherokee Sound was formerly a center for boat building and a thriving fishing community. The people are friendly and welcome visitors.

Winding Bay is about midway between the Little Harbour channel and Cherokee Sound. A private member community of town houses and homes is centered on Ocean Point where there is a clubhouse with a commanding view of the area. The community is managed by Ritz-Carleton and features a scenic links golf course. Casual visitors are generally not welcome. There is one small fair weather dock on the west side of Ocean Point.

Sail Repairs Whenever. Wherever.

Every sailor should have a portable sewing machine on board to make the inevitable sail or canvas repair. The Ultrafeed® LSZ-1 Sewing Machine is a cast iron, portable, power-house zigzag and straight stitch sewing machine designed to sew through layers of heavy canvas or sailcloth from the dock or below deck.

Learn more about the Ultrafeed® LSZ-1 at **www.sailrite.com**.

www.sailrite.com | 800.348.2769 | Free Catalog

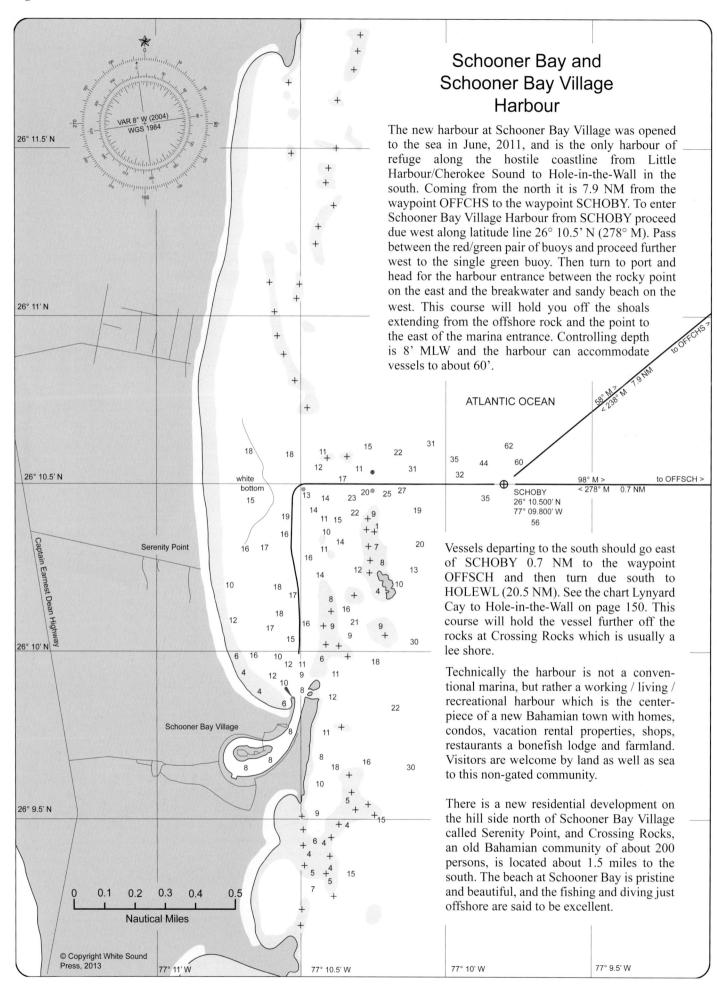

Schooner Bay and Schooner Bay Village Harbour

The new harbour at Schooner Bay Village was opened to the sea in June, 2011, and is the only harbour of refuge along the hostile coastline from Little Harbour/Cherokee Sound to Hole-in-the-Wall in the south. Coming from the north it is 7.9 NM from the waypoint OFFCHS to the waypoint SCHOBY. To enter Schooner Bay Village Harbour from SCHOBY proceed due west along latitude line 26° 10.5' N (278° M). Pass between the red/green pair of buoys and proceed further west to the single green buoy. Then turn to port and head for the harbour entrance between the rocky point on the east and the breakwater and sandy beach on the west. This course will hold you off the shoals extending from the offshore rock and the point to the east of the marina entrance. Controlling depth is 8' MLW and the harbour can accommodate vessels to about 60'.

ATLANTIC OCEAN

Vessels departing to the south should go east of SCHOBY 0.7 NM to the waypoint OFFSCH and then turn due south to HOLEWL (20.5 NM). See the chart Lynyard Cay to Hole-in-the-Wall on page 150. This course will hold the vessel further off the rocks at Crossing Rocks which is usually a lee shore.

Technically the harbour is not a conventional marina, but rather a working / living / recreational harbour which is the centerpiece of a new Bahamian town with homes, condos, vacation rental properties, shops, restaurants a bonefish lodge and farmland. Visitors are welcome by land as well as sea to this non-gated community.

There is a new residential development on the hill side north of Schooner Bay Village called Serenity Point, and Crossing Rocks, an old Bahamian community of about 200 persons, is located about 1.5 miles to the south. The beach at Schooner Bay is pristine and beautiful, and the fishing and diving just offshore are said to be excellent.

SCHOBY
26° 10.500' N
77° 09.800' W

Serenity Point

Captain Earnest Dean Highway

Schooner Bay Village

Nautical Miles

SCHOONER BAY AND SCHOONER BAY VILLAGE

Schooner Bay Village is a very interesting development in many ways. First, those cruising between Hole-in-the-Wall and the Little Harbour Cut have a possible harbour of refuge—a place to stop on the way from Abaco to North Eleuthera, Nassau, Florida or elsewhere. It will make the southern route between Florida and Abaco more comfortable by providing relief from the 100+ mile run without viable protection.

Second, the development itself is fascinating. It is not just another residential development—the goal is to create a new village—in the tradition, generally speaking, of the Puritans in Boston and the loyalists at Carleton, Abaco. Envisioned as a business center serving southern Abaco, it is to have a bank, a post office and a supermarket which will sell produce grown on adjacent farmland. Mom and Pop businesses will surround the harbour housed in two-storey buildings with the business at street level and the owner's living quarters above—similar to Manhattan 200 years ago. Those who purchase land are required to build within a certain time frame (1-3 years)—this to achieve a reasonable critical mass for the town in a short period of time, and to avoid land purchase for speculative reasons. It seems that the village has an excellent chance of success—it should become an alternative to Marsh Harbour for residents of Crossing Rocks and Sandy Point for employment as well as retail shopping and other business.

It is also interesting from an environmental point of view. Designed as a green community, a large area of coppice has been left in its natural state to accomodate local as well as migrating birds, and energy and water systems have been designed with protection of the environment in mind. That said, it should also be noted that the harbour basin irself is the product of a dredge and fill. But almost every new marina in the Bahamas is built this same way—all the really good natural deep water harbours were settled and developed many years ago (Nassau, Marsh Harbour, Hope Town). Every development takes away something that can never be recovered, but adds something that didn't previously exist. In the case of Schooner Bay Village, it seems that the positives significantly outway the negatives.

Schooner Bay Village Harbour from the north in July 2012 clearly showing the entry channel and with over a dozen residences under construction or completed. Photo courtesy of Schooner Bay Village..

The dining table and the view of Schooner Bay from the clubhouse located on the beach just west of the harbour entry channel. Photo courtesy of Schooner Bay Village.

For continuation see chart on pages 20-21

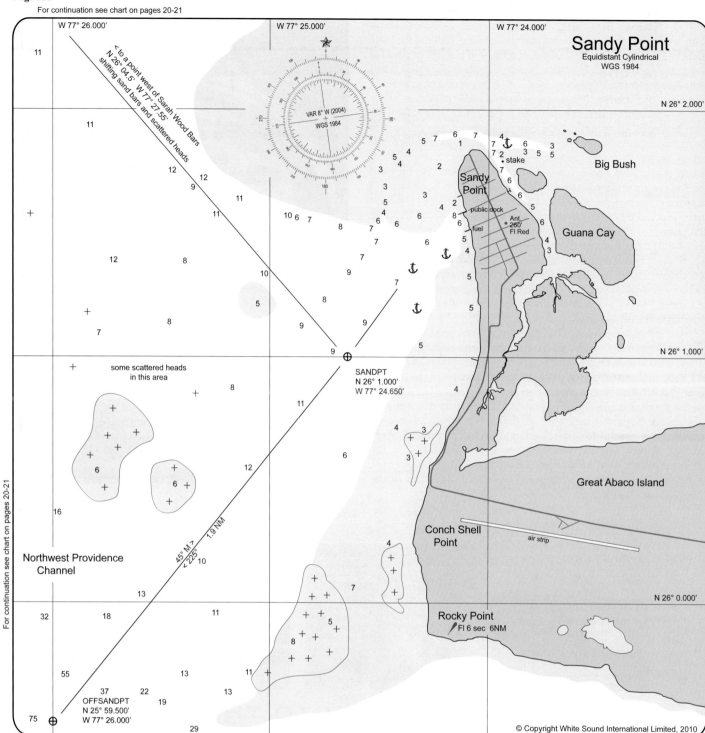

For continuation see chart on page 150

SANDY POINT

This small community, located on the SW side of the southern extremity of Great Abaco Island, is a possible stop for boats travelling between Florida and the Sea of Abaco by the southern route which rounds Hole-in-the-Wall about 20 NM SE of Sandy Point. Its advantage is its location close to this route; its disadvantage is that it has no real harbour. There is protection from SE to NE—anchor off the west side of the town. For protection from the S and SW go to the creek north of the town over a bar which carries about 3' MLW. Lightbourne's Marina is the dock south of the government dock and has fuel, power and water and room for 4 boats to about 40'. Like the anchorage, it is fully exposed to the W, actually from S through W to N. There are a couple of grocery stores and restaurants in town. Nancy's is the best known restaurant, and seems to be open more often than the others. Bahamas Fast Ferries had scheduled service to and from Nassau on Fridays and Sundays during summer, 2011; check regarding current schedule. Flights to Nassau are scheduled several times a week and there is a shuttle service for travel to Marsh Harbour via the highway.

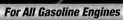

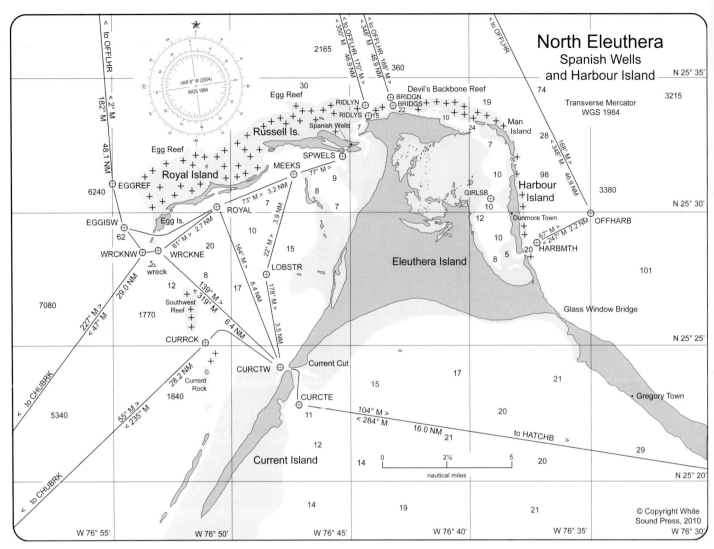

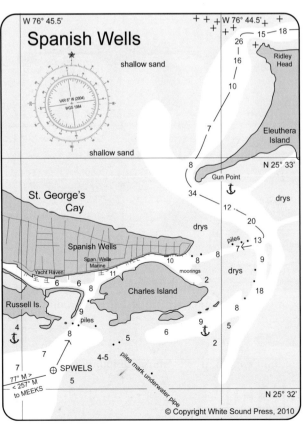

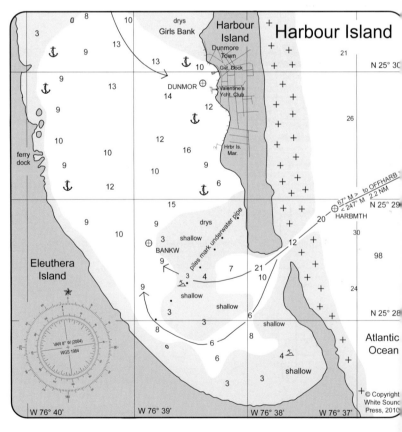

Approaches to North Eleuthera

The northern tip of Eleuthera Island is situated about 30 NM SE of Hole-in-the-Wall, Abaco. The two principal communities—Spanish Wells and Dunmore Town—are located on relatively small land masses—St. George's Cay and Harbour Island—on opposite sides of Eleuthera Island. Passage from one to the other inside Devil's Backbone Reef is challenging with a circuitous and in some places very narrow deep water channel between the beach and the reef. Local pilots are readily available and highly recommended for the first time or two. They will come to your boat in their outboard and tow it through behind yours, and then return home in their boat. Call them on VHF 16.

There are two openings in the reefs which ring the northern tip of Eleuthera—one north of Ridley Head and the other north of Bridge Point. Waypoints for these passages are provided. These are fair weather good visibility passages only. If the weather is not suitable, go west around Egg Reef and Egg Island to get to Spanish Wells, or east around Man Island and Harbour Island to get to Harbour Mouth (inlet) at the south end of Harbour Island. Royal Island, about 5 NM west of Spanish Wells, offers a good anchorage, and Current Cut, which is aptly named, is the most direct route to the various harbours and communities located further south on the west side of Eleuthera.

Spanish Wells

The harbour is long and narrow—formed by St. George's Cay on the north and Russell and Charles Islands on the south. Entry is through dredged channels at the eastern end and in the middle between Russell and Charles Islands. There is a lot of traffic in the harbour, and no room to anchor. Yacht Haven and Spanish Wells Marine have dockage, and moorings are available in a small area east of Charles Island. Anchorages can be found south of Charles Island or east of St. George's Cay. Spanish Wells is an old Bahamian fishing and boat building community.

Harbour Island

Harbour Island is most easily approached through Harbour Mouth, which has strong tidal flows. Waypoints for the approach are provided. Two routes through the sand banks on the inside are shown, one providing about 3' MLW and the other about 6'. Alternatively, the northern approach is via the natural channel between Devil's Backbone Reef and the beach on Eleuthera Island for which a local pilot is recommended. Anchorages can be found along the west shore of Harbour Island. Moorings are available as well, and Valentine's Yacht Club and Harbour Island Marina both have full service dockage available. Dunmore Town is a charming old hillside community with a beautiful beach on the eastern shore of Harbour Island. There are several resorts, restaurants and shops in this vibrant resort town.

Waypoints: *Eleuthera* **(generally listed WNW to ESE):**

WPT	Description of Position	Latitude	Longitutde
EGGREF	0.8 NM W of Egg Reef	N 25° 31.210	W 76° 55.031'
EGGISW	1.1 NM W Egg Island	N 25° 29.500'	W 76° 54.500'
WRCKNW	0.75 NM NW wreck of *Arimora*	N 25° 28.550'	W 76° 53.757'
WRCKNE	0.75 NM ENE wreck of *Arimora*	N 25° 28.680'	W 76° 53.093'
ROYAL	0.5 NM S Royal Island harbour	N 25° 30.226'	W 76° 50.635'
MEEKS	0.4 NM NNW Meeks Patch	N 25° 31.489'	W 76° 47.290
SPWELS	0.2 NM S of south ent. SpWells	N 25° 32.082'	W 76° 45.340'
LOBSTR	1 NM W of Lobster Cays	N 25° 27.734'	W 76° 48.507'
CURRCK	1.4 NM N of Current Rock	N 25° 25.180'	W 76° 51.160'
CURCTW	0.35 NM W of Current Cut	N 25° 24.275	W 76° 47.982'
CURCTE	1.2 NM S of E end Current Cut	N 25° 22.875'	W 76° 47.141'
RIDLYN	N end Ridley route thru reef	N 25° 33.986'	W 76° 44.340'
RIDKYS	S end Ridley route thru reef	N 25° 33.611'	W 76° 44.270'
BRIDGN	N end Bridge Pt. route thru reef	N 25° 34.298'	W 76° 43.344'
BRIDGS	S end Bridge Pt. route thru reef	N 25° 33.970'	W 76° 43.300'
GIRLSB	W of Girls Bank	N 25° 30.560'	W 76° 39.120'
DUNMOR	W of Govt Dock, Dunmore Twn	N 25° 29.918'	W 76° 38.389'
BANKW	W of bank N of Harbour Mouth	N 25° 28.634'	W 76° 38.897'
OFFHARB	3.0 NM NE Harbour Mouth	N 25° 30.000'	W 76° 35.000'
HARBMTH	0.5 NM NE Harbour Mouth	N 25° 28.900'	W 76° 37.200'

Waypoints not shown on charts

OFFLHB	1 NM SE ent. Little Harbour*	N 26° 18.971'	W 76° 58.858'
HATCHB	0.25 NM S of entr Hatchet Bay	N 25° 20.531'	W 76° 29.649'
CHUBRK	0.4 NM NW Chub Rock **	N 25° 06.700'	W 77° 14.700'

*Little Harbour, Abaco
**Chub Rock is N of the east end of Salt Cay about 5 NM NE Nassau

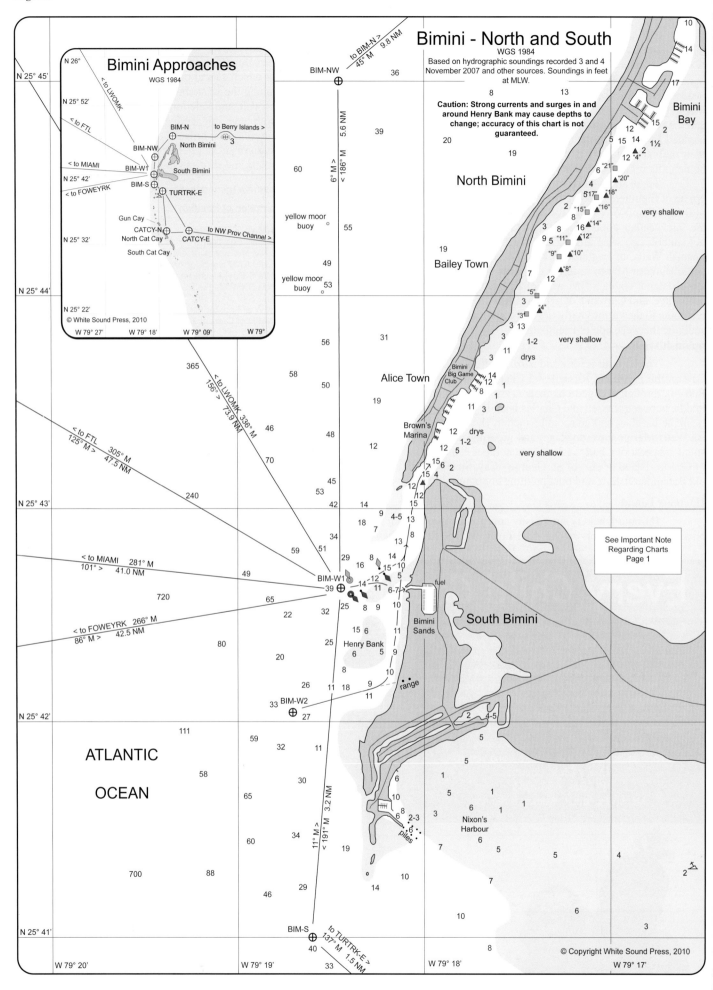

Bimini - North and South

WGS 1984
Based on hydrographic soundings recorded 3 and 4 November 2007 and other sources. Soundings in feet at MLW.

Caution: Strong currents and surges in and around Henry Bank may cause depths to change; accuracy of this chart is not guaranteed.

Bimini Approaches
WGS 1984

© White Sound Press, 2010

North Bimini

Bailey Town

Bimini Bay

very shallow

Alice Town

Bimini Big Game Club

Brown's Marina

drys

very shallow

very shallow

drys

South Bimini

fuel

Bimini Sands

Henry Bank

range

ATLANTIC

OCEAN

Nixon's Harbour

piles

See Important Note Regarding Charts Page 1

yellow moor buoy

yellow moor buoy

© Copyright White Sound Press, 2010

BIMINI

There are two ways to enter protected areas at North and South Bimini. The "old" natural channel is marked with a range on the beach on South Bimini. from the waypoint BIM-W2 approach the beach on the range and then turn to port and parallel the shore. Enter Bimini Sands on South Bimini (short breakwaters on both sides of the entrance) or continue northward and enter the main harbour at North Bimini where Alice Town is located.

The other entry is via a recently dredged channel marked with red and green buoys. Go to the waypoint BIM-W1 and proceed between the buoys, and then enter Bimini Sands or turn north to North Bimini and Alice Town.

Bimini Sands is a marina/condo development with a restaurant and a store on site. Marinas at North Bimini (in order of appearance for entering vessel) are Brown's Marina, the newly re-opened Bimini Big Game Club, and Bimini Bay.

Entrance to harbour at Alice Town, North Bimini from the south. Photo by Steve Dodge, November, 2007.

Waypoints shown on these charts (generally from north to south)

WPT	Description	Latitude	Longitude
BIM-N	0.3 NM N of North Rock	N 25° 48.250'	W 79° 15.500'
BIM-NW	1.0 NM NW cntr.North Bimini	N 25° 45.000'	W 79° 18.450'
BIM-W1	West of dredged channel	N 25° 42.630'	W 79° 18.450'
BIM-W2	entrance old channel	N 25° 42.050'	W 79° 18.700'
BIM-S	0.5 NM SSW South Bimini	N 25° 41.000'	W 79° 18.600'
CATCY-N	0.5 NM N Harbr North Cat Cy	N 25° 33.800'	W 79° 16.700'
CATCY-E	3.5 NM E of Cat Cay	N 25° 34.000'	W 79° 13.000'

Waypoints beyond area shown on these charts (generally from north to south)

LWOMK	Lake Worth outer mark	N 26° 46.340'	W 80° 00.490'
FTL	Fort Lauderdale outer mark	N 26° 05.400'	W 80° 04.700'
MIAMI	S of Govt. Cut outer mark	N 25° 45.950'	W 80° 05.000'
FOWEYRK	1NM E Fowey Rock light	N 25° 35.400'	W 80° 04.700'

Natural channel looking SSW from beach on South Bimini near Bimini Sands. Henry Bank is clearly visible with breakers on right side of photo. Range markers are on beach north of point on photo and are not clearly discernable on this photo. Photo by Steve Dodge, November, 2007.

A school of grunts (and a lone sargeant major near the right side) beneath a pretty stand of elk horn coral on Sandy Cay Reef in Pelican Cays Land and Sea Park.. Photo by Katie Dodge, July, 2011, with a Sea Life camera.

A sting ray cruising along Sandy Cay Reef. String rays are not aggressive—they do have a sharp barb near the base of the tail which can be used to cut and inject toxin in a threatening opponent—but aggressive attacks against non-threatening humans are almost unknown. Note the crawfish (spiny lobster) feelers protruding from the ledge near the stingray's tail. Photo by Katie Dodge, July, 2011, with a Sea Life camera.

A pair of spotted eagle rays cruising along just beyond the eastern edge of Sandy Cay Reef. Note the remora swimming beneath the second spotted eagle ray. Photo by Katie Dodge, July, 2011, with a Sea Life camera.

Snorkeling/Dive/Fishing
Chart Section

The Fowl Cay reef has moorings installed and maintained by Friends of the Environment for use by snorkelers and SCUBA divers. This photo was taken from the NNW and shows Fowl Cay Reef with the Froggies dive boat in the foreground, with the north Man-O-War Channel, Man-O-War Cay and Fish Hawk Cay beyond the reef, and Elbow Cay, Great Abaco Island, Eastern Shores in Marsh Harbour and Matt Lowe's Cay in the background. Photo by Steve Dodge 4 July 2008.

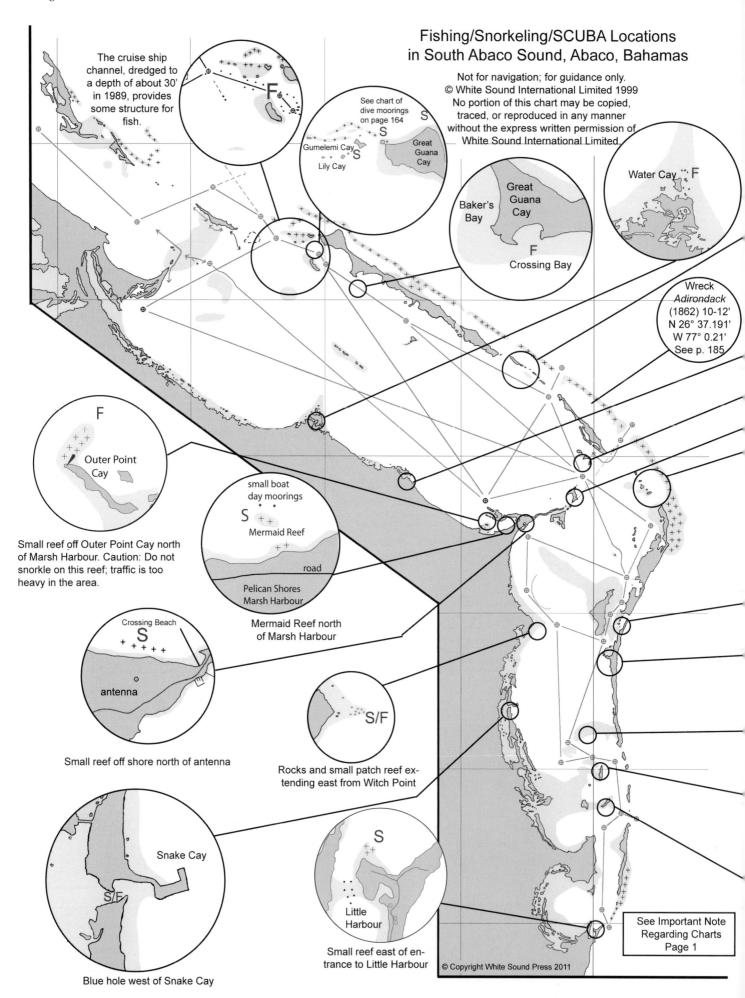

Fishing/Snorkeling/SCUBA Locations in South Abaco Sound, Abaco, Bahamas

Not for navigation; for guidance only.
© White Sound International Limited 1999
No portion of this chart may be copied, traced, or reproduced in any manner without the express written permission of White Sound International Limited.

The cruise ship channel, dredged to a depth of about 30' in 1989, provides some structure for fish.

See chart of dive moorings on page 164

Gumelemi Cay
Lily Cay
Great Guana Cay

Baker's Bay
Great Guana Cay
Crossing Bay

Water Cay

Wreck *Adirondack* (1862) 10-12' N 26° 37.191' W 77° 0.21' See p. 185

Outer Point Cay

Small reef off Outer Point Cay north of Marsh Harbour. Caution: Do not snorkle on this reef; traffic is too heavy in the area.

small boat day moorings
Mermaid Reef
road
Pelican Shores
Marsh Harbour

Mermaid Reef north of Marsh Harbour

Crossing Beach
antenna

Small reef off shore north of antenna

Rocks and small patch reef extending east from Witch Point

Snake Cay

Blue hole west of Snake Cay

Little Harbour

Small reef east of entrance to Little Harbour

See Important Note Regarding Charts Page 1

© Copyright White Sound Press 2011

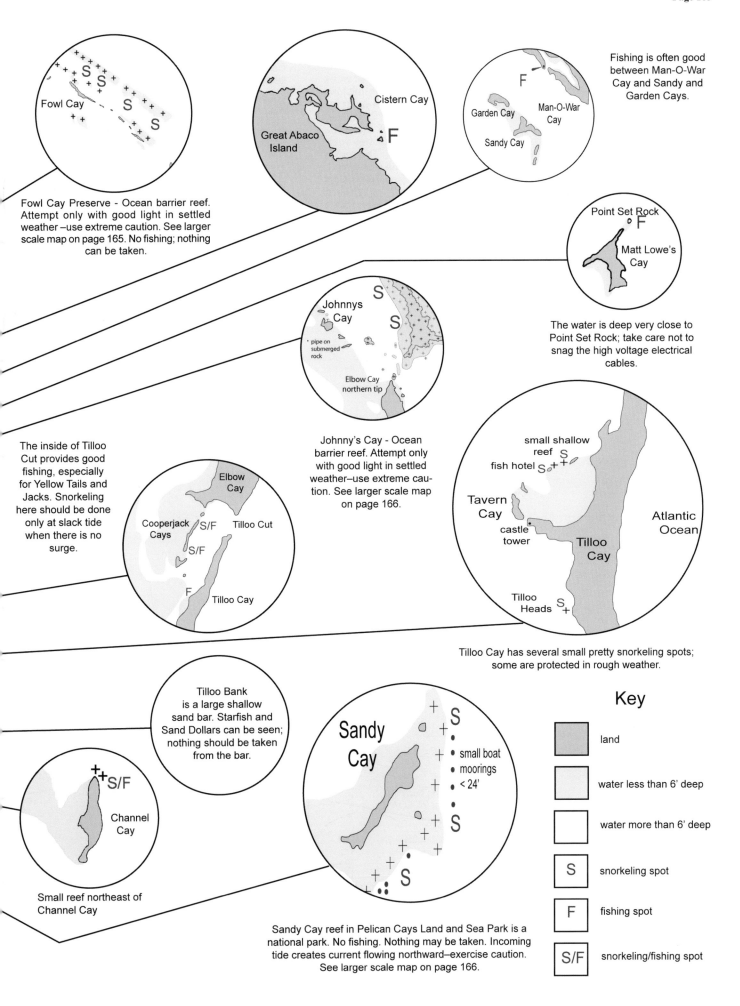

Fowl Cay Preserve - Ocean barrier reef. Attempt only with good light in settled weather –use extreme caution. See larger scale map on page 165. No fishing; nothing can be taken.

Fowl Cay

Cistern Cay

Great Abaco Island

Fishing is often good between Man-O-War Cay and Sandy and Garden Cays.

Garden Cay   Man-O-War Cay

Sandy Cay

Point Set Rock   F

Matt Lowe's Cay

The water is deep very close to Point Set Rock; take care not to snag the high voltage electrical cables.

Johnnys Cay

pipe on submerged rock

Elbow Cay northern tip

Johnny's Cay - Ocean barrier reef. Attempt only with good light in settled weather–use extreme caution. See larger scale map on page 166.

The inside of Tilloo Cut provides good fishing, especially for Yellow Tails and Jacks. Snorkeling here should be done only at slack tide when there is no surge.

Elbow Cay

Cooperjack Cays   S/F   Tilloo Cut

S/F

F

Tilloo Cay

small shallow reef   S
fish hotel   S   +   +

Tavern Cay

castle tower

Tilloo Cay

Atlantic Ocean

Tilloo Heads   S
+

Tilloo Cay has several small pretty snorkeling spots; some are protected in rough weather.

Tilloo Bank is a large shallow sand bar. Starfish and Sand Dollars can be seen; nothing should be taken from the bar.

+ + S/F

Channel Cay

Small reef northeast of Channel Cay

Sandy Cay

+   S
• •
+   small boat • moorings • < 24'
+
• •
+   S
+
+ +   •
+   S
• •

Sandy Cay reef in Pelican Cays Land and Sea Park is a national park. No fishing. Nothing may be taken. Incoming tide creates current flowing northward–exercise caution. See larger scale map on page 166.

Key

▓	land
░	water less than 6' deep
□	water more than 6' deep
S	snorkeling spot
F	fishing spot
S/F	snorkeling/fishing spot

Walker's Cay Dive Chart

This chart was developed from information and a sketch chart provided by Jon Longair of Treasure Island, Florida. He wrote:

"We watched and followed [the dive] boat in and out of the marina all week and they all went the same way as depicted on the map. The big mistake is trying to follow the dive boat out the middle of the reef. Do not even try. There is a week's worth of diving right inside what we called the horseshoe. All around "Pillars," "Utopia," and "Jon's Point." If you had a week there you would never need to leave that area. Most of the other dive locations were deeper but I did not think that they were that much better if at all. The reef is treacherous though. You can be in 50' of water and step out of the side of your boat on to a 3' deep mound. The steepness of the reef is also what makes it so beautiful. Go slow and watch the colors. The area in front of Walker's is now a preserve. There is no fishing, lobstering, or spearing, even with a pole spear or Hawaiian sling. Just enjoying the pristine beauty God created. I have not dived the world but I can say without hesitation that this is the most magnificent place I have ever been."

Coordinates for Walker's Cay Dive Sites

Name (Depth)	latitude	longitude
Near Kevin's Crack	27° 18.980'	78° 25.590'
Kevin's Crack (60/90')	27° 18.890'	78° 26.600'
Aquarium (85')	27° 18.980'	78° 25.540'
190' Blue Canyon (80/190')	27° 18.760'	78° 25.610'
80-130' Canyon (80/130')	27° 18.710'	78° 25.610'
Small Ledge - Lobsters (80')	27° 18.890'	78° 22.500'
Shark Canyon (90')	27° 18.180'	78° 22.580'
Walker's Cay Dive Buoy (80')	27° 17.880'	78° 22.500'
Jon's Point	27° 17.271'	78° 22.958'
Pillars (48')	27° 17.266'	78° 22.551'
Utopia (48')	27° 17.218'	78° 22.572'
Larry's Sharks (60')	27° 17.910'	78° 21.980'

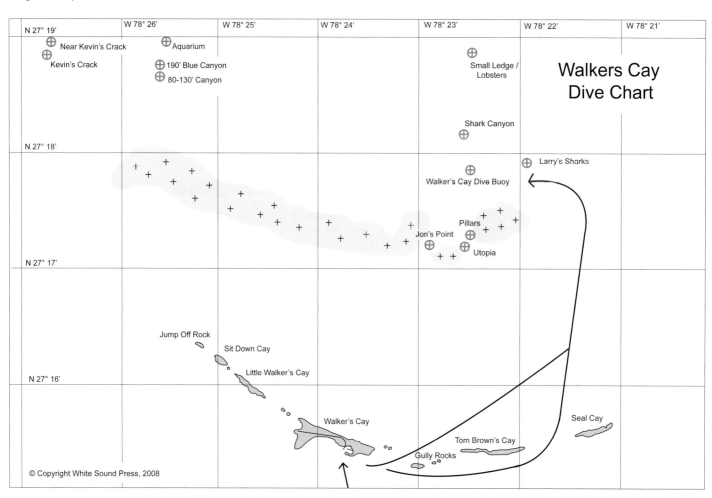

Walkers Cay Dive Chart

© Copyright White Sound Press, 2008

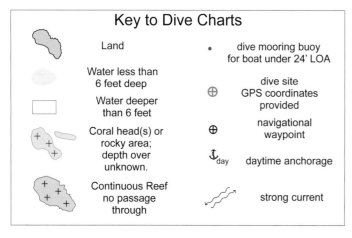

Key to Dive Charts

Land

Water less than 6 feet deep

Water deeper than 6 feet

Coral head(s) or rocky area; depth over unknown.

Continuous Reef no passage through

• dive mooring buoy for boat under 24' LOA

⊕ dive site GPS coordinates provided

⊕ navigational waypoint

⚓day daytime anchorage

〰 strong current

Turtle at Sandy Cay Reef, July 2010. Photo by Katie Dodge with Sea Life camera.

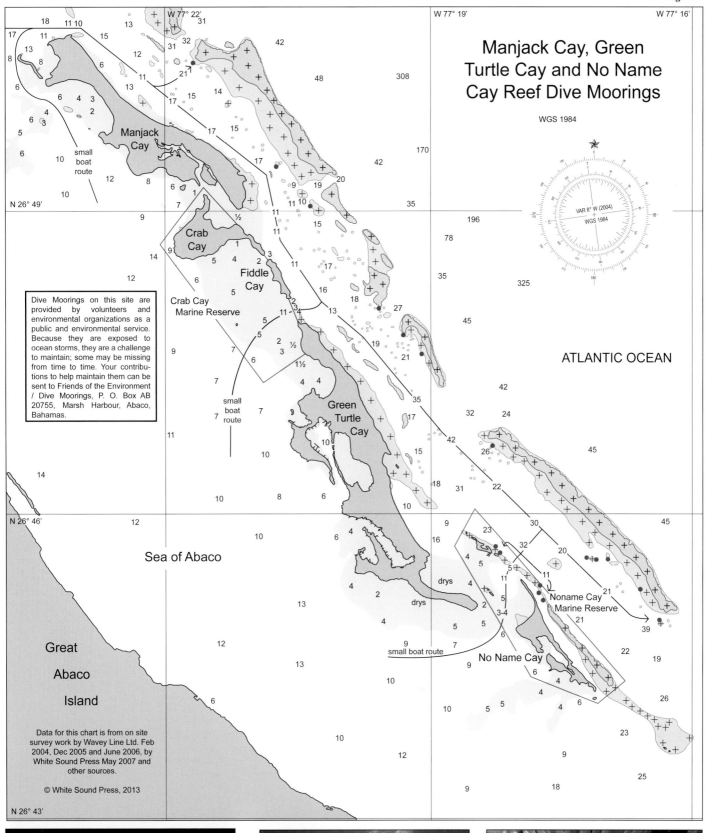

Manjack Cay, Green Turtle Cay and No Name Cay Reef Dive Moorings

WGS 1984

VAR 8° W (2004)
WGS 1984

ATLANTIC OCEAN

Manjack Cay

small boat route

N 26° 49'

Crab Cay

Fiddle Cay

Crab Cay Marine Reserve

Dive Moorings on this site are provided by volunteers and environmental organizations as a public and environmental service. Because they are exposed to ocean storms, they are a challenge to maintain; some may be missing from time to time. Your contributions to help maintain them can be sent to Friends of the Environment / Dive Moorings, P. O. Box AB 20755, Marsh Harbour, Abaco, Bahamas.

small boat route

Green Turtle Cay

N 26° 46'

Sea of Abaco

drys

drys

Noname Cay Marine Reserve

No Name Cay

small boat route

Great

Abaco

Island

Data for this chart is from on site survey work by Wavey Line Ltd. Feb 2004, Dec 2005 and June 2006, by White Sound Press May 2007 and other sources.

© White Sound Press, 2013

N 26° 43'

Juvenile Queen Angelfish.

Nassau Grouper

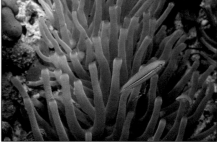

Flamefish.

photos © Mike Adair, Sports Photography, 2001

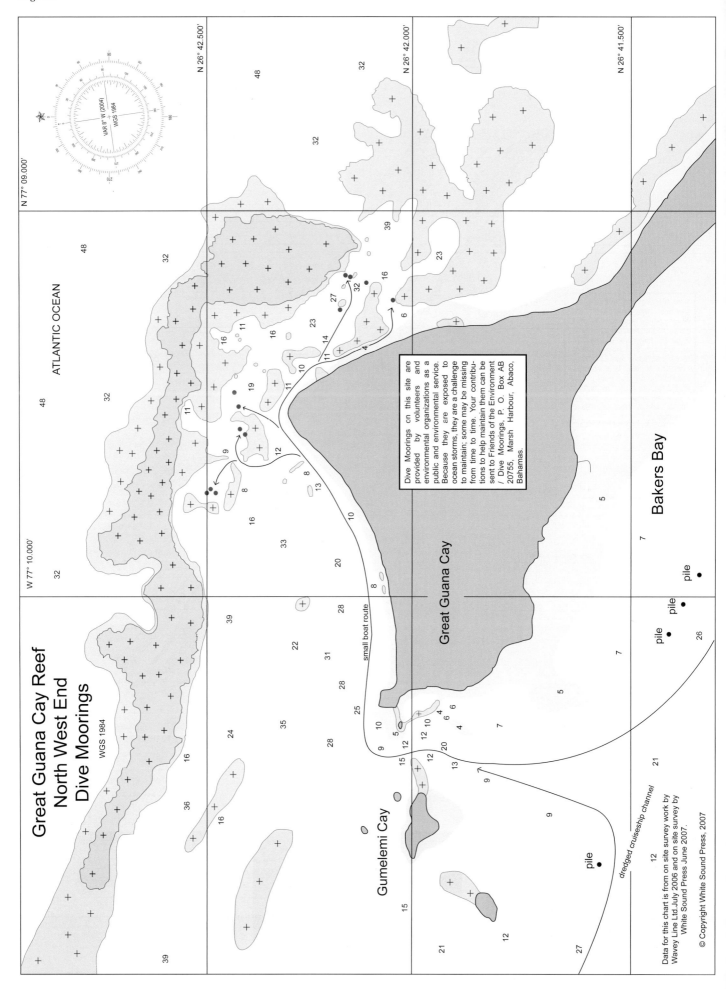

Great Guana Cay Reef
North West End
Dive Moorings

WGS 1984

ATLANTIC OCEAN

VAR 8° W (2004)
WGS 1984

N 77° 09.000'

W 77° 10.000'

N 26° 42.500'

N 26° 42.000'

N 26° 41.500'

Dive Moorings on this site are provided by volunteers and environmental organizations as a public and environmental service. Because they are exposed to ocean storms, they are a challenge to maintain; some may be missing from time to time. Your contributions to help maintain them can be sent to Friends of the Environment / Dive Moorings, P. O. Box AB 20755, Marsh Harbour, Abaco, Bahamas.

Great Guana Cay

Gumelemi Cay

Bakers Bay

small boat route

dredged cruiseship channel

pile

Data for this chart is from on site survey work by Wavey Line Ltd July 2006 and on site survey by White Sound Press June 2007.

© Copyright White Sound Press, 2007

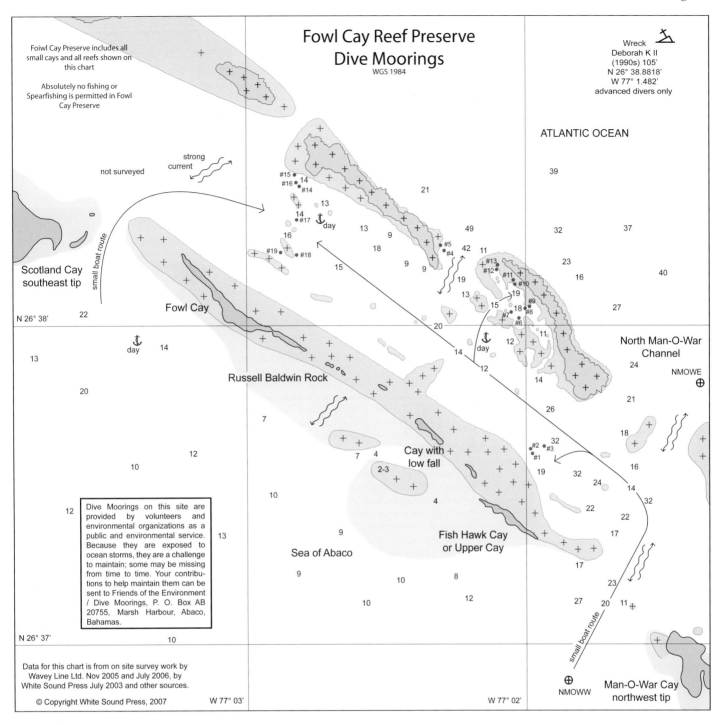

Fowl Cay Reef Preserve
Dive Moorings
WGS 1984

Foiwl Cay Preserve includes all small cays and all reefs shown on this chart

Absolutely no fishing or Spearfishing is permitted in Fowl Cay Preserve

Wreck
Deborah K II
(1990s) 105'
N 26° 38.8818'
W 77° 1.482'
advanced divers only

ATLANTIC OCEAN

not surveyed

strong current

Scotland Cay southeast tip

small boat route

N 26° 38'

Fowl Cay

day

Russell Baldwin Rock

Cay with low fall

Fish Hawk Cay or Upper Cay

Sea of Abaco

North Man-O-War Channel

NMOWE

Man-O-War Cay northwest tip

NMOWW

small boat route

Dive Moorings on this site are provided by volunteers and environmental organizations as a public and environmental service. Because they are exposed to ocean storms, they are a challenge to maintain; some may be missing from time to time. Your contributions to help maintain them can be sent to Friends of the Environment / Dive Moorings, P. O. Box AB 20755, Marsh Harbour, Abaco, Bahamas.

N 26° 37'

Data for this chart is from on site survey work by Wavey Line Ltd. Nov 2005 and July 2006, by White Sound Press July 2003 and other sources.

© Copyright White Sound Press, 2007   W 77° 03'   W 77° 02'

French Grunts and Squirrel Fish at Cooperjack Cay, July 2010. Photo by Katie Dodge with Sea Life camera.

Mooring Numbers, Names, and GPS Coordinates

#	Name	Coordinates
#1	French Grunt Alley A	N 26° 37.598' W 77° 01.985'
#2	French Grunt Alley B	N 26° 37.610' W 77° 01.988'
#3	French Grunt Alley C	N 26° 37.620' W 77° 01.992'
#4	The Wall A	N 26° 38.233' W 77° 02.300'
#5	The Wall B	N 26° 38.248' W 77° 02.310'
#6	Frog Us	N 26° 38.016' W 77° 02.031'
#7	Frog Troy	N 26° 38.043' W 77° 02.053'
#8	Frog Big Boat	N 26° 38.054' W 77° 02.005'
#9	Big Boat	N 26° 38.063' W 77° 01.990'
#10	Flywheel Bay A	N 26° 38.131' W 77° 02.037'
#11	Flywheel Bay B	N 26° 38.144' W 77° 02.044'
#12	Grouper Alley	N 26° 38.174' W 77° 02.113'
#13	Shoots & Ladders	N 26° 38.191' W 77° 02.106'
#14	Tombstone A	N 26° 38.438' W 77° 02.082'
#15	Tombstone B	N 26° 38.429' W 77° 02.829'
#16	Tombstone C	N 26° 38.449' W 77° 02.835'
#17	Twin Reef A	N 26° 38.343' W 77° 02.838'
#18	Twin Reef B	N 26° 38.320' W 77° 02.826'
#19	Boy Scout	N 26° 38.225' W 77° 02.885'

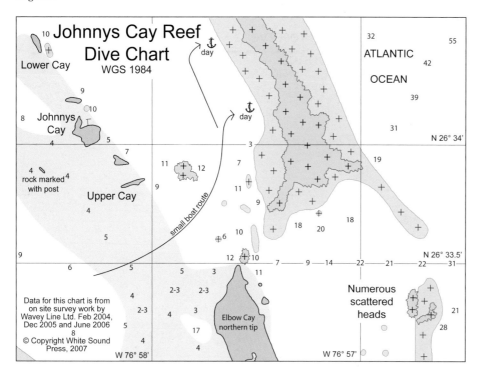

Johnnys Cay Reef
Dive Chart
WGS 1984

10
Lower Cay
9
10
8 Johnnys Cay
4   5
7
4
rock marked 4
with post
Upper Cay
4
5
9
day
day
3
11   12
7
11
9
10
6
12   10
ATLANTIC
OCEAN
32   55
42
39
31
N 26° 34'
19
small boat route
18
18
20
7   9   14   22   21   22   31
N 26° 33.5'
5
6   5
2-3   2-3
4
3
2-3   4   3
5   17
8
4
Elbow Cay
northern tip
11
5
Numerous
scattered
heads
21
28

Data for this chart is from
on site survey work by
Wavey Line Ltd. Feb 2004,
Dec 2005 and June 2006
© Copyright White Sound
Press, 2007

W 76° 58'   W 76° 57'

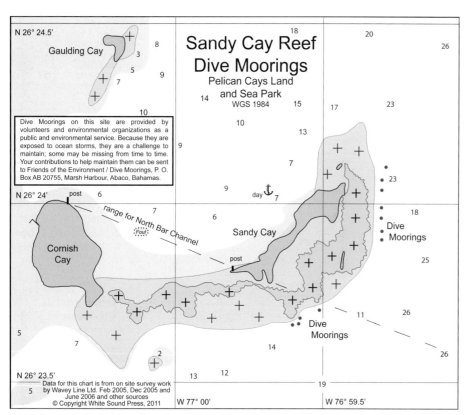

N 26° 24.5'
Gaulding Cay
8
3
5
9
7
10

Sandy Cay Reef
Dive Moorings
Pelican Cays Land
and Sea Park
WGS 1984

18
20
26

14   15   17   23
10
13
9
7

N 26° 24'   post   6
range for North Bar Channel
Foul!
7
6

Cornish
Cay

9
day   7
23

18
Dive
Moorings
25

post
Sandy Cay

5
7
2
11   26

Dive
Moorings
14
26

N 26° 23.5'
5   13   12   19
W 77° 00'   W 76° 59.5'

Data for this chart is from on site survey work
by Wavey Line Ltd. Feb 2005, Dec 2005 and
June 2006 and other sources
© Copyright White Sound Press, 2011

Yellowtail Snappers at Sandy Cay Reef, July 2010.

Spotted Eagle Ray at Sandy Cay Reef, July, 2011.

Parrot Fish, Fire Coral and Chromis at Sandy Cay Reef, July 2010.

A small piece of Sargassum seaweed floating free at Sandy Cay Reef in June, 2010. Sargassum is often found in clumps floating at the surface and it usually supports a variety of sea life which lives just beneath it. It is very thick in the Sargasso Sea, a part of the Atlantic Ocean located several hundred miles east of Abaco characterized by slow moving ocean currents surrounded by fast moving ocean currents and large masses of floating Sargassum. Early mariners believed the weed would entrap their ships and that sea monsters living benearh the Sargassum would attack them.

All photos above taken by Katie Dodge with a Sealife camera.

Sandy Cay and Sandy Cay Reef from the southwest., with the Pelican Cays and Atlantic Ocean in the background. The reef can be identified by the strip of darker water running north and south just east of the rock and the breaking waves near its southern end. Also, note the reef (dark patches of water) extending off to the west where some new moorings have been placed. Photo by Steve Dodge.

An adult male Cuvier's beaked whale lunges out of the water, preparing for a deep foraging dive.

Guide to the Most Common Whales and Dolphins of Abaco

By Diane Claridge and Olivia Patterson

Bahamas Marine Mammal Research Organisation

The Bahamas is an archipelago that boasts many natural attributes, none more spectacular than its marine life. The shallow carbonate banks and deep-water channels and basins of The Bahamas provide important habitat for marine mammals and an ideal study site for the Bahamas Marine Mammal Research Organisation (BMMRO). BMMRO is a Bahamian non-profit organisation whose mission is to promote the conservation of marine mammals in The Bahamas through scientific research and educational outreach.

Since 1991, BMMRO has been conducting small vessel surveys primarily around Abaco Island to document the occurrence, distribution and abundance of marine mammals in The Bahamas. The main goal of the project is to contribute to the conservation of marine mammals by learning more about them and sharing information with other scientists and interested parties. The majority of species found here are deep diving toothed whales that inhabit the pelagic waters surrounding the shallow Bahama banks. Many migrate through The Bahamas, but some species are year-round residents, including some of the world's least known whales. By photographing the pattern of natural nicks and scars on each animal's dorsal fin or tail flukes, a technique known as photo-identification, we are able to keep track of individuals—gaining an understanding of their social structure, habitat requirements and population status.

Over the past three years, BMMRO's research effort has expanded to include large vessel surveys in the Great Bahama Canyon. These surveys have provided a wider picture of marine mammal distribution in the northern Bahamas and have aided in identifying potentially critical habitats for beaked whales. Associated research, including genetic studies and pollutant analyses will help to identify stocks and further investigate the health of local populations.

The Bahamas Marine Mammal Research Organisation also concentrates on community education and has shared a model for an environmental summer camp with Friends of the Environment; which is now offered free of charge to local youths in three locations throughout The Abaco's each year. BMMRO is based in Sandy Point, Abaco, and created this program in the hopes that young Bahamians will grow up with a better understanding of their environment. To further expand this program, BMMRO has recently offered a "whale camp" to Bahamian teenagers so that they may have a first hand experience in marine mammal research. "Whale Camp" exposes these students to the challenges of research and

A sperm whale in the Great Abaco Canyon prepares to dive and BMMRO Researchers stand by to capture a photo of its tail flukes for photo-identification. Photo by Lindsey D. McCoy.

provides an eye-opening look at the diversity of marine mammals that can be found in The Bahamas, while investigating relevant conservation issues. The program is offered specifically to high school students with an interest in marine biology. BMMRO has partnered with Young Bahamian Marine Scientists (YBMS) to offer the program to students outside of Abaco.

Our research efforts have been greatly enhanced by sighting reports which boaters have contributed over

The shallow sand banks of Abaco provide important feeding habitat for common bottlenose dolphins.

the years. As cruisers, you have a unique opportunity to observe rarely seen marine mammal species and it is important to keep an accurate log, take photographs and/or video, while respecting the animals' needs for space; and, please never try to touch or feed them as this may cause harm to you or the animal. While The Bahama Islands are home to at least twenty-five species of marine mammals, the following is a guide to the most commonly seen whales and dolphins in the Abacos and is intended to aid and encourage boaters to continue to report sightings. The species shown represent four groups of whales and dolphins, separated into their taxonomic families: oceanic dolphins, dwarf and pygmy sperm whales, sperm whales and beaked whales. All photographs were taken in The Bahamas.

Family Delphinidae – Oceanic Dolphins
The family Delphinidae is a large diverse group of species that may not appear all that similar externally, but they share features of their internal anatomy. For example, some dolphins have a pronounced beak or rostrum while others lack a beak entirely, but internally they all have sharp, conical teeth. These highly social animals can be found in groups ranging in size from a few individuals to several thousand; and, some species are known to live in complex societies consisting of related individuals. Twelve oceanic dolphin species have been recorded in The Bahamas.

Common bottlenose dolphins (*Tursiops truncatus*), formerly called Atlantic bottlenose dolphins, are the most common marine mammals seen in Abaco. It should be noted, however, that there are at least two distinct "breeding populations" or "ecotypes" of this species: coastal or inshore bottlenose dolphins that inhabit the shallow waters of Little Bahama Bank; and, oceanic or offshore bottlenose dolphins found in the deep waters surrounding Abaco. These populations diverged genetically several hundred thousand years ago and have since developed different physiological adaptations to their respective marine environments. The coastal ecotype is smaller in length reaching just over 8 feet and has relatively larger pectoral fins and dorsal fin which helps them to maneuver more readily around rocks and reefs to catch fish, and to regulate their internal body temperature (the temperature of the shallow Bank waters fluctuates much more than the deeper Atlantic Ocean). The inshore dolphins do not travel much beyond the barrier reefs of Abaco; and, while some individuals remain in the same area for years, others are known to range all over Little Bahama Bank. The deeper diving oceanic ecotype can reach 10 feet or more in length and can remain at depth for longer than their coastal cousins due to their ability to store more oxygen in their blood. They are usually seen in larger groups and appear to have an extensive range. Photographs of individual oceanic bottlenose dolphins have shown movements between Abaco, Bimini and Exuma Sound.

Oceanic bottlenose dolphins inhabit the pelagic waters surrounding the shallow Bahama Banks.

Throughout their lifetimes, common bottlenose dolphins acquire a unique pattern of nicks and scars on their dorsal fin which researchers use to tell individuals apart and track them over time.

A common bottlenose dolphin jumps out of the water showing the large pectoral fins characteristic of the coastal ecotype.

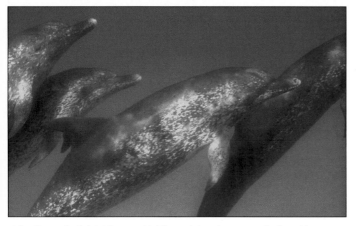

Atlantic spotted dolphins are highly social and are usually found in groups of 20 or more individuals.

Atlantic spotted dolphins (*Stenella frontalis*), are the more frequently seen of two different species of spotted dolphins found in the Abacos. Atlantic spotted dolphins are a resident species and are commonly seen in groups of 20-50 dolphins in the oceanic waters of Abaco where they feed on flying fish and squid. In some parts of Little Bahama Bank this species can also be found along the edge of the banks during the daytime where they come to rest and socialize. Spotted dolphins are not born with spots, but actually accumulate them as they mature, becoming quite mottled looking as adults. Young spotted dolphins are often confused with bottlenose dolphins, and sometimes the two species interact, which adds to the confusion. Spotted dolphins have a more slender snout, and although they can almost reach the same length as bottlenose dolphins, they have a smaller girth and thus body weight.

Risso's dolphins (*Grampus griseus*) are large light grey dolphins that can reach over 13 feet in length and have a relatively tall, dark dorsal fin. Adults are typically covered with overlapping white scars caused by the teeth of their con-specifics making them look quite battered. They have a rounded head, lacking a beak, but have

The prominent white forehead of the Risso's dolphins makes it a relatively easy species to recognize at sea.

a deep vertical crease down the centre of the forehead. As they mature, their forehead becomes prominently white, making them one of the easiest species to recognize at sea. Risso's dolphins are commonly seen in the Abacos each winter and spring, primarily on the Atlantic side of the islands. It is unknown where these groups range the rest of the year, but some individuals have been seen in Abaco repeatedly over the years.

Short-finned pilot whales (*Globicephala macrorhynchus*) can grow to 18 feet long and weigh over 5,000 pounds, with males being significantly larger than females. They have a bulbous forehead with no perceptible beak, a faint grey diagonal stripe behind each eye and a faint grey "saddle" behind and below the dorsal fin. The rest of their body dorsally is jet black, which prompted whalers to name them "blackfish", a term that also includes three other species known from The Bahamas (melon-headed whales, pygmy killer whales and false killer whales). Pilot whales can be distinguished from the other blackfish species by the position of their large, broad-based dorsal fin, which is set quite far forward on their body.

The bulbous head and forward position of the dorsal fin helps us to distinguish pilot whales from the other "blackfish".

The dorsal fins of adult male pilot whales (foreground) are much broader and taller than adult females or immature animals (background).

They live in matrilineal pods consisting of up to three generations of related females and their offspring. Pilot whales are seen in Abaco year-round but are more common during the spring and summer months. On calm days, they can be seen in tight groups lying abreast, resting at the surface for hours.

The orca is one of the easiest species to identify at sea.

An orca lunges out of the water with a dwarf sperm whale in its mouth.

Two dwarf sperm whales resting at the surface, just east of Elbow Cay.

Pygmy sperm whales can be 1-2 feet larger than dwarf sperm whales, but their dorsal fin is smaller and set farther back on the body, making them easy to confuse with beaked whales.

Killer whales (*Orcinus orca*), or orcas, are probably the easiest cetacean species to recognize at sea due to their striking black and white pigmentation patterns. Orcas are the largest member of the oceanic dolphin family, with males reaching 30 feet in length and weighing 8 tons, while females reach only 23 feet and weigh 4 tons. The most conspicuous feature of these whales is the dorsal fin, which can grow over 5 feet tall in adult males. These top predators are found in all the world's oceans but are more abundant in higher latitudes where prey resources are more plentiful. Orca pods are seen each year in Abaco usually in the late spring and summer, including one group that has returned repeatedly over 11 years. While they have been observed feeding on dolphins and dwarf sperm whales around Abaco, they are most likely in the area in response to prey migrations such as tuna.

Family Kogiidae – Dwarf and Pygmy Sperm Whales
Dwarf and pygmy sperm whales are small whales which share similar characteristics with sperm whales. All possess an under-slung toothed lower jaw, and a toothless upper jaw. The head shape ranges from triangular to square, becoming blunter with age, and all have a single nostril found on the left side of the head.

Dwarf sperm whales (*Kogia sima*) are the most common marine mammal seen in the oceanic waters around Abaco. Adults reach only 8-9 feet in length, and the dorsal fin is set mid-way down the body and is falcate or triangular in shape, so they can easily be confused with dolphins at a distance. **Pygmy sperm whales** (*Kogia breviceps*) are slightly larger reaching up to 10 feet in length, but

the dorsal fin is smaller and set further back on the body, making it easy to confuse this species with beaked whales. These small whales are often found solitary or in small groups in extremely deep water environments, and have adapted numerous ways to avoid predators such as killer whales. Both species have counter shading, being dark grey dorsally and white on the underside making it more difficult to see them from the surface or from below. They also have a white line of pigmentation on each side behind the head, known as a false gill, making them look like a shark. When threatened, they are able to expel ink which they have ingested from squid, their primary prey, creating a dark cloud in which they can escape. Their behaviour while at the surface is very cryptic, and they are most typically seen logging, or lying motionless. When a vessel approaches them, they dive and swim away, making them very difficult study subjects!

Family Physeteridae – Sperm Whales
The sperm whale is the only species in the family Physeteridae. Sperm whales are the largest toothed whales in the world and are the only common great whale seen year-round in The Bahamas.

Sperm whales (*Physeter macrocephalus*) have dark brown, wrinkled-looking skin and an enormous square-shaped head that comprises one third of their total body length. Males can attain a body length of 60 feet while females are considerably smaller, reaching 35-40 feet in length when mature. Their single blowhole on the left side of the head at the front causes a distinctive "blow" which angles to the left and forward. When a sperm whale prepares to dive, it raises its massive tail, allowing us to photograph the distinctive pattern of notches in the trailing edge of the tail flukes. Sperm whales dive to great depths (>1000 metres) for more than an hour at a time where they feed on large squid, their primary prey. Adult females form nursery groups that can be found in the Abacos year-round, while the mature males frequent the islands only during the winter breeding season and spend the rest of the year feeding in more productive Arctic waters.

Surface profiles of three beaked whale species known to The Bahamas (top to bottom): Blainville's beaked whale (Mesoplodon densirostris), Gervais' beaked whale (Mesoplodon europaeus), Cuvier's beaked whale (Ziphius cavirostris)

Family Ziphiidae – Beaked Whales

The beaked whale family is characterized by having reduced dentition; with typically only two teeth located in the lower jaw and erupting above the gum line of sexually mature males. These teeth are more appropriately described as "tusks" because they are actually used for combat with other males and not for feeding purposes. Beaked whales can be shy whales found generally in small groups that inhabit extremely deep water, making field studies difficult. As a consequence, beaked whales represent the least known large mammals that exist today; in fact, some species have never been seen at sea, and are known only from old weathered skull fragments. Of the 21 recognized species of beaked whales found worldwide, three are known from The Bahamas.

Blainville's beaked whales (*Mesoplodon densirostris*) are found in all the world's tropical and temperate waters and are one of the most common species seen around Abaco. These medium-sized whales reach 14-16 feet in length, with males being slightly larger, are brownish-grey in colour and have a spindle-shaped body that tapers at both ends. They have a small dorsal fin found almost

Adult male Blainville's beaked whales have extremely arched lower jaws with tusk-like teeth on either side of the head. Blainville's beaked whales live in a harem like society and the teeth are thought to be used for interspecific fighting with other males for dominance.

Blainville's beaked whales have a spindle-shaped body and their small dorsal fin is almost two-thirds of the way back.

A subadult male Blainville's beaked whale breaches, exposing a unique pattern of scarring on its side. The oval scars are caused by bites from the parasitic cookie cutter shark, while the linear scars are a result of interactions with adult male Blainville's beaked whales.

two thirds of the way back along their body and a well-defined beak or snout, which usually breaks the water first as the whale surfaces to breathe.

Older whales have numerous white oval scars caused by cookie cutter sharks and multiple paired linear scars caused by the "tusks" of their con-specifics. Adult males look quite bizarre as they often have clusters of stalked barnacles growing on their protruding "tusks". There are resident groups of Blainville's beaked whales inhabiting the deep submarine canyons around Abaco, although adult males seem to have a greater range than females.

Please report your marine mammal sightings to:

Bahamas Marine Mammal Research Organisation
P.O. Box AB-20714
Marsh Harbour, Abaco, Bahamas

Email: info@bahamaswhales.org
www.bahamaswhales.org

Or call
"Dolphin Research" VHF Ch65A

To report stranded, injured, or dead marine mammals call: (242) 544-5409

BAHAMAS MARINE MAMMAL RESEARCH ORGANISATION

Our Mission:

To promote conservation of marine mammals and their habitats through scientific research and educational outreach.

Fishing in Abaco

by Harry Weldon and Jon Dodge

The Abaco islands offer a beautiful and productive area for exciting fishing. The string of cays east of Great Abaco Island provide a protected to semi-protected area named the Sea of Abaco or Abaco Sound. Beyond most of the cays are rocks and reef formations up to about two miles offshore. While not continuous, a reef stretches from Walkers Cay in the north to just east of Hope Town, a distance of about 90 miles. About two to three miles offshore the bottom drops off to depths of 600 feet to over 1000 feet. The visiting fisherman to Abaco has three basic choices. Fish inside on the sound and flats, outside on the reef, or outside beyond the reef.

Fishing Inside

Almost any dock will have its resident gray snapper. Some of these will top out at three or four pounds. Trying to catch them, while entertaining, can be an exercise in frustration. The larger they are, the less likely you are to catch them. They didn't get to that size by incautious dining. The large ones have excellent eye sight and are very cautious feeders. Try using very small line (6lb or under) tied directly to the hook. With the hook fully hidden in a

Gray Snapper

suitable bait, toss several pieces of cut bait in the water along with the hook and line. Allow the line to sink with the other pieces of bait. This might get you hooked up. More than likely though, the smaller snapper will take it before the larger one. Once you manage to tie into a good sized fish, the light line will snap after a quick wrap around a piling or mangrove root. This type of fishing can be lots of fun but please release all the small fry that are not going to make it to the kitchen.

Yellowtail snapper, grunt, bar jack, and many others will be found on small patches of reef or rock along any of the keys of the Abacos. Just look for any type of hard bottom structure. On a completely flat day, the surface of the Sea of Abaco may appear as flat as glass. This does not happen often, but when it does the

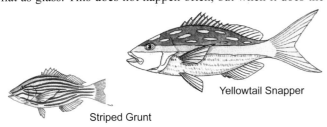

Yellowtail Snapper

Striped Grunt

bottom may be viewed as if looking into an aquarium. This is a great experience in itself and it also provides an opportunity to easily see any structure on the bottom. When the wind is up it is more difficult to identify hard structure, but it is still possible to do so.

Bait fishing with spinning gear should provide food for the table and a whole lot of fun. Frozen shrimp, conch, hermit crab, and cut ballyhoo will all work with this type of fishing. Eventually the barracuda will show up and, depending on your philosophy will either ruin the day or make it. A small live snapper with a suitable hook lightly through the back will put a barracuda on the end of your line and with six or twelve pound line give a good account

of himself. Barracuda is not normally eaten by locals and unless going to the table, release him for someone else to catch.

If you prefer to troll, just drag a small white or yellow feather along the rocky edges of most cays. Yellowtail, bar jack, needle fish, and barracuda will be your most likely catch, but when you're

Barracuda

near an opening to the ocean the surprise factor goes way up. If you're going to be fishing inside, take a good look at the fish at the dock before you leave. If they're active and excited over a bit of bait tossed in the water and if the snappers darken around the eyes, then they're in a feeding mood and hopefully the fish elsewhere are also ready to feed. If the snapper that were active this morning show little interest, you might want to read a book. Midday seems to be a slow time for this type of fishing but the time of year is not much of a factor, though obviously winds and tide will make a difference to you, if not to the fish.

If you're not looking for food for the table, you might want to try your hand at bonefishing. Bonefishing is done on the flats during the last of the ebb tide and the first few hours of the incoming tide. It takes a skilled eye to spot bonefish swimming in the shallow water in search of food. Look for their tails and dorsal fins which break the surface and give them away. Once the fish have been found, it is up to the angler to present the bait to the fish. The most common bait used is natural conch, crab, or shrimp. Artificial bait like the wiggle jig, which is flat and does not dig into the bottom,

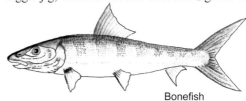

Bonefish

works well on sand or grass. Years of experience indicate that pink, which resembles shrimp, is the best color for artificial bait, but brown and yellow also seem to work well. Most bonefish are caught on spinning or fly tackle and six to twelve pound line. On the initial run, a four to six pound fish can run for a hundred yards or more- a memorable experience. Bonefish are a sport fish only and should always be released. Bonefishing is a year round sport in Abaco, but the winter months seem to provide more fish.

Fishing On the Reef

Reef fishing usually assures fish for the table. Fishing the reef is pretty much the same as fishing on the inside, it's just deeper and the fish are larger. The reefs around Abaco have a good supply of grouper, snapper, mackerel, yellowtail, and many other species that are usually easily caught. Large mutton snapper (8–15 pounds) concentrate for spawning the last of May and into June. Local fisherman have traditionally used heavy hand lines in 20-50 feet of water. You'll need some local knowledge, however, to find out just where they are. They're here all the time, but when they're spawning they can be found in large numbers if you know just where to fish the reef.

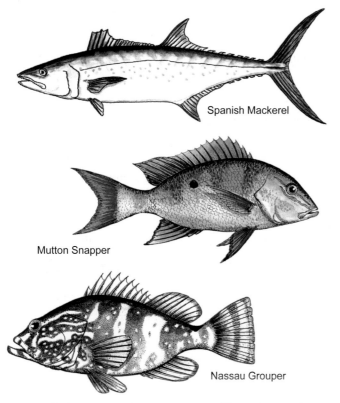

Spanish Mackerel

Mutton Snapper

Nassau Grouper

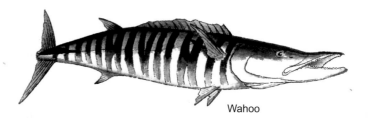

Wahoo

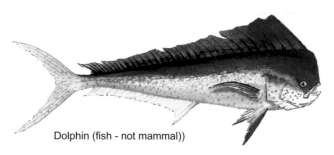

Dolphin (fish - not mammal))

Reef fishing can be done two ways: trolling or bottom fishing. Cut bait, such as ballyhoo or conch, is most commonly used. When trolling or casting with artificial bait, a small yellow lure or silver spoon is a good choice. A light wire leader is also suggested because of the possibility of spanish mackerel and barracuda. Barracuda and amberjack are found on the reef and put up a great fight, but local specimens have been found to have ciguatera, or fish poisoning, and should never be eaten.

Fishing Deep

Deep-sea fishing is for those who want to venture beyond the barrier reef and try for the "Big One." Marlin, sailfish, tuna, dolphin and wahoo can be found at the drop-off, which, in the Elbow Cay area, is approximately two to three miles east of the cay beyond the reef. The water off Hope Town goes out from the reef in steps of sixty, ninety, two hundred forty, and six hundred feet. The two hundred forty to six hundred foot break is what is referred to as the

warm water a downrigger, wire or plainer to get the bait deep will increase your success, with wahoo being a common catch. July, August, and September are only fair but catches of blackfin tuna and an occasional dolphin are always possible. Fishing picks up in October and by Christmas is normally pretty good and continues to improve through February and March. Large schools of skipjack

and cero mackerel are sometimes encountered but getting them to bite can be a challenge. For the small schooling tuna, especially the blackfin, a small white feather trolled way, way back can secure a hit. The trick then is landing the fish before a shark takes the better part. Sometimes deep jigging around the schooling tuna can result in hooking up with a nice fish. Another method is to chunk bait and drift lines deep for yellowfin and blackfin tuna. There's no question that successful ocean fishing during the quiet months requires a lot more work than at other times. If you feel like a little exercise and the weather is calm, stop the boat just at the two hundred foot mark before the drop off and deep jig for grouper, red snapper or amberjack.

Yellowfin Tuna

Blackfin Tuna

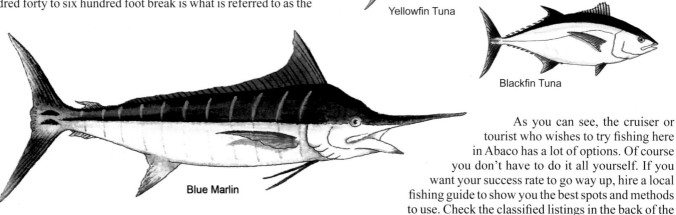

Blue Marlin

"drop off." Other than perhaps marlin, the best ocean fishing can be found at this line. Most boats troll skirted ballyhoo.

Weather permitting, mid-March through mid-April is normally the peak ocean fishing season, with large numbers of dolphin and tuna. By the end of June things have quieted down and with the

As you can see, the cruiser or tourist who wishes to try fishing here in Abaco has a lot of options. Of course you don't have to do it all yourself. If you want your success rate to go way up, hire a local fishing guide to show you the best spots and methods to use. Check the classified listings in the back of the book for a fishing guide in your area.

Anyone who fishes in the area should learn about local fishing rules and limits before going out. See page 17 for fishing regulations and pp 146 and 165 for the boundaries of the parks where no fishing is permitted. Remember to release any fish you cannot consume. If you're not going to eat it, please don't kill it.

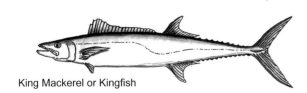

King Mackerel or Kingfish

Harry Weldon is the fishing editor for *The Cruising guide to Abaco, Bahamas*. He lives at White Sound on Elbow Cay. Jon Dodge also contributed to this article.

Kim Neilson of West Palm Beach, Florida, created the paintings of fish used in this article. He has lived in Florida for over fifty years, and first went to the Bahamas in 1971 to fish and dive. He started drawing and painting Bahama charts and scenes in 1972, and started Gulfstream Trading Company in 1987. He works full time producing custom T-shirt designs for sport fishing boats, and custom charts of the Bahamas, the Florida Keys, or the Caribbean. Gulfstream Trading Company, 4300 N. Flagler Drive #15, West Palm Beach, FL 33407 (studio- 561-863-7133; cell- 561-758-8536).

Wizard's Way, from Deerfield Beach, Florida, departing White Sound, Elbow Cay, Summer, 2006

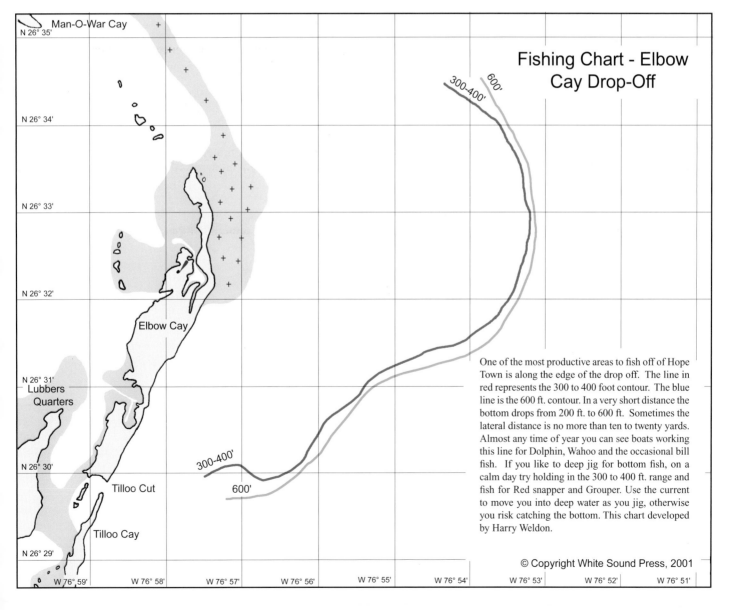

Fishing Chart - Elbow Cay Drop-Off

One of the most productive areas to fish off of Hope Town is along the edge of the drop off. The line in red represents the 300 to 400 foot contour. The blue line is the 600 ft. contour. In a very short distance the bottom drops from 200 ft. to 600 ft. Sometimes the lateral distance is no more than ten to twenty yards. Almost any time of year you can see boats working this line for Dolphin, Wahoo and the occasional bill fish. If you like to deep jig for bottom fish, on a calm day try holding in the 300 to 400 ft. range and fish for Red snapper and Grouper. Use the current to move you into deep water as you jig, otherwise you risk catching the bottom. This chart developed by Harry Weldon.

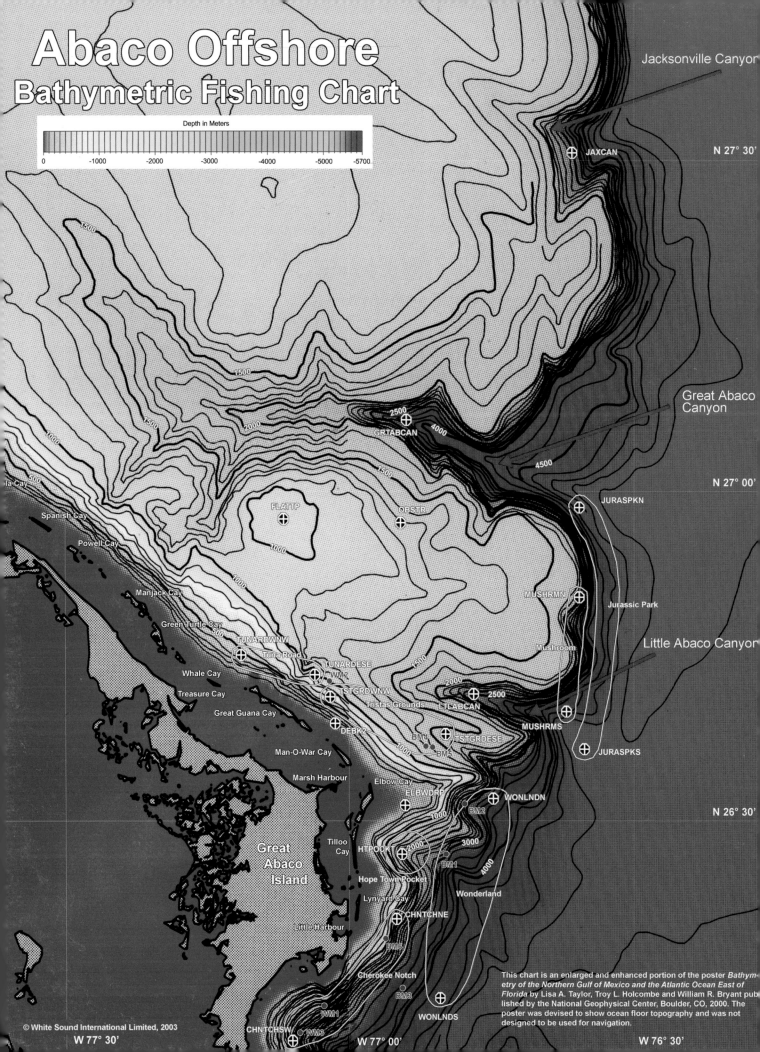

Waypoints on Abaco Offshore Bathymetric Fishing Chart:

Fishing Areas (generally from north and west to south and east):

Waypoint Name	Coordinates	
JAXCAN	N 27° 30.7205'	W 76° 63.5350'
GRTABCAN	N 27° 06.6003'	W 76° 53.8502'
FLATTP	N 26° 57.5003'	W 77° 07.0008'
OBSTR	N 26° 57.2150'	W 76° 54.8760'
JURASPKN	N 26° 58.5000'	W 76° 35.8500'
JURASPKS	N 26° 36.5000'	W 76° 35.1700'
MUSHRMN	N 26° 50.4000'	W 76° 35.7500'
MUSHRMS	N 26° 40.0000'	W 76° 37.0000'
TUNARDWNW	N 26° 45.1500'	W 77° 11.4500'
TUNARDESE	N 26° 43.3000'	W 77° 03.6000'
TRSGRDWNW	N 26° 41.2800'	W 77° 02.0000'
TRSGRDESE	N 26° 37.8800'	W 76° 49.7500'
LTLABCAN	N 26° 41.5302'	W 76° 46.7904'
DEBK2	N 26° 38.8818'	W 77° 01.4820'
ELBWDRP	N 26° 31.4000'	W 76° 54.0000'
HTPOCKT	N 26° 26.9100'	W 76° 54.3500'
WONLNDN	N 26° 32.0400'	W 76° 44.7800'
WONLNDS	N 26° 13.8500'	W 76° 50.3500'
CHNTCHNE	N 26° 21.0000'	W 76° 55.0000'
CHNTCHSW	N 26° 09.9200'	W 77° 06.1000'

Captain Perry L. Thomas' catch locations (generally from north to south—BM denotes sites of Blue Marlin catches; WM denotes sites of White Marllin catches):

Waypoint Name	Coordinates	
BM1	N 26° 36.8580'	W 76° 51.8670'
BM2	N 26° 36.7240'	W 76° 51.0060'
BM3	N 26° 31.4870'	W 76° 47.8620'
BM4	N 26° 26.9530'	W 76° 49.7410'
BM5	N 26° 19.0560'	W 76° 56.2560'
BM6	N 26° 14.6530'	W 76° 54.4770'
WM1	N 26° 42.6770'	W 77° 02.0080'
WM2	N 26° 13.0990'	W 77° 02.6460'
WM3	N 26° 10.4340'	W 77° 05.3040'

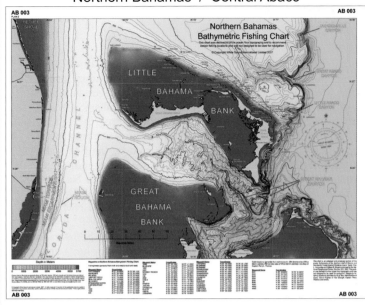

Abaco: The Year in Review - 2012

by Victor Patterson

7 May 2012 brought a general election and a new government to The bahamas. The incumbent government was headed by the Member of Parliament for North Abaco, Free National Movement (FNM) Party Leader Mr. Hubert Ingraham. He had taken over the top govenment spot in 2007 from Progressive Liberal Party (PLP) Leader Mr. Perry Christie, who was trying to get his position back. Both Abaco seats were held by the FNM and both incumbents were running to retain their seats. In addition to the opposition PLP, a new party called the Democratic National Alliance (DNA) had sprung up and fielded candidates for both seats. The DNA was made up of a mix of disgruntled FNM supporters, disaffected youth and the occasional unhappy PLP supporter. As such, they were expected to draw votes mostly from the FNM, particularly in the South Abaco seat, where they had nominated Mr. Roscoe Thompson III, who had unsuccessfully sought the FNM nomination.

The election was hard fought, but with over 50% of the seats being in Nassau, that was where the balance of power would be determined. Despite the fact that the FNM easily retained both seats in Abaco, a near PLP sweep of the capital vaulted them back into power. Mr. Ingraham, who had held the North Abaco seat since 1977, decided to follow the traditions of the Westminster system and announced that he would be stepping down from his seat. His resignation took effect on August 31st, and he will be replaced in a bye-election to be held later in the year.

One of the reasons the FNM was able to win their seats in Abaco so easily was the large amount of infrastructure spending that had happened during the year. The Leonard Thompson International Airport in Marsh Harbour began construction and work proceeded quickly. A new, modern terminal as well as an air traffic controllers' tower were built to replace the 30 year old facility that had been too small on the day it opened. Visitors to Abaco will now find an airport worthy of the second busiest airfield in the Bahamas.

A new government office building was completed and opened in 2012 as well. Previously, government offices were scattered in different locations throughout central Abaco and would often require challenges of parking and traffic to get anything done. The new complex contains the first elevator in Abaco as well as what is surely the largest paved parking lot.

A contract was also signed for a new mini hospital to be constructed in Marsh Harbour. Residents and visitors will no longer have to navigate late night emergency flights when health issues spring up suddenly and expectant mothers will be able to stay home and deliver safely right on the island.

Of course, there were still areas of concern for citizens of Abaco. While vastly improved, the electric company's new power plant still had challenges due to poor distribution lines that sometimes put the island into darkness. But unlike the previous summer when many visiting guests were inconvenienced, there were fewer complaints of that nature in 2012. There is also need for work to be done to the road network; this challenge will fall to the new government and voters will undoubtedly be looking for results.

Abaco's cellular system upgraded to 4G during 2012. Because of the numbers of people on boats and far-flung islands, wireless technology has become increasingly important for both residents and visitors. And while no one should need Google Maps to get around the streets of Man-O-War, the increased capabilities were quite welcome.

The economic situation remained mixed. While 2012 did see an increase in visitors and resulted in some much welcome strengths in some areas of the economy, most of it remained down. Real estate, construction and related industries remained mired in the Great Recession with little sign of a healthy recovery anytime soon.

There was also a tragedy on the seas in 2012. Living on Abaco are a significant percentage of Haitian nationals; economic refugees from our third world neighbor to the south. While many see Abaco as a final destination, for many it is a way station in hopes of eventually reaching the United States. This desire leads many to be taken advantage of, as there is an underground smuggling industry. The Bahamas is no stranger to smuggling, having a long history of smuggling weapons (during the Civil War), rum (during prohibition), narcotics (during the 1980s) and now refugees. However, unlike the previous cases which only posed risks to the smugglers, when large numbers of people are loaded onto vessels of questionable seaworthiness, it is only a matter of time before something tragic happens and luck ran out this year when a boat floundered in rough seas off of Little Abaco one night this spring. Because any number of the people on the boat did not know how to swim, there were multiple drownings, even more tragic because among the victims were children. Left unanswered is why—after spending a large sum to secure a slot on the trip—an investment in a lifejacket wasn't also made. One can only hope that while human nature dictates that there will always be people willing to take the chance and persons willing to assist them in it, at least a minimal attempt will be made to reduce future risks.

The year was mostly uneventful for Abaco's large developments. The Schooner Bay project met their sales targets and continued to develop. Baker's Bay saw activity with building of houses. Winding Bay, on the other hand, seems to be facing ongoing structural challenges based on their business model. Because the facilities are private, there never seems to be enough of their owners present to support the facilities and their future is somewhat up in the air.

The 39th annual Abaco Regatta was held this year. This sailing race has become one of the lynchpins of the summer boating economy, bringing large numbers of visitors to both participate in and watch the races. Along with various fishing tournaments, this event helped bring increased numbers of boaters into Abaco than the previous year. The lack of any close calls with hurricanes also contributed to a strong year in this sector.

One bit of good news; for the past couple of years, Abaco had held a Lionfish Derby, which has been sponsored by various environment friendly groups. The lionfish is an invasive species that was native to the Pacific Ocean, but somehow wound up in the tropics. Because Lionfish have no natural predators in the Atlantic, they have the potential to do great harm and efforts are be-

continued on page 190

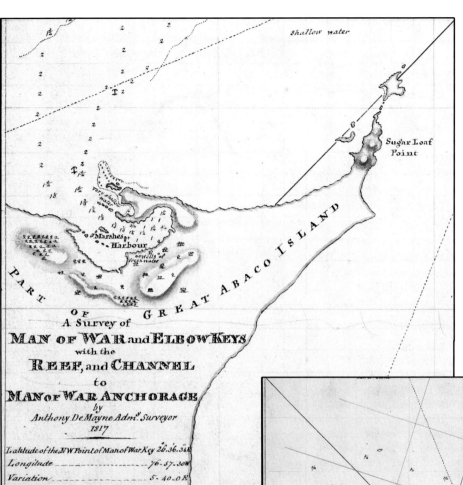

This portion of the chart **Man of War and Elbow Cays with the Reef and Channel to Man of War Anchorage** by Anthony de Mayne (1817) shows Marsh Harbour and its "wells of fresh water" in the lower left corner of the chart. Note that the harbour is drawn accurately, but that the survey vessel did not venture to Matt Lowe's Cay and Sugar Loaf Point. The suggestions for anchoring are both outside the harbour because the chart was drawn for large ships to gain shelter (and fresh water in Marsh Harbour) rather than for small boats. High quality prints of the chart can be purchased from Heritage Charts (see advertisement on page 107).

This portion of the 1817 chart **A Trigonometrical Survey of Little and Pelican Harbours Great Island of Abaco Bahama** drawn by Anthony DeMayne shows the harbours which were of interest to the British navy and merchant marine where large ships could take refuge during stormy ocean weather. Note that what we call Little Harbour today was designated as "Hurricane Hole" and what they called "Little Harbour" extended up to what we call the Lynyard Cay anchorage today. Pelican Harbour included the entire area bounded by the Pelican Cays to the east and Sandy and Channel Cays to the west. Note also that Lynyard Cay was designated as Little Harbour Cay. Excllent full-size reproductions of these early charts of Abaco can be acquired from Heritage Charts. See their advertisement on page 107.

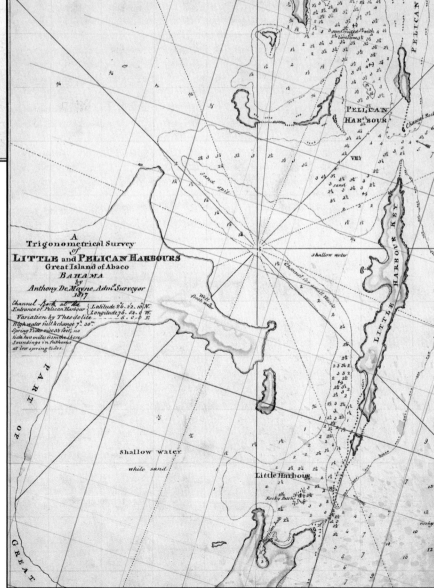

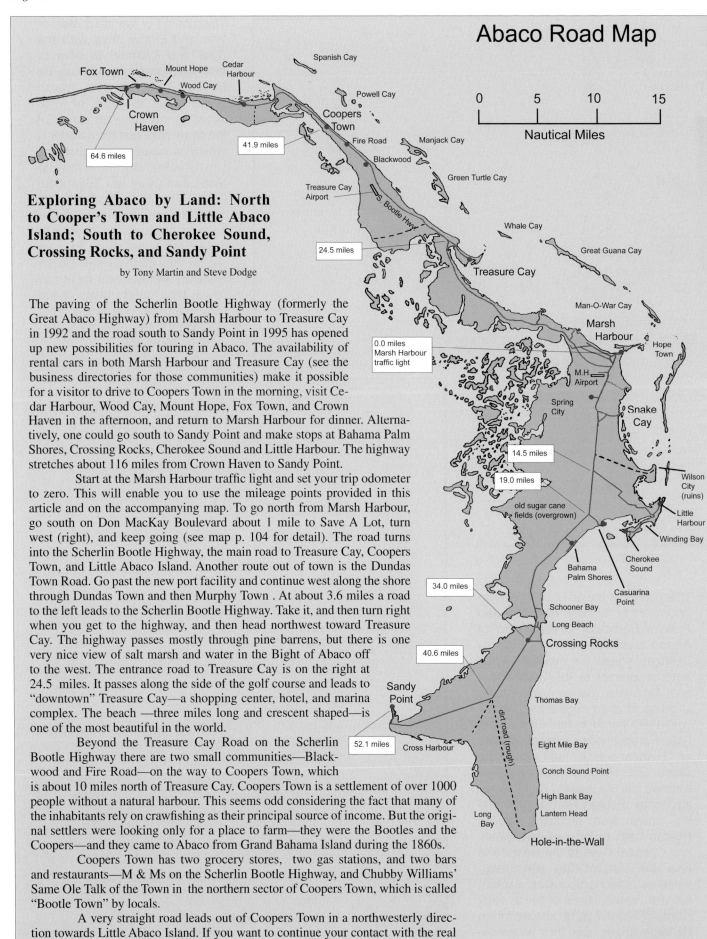

Abaco Road Map

Spanish Cay

Fox Town Mount Hope Cedar Harbour Powell Cay

Wood Cay Coopers Town

Crown Haven Fire Road Manjack Cay

64.6 miles 41.9 miles Blackwood Green Turtle Cay

Treasure Cay Airport Whale Cay

24.5 miles Great Guana Cay

Treasure Cay

Man-O-War Cay

Marsh Harbour Hope Town

0.0 miles Marsh Harbour traffic light M.H. Airport

Spring City Snake Cay

14.5 miles

19.0 miles Wilson City (ruins)

old sugar cane fields (overgrown) Little Harbour

Winding Bay

Bahama Palm Shores Cherokee Sound

34.0 miles Casuarina Point

Schooner Bay

Long Beach Crossing Rocks

40.6 miles

Sandy Point Thomas Bay

52.1 miles Cross Harbour Eight Mile Bay

dirt road (rough) Conch Sound Point

High Bank Bay

Long Bay Lantern Head

Hole-in-the-Wall

Scherlin Bootle Hwy

Nautical Miles
0   5   10   15

Exploring Abaco by Land: North to Cooper's Town and Little Abaco Island; South to Cherokee Sound, Crossing Rocks, and Sandy Point

by Tony Martin and Steve Dodge

The paving of the Scherlin Bootle Highway (formerly the Great Abaco Highway) from Marsh Harbour to Treasure Cay in 1992 and the road south to Sandy Point in 1995 has opened up new possibilities for touring in Abaco. The availability of rental cars in both Marsh Harbour and Treasure Cay (see the business directories for those communities) make it possible for a visitor to drive to Coopers Town in the morning, visit Cedar Harbour, Wood Cay, Mount Hope, Fox Town, and Crown Haven in the afternoon, and return to Marsh Harbour for dinner. Alternatively, one could go south to Sandy Point and make stops at Bahama Palm Shores, Crossing Rocks, Cherokee Sound and Little Harbour. The highway stretches about 116 miles from Crown Haven to Sandy Point.

Start at the Marsh Harbour traffic light and set your trip odometer to zero. This will enable you to use the mileage points provided in this article and on the accompanying map. To go north from Marsh Harbour, go south on Don MacKay Boulevard about 1 mile to Save A Lot, turn west (right), and keep going (see map p. 104 for detail). The road turns into the Scherlin Bootle Highway, the main road to Treasure Cay, Coopers Town, and Little Abaco Island. Another route out of town is the Dundas Town Road. Go past the new port facility and continue west along the shore through Dundas Town and then Murphy Town . At about 3.6 miles a road to the left leads to the Scherlin Bootle Highway. Take it, and then turn right when you get to the highway, and then head northwest toward Treasure Cay. The highway passes mostly through pine barrens, but there is one very nice view of salt marsh and water in the Bight of Abaco off to the west. The entrance road to Treasure Cay is on the right at 24.5 miles. It passes along the side of the golf course and leads to "downtown" Treasure Cay—a shopping center, hotel, and marina complex. The beach —three miles long and crescent shaped—is one of the most beautiful in the world.

Beyond the Treasure Cay Road on the Scherlin Bootle Highway there are two small communities—Blackwood and Fire Road—on the way to Coopers Town, which is about 10 miles north of Treasure Cay. Coopers Town is a settlement of over 1000 people without a natural harbour. This seems odd considering the fact that many of the inhabitants rely on crawfishing as their principal source of income. But the original settlers were looking only for a place to farm—they were the Bootles and the Coopers—and they came to Abaco from Grand Bahama Island during the 1860s.

Coopers Town has two grocery stores, two gas stations, and two bars and restaurants—M & Ms on the Scherlin Bootle Highway, and Chubby Williams' Same Ole Talk of the Town in the northern sector of Coopers Town, which is called "Bootle Town" by locals.

A very straight road leads out of Coopers Town in a northwesterly direction towards Little Abaco Island. If you want to continue your contact with the real

Bahamas, drive on. You will be rewarded with quizzical but friendly faces and the experiences that being "off the beaten track" often provide.

The landscape provides no pine at this point, just coppice. Five miles from Coopers Town you cross a causeway (locally known as "The Bridge"). This signals the beginning of Little Abaco, formerly a separate island. It has its own distinct character and life style.

Looking north from the causeway connecting Great and Little Abaco Islands. The Government reportedly has plans to replace the causeway with a bridge in order to resotre natural tidal flow to the Bight of Abaco.

Now you are heading generally west instead of northwest and pine begins to replace the coppice. There is a Lucayan Indian site and the ruins of an old sisal mill in this area. Both are off the paved road and should only be attempted with local knowledge and a truck with good road clearance.

Further along the road is a water tower which marks the edge of Cedar Harbour. The piles of conch shells, the fishing boats,

A dredged channel, breakwater and dock at Cedar Harbour, Little Abaco Island. Photo taken July 2002.

and the mangroves afford good photo opportunities. Four and a half miles further on (59.2 miles from Marsh Harbour) lies Wood Cay , settled by a family from Fire Road at the beginning of the century who were trying to get away from the wild hogs that kept eating their crops. The Tangelo Hotel is located here; it has twelve moderate sized, though comfortable and reasonably priced rooms, and a restaurant and bar (phone 242 365-2222). One of the most reliable local mechanics, Charley Mills, has his gas station and garage a little further along at Chuck's Auto Service. Again, the pine gives way to smaller trees and less than two miles further west we approach the smallest of Little Abaco's five settlements—Mount Hope. This is the only settlement not directly accessible by boat and appears on few maps. It is worth stopping to sample the food at B. J.'s Restaurant.

A typical scene of the Scherlin Bootle Highway passing through a pine forest. This photo was taken north of the Treasure Cay Airport.

Just a mile further along the highway is Fox Town, the largest and most scenic of Little Abaco's villages. Numerous small cays and rocks dot the harbour, and the Hawksbill Cays lie about a mile offshore. Fox Town has about 500 inhabitants, and its main winding street contains a wide variety of residences, some ultra modern with satellite dishes, others with wooden siding and little changed since the ancestors of the present inhabitants chose this site for its potential as a fishing community. Groceries and fuel are available at Fox Town Shell.

A mere half mile further on, we reach the end of the line— Crown Haven. It is 64.6 miles north of Marsh Harbour. Older members of this community once lived on Cave Cay, an isolated islet to the southwest, until a hurricane in the late thirties destroyed their homes. The authorities of the day provided land on the main island for them to start anew and Crown Haven was born. From here it is a short trip to get to Grand Bahama by boat, and local people often have closer connections with that island than the rest of Abaco. There is a passenger ferry service between Crown Haven and McLean's Town on Grand Bahama Island (see page 206).

To go south from Marsh Harbour to Sandy Point, begin by heading south on Don MacKay Boulevard from the traffic light. At the airport roundabout (about 3 miles) go straight. The road passes through pine forests. There are turnoffs to the left for Snake Cay (at about 6 miles), Cherokee Sound and Little Harbour (at 14.5 miles), Casuarina Point (19.0 miles), and Bahama Palm Shores, as well as other minor roads. Snake Cay is the old port for Owens-Illinois' lumber operation which was active during

The turnoff for Casuarina Point, 19 miles south of the Marsh Harbour traffic light.

Snake Cay: view of the inlet on the south side.

the 1960s; it is no longer in use. The road to Cherokee Sound was recently paved, but the side road from that to Little Harbour is still dirt, and it is rough. The Abaco Club on Winding Bay, operated by Ritz-Carleton Hotels is on the road to Cherokee Sound about 9 miles from the Great Abaco Highway. There is an 18-hole "links" golf course, a club house, guest rooms private homes and a beauti-

The beach at Winding Bay before development, July 2003.

ful beach. Membership is generally required for entry. Cherokee Sound, a picturesque and charming old fishing and boat building village, is 11.5 miles from the highway turnoff. Cherokee Sound's famous long dock is located to the southeast of the settlement. The Cherokee Food Fair is well stocked with groceries, and also offers apartments for transients at very reasonable rates. Pete's Pub and

Cherokee Sound is an old fishing and boat building village. The long dock is visible above the town in this photo, March 2010.

Gallery at Little Harbour offers food, drinks, bronze sculptures and other original art—all in a very casual, very friendly atmosphere. Casuarina Point is a small residential community comprised of the old executive housing built by Owens-Illinois and some new construction.

Some of Abaco's most beautiful beaches are located along the eastern coast of the island between Cherokee Sound and Hole-in-the-Wall, which is the southern tip of the island. These are difficult to access by boat because there are no harbours along this coast, but several of the beaches can now be easily accessed by land. A turnoff located about 22 miles south of Marsh Harbour (3 miles south of the Casuarina Point turnoff) leads to Bahama Palm Shores, a residential development with palm-lined streets, about 20-25 homes, and a beautiful ocean beach.

A few miles further south, at 29.7 miles from the traffic light, there is a turnoff to Serenity Point, a new development by Anco

The beach at Bahama Palm Shores.

Lands, which owns substantial acreage in southern Abaco. Serenity Point is a hillside residential development on a high ridge overlooking the wide gently curving ocean beach which forms Schooner Bay and the Atlantic Ocean beyond. Entry to the development is monitored at a gate, but visitors are welcome, and there is an observation tower which offer a commanding view of the area. The beach is beautiful and pristine. For further information see the Serenity Point advertisement on page 24.

A mile or so further south there is a turnoff to Schooner Bay Village, a very unique development in that the goal is to create a new Bahamian village to serve as a business, residential and commercial center for south Abaco. The central feature is a small (14 acre) harbour with deep water access from the Atlantic Ocean. It is the only secure harbour of refuge between Hole-in-the-Wall and Little Harbour / Cherokee Sound. The harbour has an island in the middle will have about 30 waterfront Bahamian style cottage residences. A wide promenade will circle the harbour featuring two-storey owner-occupied Mom and Pop businesses—shops, offices, restaurants and inns. All buildings will be traditional Bahamian style, and lot owners must commit to building within one or two years to guarantee that the community will reach critical mass within a reasonable period of time. Further up the ridge there will be a regional shopping center with a post office, bank, grocery store, and there is an area reserved for farmland as well. The harbour was opened to the sea in June 2011, and by September one home was completed with 8-10 more under construction. See the chart and more detailed description on pages 154-155.

Long Beach is an older development with several homes another mile or so south. The beach here is beautiful as well. The turnoff is about 33 miles south of the Marsh Harbour traffic light.

About 1 mile further south (34.0 miles from Marsh Harbour) is the road to Crossing Rocks, a small town located just off the Atlantic Ocean Beach. During 2000 the town was moved a little inland after the devastation of hurricane Floyd. There is a bar and restaurant—Trevor's Midway Motel— at the entrance road. The town is a short drive east on the road. It has a pretty beach with some off-lying rocks.

At 6.6 miles beyond the Crossing Rocks road (and 40.6 miles south of Marsh Harbour) the highway forks. The road to Hole-in-the-Wall goes southeast. It is 15 miles to the lighthouse and very rough; it should be attempted only in a truck with good road clearance. It passes through the Sandy Point Forest Preserve, which is administered by the Bahamas National Trust and is home to the endangered Abaco parrot. Eco-tours of this area are sometimes available.

The paved road to the southwest goes to Sandy Point, the only settlement on the west side of Great Abaco Island. It is 11.5 miles from the fork, and the road parallels a beautiful beach which is often used for community cookouts. Sandy Point is a small fishing village which has grocery stores, restaurants, and rooms for rent. Nancy's Sea Side Inn, located on the waterfront a block north of the public dock, is a good lunch stop. Oeisha's Resort caters mostly to bonefishermen; rooms are moderately priced (phone 242 366-4139).

Looking southeast toward Schooner Bay Village from an observation tower at Serenity Point.

Five miles northwest of Sandy Point (by water only) is Gorda Cay, developed by the Disney Corporation as a cruise ship stop they named Castaway Cay. The *Disney Magic* began regular visits to the island in July, 1998. A ferry service operated by Bahamas Ferries connects Sandy Point to Nassau for automobiles as well as passengers. See page 206 for more detail.

Two new developments on the coast of Great Abaco Island about 25 miles south of Marsh Harbour will boost the economy of the area. Serenity Point, located on a high ridge overlooking Schooner Bay and the Atlantic, is the development on the right side of this photo. Schooner Bay Village, located on the left side, is under construction and features a small harbour with deep water entry from the Atlantic Ocean. The Long Beach development, the town of Crossing Rocks and the highway leading toward Hole-in-the-Wall and Sandy Point can be seen in the distance. Photo by Steve Dodge, 15 March, 2010.

A Brief History of Abaco

by Steve Dodge
Professor Emeritus
Millikin University

The Spaniards called it Habacoa,* and they were not impressed. Although they were the first Europeans to explore Abaco and the Bahamas, they settled on larger islands further to the south such as Hispaniola and Cuba, then moved on to conquer large and wealthy Indian civilizations in Mexico and Peru. When the enslaved Indians of Cuba and Hispaniola died of smallpox and overwork, the Spaniards sailed to Habacoa and other Bahamian islands to recruit new Indian slaves. Thus, the Lucayan Indians, whom Columbus had described as gentle and kind, were victims of genocide and were gone before 1550. The sites of their numerous settlements have been discovered and various artifacts have been found, but none of the sites in Abaco have been fully excavated by archaeologists. The British eventually colonized Eleuthera Island and New Providence Island (Nassau) in the Bahamas, and claimed the entire archipelago as their colony, but no permanent settlements were made in Abaco for over 200 years after the departure of the Lucayans. The French made an attempt to establish a colony in Abaco in 1625. They called it Lucaya or Lucayonique, but it was not successful and no trace of the settlement has been found. The early French maps of Abaco are generally more accurate than others which have survived, but pirates undoubtedly knew the waters better than anyone else.

Abaco was well situated for piracy. The small cays offered excellent anchorages as well as good lookout points, and the combination of the shallow banks and the off-shore barrier reef discouraged pursuers. Few records exist concerning the haunts of pirates, but we do know that Vain the Great Pirate based himself at Green Turtle Cay in Abaco after fleeing Nassau when the first royal governor, Woodes Rogers, arrived in 1717. He was discovered by Benjamin Hornygold, a recently-converted pirate sent by Rogers, but Vain managed to escape from Green Turtle Cay and from the Bahamas. Other pirates, a few wreckers, and some transient fishermen may have made their residence at Abaco from time to time, but there were no permanent settlements by the 1770s when the British North American colonies declared their independence from Britain.

Not all the colonists supported the patriot cause during the American Revolution; from 10 to 20 percent of the population favored Great Britain. Their reasons were various. Some genuinely liked George III, some disliked the patriots, and some feared that democracy and republicanism would imperil their security or their property. These loyalists were treated badly by the patriots–their property was often confiscated and they were expelled from the villages in which they lived. Many moved to areas such as New York and Florida which were controlled by Britain during the war. When Britain conceded independence to the United States, many of the loyalists chose to move again rather than become citizens of the United States. Encouraged by exaggerated claims for the agricultural and commercial potential of Abaco, some of them became convinced that it would be a good place to build a new British Empire.

Over 600 persons left New York for Abaco in August, 1783. They settled at Carleton, named after Sir Guy Carleton, the British commanding officer in New York. The location of Carleton was unknown for many years and many wild guesses were made. While working in the Bahamas Archives and at Lands and Surveys in 1979, I found two original land grant deeds for parcels which were adjacent to Carleton, and determined that the town had been located near the north end of the Treasure Cay Beach. This was subsequently confirmed by an archaeological dig by Bob Carr and the discovery of a map of Carleton drawn in 1784 found at the Public Records Office in London by Gail Saunders. Before the loyalists had been at Carleton for three months, a minor dispute regarding each man's responsibility to work in the cooperative provisions store had escalated into a revolution. Many of the town's residents supported a Committee of Safety which overthrew the authority of Captain John Stephens and placed him under arrest. When they received word that reinforcements were on the way from the British garrison at St. Augustine, they feared these troops would support Stephens, so two-thirds of the residents left Carleton, moved six leagues (18 miles) to the southeast, and founded Marsh's Harbour. Within the next five years some of the remaining settlers at Carleton moved on to other locations, and Carleton ceased to exist.

The dissident group at Marsh's Harbour was joined by additional refugees from New York, some of whom founded Maxwell, which was named for the Governor of the Bahamas and was adjacent to Marsh's Harbour. It was probably located on the southeastern shore, perhaps at Boat Harbour, which is now the site of the Great Abaco Beach Hotel and Boat Harbour Marina. Refugees from Florida came to Abaco also. A group settled in southern Abaco at Spencer's Bight (about 10 miles south of Marsh's Harbour) and a former member of the Carolina Rangers, Lt. Col. Brown, was granted a large parcel of land at Eight Mile Bay, about eight miles south of Spencer's Bight, where he intended to establish a plantation. Within a year or two he moved his slaves from Abaco to Caicos, where he had acquired another grant of crown land. As far as can be determined this was the only attempt by a loyalist to cultivate cotton on a large scale in Abaco.

Many of the loyalists were displeased with Abaco. They had come to Abaco to farm, but they found only small pockets of soil on the limestone island. Rainfall was plentiful, but there were long, dry periods when crops dried and burned up. Life was not as easy as the promotional literature said it would be. When the free provisions provided by the Crown were exhausted, many of the new migrants decided to leave the island. About 2000 had come to Abaco during the middle 1780s, but only 400 (200 whites and 200 blacks) were left in 1790. Those who had money or influence probably left Abaco. Those who stayed probably had no alternative.

The few hundred loyalists who remained in Abaco were joined by migrants from Harbour Island, Eleuthera, an old Bahamian settlement. Young men from Harbour Island were reportedly impressed with the beauty of the Abaco girls, and also with the large and unexploited fishing grounds of Abaco. They knew that survival in the Bahamas meant that one had to fish as well as farm, and new communities were established on the outer cays which were closer to the reef and the best fishing. New Plymouth was founded on Green Turtle Cay. It was the most important settlement in Abaco during most of the nineteenth century. Its men relied on farming, fishing, and wrecking–no one became wealthy, but they made a living. According to tradition, Wyannie Malone, a widow from South Carolina, was the founder of Hope Town on Elbow Cay. During the 1820s a single young couple settled on Man-O-War Cay; in 1977 230 of Man-0-War's population of 235 could trace their ancestry to Pappy Ben and Mammy Nellie. A small settlement was also established on Great Guana Cay.

The settlers who survived in Abaco learned to be self-sufficient. They had no choice in the matter; they lacked government mail service until 1867 when the House of Assembly provided a subsidy for a privately-owned vessel to make one round trip per month between Nassau and Abaco. Nassau, capital of the Bahamas, was no great metropolis–its population was only 10,000 in 1864–but

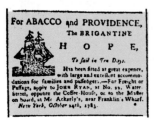

The first group of loyalists to leave New York for Abaco did so in September, 1783. This advertisement for the sailing of the *Hope*, which carried a second or third group of immigrants to Abaco, appeared in the *Royal Gazette* (New York) on October 24, 1783.

it was Abaco's only link with the outside world. The Abaconians attempted to become involved in various export operations during the late nineteenth and the early twentieth centuries–pineapples, sisal, lumber, sponge–all provided a living for a large number of Abaconians for a period of time, but failed to move the economy much beyond the subsistence level. The problem was not that the people did not work hard; the problem was that they lacked knowledge of foreign markets. They always seemed to be doing the right thing at the wrong time or in the wrong way. They shipped pineapples to the United States in bulk, and frequently lost a large portion of the crop to spoilage in the ships' holds. They shifted into sisal production just as the market for sisal was deteriorating.

One of the most reliable sources of income for Abaconians during the mid-nineteenth century was wrecking, but it declined in importance long before 1900. Wrecking did not necessarily mean luring a ship to its destruction. It meant salvaging the cargo and usable parts of ships that wandered onto the reef or the banks. Wreckers saved many sailors' lives. Because Abaco is situated adjacent to one of the busiest north-south shipping lanes in the Atlantic, a seemingly inexhaustible supply of ships were wrecked in Abaco during the 19th century. One of the best-known wrecks was that of the *U.S.S. Adirondack*, a brand new steam sloop which was the pride of the Union Navy in 1862. En route to Nassau to

The *U.S.S. Ossipee*, shown here, was a sister ship to the *U.S.S. Adirondack*, the remains of which can still be seen on the reef near Man-O-War Cay. This photograph was provided courtesy of the Naval Historical Foundation, Collection of W. Beverly Mason, Jr.

inform Union ships there to search for the infamous Confederate raider, the Alabama, the *Adirondack* struck the reef at Man-O-War Cay, where her remains can still be seen. Shortly after this wreck, the British Imperial Lighthouse Service contributed to the decline of wrecking by building lighthouses throughout the Bahamas. The lighthouse at Hope Town on Elbow Cay was completed in 1863, despite attempts by local residents to protect their livelihoods by sabotaging the construction project.

By 1900 Hope Town was the largest and most prosperous settlement in Abaco. It was the seat for a commissioner, and its population of almost 1200 lived by fishing, sponging, shipping and boat building. Abaco boats were admired for their design as well as their fine construction, and were known as the best in the Bahamas. Abaco dinghies, small open boats with a single sail, were sought by most Bahamian fishermen, and Abaco-built smacks (sloops with bowsprits) and schooners brought a premium in the marketplace. During World War I and the early 1920s, large lumber-carrying schooners of more than 200 tons were built at Hope Town and at Man-O-War Cay. There is only one boat carpenter left in Hope Town today -- Winer Malone builds Abaco dinghies in his shed near the harbour using only hand tools and providing the visitor with an accurate view of how boats were built in Abaco a century ago. Man-O-War Cay is the most active boat building center in

Abaco today. Albury Brothers Boats builds outboard powerboats. Beginning in 1979 fiberglass as well as wood hulls were made. These Bahamian-built boats are typically heavier and stronger than their US-built counterparts; they are built to withstand many years of hard use in high seas. They are sought after by fishermen and others throughout the islands, so contemporary Abaco continues to export boats as it has done since the early nineteenth century.

The first glimpse of twentieth-century life style in Abaco was Wilson City, a company town located about 10 miles south of Marsh's Harbour. Founded in 1906, it was the marvel of its

The mill at Wilson City. Photo from Gray Russell, former resident of Wilson City. Copied by Steve Dodge with assistance of Leo Savola.

age, boasting modern conveniences such as electricity and an ice plant, both rarities in the Out Islands. It was built by the Bahamas Timber Company, which operated a saw mill and dock facilities at the site. Many residents of Hope Town and Marsh's Harbour moved to Wilson City where they found steady employment, but this operation was short-lived; the company closed the mill at Wilson City in 1916. Several years later, during the early 1920s, two developments provided Abaco with improved communication with the outside world. The installation of a radio-telephone station at Hope Town made instant communication with Nassau possible, and the diesel-powered Priscilla replaced the Albertine Adoue schooner which had been serving as the mail boat.

The improved transportation and communication had only a limited impact on the Abaconians. The depression of the early 1930s inhibited economic development, and the lives of most Abaconians were still very similar to those of their ancestors some 100 years before. Boat building and fishing, supplemented by small farming, were the principle economic activities, and most Abaconians lived at or near the subsistence level. Real change did not occur until after World War II, when the lumber industry was revived by Owens-Illinois Corporation and tourists from the United States, Canada, and Britain discovered Abaco.

Owens-Illinois had acquired the 100 year lease originally granted to the Bahamas Timber Company. In 1959 the company built the first roads which connected the several communities on Great Abaco, and the first motor vehicles were introduced. An airport was built at Marsh Harbour and port facilities were constructed at Snake Cay. The company cut the Caribbean Pine forest of Abaco and exported it for use as pulpwood. Marsh Harbour boomed– several banks and a small shopping center with a supermarket were constructed. When Owens-Illinois completed its pulpwood operation in Abaco during the late 1960s, the company decided to utilize its investments and labor force in Abaco by building a huge sugar plantation. Sugar was exported from Abaco in 1968, 1969 and 1970, but the company lost money and the operation, which is the largest farm in the Bahama Islands, was closed. The land was sold to the government of the Bahamas, and the government, after considering various schemes, including converting it into a ranch for raising cattle, then leased it to B. J. Harmon, a Florida company which grew and exported citrus. A neem farm has been started and is successfully growing and producing neem products. Tourism developed slowly after World War II when cruising yachtsmen and others discovered the islands. Some bought land at very reasonable prices and built vacation or retirement homes. Many of these people have become a permanent part of Abaconian society. Dr. George Gallup's family still maintains a vacation house he built in Hope Town during the 1950s, and Randolph Johnston, an artist from New England, settled at Little Harbour, Abaco, at about the same time. He built a beachside home and studio where he produced lost wax castings in bronze for gallery shows in New York and Paris. Small resorts and hotels were established to service tourists who preferred the quiet and measured pace of a vacation in Abaco to the more active life-style of Nassau and Freeport, which became major tourist destinations during the 1950s and 1960s. Abaco is still off the beaten tourist track and offers the visitor an opportunity to enjoy unspoiled waters, reefs, and cays, good swimming, snorkeling, sailing and beachcombing -- all in an atmosphere of clean air and friendly, honest people. Though an increasing number of tourists visit Abaco each year, the charm and warmth of its environment and its people have not changed.

In 1967 the Progressive Liberal Party (PLP), led by Lynden Pindling, gained a majority in the House of Assembly and formed a government. The party represented the black majority (85% of the population of the Bahamas is black), and Abaco, which is about 50% white, voted for the opposition. When the PLP decided to seek independence for the Bahamas in 1972, many of the residents of Abaco resisted it. They petitioned Queen Elizabeth II, and asked to be separated from the Bahamas so they could remain a British Crown Colony. Citing the loyalty of their ancestors to the Crown, they begged the Queen to reciprocate. Their petition was not granted, and though a small group contemplated the possibility of a revolution to separate Abaco from the Bahamas and make it independent, those plans received little support. Although many Abaconians eventually shifted their support to the PLP government of Lynden Pindling, Abaco remained a centre of opposition activity. Its representatives in the House of Assembly were usually members of the official opposition party, the Free National Movement, and were frequently involved in debates and disputes with government representatives. The Pindling government was defeated in the general election held on 19 August 1992, and Hubert Ingraham, FNM representative for Coopers Town, Abaco, became the new Prime Minister. The change of government was achieved democratically and peacefully. Ingraham brought a new burst of economic activity and long overdue reforms such as the implementation of local government. He was re-elected in 1997 for a second five-year term. In May 2002 the FNM lost a general election and Perry Christie, leader of the PLP, became Prime Minister. Five five years later, in May 2007, the FNM which was again led by Hubert Ingraham, won control of the government. The Bahamians celebrated the 35th anniversary of their independence on 10 July 2008. The nation has been successful in achieving significant economic growth and has developed a viable democratic political system. Bahamians are rightfully proud of their achievement.

*The name Habacoa is of Taino (Indian) origin. It meant Large Upper Outlier and was originally used to refer to the island now called Andros. The name first appeared on a Spanish map in 1500 when Juan de la Cosa used it to designate a large island in the northern Bahamas. The Taino name for Abaco was Lucayoneque, which means Peoples' Distant Waters Land. See Julian Granberry, "Lucayan Toponyms," *Journal of the Bahamas Historical Society* 13 1 (October, 1991), 3-12.

Steve Dodge, who is also the author of this *Cruising Guide to Abaco, Bahamas*, is Professor Emeritus of History at Millikin University in Decatur, Illinois. He has also written *Abaco: The History of an Out Island and its Cays* (1983, 1995, 2005).

A Guide and History of Hope Town

by Barbara and Vernon Malone
and
Marjorie and Steve Dodge

Available at Vernon's Grocery in Hope Town and other fine Bahamian bookstores or at www.wspress.com
Only $5.95

continued from page 182

ing made to encourage fishermen to catch them as they are quite tasty to eat once you have mastered the art of removing the poisonous spines from their body. The Lionfish Derby offers prizes to whoever can catch the most lionfish in one day. The numbers caught were markedly down this year and fishermen report seeing fewer numbers around. While the lionfish will never be eradicated from the Bahamas, this is certainly welcome news.

Media in Abaco made some news on its own in 2012. The islands bi-weekly newspaper, The Abaconian which was published for the past 18 years by the founders, longtime residents Dave and Cathy Ralph, was sold to new owners. The new editor-in-chief is Bradley Albury, son of prominent Hope Town resident, the late Monty Albury. Mr. Albury recently returned from college and has a young and vibrant team working on the paper and improving on the excellent product that had been put out by the Ralphs, who are now enjoying a well-earned retirement.

Overall, it is fair to say that Abaco remains mired in recession along with the rest of the world. Economic activity continues, but it is really sputtering rather than the hum that Abaconians had been used to in the previous couple of decades. But it retains the opportunities and unspoiled beauty and charm that have drawn visitors to its shores. With uncertain conditions in the US and Europe, Abaco must continue to navigate the choppy seas of the world's economy, but managing storms is something the residents of these islands are very skilled and practiced at. And when the economy comes back, you can be sure that Abaco will be one of the first to harness the wind and progress forward once more.

Medical Tips
for Tropical Waters

Raymond Heimbecker
Jane Garfield
Justin Noice

It is fortunate that in the Abacos we have few serious health hazards. Our visitors should be aware of special problems that can be easily avoided, which would otherwise spoil a wonderful vacation. Do take simple precautions to prevent or at least mitigate what could become serious problems.

The problems we see most frequently in the Abacos are:

1. Ear infections, both acute and chronic, usually only in the ear canal, but can be SCUBA diving injury
2. Ciguatera fish poisoning, and, rarely, fish spoilage
3. Serious sunburn due to excessive U. V. exposure
4. Skin reactions due to poison wood, jelly fish, sea lice, and, rarely, from Portuguese Man-O'War
5. Trauma, mostly face and hand lacerations, often fish hooks, but also fish fillet knives! Also, we see sprains and fractions which occur while boating.

Before travelling each year you should have your ear canals checked and cleared of all wax. Tetanus Toxoid is the only immunization often required before you travel (every ten years).

Only rarely do we see patients with acute heart or abdominal problems, strokes, major fractures or life threatening accidents. But when these emergencies occur there are physicians available in Marsh Harbour to provide immediate care and arrange for transfer to a hospital if need be. A number of air ambulance services will come to the Bahamas to pick up patients. The local physicians can call these when needed. The patient or the family must be able to provide a credit card which has the funds available to cover the six to ten thousand dollar bill which will be incurred. If the medical situation is urgent but not life threatening, arrangements can often be made for one of the charter airlines to fly the patient out. In all but the most severe weather a patient can be in a hospital within two hours.

Sun Protection ... whenever possible!

EAR PROBLEMS

Ear problems occur all too frequently. In most cases these involve the ear canal and are caused by a fungus. We advise those swimmers who are prone to these itchy, painful, sometimes discharging ear infections to treat them preventively by placing a few drops of white vinegar and clean water, half and half, in the ear canal. This solution should be used before and after each and every snorkeling trip or dive. This will go a long way toward preventing serious ear canal infections. Scuba divers can and do develop middle ear problems due to poor equalization. Even though diving in the Abacos is usually quite shallow, the routine SCUBA precautions are important. If the diver has any mild nasal congestion, the use of a decongestant before each dive would be helpful. No one with a cold should dive, and no one should continue a dive if equalization is difficult. Most important of all, a dive must be immediately aborted if the diver experiences pain, bleeding, or dizziness. Each year there are three to four perforated ear drums as a result of ignoring these basic precautions. Finally, in regard to diving, all should be aware that blue holes can be extremely dangerous for even experienced divers.

FISH POISONING

The second medical problem, and one that is not uncommon, is tropical fish poisoning or ciguatera. It is caused by a photosynthetic dinoflagellate (a microscopic free swimming organism). The flagellates live among the algae on coral reefs. Especially (but not only) when the reefs are stirred up, these organisms are eaten by small fish and enter the food chain. Larger reef fish eventually harbour the toxin which accumulates in the flesh of the fish. The unwary person who eats the ciguateric fish may become ill. The reef fish most commonly involved are the larger grouper, barracuda, and snappers. The free swimmers, that is, fish that do not feed on the reef, are not involved. The smaller reef feeders are usually less dangerous because both by weight and age they accumulate less poison.

There is no way to detect or neutralize the toxin in an affected fish, and no amount of cooking or freezing will detoxify an affected fish. All of the old wives tales of how to test fish meat for ciguatera are just myths and do not work. Obviously the best way to deal with ciguatera is to avoid it. The best way to do that is to ask local Abaconians what kind of fish to avoid before eating fish, and do not eat fish if you do not know what kind it is.

Occasionally someone may eat a "mystery" fish and toxic fish poisoning may follow. The first symptom is often numbness and tingling, especially around the mouth, lips, and tongue. This may be followed by nausea, vomiting, diarrhea, severe aches and pains, and generalized weakness. The poison is neurotoxic. A unique symptom is heat/cold reversal. Hot water or warm weather may feel cold and vice versa. Each person seems to react differently. Some will recover in a few weeks; some will be debilitated for many months. Although we haven't seen this in the Abacos, the person may become comatose and die. The most serious chronic effects are prolonged muscle weakness and temperature inversion. Once a person has developed ciguatera, that person will remain hypersensitive for the rest of their lives.

There have been two recent breakthroughs in our knowledge of ciguatera. First, an easily used colorimetric test to determine whether or not a fish is ciguateric is now available. Second, we now have a treatment for the severely ill comatose patients. This is Mannitol, a solution that must be given intravenously. Unfortunately, it is of no use for the other symptoms of the poisoning. .

The other common fish poisoning is simply spoilage caused by inadequate refrigeration. The well known symptoms of nausea, vomiting and diarrhea are usually short lasting. The only treatment is oral fluid replacement. All the members of the mackerel family are extremely susceptible to this type of spoilage. It is extremely important especially in the summer to put fish on ice as soon as they are caught, and to cook them immediately after they come off the ice.

SKIN PROBLEMS

The most common problems doctors encounter in the Abacos involve the skin. Severe sun burn, poison wood, and stings from Portuguese Men O'War, other jelly fish, or sea lice can all cause skin inflammations that can make a person miserable.

Sunburn: Visitors from northern climates are often unaware that even in the winter the Abaco sun is strong and can produce severe burns. Proper clothing and modern barrier creams that cut down on both ultraviolet A and B exposure are vital. For swimmers and divers water resistant sunblock creams are a must. Severe burns will require fluid replacement and a trip to the clinic. Local aloe plants, when sliced length wise and applied directly to the burned area, may provide some relief.

Poison wood is a bush or a tree that has clusters of five, seven or nine dark green shiny green leaves (see illustration). The bark is gray, but is mottled with black stains caused by sap, which seeps through the bark and then turns black. Walking through the thick bush, or clearing land, are the usual ways for the susceptible person to get a poisonwood rash. The oily sap, transferred to the skin by

Poison Wood (Metopium Toxiferum) is a tree which has clusters of five, seven or nine shiny leaves and mottled gray, tan and black bark. It is more volatile than Poison Ivy and is common throughout Abaco.

contact with the leaves or bark, causes the rash. It is similar to, but far more intense than, poison ivy. Within three days extreme itching and burning occur, and redness and blisters appear. Some persons report success in removing the sap from the skin shortly after contact with WD-40, which is apparently much more effective than soap and water. Local resident Dave Gale reports that Abaco Neem body lotion, salve, or oil stops poison wood itch immediately, and that it is much more effective than cortisone cream. If the rash is severe, widespread, or around the eyes, a trip to the clinic is indicated. If the juice gets into the eyes it may cause loss of vision and even blindness. The **Manchineel** tree (rare) is even more dangerous than poisonwood.

The **Portuguese Man O'War** can cause a severe stinging burning rash that may be painful for several days. Be sure to warn your children who otherwise would be attracted by the bright and iridescent blue colours of the balloon shaped Man O'War as it drifts

up on the beaches. These "balloons" are difficult to see while swimming and may cause severe burning if one swims through the long tentacles. They may appear on ocean beaches after strong onshore winds; they are rare in sheltered waters. If stung, leave the water and carefully remove any tentacles remaining on your skin with tweezers or a gloved hand to minimize the bursting of additional stinging capsules. There is no magic potion to cure these stings. Scrub-

The Portuguese Man O'War looks like a clear bluish or purple balloon floating on the surface. Its tentacles can be over ten feet long. Photo used with the permission of key-biscayne.com.

bing and rubbing the area could well make things worse; rubbing alcohol, once thought to be a "cure" does not really help, but some say vinegar brings relief. Usually the sharp stinging pain subsides within a few hours, and is completely gone after a few days. If the stung person develops shortness of breath, backache or muscle pain

he/she should be brought to the nearest clinic.

Fire coral and fire sponges may be encountered on the reefs. They can cause a painful rash. The most important rule is to wear gloves at all times and DON'T touch or pick up anything.

An itchy skin rash has become a problem for some summer visitors during recent years. It is popularly attributed to "**sea lice,**" but no such animal actually exists. The rash is most likely caused by the larvae of the Thimble Jellyfish (Linuche Unguiculata). These almost invisible larvae are produced in large clusters called "blooms" by the adult jellyfish during the summer months. They may be carried by wind and currents into shore. When the larvae contact with people the larvae discharge stinging nematocysts which may persist for several days (for further information see *The Journal of the American Medical Association*, vol. 269, no. 13, April 7, 1993, p. 1669). Usually nothing is felt at the time; the rash develops several hours after contact. It is always most pronounced in the areas covered by swimwear, and small children are particularly vulnerable, often developing a severe rash accompanied by a fever, nausea, and vomiting. And this can happen even if the child has just been playing at the edge of the sea rather than actually swimming in the water. These severe cases should be seen by a phsysician. In general the rash subsides in 96 hours.

Avoid sea lice if possible; rely on local knowledge. Recently a number of Abaconians have applied meat tenderizer to susceptible areas before swimming and have avoided trouble altogether. Others have found that the use of a product named Safe Sea, applied before swimming, has kept them free of the rash. A fresh water and soap shower after removing the bathing suit or trunks taken as soon as possible after swimming may wash away enough larvae so that a rash will not occur. If a rash does develop, cortisone cream may help the itchiness. Some who have been stung by sea lice or jellyfish, have found that a product named Lands End Oil alleviates the itching and discomfort. A clinic visit is only necessary for severely affected patients. There is evidence that a previous bout with sea lice sensitizes the person, and that the next exposure may result in an instant stinging sensation while in the water.

SPINES AND BARBS, CUTS AND LACERATIONS

Sea urchin spines and sting ray barbs cause discomfort and pain. The sea urchin that is most likely to cause problems in Abaco is the one with short white spines. The unwary wader or swimmer may step on or touch one of these--the spines penetrate the skin and break off to become very painful. There are usually many imbedded spines that require individual removal. The old remedy of immediately applying lemon juice or other more easily available acid softens the spines but doesn't help extract them. An infection often sets in around the spines. Obviously, prevention

is best--wear flippers and gloves and water shoes--but also, beware that sea urchin spines can penetrate these, so watch where you walk and what you touch.

A much more painful problem is caused by sting ray barbs. Rays often bury themselves in the sand in shallow water. An unwary person walking quietly may surprise the ray by stepping on it. The ray then objects

Sea Urchins are frequently found in crevices with their toxin-laden spines sticking out. Photo © Teresa Zubi; used with permission.

strenuously and struggles to free itself by flipping its barbed tail into the person's foot, ankle, or leg. The pain is immediate, intense, and unless treated, long-lasting. Application of heat (hot water) may provide relief. A person who has not been stung should "test the waters" to avoid complicating the patient's problems by scaulding. In the field, it may be possible to provide relief by utilizing the hot water exhausted from the outboard motor. Use a bucket to collect the water, and remember to check the temperature before applying it. Local physicians sometimes inject local anesthetic into the area to provide pain relief. Also, meticulous cleaning and removal of any barb fragments is important. Prevention is best--look before you walk, and shuffle and splash some water around--enough to awaken and frighten a buried ray into finding another spot for napping.

The strange-looking but beautiful lion fish carries a toxin in its sprines. Photo © John White, used with permission.

A new potential hazard for snorkelers and divers in Abaco is the lion fish. A recent migrant to the southeastern United States (2000) and to Abaco (2005), the fish is native to the Pacific and Indian Oceans. It is a strange-looking but beautiful fish with dark red stripes and various protruding tentacle-like body parts. Long spines comprise its dorsal fin (on top of its back)—these point forward as well as up, and carry a poisonous toxin. If contact occurs with humans, immediate intense pain results making movement of limbs difficult, and sometimes paralysis and nausea occurs as well. According to one website, treatment is immersing the affected area in hot water to increase blood flow, possibly local anesthesia to reduce pain, and an x-ray to determine if there are any broken spine fragments. If present, they should be removed to prevent infection. In general, lion fish are not aggresive. Do not touch.

Visitors often acquire coral cuts while swimming or exploring. The best treatment is immediate and frequent cleaning with soap and water. Antiseptic and antibiotic creams are useless and provide a wonderful culture medium for skin bacteria. Leave the cut open if possible, or bandage it loosely and change the bandage frequently.

More serious lacerations, especially those that are bleeding heavily, require immediate attention. STOP the bleeding by direct pressure. Don't bother with pressure points. Five minutes of uninterrupted pressure (time it) right over the bleeding area will stop 99% of all bleeding. Don't peek--just keep strong pressure on, and if possible elevate the bleeding area above the heart. Follow this with bulky dressing firmly applied with tape, but keep the pressure on as much as possible. Tournequets are considered obsolete and can be dangerous. If necessary the local doctors will close the wounds. If there is numbness or inability to move any injured part, go to the nearest physician as soon as possible.

For small lacerations there are excellent bandages available. They can be acquired from a doctor or pharmacy at home and should be in everyone's first aid kit. These bandages are called SteriStrips and are produced by 3M. The most useful ones are one-quarter inch in width. Use these to close small lacerations closely and accurately. They look like regular bandages with a narrow center section. If you do not have SteriStrips on hand, you can make your own from regular bandaids .

FINDING MEDICAL HELP

Finding medical help in Abaco is not difficult but serious medical problems often require emergency air evacuation to hospitals in Nassau or Florida.

The Ministry of Health operates clinics in Coopers Town, Green Turtle Cay, Man-O-War, and Hope Town which are staffed by nurses. These clinics are open at certain times and can also open when emergencies occur. A physician occasionally attends these clinics. The Government Clinic in Marsh Harbour is staffed by physicians and nurses and is the central clinic for South Abaco.

In Marsh Harbour and Treasure Cay there are also excellent private medical clinics staffed by experienced physicians and nurses. Hours vary but they are usually open Mon-Fri from 9-5. Walk-in patients during office hours are generally welcomed, subject to the clinic's existing appointment schedule. If you can, please call ahead. After hours emergency assistance **is not available** from the private clinics unless the individual has already established a patient relationship with the clinic; this is a result of insurance company rules. If a visitor wants to assure that emergency service will be available from a private clinic, he or she should establish a patient relationship prior to the emergency.

During the past few years several of the volunteer Fire & Rescue organizations have developed the capability to respond to medical emergencies, provide paramedical assistance if necessary and to transport patients to medical facilities. Such units exist in Hope Town, Guana Cay, Man-O-War and Green Turtle Cay. Hope Town Fire Rescue also provides waterborne medical response capability for Bahamas Air Sea Rescue (BASRA).

If you experience an emergency, broadcast your emergency on VHF 16 stating your location and the nature of the problem. The appropriate organization will then respond and you will be switched to their working channel. Although you will hear mention of the working channels used by various organizations on the Cruisers Net each morning, they are not monitored 24 hours a day and **VHF 16 is the ONLY channel on which to make an emergency call.** You should however avoid using the working channels reserved for emergency use for normal conversation because you might block important communications during an emergency response.

We hope you won't need this information and that with awareness of some of the avoidable hazards you will not encounter them. Please have a healthy, happy and safe time in this wonderful area.

CLINICS AND EMERGENCY ORGANIZATIONOS
List Arranged North to South

Fox Town Clinic, 365-2172
Coopers Town Clinic and Hospital, 365-0300
North Abaco Crash Fire Rescue, 365-9111
Green Turtle Govt. Clinic, 365-4028, (after hours call nurse's residence - 365-4148)
Green Turtle Fire & Rescue, 365-4133, VHF 16
Guana Cay Fire and Rescue, 365-5121, VHF 16
Man-O-War Community Clinic, 365-6081
Man-O-War Emergency Fire and Rescue, contact Walter Sweeting-365-6015
Marsh Harbour Government Clinic, 367-2510
Marsh Harbour Fire Department, 367-2000
Marsh Harbour Med. Centre (Prvt. Clinic) - 367-0049
Abaco Family Medince, Marsh Harbour, (Private Clinic) - 367-2295
Auskell Clinic, Marsh Harbour, (private Clinic), emerg. 577-0113 reg 367-0020
Hope Town Government Clinic, 366-0108
Hope Town Fire and Rescue - **Call on VHF 16 first,**   366-0500

Dr. Raymond Heimbecker has been doing volunteer medical work in Abaco for over three decades and has been Honorary Out Island Surgeon in The Bahamas since 1996. Dr. Jane Garfield was the resident physician in Hope Town and Man-O-War Cay for several years and is now operating a clinic in Blue Hill, Maine. She visited Abaco in 2007 and updated this article. Justin Noice is a member of Hope Town Fire and Rescue and lives on Elbow Cay.

Marsh Harbour Classified Business Directory

EMERGENCY SERVICES
Marsh Harbour Police, 367-2560
Marsh Harbour Fire, 367-2000

AIR CONDITIONING
See Refrigeration/Sales and Repairs

AIRLINES AND CHARTERS
Abaco Air Ltd, Airport, AB-20492, 367-2266, 367-2205, fax 367-3256
Airgate Aviation, Airport 367-3636, Reservations 386-292-2222, info@flyairgate.com
American Eagle, Airport, AB-20259, 367-2231
Bahamas Express, 954 356-1540
Bahamasair, Airport, AB-20488, 367-2095, fax 367-2039
Bimini Island Air, 954 938-8991
Cherokee Air Ltd, Airport, AB-20485, 367-3450, fax 367-3451
Go Charter Air, 843 737-6234
Majors Air Services Ltd, Airport, 367-4826
Silver Air, Airport, 367-3415
Sky Limo Charter, 1 866-SKY-LIMO
Twin Air Calypso, 367-0140
Zig Zag, Airways, Airport Road, AB-20422, 367-2889

AIRPLANE SERVICE AND FUEL
Abaco Flight Services Ltd, Airport, AB-20492, 367-2205, fax 367-3256
Abaco Petroleum Co Ltd, School Lane, AB-20899 , 367-3953, fax 367-3954
Cherokee Aviation, Airport, AB 20486, 367-0525, fax 367-0526
Zig Zag Airways, Airport Road, AB-20422, 367-2889

APPLIANCES
Abaco Hardware Ltd, Don MacKay Blvd, AB-20577, 367-2170, fax 367-2928
Abaco Stereo, Don MacKay Blvd, AB-20577, 367-2265, fax 367-3043
Corner Value, Queen Elizabeth Dr, AB-20490, 367-2250, fax 367-3810
Marco , Don MacKay Blvd, AB-20521, 367-3186, fax 367-3469
Standard Hardware, Queen Elizabeth Dr, AB-20498, 367-2811, fax 367-2645

ARCHITECTS
AB Architects, Queen Elizabeth Dr, AB-20676, 367-4355
Cooper's Architect Services, Memorial Plaza, 367-2810
Key's Architectural Design, Dove Plaza , 367-4143
Ryan's Architect Consultant, Stratton Drive, AB-20579, 367-2001, fax 367-3001
Timothy Neil, RIBA , Marsh Harbour, AB-20006, 367-2076

ART GALLERIES
Blue Sky Gallery, Don MacKay Blvd., 367-0579
Don Wood, east of Memorial Plaza
Tim Higgs Photography, 367-2213

ATTORNEYS
Alexiou Knowles & Co, Stratton Drive, AB-20409, 367-2010, fax 367-2394
E. P. Toothe & Assoc., AB-20088, 367-3368, fax 367-3923
Callenders & Co., Dove Plaza, AB-20415, 367-2991, fax 367-3013
Frederik Gottlieb, Sands Corner, AB-20405, 367-3120, fax 367-3118
Michael A. Dean & Co., Don MacKay Blvd., AB 20377, 367-2611
Rhonda Hull, Don Mackey Blvd., 367-2030
Marvin Pinder, Queen Elizabeth Drive
V. M. Lightbourn & Co, Damianos Building, AB 20365, 367-0300, 367-0301

AUTOMOBILE PARTS, SERVICE AND REPAIRS
Abaco Starters, SC Bootle Highway, AB-20347, 367-4970
AID, Don MacKay Blvd, AB-20407, 367-2077, fax 367-3296
Bodie's Engine Repair, 367-2108
Davis Auto Repairs, Forest Drive, 367-3311
Epic Batteries, Queen Elizabeth Dr., 367-0064
General's Auto, Forest Drive, 367-2411
Getafix, Airport Road, 367-3166
K & S Auto Service, Don MacKay Blvd, AB-20520, 367-2655
Lou's Video, Bay Street, 367-2043
Marsh Harbour Auto Parts, Don Mackay Blvd, AB-20446, 367-2111

Marsh Harbour Service St, Don MacKay Blvd AB-20438, 367-2840
Pinder's Marine and Auto , Bay Street, 367-2274
Pinder's Auto Body & Paint, Marsh Harbour, 367-3121
Quality Star Auto Centre, Don McKay Blvd, 367-2979, fax 367-2977
Rainbow Paint and Body, Marsh Harbour, AB-20523, 367-4900, fax 367-3462
Shell Dundas Town, Dundas Town, AB-20726, 367-3883, fax 367-3882
TNT Service Station, SC Bootle Highway, AB-20437, 367-4970

AUTOMOBILE RENTALS & SALES
A & A Auto Sales, Don MacKay Blvd, AB-20484, 367-2022
A & A Car Rentals, AB-20463, 367-2148
A & P Auto Rentals, Don MacKay Blvd, AB-20520, 367-2655, fax 367-2464
Abaco Motor Mall, Don MacKay Blvd. 367-2916
Bargain Car Rental, AB 20976, Don MacKay Blvd., 367-0555
Covenant Car Rentals, Murphy Town, AB-20652, 367-4007
D's Minivan Rentals, AB-20655, 367-3980
Dolphin Auto Sales, Queen Elizabeth Drive, AB-20060, 367-4406, fax 367-3365
Flamingo Car Rentals, SC Bootle Highway, AB-20325, 367-4787
Reliable Car Rental, Abaco Towns, AB-20089, 367-4234
Rental Wheels, East Bay Street, 367-4643
SeaStar Car Rentals, Airport, AB-20467, 367-4887
Veronica's Car Rentals, AB-20463, 367-2725

BAKERIES
Da Best Yet Bakery,Don MacKay BLvd., 367-3616
Island Bakery , B & V Plaza, AB-20479, 367-2129
Java Coffee Shop, East Bay Street, 367-5523

BANKS
Bank of Nova Scotia, Abaco Shopping Ctr, AB-20567, 367-2142, fax 367-2565
First Caribbean, Don MacKay Blvd, AB-20402, 367-2166, fax 367-2156
Commonwealth Bank, Traffic Light, AB-20582, 367-2370, fax 367-2372
Royal Bank of Canada, Don MacKay Blvd, AB-20417, 367-2420, fax 367-2547

BARS/TAVERNS
Ambassador Motel, Dundas Town, , AB-20484, 367-2022, fax 367-2133
Angler's Pub, Boat Harbour, AB-20511, 367-2158
Curly Tails, East Bay Street, 367-4444
Bustick Bay Resort, SC Bootle Highway
Corner Restaurant & Bar, Christie St DT, AB-20112, 367-4346
Emerald's, Airport, 367-4973
Jib Room, Marsh Harbour, AB-20518, 367-2700
The Lazy Parrot, SC Bootle Highway,367-5331
Mangoes, East Bay Street, AB-20529, 367-2366
The Ranch, Don MacKay Blvd, AB-20446, 367-2733
Rum Runners Bar and Grill, Queen Elizabeth Drive next to Insurance Management
Sea Shells, Don McKay Blvd., 367-4460
Sid's Pub, Spring City, 367-7333
Snappas, Harbor View Marina,367-2278
Surf Side Club, Dundas Town, 367-2762
Wally's , East Bay Street, AB-20455, 367-2074

BEAUTY SALONS/BARBERS
Creations Barber Shop, Don Mackay Blvd, 367-4850,
Essence Beauty Shop, Queen Elizabeth Dr, 367-2386
Glamour Rama, Dundas Town, 367-3966,
Hair Affair, Dove Plaza, 367-2378
Island Image, Dundas Town, AB-20112, 367-3507
Laine's Kuts & Kurls, Memorial Plaza, 367-3623
Pretty Hands and Feet, Abaco Shopping Center, 367-0126
Rosalyn's Beauty Salon, Dundas Town, 367-2030
Snazzie's Beauty Salon, Pole Line Road, AB-20557, 367-4781
Special Touch - Unisex Salon, Abaco Shopping Center, 367-3977

BEVERAGES
Island Delight, AB-20585, 367-3384, fax 367-

3298

BICYCLE SALES, RENTAL
Rental Wheels, East Bay Street, AB-20871, 367-4643

BOAT ENGINE REPAIR
Abaco Alternators and Generators, Basil Whitmore, 458-0515
Abaco Marine Propeller, AB 20070, 367-4276, fax 367-4259
Bodie's Engine Repair, 242 554-9241
Gratitude Marine, 367-2480, cell 357-6659
Hartwell Russell, Caribbean Constr, AB-20403, 367-2502
Master Marine, Bay Street, 367-4760, cell 577-0232
Pinder's Marine and Auto , Bay Street, 367-2274

BOAT RENTALS AND CHARTERS
B & B Boat Rentals, 367-RENT
Blue Wave Boat Rentals, East Bay Street, 367-3910, fax 367-3911
CJ's Abaco Dorado Boat Rentals, Conch Inn Marina, 367-1035, fax 367-1036
Concept Boat Rentals, Conch Inn Complex, 242 367-5570
Moorings Yacht Charter, Conch Inn Complex, 367-4000, fax 367-4004
Rainbow Rentals, Bay Street, AB-20070, 367-4602, fax 367-4601,
Rich's Rentals, Harbour, AB-20419, 367-2742, fax 367-2682
Sail and Dive, *Dream Catcher*, 577-0867, www.SailandDive.net
Sea Horse Rentals, Boat Harbour Marina, 367-2513, fax 367-2516
See the Sea of Abaco, 375-8246

BOAT REPAIR AND STORAGE
Abaco Outboard Engines Ltd, Dundas Town, AB-20430, 367-2452, fax 367-2354
Marsh Harbour Boat Yard Storage and Lift, 367-5205
OutBoard Shop, Pelican Shores, AB-20419, 367-2703
Rich's Rentals, Harbour, AB-20419, 367-2742, fax 367-2682

BOOKS
Abaco Treasures, Don Mackay Blvd, AB-20523, 367-3460, fax 367-3462
Bellevue Business Depot, Don Mackay Blvd, AB-20823, 367-2701, fax 367-3654
Fruit of the Vine Christian Bookstore, Don MacKay Blvd, 367-3288

BUILDERS/ CONTRACTORS
Abaco Tug and Transport, Calcutta, 367-2933
Al Key , AB-20261, 367-2293
P. G. Archer, AB-20484, 367-2113
Bahamas Building Systems, 367-2848, fax 367-2708
Bahamas Hot Mix, Queen Elizabeth Drive, 367-2337, fax 367-2354
Caribbean Construction Ltd, Don MacKay Blvd, AB-20403, 367-2502
Caribbean Marine Construction, AB-20757, 367-4842
Coastline Construction, East Bay St., 367-0715
Drill Rig Dock / Boat Lifts, AB 20872, 367-4769, 367-2704
Duane Wells, 367-2821,366-0259
JFA Construction, 359-6994
LBT Marine, Ltd., PO Box AB 20127, 357-6532
Nixon Brothers Builders, Dundas Town, AB-20252, 367-2605
Pinder's Construction, AB-20061, 367-2063
Scandi Homes, Key Club Drive, AB-20277, 367-3241,
Bill Swain & Sons, B & L Plaza, AB-20546, 367-2120,
Williams Construction, Dundas Town, AB-20527, 367-4472,

BUILDING SUPPLIES
Abaco Block and Concrete, Murphy Town, 367-2891
Abaco Glass Co, Don MacKay Blvd, AB-20507, 367-2442
Abaco Hardware, Don MacKay Blvd, AB-20488, 367-2927, fax 367-2928
Caribbean Constructors, AB20403, 367-2502
Rock & Fill Ltd, Don MacKay Blvd, AB-20207, 367-3650, fax 367-2988
Standard Hardware, Queen Elizabeth Dr, AB-20498, 367-2660, fax 367-2645

BUS SERVICES
Enovah's Bus Service, Murphy Town to Ferry Dock
Great Abaco Express, Marsh Harbour to North Abaco, 367-2165

CARPENTERS/CABINET MAKERS
Bobby's Carpentry, Don MacKay Blvd., 367-0991, 367-2316, 475-1251
Donald Russell, 367-2436
Stewart Sands, 367-2328
Tim Duggan, 367-2631

CELL PHONES
See Telephones

CHILD CARE, PRE-SCHOOL AND KINDERGARTEN
Agape, MH Gospel Chapel, AB-20426, 367-4777
Early Learning Academy, Murphy Town, 367-3307
Grace Baptist, Forest Drive, AB-20048, 367-2926
New Direction, Dundas Town
Shjanea - Bethany Gospel, Murphy Town, 367-3608
Ms Stoodley, Government Sub, AB-20165, 367-2436

CHURCHES
AB Apostilic, Crockett Drive, 367-2082
Aldersgate Methodist, Don McKay Blvd, AB-20443, 367-2009, 367-2566,
1st Assembly of God, Stratton Drive, AB-20560, 367-2130
Bethany Gospel Chapel, Murphy Town, 367-4472
Bible Truth Hall, Pelican Shores, AB-20472, 367-2579
Calvary Baptist Church, Stratton Drive Area, 367-2105
Church of Christ, Don MacKay Blvd, 367-3381
Church of God, (MRF Bible), Dundas Town, 367-2740
Church of God of Prophecy, Dundas Town, 367-2071
Church of God of Prophecy, Forest Drive
Church of the Latter Rain, Dundas Town, 367-4557
Creole Gospel Chapel, Crockett Drive, 367-3784
Faith Chapel, Queen Elizabeth Dr, 367-2508
Friendship Tabernacle, Dundas Town, 367-4238
Grace Baptist Church, Forest Drive, AB-20048, 367-2926
Kingdom Hall (JW), Forest Drive
M. H. Gospel Chapel, Don MacKay Blvd, AB-20426, 367-2204
MRF Bible Movement, Dundas Town, 367-2605
New Vision Ministries, Abaco Shopping Ctr, AB-20183, 367-3242, fax 367-3474
Seventh Day Adventist, Queen Elizabeth Dr, 367-4501
Soul Saving Ministries, Forest Drive, 367-4497
St Andrews Methodist, Dundas Town, 367-4647
St Francis De Sales (RC), Don MacKay Blvd, 367-2714
St John the Baptist Anglican, Don MacKay Blvd, AB-20543, 367-2518
Trumpet Assemblies of God, Forest Drive, 367-2914
Zion Baptist, Murphy Town, 367-3563

CLOTHING
Adam & Eve, Flamingo Place, 367-5792
Alexis Fashion, Queen Elizabeth Dr, AB-20484, 367-2241
Bahamas Outfitters, East Bay Street, 367-3312
The Clothesline, Simmons Place, 367-0105
Corner Value, Queen Elizabeth Dr, AB-20490, 367-2250
Dishy, Just Us Girls, Queen Elizabeth Drive
Gashea's Handbags & Accs, Hudson Building, 367-2828
His & Her Jeans, Abaco Shopping Ctr, AB-20539, 367-2011
Iggy Biggy, East Bay Street, AB-20121, 367-3596

Marsh Harbour Classified Business Directory (cont.)

Island Girl Boutique, East Bay Street, 367-0283
Kaleb's, Don MacKay Blvd., 367-6548
Kara's Fashions, Don MacKay Bld, AB-20546, 367-2195
Mangoes Boutique, East Bay Street, AB-20529, 367-2366
Mr Mister, Airport Roundabout, AB-20657, 367-4308
Sand Dollar Shop, East Bay Street, AB-20473, 367-4405
Sports World, 367-4693
Step-N-Style, Hudson Building, AB-20720, 367-4041
Victor's, Don MacKay Blvd, AB-20388, 367-3853
Vyrona's Health & Variety, Queen Elizabeth Dr, AB-20597, 367-3002
Wally's Boutique, East Bay Street, AB-20455, 367-2074

COMPUTER SALES AND SERVICE
Abacom Computer Service, D & S Shopping Ctr, AB-20078, 367-3475, fax 367-3771
Computer Creations, Don MacKay Blvd, 367-2004
Epyon Technologies, Don MacKay Blvd., 367-1329
Intelligent Tchnology Solutions, 357-6529
(See also INTERNET SERVICES)

CRAFT SUPPLIES, FABRICS
Home Fabrics, Don MacKay Blvd., AB20036, 367-6003

CUSTOMS AGENTS, BROKERS
Arawak Agency, Bay Street, AB-20485, 367-2089, fax 367-2530
Frederick's Agency, Queen Elizabeth Dr, AB-20468, 367-2333, fax 367-3136
Trinity Customs Brokers, Queen Elizabeth Drive, AB-20253, 367-4297

DELIVERY, COURIER SERVICES
Abaco Express, Cherokee Air at Airport, 367-3450
FedEx, Don MacKay Blvd., 367-4339
Frederick's Agency (UPS), Queen Elizabeth Dr, AB-20468, 367-2333, fax 367-3136
GWS Worldwide Exp, Abaco Shopping Ctr, AB-20552, 367-2722, fax 367-3207
Locair, air cargo, Ft.L., 954 767-6007

DENTISTS
Agape Dental Centre, Don MacKay Blvd., AB-20676, 367-4355
Diamante Dental, Queen Elizabeth Dr, AB-20579, 367-4968
Greater Abaco Dental Clinic, Don MacKay Blvd, AB-20288, 367-4070

DIVING
Abaco Dive Adventures, 367-2213
Bahamas Underground, 359-6128
Dive Abaco, Conch Inn Marina, AB-20555, 367-2787, fax 367-4779

DRUG STORES, PHARMACIES
Chemist Shoppe, D & S Shopping Ctr, AB-20459, 367-3106
Island Pharmacy, 367-2544
(See also Supermarkets)

ELECTRICIANS, ELECTRICAL SUPPLIES
Edwards Electric, Queen Elizabeth Dr, AB-20590, 367-2314
Ellis Stuart, Bay & Maxwell, AB-20053, 367-3790
J & J Electric, AB-20413, 367-5145
Key's Electric, Dove Plaza, AB-20458, 367-2640

ELECTRONICS, REPAIRS AND SALES
Abaco Stereo, Don MacKay Blvd, AB-20577, 367-2265, fax 367-3043
Avtech, Don MacKay Blvd, 367-4262, fax 367-4262
Doug's Place, D & S Shopping Ctr, AB-20310, 367-2672
Electronics Service Centre, Queen Elizabeth Dr, AB-20421, 367-2830
Marsh Harbour Electronics & Satellite Limited, Abaco Shopping Center, AB-20265, 367-2894, fax 367-3538
Sight & Sound Electronics, Abaco Shopping Ctr, AB-20183, 367-3242, fax 367-3474
Super Beeper, 367-4345

ENGINEERING
Islands by Design, Keith Bishop, 242 304-5544

EXTERMINATORS
The Bug Reaper, Marsh Harbour, AB-20919, 367-4202
The Exterminators, Marsh Harbour, AB-20185, 367-3021
Revie's Pest Control, Abaco Shopping Ctr., 367-6475, 359-6475

FARMS
Abaco Big Bird Farm, Abaco Highway, AB-20435, 367-4540, fax 367-7004
Bahama Palm, Abaco Highway
Bahama Neem, Abaco Highway, 367-4117
Harmon Farms, Abaco Highway
Rocky Farms, Cherokee Road

FERRIES
Albury's Ferry Service, Crossing Beach, 367-3147

FISH, RETAIL & WHOLESALE
Long's Landing Seafoods, Bay & William, 367-3079
MH Exporters & Importers, Harbour, AB-20585, 367-2697, fax 367-3937
Star Lite Sea Food, Dundas Town, 367-2384

FISHING GUIDES
Crestwell Archer, Conch Inn Marina, 367-2775
Fish Abaco (Ira Russell), 367-3419
Pinder, Chris & Buddy , Marsh Harbour, AB-20303, 367-2234, 366-2163
Jay Sawyer, Marsh Harbour, 367-2089
Terrance Davis, Dundas Town, AB-20227, 367-4464
Tom Albury, OnDaFly (bonefish and light tackle), 366-3141 / 477-5243

FISHING TACKLE
Abaco Hardware, Don MacKay Blvd, AB-20488, 367-2927, fax 367-2928
Island Boy Tackle and Marine, East Bay Street (above Jamie's Place), 367-3228, VHF 16
National Marine, Don MacKay Blvd, AB-20535, 367-2326, fax 367-2326
Standard Hardware, Queen Elizabeth Dr, AB-20498, 367-2660, fax 367-2645

FLORISTS
See Nurseries/Florists

FUEL, AUTOMOBILE
K & S Auto Service, Don MacKay Blvd, AB-20520, 367-2655
Marsh Harbour Auto Parts, Don MacKay Blvd, AB-20446, 367-2111
Quality Star Auto Centre, Don MacKay Blvd, 367-2979, fax 367-2977
Shell (MH)Service Station , Don MacKay Blvd, AB-20438, 367-2840
Shell (DT) Service Station, Royal Plaza DT, 367-3883
Texaco, Don Mackey Blvd., 367-2979
TNT Service Station, SC Bootle Highway, AB-20347, 367-4970

FUEL, BOAT
Boat Harbour Marina, Boat Harbour, AB-20511, 367-2736, fax 367-2979
Conch Inn Marina, East Bay Street, AB-20434, 367-4000, fax 367-4004
Harbour View Marina, East Bay Street, AB-20457, 367-2175
Marsh Harbour Marina, Pelican Shores, AB-20518, 367-2700, fax 367-2033

FURNITURE
Furniture Gallery, 367-0521
Furniture Plus, Maxwell's Plaza, 367-7287, fax 367-1237
Indie Furniture, Queen Elizabeth Dr., 367-0521
Palm Cottage, Don MacKay Blvd., 367-2300
Wood You, Don MacKay Blvd., 367-9663

GIFT SHOPS
Abaco Gold, East Bay Street, AB-20473, 367-4405, fax 367-4404
Abaco Treasures, Don MacKay Blvd, AB-20523, 367-3460, fax 367-3462
B's Sunrise, Bay Street, 367-4822
Bahamas Outfitters, East Bay Street, 367-3312
Brass & Leather Shop, Abaco Shopping Ctr, AB-20382, 367-3643
Buds and Blooms, Memorial Plaza, 367-2837
Conch Pearl Gallery, East Bay St., 367-0137
Iggy Biggy, East Bay Street, AB-20121, 367-3596
Island Petals, Abaco Shopping Ctr., 367-2260
Java Coffee Shop, East Bay Street, 367-5523
John Bull, East Bay Street, AB-20529, 367-2473, fax 367-2954
Passion Flower, Don MacKay Blvd., 367-3166
Pine Woods Nursery, Don MacKay Blvd, AB-

20422, 367-2674, fax 367-4755
Sunset Souvenirs, East Bay Street, AB-20404, 367-2658

GROCERY STORES / SUPERMARKETS
Abaco Groceries,Don MacKay Blvd,367-0278
Maxwell's Supermarket, Nathan Key Drive, 367-2601/2, fax 367-2731
M&R Grocery, Crockett Drive, 367-5196
Price Right / Save A Lot, Stratton Drive, 367-7283
Sea Shore Meats and Sea Food, Dundas Town Road, 367-5149

GROCERY CONVENIENCE STORES (EXTENDED HOURS)
A & A Food Store, Crockett Drive, 367-4521
Abaco Saver's Mart, Don MacKay Blvd
Bahamas Family Market,Traffic Light,AB-20423, 367-3714
Brown Bay Food Store, Dundas Town
Cash & Carry, Murphy Town
Central Convenience Store, Forest Drive, 367-4290
Mannie's Convenience St, Murphy Town
Muriel's Food Store, Murphy Town
Roderick's Convenience St, Crockett Drive, 367-3237
Shell Shop, Royal Plaza DT, AB-20726, 367-3883, fax 367-3882
Texaco, Don Mackey Blvd., 367-2979

HAIR SALONS
See Beauty Salons

HARDWARE AND PAINT
Abaco Ace Hardware, Don MacKay Blvd, AB-20488, 367-2927, 367-2170, fax 367-2928
AID, Don MacKay Blvd, AB-20407, 367-2077, fax 367-3296
Brand Parts, Queen Elizabeth Dr, AB-20306, 367-4185
Standard Hardware, Queen Elizabeth Dr, AB-20498, 367-2660, fax 367-2645
The Paint Place, Don MacKay Blvd., 367-2271

HOTELS, RESORTS, MOTELS AND GUEST HOUSES
Abaco Beach Hotel & Resort, Boat Harbour, AB-20669, 367-2158, fax 367-2819
Ambassador Motel, Crockett Drive, AB-20484, 367-2022, fax 367-2113
Bustick Bay Resort, S C Bootle Hwy., 367-3980
Conch Inn Resort, East Bay Street, AB-20434, 367-2800, fax 367-4004
D's Guest House, Crockett Drive, 367-3980
Island Breezes Motel, East Bay Street, AB-20036, 367-3776, fax 367-4179
Lofty Fig Villas, East Bay Street, AB-20437, 367-2681
Mermaid Reef Villas, Pelican Shores, 367-0518
Pelican Beach Villas, Pelican Shores, AB-20304, 367-3600

HOUSE/APARTMENT RENTALS
Abaco Real Estate, Stratton Drive, AB-20404, 367-2719, fax 367-2359
Regattas, East Bay Street, AB-20486, 367-2227, fax 367-3927
Bahamas Realty, East Bay Street, AB-20856, 367-3262, fax 367-3260
Great Abaco Club, 367-4151

HOUSEHOLD ITEMS
Abaco Ace Hardware, Don MacKay Blvd, AB-20488, 367-2927, 367-2170, fax 367-2928
AID, Don MacKay Blvd, AB-20407, 367-2077, fax 367-3296
Bed, Bath & Between, at traffic light, AB 20487, 367-0555
Corner Value, Queen Elizabeth Drive, AB 20490, 367-2250, fax 367-3810
Standard Hardware, Queen Elizabeth Dr, AB-20498, 367-2660, fax 367-2645

ICE
Abaco Choice, Don MacKay Blvd, AB-20757, 367-4842, fax 367-4841
Abaco Ice, East Bay Street, AB-20585, 367-3384, fax 367-3298
Boat Harbour Marina, Boat Harbour, AB-20511, 367-2736, fax 367-2979
Conch Inn Marina, East Bay Street, AB-20434, 367-2800
Harbour View Marina, East Bay Street, AB-20457, 367-2175
Marsh Harbour Marina, Pelican Shores, AB-20518, 367-2700, fax 367-2033
Standard Hardware,Queen Elizabeth Drive, 367-2660
(Also at all Liquor Stores)

INSURANCE
Abaco Insurance Agency, Stratton Drive, AB-20404, 367-2549, fax 367-3075
Family Guardian, B & L Plaza, AB-20901, 367-

3264, fax 367-3265
Imperial Life of Canada, Flamingo Plaza, AB-20471, 367-3432, fax 367-3299
Insurance Management Ltd, Queen Elizabeth Dr, AB-20666, 367-4204, fax 367-4206
J.S. Johnson Ltd, Dove Plaza, AB-20521, 367-2688, fax 367-3083
Nassau Underwriters Agency, Queen Elizabeth Dr, AB-20471, 367-2222, fax 367-2888
Star Insurance, Hudson Building, 367-3418, fax 367-4086
Van Stratton Insurance Agency, Queen Elizabeth Drive, 367-2222

INTERNET SERVICES
Bahamas WIMAX, 367-3717
Out Island InterNet, Queen Elizabeth Dr, AB-20991, 367-3006, 367-3007

INTERIOR DESIGN
Commercial Interior Design, Traffic Light, AB-20737, 367-2031

JANITORIAL SERVICES
C & P Janitorial, Little Orchard, AB-20460, 367-2814

JEWELERY
Abaco Gold, East Bay Street, AB-20473, 367-4405, fax 367-4404
Abaco Treasures, Don MacKay Blvd, AB-20523, 367-3460, fax 367-3462
John Bull, East Bay Street, AB-20084, 367-2473, fax 367-2954
Simcoe Jewellers, Memorial Plaza

JUSTICE OF THE PEACE
Elaine Thompson, 367-2719

LAUNDRIES, CLEANERS AND LAUNDROMATS
Classic Coin Wash, Stratton Drive, AB-20453, 367-2750
Express Dry Cleaner, Forest Drive, 367-4012
Harbour View Marina, East Bay Street, AB-20457, 367-2175
367-2163, fax 367-3388
Viola's Laundrymat, Johnson St DT

LIQUOR STORES
A & K Liquor Store, Queen Elizabeth Dr, AB-20565, 367-2179
Archer Brothers, Crockett Drive, AB-20484, 367-2022
Bristol Wines & Spirits,Queen Elizabeth Drive, 367-2180, fax 367-5241
Burns House #1, Don MacKay Blvd, AB-20444, 367-2135, fax 367-2151
Burns House #3, Queen Elizabeth Dr, AB-20444, 367-2172
Tupp's, East Bay Street, 367-2936
Valacq Liquors, Don McKay, Airport Rd.,367-4460

MARINAS
Boat Harbour Marina, Boat Harbour, AB-20511, 367-2158, fax 367-2819
Conch Inn Marina, East Bay Street, AB-20469, 367-4000, fax 367-4004
Harbour View Marina, East Bay Street, AB-20457, 367-2182
Mangoes, East Bay Street, 367-4255, fax 367-2519
Marsh Harbour Marina, Pelican Shores, 367-2700, fax 367-2033

MARINE STORES
Abaco Ace Hardware, Don MacKay Blvd, AB-20488, 367-2927, fax 367-2928
Abaco Marine Props, Dundas Town Road, 367-4276
Marsh Harbour Boat Yard, Calcutta, 367-5205
National Marine, Queen Elizabeth Dr., AB-20535, 367-2326, fax 367-2326
Standard Hardware, Queen Elizabeth Dr, AB-20498, 367-2660, fax 367-2645

NEWSPAPERS, MAGAZINES
Abaconian, Dove Plaza, AB-20213, 367-3200, Fax 367-3677
Destination Abaco, Abaco Shopping Ctr.

NURSERIES, FLORISTS
Buds & Blooms, Memorial Plaza, AB-20438, 367-2837, fax 367-4887
Island Petals, Abaco Shopping Ctr.,367-2260
Passion Flower, Don MacKay Blvd., 367-3166
Pine Woods Nursery, Don MacKay Blvd, AB-20422, 367-2674, fax 367-4755
Tropical Farm Nursery, Rear Abaco Whsle, 367-2783
Wonderland Gardens, 367-6663

OFFICE SUPPLIES & STATIONERY
Bellevue Business Depot, Don MacKay Blvd, AB-20823, 367-3915, 367-2701, fax 367-3914

Marsh Harbour Classified Business Directory (cont.)

OPTICAL

Abaco Optical Services, Lowe's Shopping Ctr, AB-20091, 367-3546

OUTBOARD MOTOR SALES AND SERVICE

Abaco Outboard (Yamaha), Dundas Town, AB-20430, 367-2452, fax 367-2354
Master Marine (Honda), Bay St., AB-20229, 367-4760, cell 577-0232 mastermarine242@gmail.com
National Marine (Mercury), Queen Elizabeth Drive, AB-20535, 367-2326, cell 577-0232
Outboard Shop (Evinrude/Johnson), Pelican Shores, AB-20098, 367-2703, fax 367-3709

PAINTING

Midway Painting Contractors, Government Sub, AB-20622, 367-3849
The Paint Place, Don MacKay Blvd., 367-2271

PARTY SUPPLIES

Party Time, Queen Elizabeth Dr, AB-20025, 367-2785

PETROLEUM DISTRIBUTORS

Abaco Petroleum Co Ltd, Don MacKay Blvd., AB-20899, 367-2951, fax 367-3271
Shell Bahamas Ltd, Murphy Town, AB-20508, 367-2253, fax 367-4188
Tropical Petroleum Distr, Murphy Town, AB-20247, 367-4929

PETS & PET SUPPLIES

Caribbean Veterinary Centre, Don MacKay Blvd., 367-3551
Community Animal Hospital, Don MacKay Blvd, 367-3647
Island Vet, Don Mackey Blvd., 367-0062
Pine Woods Nursery, Don MacKay Blvd, AB-20095, 367-2674, fax 367-4755

PHOTOGRAHY

Kevin Carroll, 367-3707, 477-6200
Snap Shop, D & S Shopping Ctr, AB-20459, 367-3020

PHYSICIANS, CLINICS

Abaco Auskell Advanced Medical Clinic, Queen Elizabeth Dr., 367-0020, auskellmedical@yahoo.com
Abaco Family Medicine, Lowe's Shopping Ctr, 367-2295
Abaco Medi Center, Dr. Latesha McIntosh, Queen Elizabeth Drive, 367-9999, emergency 577-9999
Dr. Hull (MD), Memorial Plaza, AB21056, 367-0050
Integrated Medical Centre, Dr. George Charite, 911 Dove Plaza, Don MackKay, Blvd., 367-1304, emergency 458-1234
Kidney Centre, Don Mackay Boulevard
Dr. William Koch, Chiropractor, 367-2584
Marsh Harbour Government Clinic, Don MacKay Blvd, 367-2510
Marsh Harbour Medical Centre, 367-0049

PLUMBERS

Clifford Henfield, Dundas Town
Pinders Plumbing, Key Club Road, 367-2598
Twins Plumbing, Dundas Town, 367-3456
Whymns Plumbing Co, Dundas Town, 367-4759

PRINTING

Abaco Custom Signs, Stratton Drive, AB-20404, 367-3081, fax 367-3075
Abaco Print Shop, Abaco Shopping Ctr, AB-20551, 367-3202
Out Island Printing, Dove Plaza, Ste. 103, 367-0780

PROPANE GAS

Abaco Gas Co, Corner Value Store, AB-20490, 367-2250, fax 367-3810

RADIO STATIONS AND BROADCAST COMPANIES

Radio Abaco, Dundas Town, 367-2935, fax 367-4242
ZNS, Loyalist Centre, 367-4044, fax 367-4025
100 Jamz

REAL ESTATE SALES

Abaco Cays Real Estate, Faron Sawyer, 367-3450
Abaco Real Estate Agency, Queen Elizabeth Dr., AB-20404, 367-2719, fax 367-2359
Abaco Realtors, Marsh Harbour, AB-20496, 367-7248, fax 367-7248
Adler Realty, Perry Thomas, 367-3231
Aisle of Palm Realty, 367-0080
Anco Lands, 242 342-1476

Bahamas Realty, East Bay Street, AB-20856, 367-3262, fax 367-3260
Coldwell Banker, Queen Elizabeth Drive, 367-2992
Damianos Sotheby's, East Bay, 367-5046
Dupuch Real Estate, AB 20340, 367-0288
Fred Kanitsch & Assoc., MH Boatyard, 367-2013
Graham Real Estate, 367-0100
H G Christie Ltd, AB-20777, 367-5454, fax 367-4885
Island Properties Bahamas, James & Donna Rees, East Bay / Schooner Bay, 366-2048, cell 458-6822
Land and Sea Realty, 367-4962
Living Easy, Memorial Plaza, 367-2202
Mosko Realty, Ltd., AB-20473 367-3420
Paradise Real Estate, 367-7653
Sea Grape Realty, Queen Elizabeth Dr, AB-20123, 367-2749, fax 367-2748

REFRIGERATION SALES & REPAIRS

Arctic Breeze, Don MacKay Blvd, AB-20559, 367-2458
Burrow's Air Conditioning & Refrigeration, 367-0652, 577-6313
Darville, Henry, 359-6012
K & W Refrigeration, Off Don MacKay, AB-20454, 367-4949, fax 367-4949
Marco Air Conditioning, Don MacKay Blvd, AB-20192, 367-3186, fax 367-3469
Nixon, Shawn, 367-5219, 577-6951
TropicKool, AB 20251, 3 Sawyers Market Building, 367-5717, 475-8000

RESTAURANTS, TAKE AWAYS AND SNACKS

Abaco Snacks, Don MacKay Blvd.
Abaco Souse House, Queen Elizabeth Drive, near port, 551-7094
Airport Restaurant, Airport, 367-4973
Ambassador Inn, Crockett Drive, AB-20484, 367-2022, fax 367-2113
Angler's Restaurant, Boat Harbour Marina, AB-20511, 367-2158
Arnold's Poinciana T-A, Dundas Town, 367-2517
Back Street Cafe and Catering, Dundas Town, 367-2782
Bay View, Dundas Town, AB-20029, 367-3738 (take-away only)
Beijing Bistro, Don MacKay Blvd., 367-3663 Chat and Chill, Dundas Town
Conch Crawl, East Bay Street, 367-4444
Curly Tails, East Bay Street at Conch Inn Marina, 367-4444
Dis We Style Take Out, Crockett Drive, 367-4244
Early Bird Breakfast Cafe, #8 Colina Building, 367-5310
Geno's, Abaco Shopping Center, 367-7272
God Bless Church Chicken, Front Street, Dundas Town, 367-3162
Golden Grouper, Dove Plaza, AB-20557, 367-2301
Island Family Restaurant, Abaco Shopping Center, 367-3778
Jamie's Place, East Bay Street, 367-2880
Java Coffee Shop, East Bay Street, 367-5523
Jib Room, Pelican Shores, AB-20518, 367-2700
Julie's Snack Shop, Dundas Town
KFC, Abaco Shopping Ctr, 367-2615, fax 367-2953
L & T Take Away, Dundas Town
Living Easy, Memorial Plaza
Mangoes, East Bay Street, AB-20529, 367-2626, fax 367-3336

Mother Merle's Fishnet, Dundas Town, AB-20476, 367-2770
Pop's Place, 367-3796
Snack Shack, East Bay Street, 367-4005
Shany's Take-Out, Dundas Town next to Platinum Car Wash, 367-0775 or 458-4698
Snappas, Harborview Marina, 367-2278
Veronica's Take-Away, Murphy Town, 367-3380
Wally's , East Bay Street, AB-20455, 367-2074, fax 367-3073

SAILBOAT CHARTERS

Cruise Abaco, Lubbers Quarters, 577-0148
Moorings, Conch Inn Marina, AB-20469, 367-4000, fax 367-4004
See the Sea of Abaco, 375-8246

SCHOOLS

Abaco Academy, Queen Elizabeth Dr, AB-20533, 367-3484
Abaco Central Secondary, Forest Drive, AB-20425, 367-2334, fax 367-3997
Agape Christian, Gospel Chapel Road, AB-20210, 367-4777, fax 367-3020
Central Abaco Primary, Forest Drive, 367-2718
Every child Counts, 367-2505
Forest Heights Academy, Don MacKay Blvd, AB-20096, 367-3539
Long Bay School, Forest Drive, AB-20377, 367-2436
St Francis de Sales, Don MacKay Blvd, 367-4399
Wesley College, Don MacKay Blvd, AB-20443, 367-2009, fax 367-2566

SECURITY SYSTEMS & SERVICES

Abaco Alarm Systems, AB-20757, 367-4841

SEPTIC TANK/SANITATION

Abaco Sanitation Service, Don MacKay Blvd, 367-4422
Lou's Tank Service, East Bay Street, 367-2043

SHIPPING / FREIGHT COMPANIES

Abaco Shipping Co, Traffic Light, AB-20737, 367-2091, fax 367-2235
Dean's Shipping Company, East of Port, M.V. *Legacy*, 367-2653, fax 367-5642
Tropical Shipping, 367-0225, fax 367-2645
See page 206 for complete shipping and freight information.

SHOES

Abaco Shoe Gallery, D &S Plaza
Brass & Leather Shop, Abaco Shopping Ctr, AB-20382, 367-3643

SIGNS, ETC

Abaco Custom Signs, 367-3081
Three D's Custom Signs, Don MacKay Blvd, 367-SIGN

STORAGE

Abaco Spaces, Don MacKay Blvd, 367-2414
Tropical Self Storage, Key Club Road, 365-6407, fax 365-6407

STRAWWORK

Sunset Straw & Souvenir, East Bay Street, AB-20404, 367-2658

SUNDRIES AND NOTIONS

Abaco Price Slashers, Dove Plaza, 367-4432
Chemist Shoppe, D & S Shopping Center, Don MacKay Blvd., 367-3106
Classic Beauty Supplies, Loyalist Centre, 367-4221
Evergreen Beauty Supplies, Queen Elizabeth Dr, 367-4856
Nix & Naxs, Abaco Shopping Ctr, AB-20194, 367-3085

SURVEYORS

Lucayan Surveying Co, Memorial Plaza, AB-20123, 367-2749, fax 367-2748
Riviere & Associates, Don Mackay Blvd, AB-20188, 367-4585, fax 367-3091

TELEPHONES

Bahamas Telecommunications Corp. (BTC), Marsh Harbour, 3672200, 367-3399
Island Care Wireless, Don Mackay Blvd. near traffic light, 367-0429
Island Cellular, Don MacKay Blvd., 367-5997

TILES

Abaco Ace Hardware, DonMackay Blvd., 367-2927
Light Impressions, Abaco Shopping Ctr, AB-20183, 367-3242, fax 367-3474
Standard Hardware, 367-2660

TOURS

Friends of the Environment, AB 20755, 367-2721
Glenda Knowles, 367-2165, 646-7072, greatabacoexpress@yahoo.com
contact dive shops

TRAVEL AGENCIES

A & W Travel, Abaco Shopping Ctr, AB-20521, 367-2806, fax 367-3219
Travel Spot, B & V Plaza, AB-20504, 367-2817, fax 367-3018
Trinity Travel & Tour, Hudson Building, 367-2606, fax 367-2607

TRUCKING

Abaco Trucking, AB-20207, 367-3650, fax 367-2988
Albury's Trucking, Key Club Road, AB-20068, 367-2976, fax 367-3930
E & D Trucking, AB-20597, 367-2480
Jerry's Trucking, Dundas Town, 367-2457

UPHOLSTERY/MARINE

Abaco Awning & Marine Up, Hudson Building, 367-4846
AC Upholstery, Dundas Town, AB-20463, 367-2292
David Williams
Island Upholstery, Kayla Gates, 367-4550

VETERINARIANS/PET SUPPLIES

Caribbean Veterinary Health and Healing Centre, Abaco Shopping Center, Don MacKay Blvd., Dr. Owen Hanna, 367-3551
Community Animal Hospital, Don MacKay Blvd., 367-3847
Island Veterinary Clinic, Don MacKay Blvd., 367-0062
Derrick Bailey, DVM, 367-0002, 577-0397
Pine Woods Nursery, Don MacKay Blvd., AB 20095, 367-2674, fax 367-4755

WASTE DISPOSAL

E & D Waste Service, Crockett Drive, AB-20064, 367-2784

WATER, BOTTLED

Abaco Water Systems Ltd, AB-20135, 367-3344
Chelsea's Choice, Don MacKay Blvd, AB-20757, 367-4842, fax 367-4841

WELDING

Abaco Marine Props, Don MacKay Blvd, 367-4276, fax 367-4259
CJ's Welding, AB-20540, 367-4011, fax 367-4018
Hartwell Russell, Caribbean Constr, AB-20403, 367-2502

Friends of the Environment

Membership open to all!
Please contact via tel: (242) 367-2721
E-mail: info@friendsoftheenvironment.org
Web Site: www.friendsoftheenvironment.org

Manjack Key from SW

Hope Town Classified Business Directory

AIR CONDITIONING
Richard Cook "Down Below" VHF 16, 577-0662
Rick Thompson, 366-0262
Shawn Thompson, VHF 16, 366-0880

ARTISTS / ART GALLERIES
Abaco Inn, White Sound, 366-0133
Da Crazy Crab, Bay Street, 366-0537
Ebb Tide, Back Street, 366-0088
Edith's Straw Shop, Back Street
Hope Town Harbour Lodge, 366-0095
Hummingbird Gallery, Back Street
Iggy Biggy, Bay Street, 366-0354
Sea Spray Marina, White Sound, 366-0065
Wyannie Malone Museum, Back Street

BAKED GOODS
Harbour View Grocery (bread), Bay Street, 366-0033
Hope Town Coffee House, Bay St., 366-0760
LVA Convenience Store, 366-0056
The Food Store, White Sound, 366-0391
Vernon's Grocery, Back Street, 366-0037

BANK
First Caribbean Bank, Fig Tree Lane (Tuesdays only), 366-0296

BARS/TAVERNS
Abaco Inn, White Sound, 366-0133
Cap'n Jack's, Bay Street, 366-0247
Firefly, Centerline Road, 366-0145
Garbonzo Reef Bar, Sea Spray Marina, White Sound, 366-0569
Harbour's Edge, 366-0087 / 366-0292
Hope Town Harbour Lodge, 366-0095
On Da Beach, Turtle Hill, 366-0558
Wine Down Sip Sip, Back Street, 366-0399

BEAUTY SALON/BARBER
The Chopping Block, Russel's Lane, 366-0052

BICYCLE RENTALS
Jack's Bikes, White Sound, 366-0635
Sun-Dried T's, Queen's Hwy., 366-0616

BOAT BUILDING / REPAIR
Classic Marine, White Sound, 366-0106
Great Harbour Boat Restoration, 366-0256
Winer Malone (wood only), Back Street

BOAT RENTALS AND CHARTERS
Captain Plug's Adventures, 366-0023, 577-0273, 366-0554
Cat's Paw Boat Rentals, 366-0380
Cruise Abaco, Lubbers Quarters, 577-0148
Island Marine, Parrot Cay, 366-0282
Maine Cat Bahamas, 1 888-832-CATS
Sea Horse Marine, Back Creek, 367-2513

BOAT STORAGE
Hope Town Marina (wet), 366-0003
Lighthouse Marina (wet/dry), 366-0154

BOOKS
Abaco Inn, White Sound, 366-0133
Ebb Tide, Back Street, 366-0088
Hope Town Harbour Lodge, 366-0095, fax 366-0286
Kemp's Souvenir Center, Back Street, 366-0423
Lighthouse Marina, 366-0154
Sea Spray Marina, White Sound, 366-0065
Vernon's Grocery, Back Street, 366-0037
Wyannie Malone Museum

BUILDERS / CONTRACTORS
Abaco Rock, 366-0168, 375-8168
Andrew Russell
Damien Cole
Greg Russell
Malone's Construction, 366-0617
Mark Malone (True Cuts)
Pat McCully Construction, 366-0309
Ronnie Sands, 366-0657
Stephen Moss, 366-0695

BUILDING MATERIALS
Abaco Rock, 366-0228
Imports Unlimited, White Sound, 366-0136

CARPENTRY / BUILDING REPAIR
Bill Fuller (cabinetry), White Sound, 366-0116
Inside/Outside (Marty Cash), 366-0122
Donnie Maura, 366-0042

CHURCHES
Assembly of God, Cemetery Road
Lighthouse Ministries, White Sound
St. Francis de Sales (Roman Catholic) Marsh Harbour
St. James Methodist, Back Street

CLINIC
Hope Town Clinic, 366-0108

CLOTHING
Abaco Inn, White Sound, 366-0133
Da Crazy Crab, Bay Street, 366-0537
Ebb Tide, Back Street, 366-0088
El Mercado, Back Street, 366-0053
Iggy Biggy, Bay Street, 366-0354
Sea Spray Marina, White Sound, 366-0065
Sun Dried Ts, Queens Hwy., 366-0616

COFFEE ROASTERS
Hope Town Coffee House, Bay St., 366-0760

DIVING
Froggies, Queen's Highway, 366-0431

ELECTRICIANS
Richard Cook "Down Below" VHF 16, 577-0662
Shawn Thompson and Bryan Roberts, 366-0880

ENGINE REPAIR
Tom Cat Enterprises, White Sound, 366-0135

FERRY
Albury's Ferry Service, 367-3147

FISH - RETAIL
Down Deep, some Fridays, Post Office Dock

FISHING GUIDES / CHARTERS
Captain Plug's Adventures, 366-0023, 577-0273, 366-0554
Ira Key, *A Salt Weapon*, 366-0245
Justin Russell, *Local Boy*, 366-0528
Maitland Lowe (bonefishing), 366-0234
Robert Lowe, *Sea Gull* Nigh Crk, 366-0266, VHF 16
Tom Albury, *OnDaFly* (bonefish and light tackle), 366-3141 / 477-5243
Truman Major, *Lucky Strike*, Hurricane Hole, 366-0101

FISHING TACKLE
Lighthouse Marina, 366-0154

FLORAL DESIGN
Bonnie Hall, Back Street, 366-0058

FUEL - AUTOMOBILE
Sea Spray Marina, White Sound, 366-0065

FUEL - BOAT (GAS AND DIESEL)
Lighthouse Marina, 366-0154
Sea Spray Marina, White Sound, 366-0065

GIFT SHOPS
Abaco Inn, White Sound, 366-0133
Da Crazy Crab, Bay Street, 366-0537
Ebb Tide, Back Street, 366-0088
Edith's Straw Shop, Back Street
El Mercado, Back Street, 366-0053
Hope Town Harbour Lodge, 366-0095
Iggy Biggy, Bay Street, 366-0354
Sea Spray Marina, White Sound, 366-0065
Wyannie Malone Museum

GOLF CART RENTAL
Elbow Cay Cart Rentals, 366-0530
Hope Town Cart Rentals, 366-0064
Island Cart Rentals, 366-0448
JR's Cart Rentals, 366-0361
T & N Cart Rentals, 366-0069

GOVERNMENT
Hope Town District Council, 366-0600
Post Office, 366-0098

GROCERY STORES
Harbour View Grocery, Bay Street, 366-0033
LVA Convenience Store, White Sound Road, 366-0056
The Food Store, White Sound Road, 366-0391
Vernon's Grocery, Back Street, 366-0037

HARDWARE
Imports Unlimited, Centerline Road, White Sound, 366-0136
Lighthouse Marina, 366-0154

HOTELS / RESORTS
Abaco Inn, White Sound, 366-0133
Hope Town Harbour Lodge, 366-0095, fax 366-0286
Hope Town Inn and Marina, 366-0003
Sea Spray Marina, White Sound, 366-0065
Turtle Hill Resort, Queen's Highway, voice/fax 366-0557

HOUSE / APT. RENTALS
Elbow Cay Properties, Bay Street, 366-0569
Hope Town Hideaways, Fax/Phone 366-0224
Hope Town Villas, 366-0030, fax 366-0377
Island View Properties
Parrot Cay Cottages, Parrot Cay, 366-0282,

fax 366-0281
Sea Gull Cottages, Nigh Creek, 366-0266, fax 366-0268
Sea Spray Resort & Marina, White Sound, 366-0065
Tomato Paste Rentals, 366-0256
Tanny Key Rentals, 366-0140, www.come-2hopetown.com
Westview Cottage, Lighthouse Marina, 366-0154

HOUSEHOLD GOODS
Imports Unlimited, Centerline Road, White Sound, 366-0136
Lighthouse Marina, 366-0154

ICE
Harbour's Edge, 366-0087 / 366-0292
Harbour View Grocery, Bay Street, 366-0033
Hope Town Inn and Marina, 366-0003
Lighthouse Liquors, Back Street, 366-0157
Lighthouse Marina, 366-0154
LVA Convenience Store, White Sound Road, 366-0056
Sea Spray Marina, White Sound, 366-0065
The Food Store, White Sound, 366-0391

INSURANCE
Hope Town Hideaways, Fax/Phone 366-0224

JEWELRY
Abaco Inn, White Sound, 366-0133
Da Crazy Crab, Bay Street, 366-0537
Ebb Tide, Back Street, 366-0088
El Mercado, Back Street, 366-0053
Iggy Biggy, Bay Street, 366-0354
Sea Spray Marina, White Sound, 366-0065

JUSTICE OF THE PEACE
Vernon Malone, 366-0058

LAUNDRY
Lighthouse Marina, 366-0154
Hope Town Inn and Marina, 366-0003t

LIQUOR STORES
Hope Town Wines &Spirits, Lighthouse Marina, 366-0154
Lighthouse Liquors, Queen's Hwy., 366-0567
A & E Liquors, White Sound, 366-0625

MARINAS
Hope Town Hideaways, Fax/Phone 366-0224
Hope Town Inn and Marina, 366-0003
Lighthouse Marina, 366-0154
Sea Spray Marina, White Sound, 366-0065

MARINE STORE
Lighthouse Marina, 366-0154

MARRIAGE OFFICER
Vernon Malone, , 366-0058

MECHANICS
Tom Cat Enterprises, diesel/generators/water-makers, 366-0135

NOTARY SERVICES
Vernon Malone, 366-0058

OUTBOARD MOTOR SALES / SERVICE
Classic Marine, White Sound
Island Marine (Evinrude), Parrot Cay, 366-0282
Lighthouse Marina (Yamaha), 366-0154
Sea Horse Marine (Johnson), Back Creek, 366-0023

PAINTING
Island Colours Painting Co. (Tim Albury), 366-0290

PROPANE
Willard Bethel, 366-0033 / 366-0086

PROPERTY MANAGEMENT
Elbow Cay Properties, Bay Street, 366-0569, 366-0039
Hope Town Hideaways, Fax/Phone 366-0224
Inside Outside, 366-0122
Paradise Found, 366-0606
Sea Glass Properties, 366-0290

REAL ESTATE SALES
Coldwell Banker, Pleasants Higgs, 366-0797
Damianos Sothebys, 366-0163, 366-0035
Dupuch Real Estate, Ricky Sweeting, 366-0193
Elbow Cay Properties, Jane Patterson, 366-0569
Graham Realty, Patti Love, 366-0601
H G Christy, Robbie Bethel, 366-0700
Hope Town Hideaways, Chris Thompson, Fax/Phone 366-0224
Junior Mernard, 366-0361, 577-1735
Paradise Real Estate, Frank Knowles, 577-0339

RESTAURANTS
Abaco Inn, White Sound, 366-0133
Boat House, Sea Spray Marina, White Sound, 366-0065
Cap'n Jack's, Bay Street, 366-0247
Cracker P's, Lubbers Quarters Cay, 366-3139
Conchy Joe's Take Away, 366-0583
Firefly, Centerline Road, 366-0145
Harbour's Edge, 366-0087 / 366-0292
Hope Town Coffee House, Bay St., 366-0760
Hope Town Harbour Lodge, 366-0095, fax 366-0286
Hope Town Inn and Marina, 357-6775, VHF 16, water taxi
Lubber's Landing, Lubbers Quarters, 577-2000
Mackey's Takeout, White Sound (north), 366-0396
Munchies Take Away, 366-0423, VHF 16
On Da Beach, Turtle Hill, 366-0558
Sugar Shack, Queen's Highway, 366-0788

SAILBOAT CHARTERS
Cruise Abaco, Lubbers Quarters, 577-0148
Maine Cat, 1 888 832-2287

SERVICE CLUBS / ASSOCIATIONS
Hope Town Association
Friends of the Environment, contact Island Marine, 366-0280
Hope Town Fire and Rescue, 366-0500, 366-0087 (Harbour's Edge), 366-0037/58

SEWING / CANVAS WORK
Hope Town Sewing and Canvas, Dominique, 553-7583

SHIPPING COMPANIES
Abacays, Carib Freight, 365-6247

TELEPHONE COMPANY
BTC, Back Street, 366-0000

TOURS
Abaco Eco (kayak), 366-0398
Captain Plug (powerboat), 366-0023, 577-0273

WATER SPORTS
Abaco Eco, 366-0398
Abaco Paddleboard, 475-0794, 357-6554
Captain Plug, 366-0023, 577-0273
Frogggies, 366-0431

Green Turtle Cay Classified Business Directory

ADMINISTRATOR
Administrator's Office, 365-4211

ART GALLERY
Alton Lowe Gallery, 365-4264
Alton Lowe Museum, 365-4094
Memorial Sculpture Garden
Ocean Blue Gallery, Plymouth Rock Bar & Restaurant, 365-4234

BAKERY
McIntosh Restaurant & Bakery, 365-4625
Wreckin' Tree Bakery and Take Away, 365-4228

BANK
First Caribbean, 365-4144

BARS / TAVERNS
Blue Bee Bar, 365-4181
Bluff House Club and Marina, 365-4247
Green Turtle Club, 365-4271
New Plymouth Inn, 365-4161
Pineapples Bar and Grill, Other Sh. Club, 365-4226
Plymouth Rock Restaurant & Bar, 365-4234
Rooster's Rest Pub & Restaurant, 365-4066
Sundowner Restaurant & Bar, 365-4060
Wreckin' Tree Bakery and Take Away, 365-4228

BEAUTY SALONS / BARBERS
Hubert's Cut & Curls, 365-4100
Sharon's Salon, 365-4131

BICYCLE RENTALS
Brendal's Bike Rental, 365-4411
Curtis Bike Rental, 365-4128
D & P Bike Rental, 365-4655

BOAT BUILDING / REPAIR
Abaco Yacht Services, 365-4033 / 365-4216

BOAT RENTALS
Dames Boat Rentals, Bluff House, White Sound, 365-4247
Donny's Rentals, Black Sound, 365-4119
Reef Boat Rentals
Robert's Hardware and Marine, 365-4122
Sunset Marine, Black Sound, 365-3644

BOAT SALES
Dolphin Marine, White Sound, 365-4262
Robert's Hardware and Marine, 365-4122

BOAT STORAGE
Abaco Yacht Services Ltd., 365-4033 / 365-4216
Bluff House Club & Marina, 365-4247
Donny's Rentals, Black Sound, 365-4119
Green Turtle Club, 365-4271
Other Shore Club & Marina, 365-4195
Robert's Hardware and Marine, 365-4122

BOOKS
Curry's Food Store, 365-4171
Lowe's Grocery Store, 365-4243
Loyalist Rose Shoppe, 365-4037
Sid's Food Store, 365-4055

BUILDERS / CONTRACTORS
3T's Construction, 365-4375, cell 577-0368
Alphonso McIntosh, 365-4030
Jonathan Curry
Lonnie Lowe, 365-4135
Maxwell McIntosh
Michael Levarity, 365-4228
Reggie Sawyer, 365-4268
Wayne Reckley, 365-4203

CHURCHES
Church of God, 365-4505
Gospel Chapel (Plymouth Brethren), 365-4198
Methodist, 365-4293
St. Peter's Anglican

CLINIC
Government Clinic, 365-4028 (after hours phone, nurse's residence, 365-4148)
Green Turtle Dental Clinic, 365-4548

CLOTHING
Bluff House Club & Marina, 365-4247
Brendal's Dive Shop, 365-4411
Green Turtle Club Boutique, 365-4271
Lowe's Grocery Store, 365-4243
Loyalist Rose Shoppe, 365-4037
Sid's Food Store, 365-4055

CUSTOMS
Customs Office, 365-4077

DIVING
Brendal's Dive Shop, 365-4411 / 800 780-9941

Green Turtle Club, 365-4271

FERRY
Green Turtle Ferry, 365-4166 or 365-4128 sometimes

FISH - RETAIL AND WHOLESALE
Abaco Seafoods, 365-4011 / 365-4012 / 365-4054
B & M Seafoods, 365-4387/365-4595
Curtis Seafood, 365-4128

FISHING GUIDES / CHARTERS
Eddie Bodie, 365-4069,357-6784
Lincoln Jones, 365-4223
Joe Sawyer, 365-4173
Rickie Sawyer, 365-4261

FISHING TACKLE
Roberts' Hardware and Marine, 365-4122

FLOWERS
Native Creations, 365-4206

FUEL
Bluff House Club & Marina, 365-4247
Green Turtle Club Marina, 365-4271
Other Shore Club & Marina, 365-4195

GIFT SHOPS
Bluff House Club & Marina, 365-4247
Golden Reef, 365-4511
Green Turtle Club Marina, 365-4271
Native Creations, Parliament St., 365-4206
Ocean Blue Gallery, Plymouth Rock Bar & Restaurant, 365-4234
Shell Hut, 365-4188

GOLF CART RENTALS
Bay Street Cart Rental, Bluff House, 365-4070
D & P Golf Carts, Green Turtle Club, 365-4655
Island Property Management Renals, 365-4465
New Plymouth Rentals, 365-4161
Sea Side Rentals, 365-4120
Shell Hut Rentals, 365-4188
South Beach Golf Cart Rentals, 365-4375
T & A Rentals, Black Sound, 365-4259

GROCERY STORES
Curry's Food Store, 365-4171
Lowe's Grocery Store, 365-4243
Sid's Groceries, 365-4055
Roberta Food Store, 365-4284

HARDWARE
New Plymouth Hardware, 365-4305
Roberts' Hardware and Marine, 365-4122

HOTELS / RESORTS
Bluff House Club & Marina, 365-4247
Green Turtle Club, 365-4271
New Plymouth Inn, 365-4161

HOUSE / APT. RENTALS
E. A. Roberts Cottages, 365-4274
Green Turtle Rentals, 365-4120, 365-4055
Linton's Beach Cottages, 365-4003
Island Property Management, 365-4047
Martha Lowe, 365-4055
Other Shore Club & Marina, 365-4195
Golden Reef Apartments, 365-4221,365-4511
Susan Roberts, 365-4105
Walter Sands, 365-4178

HOUSEHOLD GOODS
Curry's Food Store, 365-4171
Lowe's Grocery Store, 365-4243
Sid's Food Store, 365-4055
Roberta Food Store, 365-4284
Tropic Topic, 365-4284

ICE
Abaco Yacht Services Ltd., 365-4033 / 365-4216
Bluff House Club & Marina, 365-4247
B & M Seafoods, 365-4387
Curry & Sons Liquor Store, 365-4155
Curry's Food Store, 365-4171
Green Turtle Club, 365-4271
Lowe's Grocery Store, 365-4243
Other Shore Club & Marina, 365-4195
Roberts' Hardware and Marine, 365-4122
Sid's Food Store, 365-4055

JEWELRY
Native Creations, 365-4206
Sid's Food Store, 365-4055

LAUNDRY
Abaco Yacht Services Ltd., 365-4033 / 365-4216
Bluff House Club and Marina, 365-4247
Green Turtle Club, 365-4271

LIQUOR STORES

Curry & Sons Liquor Store, 365-4155
Plymouth Rock Restaurant & Bar, 365-4234

MARINAS
Abaco Yacht Services Ltd., Black Sound, 365-4033 / 365-4216
Black Sound Marina, 365-4531
Bluff House Club & Marina, White Sound, 365-4247
Green Turtle Club and Marina, White Sound, 365-4271
Leeward Yacht Club, Black Sound, 365-4111
Other Shore Club & Marina, Black Sound, 365-4195, 365-4226

MARINE STORES
Dolphin Marine, White Sound, 365-4262 / VHF 16
Green Turtle Club, 365-4271
Roberts' Hardware and Marine, 365-4122

MUSEUM
Albert Lowe Museum, 365-4094

OUTBOARD MOTOR SALES / SERVICE
Abaco Yacht Services Ltd. (Yamaha), 365-4033 / 365-4216
Dolphin Marine (Evinrude/Johnson), White Sound, 365-4262 / VHF 16
Roberts' Hardware and Marine (Evinrude/Johnson), 365-4122

PHOTOGRAPHIC SUPPLIES
Golden Reef, 365-4511
Also see Grocery Stores

POLICE DEPARTMENT
Police Department, 365-4450

POST OFFICE
Post Office, 365-4242

POWER COMPANY
Bahamas Electricity Corporation (BEC), 365-4087 / 365-4088

PROPANE
Lowe's Food Store, 365 4243
New Plymouth Hardware, 365-4305
Sid's Food Store, 365-4055

REAL ESTATE SALES
Abaco Cays Realty Ltd., Chris Plummer, 365-4648, 475-8511
Damianos Sothebys, 367-5046
Green Turtle Real Estate, Chris Farrington, 365-4695, cell 559-8800
Leeward Yacht Club, 365-4111
Lowe's Real Estate, 365-4054
Ocean Blue Prop., 365-4636

RESTAURANTS
Blue Bee Bar, 365-4181
Bluff House Club & Marina, 365-4247
Green Turtle Club, 365-4271
Harvey's Island Grill, 365-4389
Lizard Bar and Grill, Leeward Yacht Club, 365-4191
McIntosh Restaurant and Bakery, 365-4625
New Plymouth Inn, 365-4161
Pineapples at The Other Shore Club, 365-4226
Plymouth Rock Restaurant & Bar, 365-4234
Rooster's Rest Pub & Restaurant, 365-4066
Sea Side Snacks, 365-4209
Sundowner, 365-4060
Wreckin' Tree Bakery and Take Away, 365-4228

SHIPPING
Moonraker Enterprises, 365-4305 / FAX 365-4372

TELEPHONE
Batelco, 365-4113 / 365-4114 / 365-4115

TRAVEL AGENCY
A & W Travel, 365-4238

TOURS
Brendal's Dive Shop, 365-4411 / 800 780-9941
Tom Sawyer Sea Adventures, 365-4019

New Plymouth and Settlement Harbour, Green Turtle Cay from the south with Black Sound (right) and White Sound (rear left) from the south. Photo by Steve Dodge, 27 May 2011.

Treasure Cay Classified Business Directory

AIR CONDITIONING
See Refrigeration

AIRLINES AND CHARTERS
...gate Aviation, 365-9137, 407 585-3545, 386
...0-0440
...amasair, 365-8600
...tinental Connection (Gulfstream) 365-8615
...g Air, 904 641-0300
... Air, Calypso, 367-0140, 866 325-9776

...CHITECT
...an Cooper Jr, 365-0137

...MOBILE RENTAL
... Car Rentals, 365-8623
... Edgecombe, VHF-16
...ure Cay Airport Car Rental, 365-8961
... J Car Rental, 365-8761

...AKERIES/COFFEE HOUSES
Café La Florence, 365-8354
Simply The Best, 365-8258

BANKS
Royal Bank of Canada (Tues & Thurs), 365-8119

BARS, TAVERNS
Island Boil, 365-8849
Spinnaker, 365-8469
Tipsy Seagull
Touch of Class, 365-8195
...raveller's Nest, (Airport)
...reasure Sands Club, 365-9385

...ICYCLE RENTALS
...Wendell's Bike Rentals, 365-0590

BOAT RENTALS/CHARTERS
C & C Rentals, 365-8582, 365-8506
J.I.C. Rentals, 365-8582

BOAT REPAIR & STORAGE

Harold's MARINE, LTD
EVINRUDE   Johnson
SALES & SERVICE · DRY BOAT STORAGE
Monday-Friday 8AM - 4PM · Phone (242) 365-8556
VHF 16   Email: haroldsmarine@batelnet.bs

C & C Rentals, 365-8582
Edgecombe's Marine Service, 365-8245, cell 375-8211
Treasure Cay Marina, 365-8578

CHURCHES
Full Gospel Assembly, 365-8097
Sts Mary and Andrew (RC), 367-2714
St Simon's by the Sea (Anglican), 365-8422
Unity Baptist Church, 365-8371
Treasure Cay Community Church (Non-Denominational), 365-8318

CLOTHING
Delly's Variety Store
Lowe's Food Store, 365-8663
The Harbour Shoppe, 365-8757

COMPUTER SALES AND SERVICE
Simple Solutions, 365-8881, 357-6850

CRUISES, GUIDED TOURS, DIVING
C & C Boat Rentals, 365-8582, 365-8506
J.I.C. Boat Rentals, 365-8465
Treasure Cay Marina, 365-8535

DENTISTS
Howard R. Spencer, 365-8625

DIVING
Treasure Divers, 365-8571

DRUGS AND NOTIONS
G & M Variety Store, 475-0638
Golden Harvest, 365-8350

ELECTRICIANS
Deolie's Electrical Company, 365-0590, 554-9823

ELECTRONICS, APPLIANCES, ETC
GIF Home Centre, 365-8200, 365-8226

FERRY AND TOURS
Abaco Advenures - Prozac the Ferry, 375-8123, 365-8749
Abaco Gal Island Adventures, 365-8571, cell 551-4436
The Great Abaco Express, 367-2165, 646-7072

FUEL
Marina Fuel Dock, 365-8869

HOTELS
TC Resort and Marina, 365-8801, 368-8250

GIFT SHOPS
Abaco Ceramics, 365-8489
The Harbour Shoppe, 365-8757
Triple J Car Rental and Gift Shop, 365-8761

GOLF CART RENTALS
Cash's Carts, 365-8771
Chris Carts, 365-8053
Resort Cart Rentals, 365-8465

GOLF COURSE
TC Golf Course, 365-8045

GROCERY STORES/ SUPERMARKETS
Friendly Food Mart
Golden Harvest, 365-8350
Lowe's Food Store, 365-8663
G & M Variety Store, 475-0638

HAIRDRESSING / SPA
Julia's Spatique (hair and nails), 365-8198, 577-0298

HARDWARE AND PAINT
Treasure Cay Home Centre, 365-8258

HOUSE/CONDO/ APARTMENT RENTALS
Bahama Beach Club, 365-8500
Brigantine Bay Villas, 365-8033, 877-786-8455
Four Winds Cottage, 365-8568, 554-8434
Island Dreams, 365-8507, 365-8508,
Ocean Villas, 365-8200, 365-8226
Pineapple Point, 475-7464
Silver Sands, 365-8039
Treasure Cay Real Estate, 365-8538
William Hertz Ltd, 365-8061, 365-8061

INSURANCE
Abaco Insurance Agency, 365-8650
J.S. Johnson, 367-2688

LIQUOR STORES
Bristol Wines and Spirits, 365-8611
Spanky's Liquor Store, 365-8385

MARINAS
Treasure Cay Marina, 365-8250

NURSERIES
Carrollville Nursery, 365-8674
Great Abaco Nursery

PHYSICIANS
Corbett Clinic, 365-8288, 577-0606

PLUMBERS
John's Plumbing, 577-6579, 365-8714
JR Hodgkins, 365-8657
Arthur Roberts, 365-8487

PROPERTY MANAGEMENT
GIF Property Management, 359-6087, 365-8621
Island Dreams, 365-8777, 365-8507
Treasure Keys, 365-8472, 365-8472

REAL ESTATE
Anne Albury, Buyers Advisor/Broker, 365-8568, 554-8434
Damianos Sothebys, 577-0298
GIF Realty & Property, 359-6087, 365-8621
John Cash Realty, 477-5056
Pineapple Point, 475-7464
Treasure Cay Real Estate, 365-8538, fax 365-8587
William Hertz Ltd, 365-8061, 365-8061

Anne Albury
Broker   Director
If you need answers or assistance ... "Ask Anne"
"Four Winds" Treasure Cay   Ph/Fax: 242 365-8568
AskAnneAlbury@yahoo.com   Cell: 242 554-8434

REFRIGERATION
Complete Care Air Conditioning and Refrigeration, 365-8622

RESTAURANTS
Café La Florence. 365-8354
Coco Beach Bar and Grill, 365-8470
Junkanoo Cafe, Airport, 365-8961
Spinnaker, 365-8469
Tipsy Seagull
Touch of Class, 365-8195
Treasure Sands Club, 365-9385

SECURITY
Miller's Locksmithing, 365-8687
Sawyer Security Systems, 365-8198, 577-0298

TOURS
See Ferry and Tours

Man-O-War Classified Business Directory

BAKERIES
Lola's Bakery, 365-6073

BANKS
First Caribbean, 365 6098

BEAUTY SALONS / BARBERS
Bahama Waves 365-6310

BOAT BUILDERS
Albury Brothers, 365-6086

BOAT RENTALS
Conch Pearl Rentals, 365-6059
Waterways, 365-6143, 357-6540

BOAT STORAGE
Albury Brothers, 365-6086
Edwin's Boat Yard, 365-6007 / 365-6006
Man-O-War Marina, 365-6008

BOOKS
Joe's Studio, 365-6082
The Painted Fish, 365-6013

BUILDERS/CONTRACTORS
Bill Albury, 365-6009
Neville Albury, Special K, 365-6063
Warren Albury, 365-6057
Kent Bethel, 365-6246
Wallace McDonald, 365-6048
Quality Construction, Rowan Sands, 365-6061

BUILDING SUPPLIES
Man-O-War Hardware and Building Supply Ltd., 365-6011

CARPENTERS/CABINET MAKERS
Andy Albury, 365-6267
Joe Albury, 365-6082

CHURCHES
Brethren Church, 365-6048
Church Of God parsonage, 365-6088
New Life Bible Church

CLINIC
Community Clinic, 365-6081

CLOTHING
Albury's Sail Shop, 365-6014
Belle-Ena, 365-6077
Joe's Studio, 365-6082
The Painted Fish, Man-O-War Marina, 365-6013
Sally's Seaside Boutique and Fabrics, 365-6044

DIVE RENTAL EQUIPMENT
Dive Time, 365-6235

ELECTRICIANS & ELECTRICAL SUPPLIES
Man-O-War Hardware and Building Supply Ltd., 365-6011
Roberts Electrical, 365-6118

FERRY
Albury's Ferry Service, 367-3147

FISHING GUIDES/CHARTERS
David Albury, 365-6502, 365-6059

FISHING TACKLE
Man-O-War Hardware and Building Supply Ltd., 365-601
Waterways, 365-6143

FUEL
Man-O-War Marina, 365-6008

GIFT SHOPS
Albury's Designs, 365-6267, 365-6037
Albury's Sail Shop, 365-6014
Joe's Studio, 365-6082
Seaside Shop, 365-6044
The Painted Fish, 365-6013

GOLF CART RENTALS
Chariots for Hire, MOW Marina, 365-6008
Paul Albury, 365-6024

Waterways Rentals, 365-6143

GROCERY STORES
Albury's Harbour Store, 365-6004
Man-O-War Grocery Store, 365-6016

HARDWARE
Man-O_War Hardware and Building Supply Ltd., 365-6011

HOTELS/RESORTS
Schooner's Landing Ocean Club, 365-6143, 367-4469

HOUSE / APARTMENT RENTALS
Bill and Sherry Albury, 365-6009 / FAX 365-6126
David Albury, 365-6502
Denise McDonald, 365-6048
Joann Sands, 365-6093
Joe's Studio, 365-6082
Micahel Sherratt, 365-6235
Molly Sawyer, 365-6022
"Outrageous", 561 352-5999, 561 776-9229
Sweeting's Cottages, 365-6056

HOUSEHOLD GOODS
Belle-Ena, 365-6077
Man-O-War Hardware and Building Supply Ltd., 365-6011

ICE
Albury's Harbour Store, 365-6004
Man-O-War Grocery, 365-6016
Man-O-War Marina, 365-6008

JEWELRY
Joe's Studio, 365-6082
Painted Fish, Man-O-War Marina, 365-6013

LAUNDRY
Man-O-War Marina, 365-6008

MARINAS
Man-O-War Marina, 365-6008

MARINE STORES
Edwin's Boat Yard, 365-6007 / 365-6006
Painted Fish, Man-O-War Marina, 365-6013
Man-O-War Hardware and Building Supply Ltd., 365-6011

OUTBOARD MOTOR SALES & SERVICE
Albury Brothers, 365-6086
Waterways, 365-6143

PHOTOGRAPHY SUPPLIES
Joe's Studio, 365-6082
The Painted Fish, 365-6013

PLUMBERS & PLUMBING SUPPLIES
Man-O-War Hardware and Building Supply Ltd., 365-6011
Roberts Electrical, 365-6020

PROPANE
Man-O-War LP Gas, 365-6138

REAL ESTATE SALES
Abaco Cays Realty, James Pleydell-Bouverie, 365-6416
Coldwell Banker, Mailin Sands, 367-2992
Damianos Sothebys, Chris Albury 365-6885

RESTAURANTS
Dock and Dine, 365-6008
Island Treats, 365-6501

SAIL MAKER
Jay Manni, Dickie's Cay, 365-6171

SHIPPING COMPANIES
Abacays, 365-6247

TELEPHONE COMPANY
Batelco, 365-6001 / 365-6002

Great Guana Cay

EMERGENCY SERVICES
Guana Fire and Rescue, 365-5121
Marsh Harbour Police, 367-2560
Marsh Harbour Fire, 367-2000

BARS/TAVERNS
Conch Shack Raw Bar, Bakers Bay Marina
Grabbers, 365-5133
Nippers, 365-5143
Pirates Cove at Sea Shore Villas, 365-5006

BOAT RENTALS
Dive Guana, 365-5178

BOOKS
Dive Guana, 365-5178
Guana Harbour Grocery, 365-5067
Guana Drug Store, 365-5050

CHURCHES
Seaside Gospel Chapel

CLOTHING
Grabbers, Sunset Beach

Nippers Gift Shop
Orchid Bay Marina

DIVING
Dive Guana, 365-5178

DRUG STORE
Guana Drugstore, 365-5050

FERRY
Albury's Ferry Service, 367-3147

FREIGHT/SHIPPING COMPANIES
Guana Frieght, 365-5190

FUEL
Orchid Bay Marina, 365-5175

GIFT SHOPS
Dive Guana, 365-5178
Dolphin Beach Resort, 365-5137
Donna's Golf Cart Rentals, 365-5195
Grabbers, 365-5133
Nippers, 365-5143
Orchid Bay Marina, 365-5175

GOLF CART RENTALS
Dive Guana, 365-5178
Donna's Golf Cart Rental, 365-5195

GROCERY STORES
Guana Harbour Grocery, 365-5067

HARDWARE AND LUMBER
Guana Lumber and Supplies, 365-5130

HOTELS, RESORTS
Dolphin Beach Resort, 365-5137
Grabbers, , 365-5133
Oceanfrontier Hideaway, 519 389-4846

ICE
Fig Tree Wine and Spirits, 365-5058
Orchid Bay Marina, 365-5175

LAUNDRY
Sea Shore Villas Shop, 365-5006

LIQUOR STORES
Fig Tree Wine and Spirits, 365-5058

MARINAS / DOCKAGE
Bakers Bay Marina, 365-5802
Guana Hideaways Marina, 577-0003
Orchid Bay Marina, 365-5175

REAL ESTATE
Aisle of Palm Real Estate, 365-5003
Baker's Bay Club, 367-0612
Damianos, Chris Albury, 359-6885
Edmond Pinder Real Estate, 365-5181
H. G. Christie, 365-5454

RESTAURANTS
Bambi's Cafe
Conch Shack Raw Bar, Baker's Bay Ma
Grabbers, 365-5133
Market Restaurant, Baker's Bay Marina
Village
Nippers, 365-5143
Orchid Bay Marina, 365-5175
Pirates Cove at Sea Shore Villas, 365-5006

Abaco Government Offices

AGRICULTURE AND FISHERIES
Marsh Harbour, 367-2240

AUDITORS GENERAL
Marsh Harbour, 367-3688

BAHAMASAIR
Marsh Harbour, 367-2095, 367-2039

BAHAMAS ELECTRICITY CORPORATION
Marsh Harbour, 367-2740, Emergency Service, 367-2727, Fax 367-2183
Coopers Town, 365-0033
Fox Town, 365-2151
Green Turtle Cay, 365-4087, 365-4088
Moores Island, 366-6300
Sandy Point, 366-4397

BAHAMAS TELECOMMUNICATIONS CORP.
Marsh Harbour, 367-2200, 367-3399, Fax 367-2994
Cedar Harbour, 365-0290
Cherokee Sound, 366-2000, Fax 366-2250
Coopers Town, 365-0044, Fax 365-0294
Crossing Rocks, 366-2198, Fax 366-2199
Fox Town, 365-2000, Fax 365-2290
Great Guana Cay, 365-5000, Fax 365-5098
Green Turtle Cay, 365-4113, Fax 365-4390
Hope Town, 366-0000, Fax 366-0366
Man-O-War Cay, 365-6001, Fax 365-6266
Moores Island, 366-6015, Fax 366-6079
Sandy Point, 366-4000, Fax 366-4390
Treasure Cay, 365-8000, Fax 365-8490

BROADCASTING CORPORATION
Marsh Harbour, 367-4044, 367-4895, Fax 367-4025

CUSTOMS
Marsh Harbour, 367-2524, 367-2522, Airport, 367-2026
Green Turtle Cay, 365-4077

FINANCE AND PLANNING DEPARTMENT
Marsh Harbour, 367-3700

HEALTH CLINICS
Marsh Harbour, 367-2510, 367-2586, 367-2867, 367-4480
Coopers Town, 365-0019, 365-0300
Green Turtle Cay, 365-4028
Hope Town, 366-0108
Moores Island, 366-6105
Sandy Point, 366-4010

IMMIGRATION
Marsh Harbour, 367-2675, 367-2536

ISLAND ADMINISTRATOR
Marsh Harbour, 367-2343, 367-2344
Deputy, Coopers Town, 365-0000
Deputy, Sandy Point, 366-4001

LABOUR DEPARTMENT
Marsh Harbour, 367-2133

LANDS AND SURVEYS DEPARTMENT
Marsh Harbour, 367-2013

LOCAL GOVERNMENT
Northern Disrict Council, 365-0401
Central District Council, 367-4957/8, Fax 367-4984
Southern District Council, 366-4001

NATIONAL INSURANCE BOARD
Coopers Town, 365-0225, 365-0055, Fax 365-0245
Dundas Town, 367-2550, 367-2639, Fax 367-2970

POLICE DEPARTMENT
Marsh Harbour, 367-2560, 367-2594, Airport, 367-3500
Coopers Town, 365-0002
Crown Haven, 365-2111
Green Turtle Cay, 365-4450
Moores Island, 366-6100
Sandy Point, 366-4044
Treasure Cay, 365-8048

POST OFFICES
Marsh Harbour, 367-2571
Coopers Town, 365-0000
Green Turtle Cay, 365-4242
Hope Town, 366-0098
Man-O-War Cay, 365-6108
Sandy Point, 366-4001

ROAD TRAFFIC DEPARTMENT
Marsh Harbour, 367-2121
Coopers Town, 365-0198

SCHOOLS
District Supervisor, 367-2342
Abaco Central Primary (Dundas Town), 367-2718, (Marsh Harbour), 367-2757
Abaco Central Secondary (Murphy Town), 367-2334, Fax 367-3997
Amy Roberts School (Green Turtle Cay), 365-4108
Hope Town, 366-0177
James A. Pinder School (Sandy Point), 366-4015
Man-O-War Cay, 365-6049
Moores Island, 366-6012
SC Bootle Secondary (Coopers Town), 365-0065

SOCIAL SERVICES DEPARTMENT
Marsh Harbour, 367-2246
Coopers Town, 365-0055

TOURIST OFFICE
Marsh Harbour, 367-3067, Fax 367-3068

WATER AND SEWERAGE CORPORATION
Marsh Harbour, 367-2995, 367-3974, Fax 367-2993

WORKS
Marsh Harbour, 367-2540

YOUTH, SPORTS & CULTURE
Dundas Town, 367-2220

EMERGENCY

List Arranged North to South

Fox Town Clinic, 365-2172
Coopers Town Clinic and Hospital, 365-0300
North Abaco Crash Fire Rescue, 365-9111
Green Turtle Govt. Clinic, 365-4028, (after hours call nurse's residence - 365-4148)
Green Turtle Fire & Rescue, 365-4133, VHF 16
Guana Cay Fire and Rescue, 365-5121, VHF 16
Man-O-War Community Clinic, 365-6081
Man-O-War Emergency Fire and Rescue, contact Walter Sweeting-365-6015
Marsh Harbour Government Clinic, 367-2510
Marsh Harbour Fire Department, 367-2000
Marsh Harbour Med. Centre (Prvt. Clinic) - 367-0049
Abaco Family Medince, Marsh Harbour, (Private Clinic) - 367-2295
Auskell Clinic, Marsh Harbour, (private Clinic), emerg. 577-0113 reg 367-0020
Hope Town Government Clinic, 366-0108
Hope Town Fire and Rescue - **Call on VHF 16 first,** 366-0500

Not a day for a relaxing ocean cruise. Wave breaking on the rock outcropping at Abaco Inn, White Sound, Elbow Cay on 20 November 2008. Photo by Steve Dodge.

Tide Tables - 2013

Sea of Abaco • Abaco • Bahamas

NOAA Tide Station at Pelican Harbour (Sandy Cay at Pelican Cays Land and Sea Park)

Times are given for the Sea of Abaco at Pelican Harbour, but tides throughout Abaco vary by only a few minutes. Heights are in reference to Mean Lower Low Water (MLLW). Times are in Eastern Standard Time (EST) from 1 January through 9 March, in Eastern Daylight Time from 10 March through 2 November, and in Eastern Standard Time (EST) from 3 November through 31 December.

January

Day	Time	Ht		Day	Time	Ht
1 Tu	04:20 AM	0.0		16 W	05:31 AM	-0.2
	10:28 AM	2.7			11:31 AM	2.7
	04:59 PM	-0.1			06:00 PM	-0.4
	10:54 PM	2.3				
2 W	05:04 AM	0.1		17 Th	12:08 AM	2.6
	11:08 AM	2.6			06:25 AM	0.0
	05:39 PM	-0.1			12:21 PM	2.4
	11:40 PM	2.4			06:48 PM	-0.2
3 Th	05:53 AM	0.1		18 F	01:02 AM	2.4
	11:53 AM	2.5			07:22 AM	0.2
	06:23 PM	-0.1			01:12 PM	2.2
					07:38 PM	-0.1
4 F	12:32 AM	2.4		19 Sa	01:57 AM	2.4
	06:48 AM	0.2			08:22 AM	0.3
	12:43 PM	2.4			02:06 PM	2.0
	07:12 PM	-0.2			08:30 PM	0.0
5 Sa	01:28 AM	2.5		20 Su	02:54 AM	2.3
	07:50 AM	0.2			09:23 AM	0.4
	01:40 PM	2.3			03:03 PM	1.9
	08:07 PM	-0.2			09:23 PM	0.1
6 Su	02:29 AM	2.6		21 M	03:50 AM	2.3
	08:57 AM	0.2			10:22 AM	0.4
	02:42 PM	2.2			03:59 PM	1.8
	09:06 PM	-0.3			10:16 PM	0.0
7 M	03:32 AM	2.8		22 Tu	04:42 AM	2.4
	10:04 AM	0.0			11:15 AM	0.3
	03:47 PM	2.3			04:53 PM	1.9
	10:08 PM	-0.4			11:06 PM	0.0
8 Tu	04:34 AM	3.0		23 W	05:30 AM	2.5
	11:08 AM	-0.1			12:03 PM	0.2
	04:51 PM	2.3			05:42 PM	1.9
	11:09 PM	-0.6			11:53 PM	-0.1
9 W	05:34 AM	3.2		24 Th	06:14 AM	2.6
	12:08 PM	-0.3			12:46 PM	0.1
	05:52 PM	2.5			06:27 PM	2.0
10 Th	12:08 AM	-0.7		25 F	12:37 AM	-0.1
	06:30 AM	3.3			06:55 AM	2.7
	01:04 PM	-0.5			01:26 PM	0.0
	06:50 PM	2.6			07:09 PM	2.1
11 F	01:05 AM	-0.8		26 Sa	01:19 AM	-0.2
	07:24 AM	3.4			07:34 AM	2.8
	01:57 PM	-0.6			02:04 PM	-0.1
	07:46 PM	2.7			07:50 PM	2.3
12 Sa	02:00 AM	-0.8		27 Su	01:59 AM	-0.2
	08:16 AM	3.4			08:11 AM	2.8
	02:48 PM	-0.7			02:40 PM	-0.2
	08:39 PM	2.8			08:29 PM	2.4
13 Su	02:54 AM	-0.8		28 M	02:39 AM	-0.3
	09:06 AM	3.3			08:48 AM	2.8
	03:37 PM	-0.7			03:16 PM	-0.3
	09:32 PM	2.8			09:08 PM	2.4
14 M	03:46 AM	-0.7		29 Tu	03:20 AM	-0.2
	09:55 AM	3.2			09:25 AM	2.8
	04:25 PM	-0.7			03:52 PM	-0.3
	10:23 PM	2.8			09:48 PM	2.5
15 Tu	04:38 AM	-0.5		30 W	04:01 AM	-0.2
	10:43 AM	3.0			10:03 AM	2.7
	05:12 PM	-0.5			04:29 PM	-0.3
	11:15 PM	2.7			10:30 PM	2.6
				31 Th	04:46 AM	-0.1
					10:44 AM	2.6
					05:09 PM	-0.3
					11:16 PM	2.6

February

Day	Time	Ht		Day	Time	Ht
1 F	05:35 AM	-0.1		16 Sa	12:19 AM	2.5
	11:29 AM	2.5			06:43 AM	0.2
	05:54 PM	-0.3			12:31 PM	2.1
					06:52 PM	0.0
2 Sa	12:07 AM	2.6		17 Su	01:10 AM	2.4
	06:29 AM	0.0			07:38 AM	0.3
	12:19 PM	2.3			01:22 PM	1.9
	06:44 PM	-0.3			07:42 PM	0.1
3 Su	01:03 AM	2.7		18 M	02:05 AM	2.3
	07:30 AM	0.1			08:36 AM	0.4
	01:17 PM	2.2			02:18 PM	1.8
	07:41 PM	-0.3			08:36 PM	0.2
4 M	02:06 AM	2.7		19 Tu	03:03 AM	2.3
	08:38 AM	0.1			09:37 AM	0.5
	02:22 PM	2.2			03:17 PM	1.8
	08:44 PM	-0.3			09:33 PM	0.2
5 Tu	03:12 AM	2.8		20 W	04:00 AM	2.3
	09:47 AM	0.1			10:34 AM	0.4
	03:31 PM	2.2			04:15 PM	1.9
	09:51 PM	-0.3			10:29 PM	0.2
6 W	04:18 AM	2.9		21 Th	04:52 AM	2.4
	10:53 AM	-0.1			11:25 AM	0.3
	04:38 PM	2.3			05:08 PM	2.0
	10:56 PM	-0.4			11:21 PM	0.1
7 Th	05:20 AM	3.0		22 F	05:40 AM	2.5
	11:53 AM	-0.2			12:10 PM	0.2
	05:41 PM	2.4			05:56 PM	2.1
	11:58 PM	-0.6				
8 F	06:17 AM	3.1		23 Sa	12:09 AM	0.0
	12:48 PM	-0.4			06:23 AM	2.6
	06:39 PM	2.6			12:51 PM	0.0
					06:40 PM	2.3
9 Sa	12:55 AM	-0.6		24 Su	12:53 AM	-0.1
	07:09 AM	3.2			07:03 AM	2.7
	01:39 PM	-0.6			01:29 PM	-0.1
	07:32 PM	2.8			07:21 PM	2.5
10 Su	01:48 AM	-0.7		25 M	01:36 AM	-0.2
	07:59 AM	3.2			07:42 AM	2.8
	02:27 PM	-0.6			02:06 PM	-0.2
	08:23 PM	2.8			08:02 PM	2.6
11 M	02:39 AM	-0.7		26 Tu	02:18 AM	-0.3
	08:46 AM	3.1			08:21 AM	2.8
	03:12 PM	-0.7			02:43 PM	-0.4
	09:11 PM	2.9			08:42 PM	2.8
12 Tu	03:28 AM	-0.6		27 W	03:00 AM	-0.3
	09:31 AM	3.0			09:00 AM	2.8
	03:56 PM	-0.6			03:21 PM	-0.4
	09:58 PM	2.8			09:24 PM	2.9
13 W	04:16 AM	-0.4		28 Th	03:44 AM	-0.3
	10:15 AM	2.8			09:41 AM	2.7
	04:39 PM	-0.5			04:01 PM	-0.4
	10:44 PM	2.7			10:08 PM	2.9
14 Th	05:04 AM	-0.2				
	10:59 AM	2.6				
	05:22 PM	-0.3				
	11:31 PM	2.6				
15 F	05:52 AM	0.0				
	11:44 AM	2.3				
	06:05 PM	-0.2				

March

Day	Time	Ht		Day	Time	Ht
1 F	04:30 AM	-0.3		16 Sa	06:20 AM	0.0
	10:24 AM	2.6			12:09 PM	2.3
	04:43 PM	-0.4			06:24 PM	0.0
	10:55 PM	2.9				
2 Sa	05:20 AM	-0.2		17 Su	12:38 AM	2.6
	11:11 AM	2.5			07:06 AM	0.2
	05:31 PM	-0.4			12:53 PM	2.1
	11:47 PM	2.9			07:08 PM	0.1
3 Su	06:15 AM	-0.1		18 M	01:25 AM	2.4
	12:04 PM	2.4			07:56 AM	0.4
	06:24 PM	-0.3			01:41 PM	2.0
					07:56 PM	0.3
4 M	12:45 AM	2.8		19 Tu	02:17 AM	2.3
	07:17 AM	0.1			08:51 AM	0.5
	01:04 PM	2.3			02:36 PM	1.9
	07:24 PM	-0.2			08:50 PM	0.4
5 Tu	01:49 AM	2.8		20 W	03:14 AM	2.3
	08:24 AM	0.1			09:49 AM	0.5
	02:11 PM	2.2			03:35 PM	1.9
	08:31 PM	-0.1			09:50 PM	0.4
6 W	02:57 AM	2.8		21 Th	04:12 AM	2.3
	09:33 AM	0.1			10:46 AM	0.5
	03:22 PM	2.3			04:35 PM	2.0
	09:41 PM	-0.1			10:49 PM	0.4
7 Th	04:03 AM	2.8		22 F	05:07 AM	2.4
	10:38 AM	0.0			11:38 AM	0.4
	04:30 PM	2.4			05:30 PM	2.1
	10:48 PM	-0.2			11:45 PM	0.2
8 F	05:05 AM	2.9		23 Sa	05:57 AM	2.5
	11:37 AM	-0.2			12:25 PM	0.2
	05:31 PM	2.6			06:20 PM	2.3
	11:49 PM	-0.3				
9 Sa	06:01 AM	3.0		24 Su	12:37 AM	0.1
	12:29 PM	-0.3			06:43 AM	2.6
	06:26 PM	2.7			01:08 PM	0.0
					07:06 PM	2.5
10 Su	12:45 AM	-0.4		25 M	01:24 AM	-0.1
	07:52 AM	3.0			07:27 AM	2.7
	02:17 PM	-0.4			01:49 PM	-0.1
	08:16 PM	2.9			07:49 PM	2.7
11 M	02:36 AM	-0.5		26 Tu	02:10 AM	-0.2
	08:39 AM	3.0			08:09 AM	2.8
	03:02 PM	-0.5			02:29 PM	-0.3
	09:03 PM	3.0			08:32 PM	2.9
12 Tu	03:24 AM	-0.5		27 W	02:55 AM	-0.3
	09:23 AM	2.9			08:52 AM	2.8
	03:44 PM	-0.5			03:09 PM	-0.4
	09:47 PM	3.0			09:16 PM	3.1
13 W	04:09 AM	-0.4		28 Th	03:41 AM	-0.4
	10:05 AM	2.8			09:35 AM	2.8
	04:24 PM	-0.5			03:51 PM	-0.5
	10:30 PM	2.9			10:01 PM	3.2
14 Th	04:53 AM	-0.3		29 F	04:27 AM	-0.4
	10:47 AM	2.6			10:19 AM	2.8
	05:04 PM	-0.3			04:35 PM	-0.5
	11:12 PM	2.8			10:47 PM	3.2
15 F	05:36 AM	-0.2		30 Sa	05:16 AM	-0.4
	11:27 AM	2.4			11:07 AM	2.7
	05:43 PM	-0.2			05:22 PM	-0.5
	11:54 PM	2.7			11:37 PM	3.2
				31 Su	06:08 AM	-0.3
					11:58 AM	2.6
					06:13 PM	-0.4

April

Day	Time	Ht		Day	Time	Ht
1 M	12:31 AM	3.1		16 Tu	12:46 AM	2.5
	07:05 AM	-0.1			07:21 AM	0.3
	12:54 PM	2.4			01:07 PM	2.0
	07:10 PM	-0.2			07:16 PM	0.3
2 Tu	01:30 AM	2.4		17 W	01:34 AM	2.4
	08:06 AM	0.0			08:10 AM	0.4
	01:57 PM	2.4			01:59 PM	2.0
	08:13 PM	-0.1			08:09 PM	0.4
3 W	02:34 AM	2.9		18 Th	02:26 AM	2.4
	09:11 AM	0.0			09:03 AM	0.4
	03:05 PM	2.3			02:55 PM	2.0
	09:22 PM	0.0			09:07 PM	0.5
4 Th	03:41 AM	2.8		19 F	03:21 AM	2.3
	10:17 AM	0.0			09:56 AM	0.4
	04:15 PM	2.4			03:53 PM	2.1
	10:33 PM	0.0			10:07 PM	0.4
5 F	04:46 AM	2.8		20 Sa	04:16 AM	2.4
	11:19 AM	0.0			10:47 AM	0.3
	05:20 PM	2.5			04:49 PM	2.2
	11:39 PM	0.0			11:06 PM	0.3
6 Sa	05:47 AM	2.8		21 Su	05:09 AM	2.4
	12:15 PM	-0.1			11:36 AM	0.2
	06:18 PM	2.7			05:41 PM	2.5
7 Su	12:39 AM	-0.1		22 M	12:01 AM	0.2
	06:41 AM	2.8			06:00 AM	2.5
	01:06 PM	-0.2			12:22 PM	0.0
	07:11 PM	2.8			06:30 PM	2.7
8 M	01:33 AM	-0.2		23 Tu	12:53 AM	0.0
	07:31 AM	2.8			06:48 AM	2.6
	01:51 PM	-0.3			01:07 PM	-0.2
	07:58 PM	2.9			07:17 PM	3.0
9 Tu	02:21 AM	-0.3		24 W	01:43 AM	-0.2
	08:16 AM	2.7			07:35 AM	2.7
	02:34 PM	-0.4			01:52 PM	-0.4
	08:41 PM	3.0			08:04 PM	3.2
10 W	03:06 AM	-0.3		25 Th	02:32 AM	-0.4
	08:58 AM	2.6			08:23 AM	2.7
	03:14 PM	-0.4			02:38 PM	-0.6
	09:22 PM	3.0			08:51 PM	3.3
11 Th	03:49 AM	-0.2		26 F	03:21 AM	-0.5
	09:39 AM	2.5			09:11 AM	2.8
	03:52 PM	-0.3			03:24 PM	-0.6
	10:02 PM	2.9			09:40 PM	3.4
12 F	04:30 AM	-0.2		27 Sa	04:11 AM	-0.5
	10:18 AM	2.4			10:00 AM	2.7
	04:30 PM	-0.2			04:13 PM	-0.6
	10:41 PM	2.9			10:30 PM	3.4
13 Sa	05:11 AM	-0.1		28 Su	05:03 AM	-0.5
	10:58 AM	2.3			10:52 AM	2.7
	05:08 PM	-0.1			05:04 PM	-0.6
	11:21 PM	2.8			11:22 PM	3.4
14 Su	05:52 AM	0.1		29 M	05:57 AM	-0.4
	11:38 AM	2.2			11:46 AM	2.6
	05:47 PM	0.0			05:59 PM	-0.4
15 M	12:02 AM	2.6		30 Tu	12:17 AM	3.2
	06:35 AM	0.2			06:53 AM	-0.3
	12:21 PM	2.1			12:45 PM	2.5
	06:30 PM	0.2			06:59 PM	-0.2

Tide Table for December 2012 can be found on page 204

Tide Tables - 2013

Sea of Abaco • Abaco • Bahamas

NOAA Tide Station at Pelican Harbour (Sandy Cay at Pelican Cays Land and Sea Park)

Times are given for the Sea of Abaco at Pelican Harbour, but tides throughout Abaco vary by only a few minutes. Heights are in reference to Mean Lower Low Water (MLLW). Times are in Eastern Standard Time (EST) from 1 January through 9 March, in Eastern Daylight Time from 10 March through 2 November, and in Eastern Standard Time (EST) from 3 November through 31 December.

May

Day	Time	Ht	Day	Time	Ht
1 W	01:16 AM	3.1	16 Th	12:56 AM	2.5
	07:53 AM	-0.2		07:33 AM	0.3
	01:49 PM	2.5		01:25 PM	2.1
	08:03 PM	-0.1		07:32 PM	0.4
2 Th	02:18 AM	2.9	17 F	01:43 AM	2.4
	08:55 AM	-0.1		08:19 AM	0.3
	02:56 PM	2.5		02:18 PM	2.1
	09:12 PM	0.1		08:27 PM	0.5
3 F	03:22 AM	2.8	18 Sa	02:33 AM	2.4
	09:56 AM	-0.1		09:08 AM	0.3
	04:02 PM	2.5		03:12 PM	2.2
	10:21 PM	0.1		09:26 PM	0.5
4 Sa	04:24 AM	2.6	19 Su	03:27 AM	2.4
	10:55 AM	-0.1		09:58 AM	0.2
	05:04 PM	2.6		04:08 PM	2.4
	11:26 PM	0.1		10:27 PM	0.4
5 Su	05:23 AM	2.6	20 M	04:22 AM	2.4
	11:49 AM	-0.1		10:48 AM	0.0
	06:01 PM	2.7		05:02 PM	2.6
				11:26 PM	0.2
6 M	12:24 AM	0.1	21 Tu	05:17 AM	2.4
	06:17 AM	2.5		11:38 AM	-0.1
	12:38 PM	-0.2		05:55 PM	2.9
	06:51 PM	2.8			
7 Tu	01:17 AM	0.0	22 W	12:23 AM	0.0
	07:06 AM	2.5		06:11 AM	2.5
	01:23 PM	-0.2		12:29 PM	-0.3
	07:36 PM	2.9		06:47 PM	3.1
8 W	02:04 AM	-0.1	23 Th	01:17 AM	-0.2
	07:51 AM	2.4		07:04 AM	2.6
	02:04 PM	-0.2		01:19 PM	-0.5
	08:18 PM	2.9		07:38 PM	3.3
9 Th	02:47 AM	-0.1	24 F	02:10 AM	-0.3
	08:33 AM	2.4		07:57 AM	2.7
	02:44 PM	-0.2		02:10 PM	-0.6
	08:57 PM	2.9		08:30 PM	3.5
10 F	03:28 AM	-0.1	25 Sa	03:03 AM	-0.5
	09:13 AM	2.3		08:49 AM	2.7
	03:22 PM	-0.2		03:02 PM	-0.7
	09:36 PM	2.9		09:21 PM	3.6
11 Sa	04:07 AM	-0.1	26 Su	03:55 AM	-0.5
	09:52 AM	2.3		09:43 AM	2.8
	03:59 PM	-0.1		03:55 PM	-0.7
	10:14 PM	2.9		10:13 PM	3.6
12 Su	04:47 AM	0.0	27 M	04:48 AM	-0.5
	10:31 AM	2.2		10:37 AM	2.8
	04:37 PM	0.0		04:50 PM	-0.6
	10:53 PM	2.8		11:07 PM	3.5
13 M	05:26 AM	0.1	28 Tu	05:42 AM	-0.5
	11:11 AM	2.2		11:34 AM	2.7
	05:16 PM	0.1		05:47 PM	-0.4
	11:32 PM	2.7			
14 Tu	06:07 AM	0.2	29 W	12:02 AM	3.3
	11:53 AM	2.1		06:37 AM	-0.4
	05:58 PM	0.2		12:33 PM	2.7
				06:46 PM	-0.2
15 W	12:13 AM	2.6	30 Th	12:58 AM	3.1
	06:49 AM	0.2		07:34 AM	-0.3
	12:37 PM	2.1		01:35 PM	2.7
	06:42 PM	0.3		07:50 PM	0.0
			31 F	01:57 AM	2.9
				08:31 AM	-0.2
				02:38 PM	2.6
				08:55 PM	0.1

June

Day	Time	Ht	Day	Time	He
1 Sa	02:57 AM	2.7	16 Su	01:52 AM	2.5
	09:29 AM	-0.1		08:24 AM	0.2
	03:41 PM	2.7		02:34 PM	2.4
	10:02 PM	0.2		08:50 PM	0.5
2 Su	03:57 AM	2.5	17 M	02:44 AM	2.4
	10:25 AM	-0.1		09:13 AM	0.1
	04:41 PM	2.7		03:30 PM	2.6
	11:05 PM	0.3		09:52 PM	0.4
3 M	04:54 AM	2.4	18 Tu	03:40 AM	2.4
	11:18 AM	-0.1		10:06 AM	0.0
	05:37 PM	2.7		04:27 PM	2.8
				10:54 PM	0.3
4 Tu	12:04 AM	0.2	19 W	04:39 AM	2.4
	05:49 AM	2.3		11:01 AM	-0.1
	12:07 PM	-0.1		05:25 PM	3.0
	06:26 PM	2.8		11:56 PM	0.1
5 W	12:56 AM	0.2	20 Th	05:39 AM	2.5
	06:38 AM	2.3		11:57 AM	-0.3
	12:52 PM	-0.1		06:21 PM	3.2
	07:12 PM	2.8			
6 Th	01:43 AM	0.1	21 F	12:54 AM	0.0
	07:24 AM	2.2		06:38 AM	2.6
	01:35 PM	-0.1		12:54 PM	-0.5
	07:54 PM	2.9		07:17 PM	3.5
7 F	02:26 AM	0.1	22 Sa	01:51 AM	-0.2
	08:07 AM	2.2		07:35 AM	2.7
	02:15 PM	-0.1		01:49 PM	-0.6
	08:33 PM	2.9		08:11 PM	3.6
8 Sa	03:06 AM	0.1	23 Su	02:45 AM	-0.4
	08:47 AM	2.2		08:31 AM	2.8
	02:54 PM	-0.1		02:45 PM	-0.6
	09:12 PM	2.9		09:04 PM	3.7
9 Su	03:45 AM	0.1	24 M	03:38 AM	-0.5
	09:27 AM	2.2		09:27 AM	2.9
	03:33 PM	0.0		03:40 PM	-0.6
	09:49 PM	2.9		09:57 PM	3.7
10 M	04:23 AM	0.1	25 Tu	04:31 AM	-0.5
	10:06 AM	2.2		10:22 AM	2.9
	04:11 PM	0.1		04:36 PM	-0.5
	10:27 PM	2.9		10:50 PM	3.6
11 Tu	05:01 AM	0.1	26 W	05:23 AM	-0.5
	10:46 AM	2.2		11:18 AM	3.0
	04:50 PM	0.1		05:32 PM	-0.4
	11:05 PM	2.8		11:42 PM	3.4
12 W	05:39 AM	0.2	27 Th	06:15 AM	-0.4
	11:26 AM	2.1		12:15 PM	2.9
	05:31 PM	0.2		06:30 PM	-0.2
	11:43 PM	2.7			
13 Th	06:17 AM	0.2	28 F	12:36 AM	3.2
	12:08 PM	2.2		07:08 AM	-0.3
	06:14 PM	0.3		01:13 PM	2.9
				07:30 PM	0.1
14 F	12:22 AM	2.6	29 Sa	01:31 AM	2.9
	06:57 AM	0.2		08:02 AM	-0.2
	12:53 PM	2.3		02:12 PM	2.8
	07:00 PM	0.4		08:32 PM	0.3
15 Sa	01:05 AM	2.6	30 Su	02:27 AM	2.7
	07:39 AM	0.2		08:56 AM	0.0
	01:42 PM	2.3		03:12 PM	2.8
	07:53 PM	0.5		09:35 PM	0.4

July

Day	Time	Ht	Day	Time	Ht
1 M	03:24 AM	2.5	16 Tu	02:10 AM	2.5
	09:50 AM	0.1		08:37 AM	0.2
	04:11 PM	2.7		02:58 PM	2.9
	10:37 PM	0.5		09:23 PM	0.6
2 Tu	04:21 AM	2.3	17 W	03:08 AM	2.5
	10:43 AM	0.1		09:33 AM	0.1
	05:07 PM	2.7		03:59 PM	3.0
	11:36 PM	0.5		10:29 PM	0.5
3 W	05:17 AM	2.2	18 Th	04:12 AM	2.5
	11:34 AM	0.2		10:33 AM	0.0
	05:58 PM	2.8		05:00 PM	3.2
				11:33 PM	0.4
4 Th	12:30 AM	0.5	19 F	05:16 AM	2.6
	06:09 AM	2.2		11:35 AM	-0.1
	12:22 PM	0.2		06:01 PM	3.4
	06:45 PM	2.8			
5 F	01:18 AM	0.4	20 Sa	12:35 AM	0.2
	06:56 AM	2.2		06:19 AM	2.7
	01:06 PM	0.2		12:35 PM	-0.2
	07:28 PM	2.9		06:59 PM	3.6
6 Sa	02:01 AM	0.3	21 Su	01:33 AM	0.0
	07:40 AM	2.3		07:18 AM	2.9
	01:49 PM	0.1		01:34 PM	-0.4
	08:09 PM	2.9		07:54 PM	3.7
7 Su	02:41 AM	0.3	22 M	02:27 AM	-0.2
	08:22 AM	2.3		08:16 AM	3.0
	02:30 PM	0.1		02:31 PM	-0.4
	08:47 PM	3.0		08:48 PM	3.8
8 M	03:20 AM	0.2	23 Tu	03:19 AM	-0.3
	09:02 AM	2.4		09:11 AM	3.2
	03:09 PM	0.1		03:26 PM	-0.4
	09:25 PM	3.0		09:39 PM	3.7
9 Tu	03:57 AM	0.2	24 W	04:09 AM	-0.3
	09:42 AM	2.4		10:05 AM	3.2
	03:48 PM	0.2		04:21 PM	-0.3
	10:01 PM	3.0		10:30 PM	3.6
10 W	04:33 AM	0.2	25 Th	04:59 AM	-0.3
	10:20 AM	2.5		10:58 AM	3.2
	04:27 PM	0.2		05:15 PM	-0.2
	10:37 PM	3.0		11:19 PM	3.4
11 Th	05:08 AM	0.2	26 F	05:48 AM	-0.2
	10:59 AM	2.5		11:51 AM	3.2
	05:07 PM	0.3		06:09 PM	0.0
	11:14 PM	2.9			
12 F	05:44 AM	0.2	27 Sa	12:09 AM	3.2
	11:39 AM	2.6		06:37 AM	-0.1
	05:49 PM	0.4		12:44 PM	3.1
	11:52 PM	2.8		07:04 PM	0.3
13 Sa	06:21 AM	0.2	28 Su	01:00 AM	2.9
	12:22 PM	2.6		07:27 AM	0.1
	06:34 PM	0.5		01:39 PM	3.0
				08:02 PM	0.5
14 Su	12:33 AM	2.7	29 M	01:53 AM	2.7
	07:01 AM	0.2		08:18 AM	0.2
	01:09 PM	2.7		02:36 PM	2.9
	07:24 PM	0.5		09:02 PM	0.6
15 M	01:18 AM	2.6	30 Tu	02:48 AM	2.5
	07:46 AM	0.2		09:11 AM	0.4
	02:01 PM	2.8		03:34 PM	2.8
	08:21 PM	0.6		10:03 PM	0.7
			31 W	03:45 AM	2.3
				10:05 AM	0.5
				04:31 PM	2.8
				11:03 PM	0.8

August

Day	Time	Ht	Day	Time	Ht
1 Th	04:43 AM	2.3	16 F	03:54 AM	2.7
	10:59 AM	0.5		10:15 AM	0.3
	05:25 PM	2.8		04:42 PM	3.3
	11:58 PM	0.8		11:16 PM	0.6
2 F	05:37 AM	2.3	17 Sa	05:02 AM	2.8
	11:51 AM	0.5		11:21 AM	0.2
	06:14 PM	2.9		05:45 PM	3.5
3 Sa	12:47 AM	0.7	18 Su	12:18 AM	0.4
	06:27 AM	2.4		06:06 AM	2.9
	12:39 PM	0.5		12:24 PM	0.1
	06:59 PM	3.0		06:43 PM	3.6
4 Su	01:31 AM	0.6	19 M	01:15 AM	0.2
	07:13 AM	2.5		07:06 AM	3.1
	01:23 PM	0.4		01:24 PM	-0.1
	07:41 PM	3.1		07:38 PM	3.7
5 M	02:11 AM	0.5	20 Tu	02:07 AM	0.0
	07:55 AM	2.6		08:02 AM	3.3
	02:06 PM	0.3		02:20 PM	-0.1
	08:20 PM	3.1		08:30 PM	3.7
6 Tu	02:49 AM	0.4	21 W	02:57 AM	-0.1
	08:36 AM	2.7		08:54 AM	3.4
	02:46 PM	0.3		03:13 PM	-0.2
	08:57 PM	3.2		09:19 PM	3.7
7 W	03:25 AM	0.4	22 Th	03:44 AM	-0.1
	09:14 AM	2.8		09:45 AM	3.5
	03:25 PM	0.3		04:04 PM	-0.1
	09:33 PM	3.2		10:07 PM	3.6
8 Th	04:00 AM	0.3	23 F	04:31 AM	-0.1
	09:52 AM	2.9		10:34 AM	3.5
	04:05 PM	0.3		04:55 PM	0.0
	10:09 PM	3.1		10:54 PM	3.4
9 F	04:35 AM	0.3	24 Sa	05:16 AM	0.0
	10:31 AM	2.9		11:22 AM	3.4
	04:45 PM	0.4		05:45 PM	0.2
	10:46 PM	3.1		11:40 PM	3.2
10 Sa	05:10 AM	0.3	25 Su	06:02 AM	0.1
	11:11 AM	3.0		12:11 PM	3.3
	05:27 PM	0.4		06:35 PM	0.4
	11:24 PM	3.0			
11 Su	05:47 AM	0.3	26 M	12:28 AM	2.9
	11:53 AM	3.0		06:48 AM	0.3
	06:12 PM	0.5		01:02 PM	3.1
				07:28 PM	0.7
12 M	12:06 AM	2.9	27 Tu	01:17 AM	2.7
	06:29 AM	0.3		07:37 AM	0.5
	12:40 PM	3.0		01:55 PM	3.0
	07:02 PM	0.6		08:24 PM	0.8
13 Tu	12:52 AM	2.8	28 W	02:10 AM	2.5
	07:15 AM	0.3		08:29 AM	0.7
	01:33 PM	3.1		02:51 PM	2.9
	07:59 PM	0.7		09:23 PM	1.0
14 W	01:46 AM	2.7	29 Th	03:07 AM	2.4
	08:09 AM	0.3		09:24 AM	0.8
	02:32 PM	3.1		03:49 PM	2.8
	09:03 PM	0.7		10:23 PM	1.0
15 Th	02:47 AM	2.6	30 F	04:06 AM	2.4
	09:09 AM	0.3		10:22 AM	0.8
	03:37 PM	3.2		04:46 PM	2.8
	10:10 PM	0.7		11:20 PM	1.0
			31 Sa	05:04 AM	2.4
				11:17 AM	0.8
				05:38 PM	2.9

Tide Table for December 2012 can be found on page 204

Tide Tables - 2013
Sea of Abaco • Abaco • Bahamas
NOAA Tide Station at Pelican Harbour (Sandy Cay at Pelican Cays Land and Sea Park

Times are given for the Sea of Abaco at Pelican Harbour, but tides throughout Abaco vary by only a few minutes.
Heights are in reference to Mean Lower Low Water (MLLW). Times are in Eastern Standard Time (EST) from 1 January through 9 March, in Eastern Daylight Time from 10 March through 2 November, and in Eastern Standard Time (EST) from 3 November through 31 December.

September

Day	Time	Ht	Day	Time	Ht
1 Su	12:10 AM / 05:56 AM / 12:09 PM / 06:25 PM	0.9 / 2.5 / 0.7 / 3.0	**16** M	12:02 AM / 05:57 AM / 12:16 PM / 06:28 PM	0.5 / 3.1 / 0.3 / 3.5
2 M	12:54 AM / 06:42 AM / 12:56 PM / 07:07 PM	0.8 / 2.7 / 0.6 / 3.1	**17** Tu	12:56 AM / 06:54 AM / 01:15 PM / 07:21 PM	0.3 / 3.3 / 0.2 / 3.6
3 Tu	01:34 AM / 07:25 AM / 01:39 PM / 07:47 PM	0.7 / 2.8 / 0.5 / 3.2	**18** W	01:46 AM / 07:47 AM / 02:08 PM / 08:10 PM	0.1 / 3.5 / 0.1 / 3.5
4 W	02:12 AM / 08:06 AM / 02:21 PM / 08:25 PM	0.5 / 3.0 / 0.4 / 3.2	**19** Th	02:33 AM / 08:36 AM / 02:59 PM / 08:57 PM	0.0 / 3.6 / 0.1 / 3.5
5 Th	02:48 AM / 08:45 AM / 03:02 PM / 09:03 PM	0.4 / 3.1 / 0.4 / 3.3	**20** F	03:17 AM / 09:23 AM / 03:47 PM / 09:42 PM	0.0 / 3.6 / 0.1 / 3.4
6 F	03:24 AM / 09:23 AM / 03:42 PM / 09:40 PM	0.3 / 3.2 / 0.4 / 3.2	**21** Sa	04:01 AM / 10:08 AM / 04:33 PM / 10:26 PM	0.0 / 3.6 / 0.2 / 3.2
7 Sa	04:00 AM / 10:03 AM / 04:24 PM / 10:19 PM	0.3 / 3.3 / 0.4 / 3.2	**22** Su	04:43 AM / 10:52 AM / 05:19 PM / 11:10 PM	0.1 / 3.5 / 0.3 / 3.0
8 Su	04:37 AM / 10:44 AM / 05:07 PM / 11:00 PM	0.3 / 3.4 / 0.4 / 3.1	**23** M	05:25 AM / 11:37 AM / 06:06 PM / 11:55 PM	0.3 / 3.3 / 0.5 / 2.8
9 M	05:17 AM / 11:28 AM / 05:54 PM / 11:44 PM	0.3 / 3.4 / 0.5 / 3.0	**24** Tu	06:09 AM / 12:23 PM / 06:54 PM	0.5 / 3.2 / 0.7
10 Tu	06:02 AM / 12:17 PM / 06:46 PM	0.3 / 3.4 / 0.6	**25** W	12:41 AM / 06:55 AM / 01:12 PM / 07:46 PM	2.6 / 0.7 / 3.0 / 0.9
11 W	12:34 AM / 06:52 AM / 01:12 PM / 07:44 PM	2.9 / 0.4 / 3.3 / 0.7	**26** Th	07:45 AM / 07:45 AM / 02:05 PM / 08:41 PM	2.5 / 0.8 / 2.9 / 1.0
12 Th	01:31 AM / 07:50 AM / 02:14 PM / 08:49 PM	2.8 / 0.5 / 3.3 / 0.7	**27** F	02:28 AM / 08:41 AM / 03:02 PM / 09:39 PM	2.4 / 0.9 / 2.8 / 1.0
13 F	02:36 AM / 08:55 AM / 03:20 PM / 09:56 PM	2.7 / 0.5 / 3.3 / 0.7	**28** Sa	03:28 AM / 09:40 AM / 03:59 PM / 10:34 PM	2.4 / 1.0 / 2.8 / 1.0
14 Sa	03:46 AM / 10:04 AM / 04:25 PM / 11:01 PM	2.8 / 0.5 / 3.4 / 0.6	**29** Su	04:26 AM / 10:39 AM / 04:53 PM / 11:25 PM	2.5 / 0.9 / 2.8 / 0.9
15 Su	04:54 AM / 11:13 AM / 05:30 PM	2.9 / 0.4 / 3.4	**30** M	05:19 AM / 11:34 AM / 05:43 PM	2.6 / 0.9 / 2.9

October

Day	Time	Ht	Day	Time	He
1 Tu	12:10 AM / 06:07 AM / 12:24 PM / 06:28 PM	0.8 / 2.8 / 0.7 / 3.0	**16** W	12:34 AM / 06:41 AM / 01:05 PM / 07:02 PM	0.2 / 3.3 / 0.3 / 3.2
2 W	12:52 AM / 06:51 AM / 01:10 PM / 07:10 PM	0.6 / 3.0 / 0.6 / 3.1	**17** Th	01:23 AM / 07:31 AM / 01:56 PM / 07:50 PM	0.1 / 3.4 / 0.2 / 3.2
3 Th	01:31 AM / 07:33 AM / 01:54 PM / 07:50 PM	0.5 / 3.2 / 0.4 / 3.1	**18** F	02:08 AM / 08:17 AM / 02:44 PM / 08:35 PM	0.0 / 3.5 / 0.1 / 3.1
4 F	02:09 AM / 08:14 AM / 02:37 PM / 08:31 PM	0.3 / 3.3 / 0.3 / 3.2	**19** Sa	02:50 AM / 09:01 AM / 03:29 PM / 09:18 PM	0.0 / 3.5 / 0.1 / 3.0
5 Sa	02:47 AM / 08:54 AM / 03:20 PM / 09:12 PM	0.2 / 3.5 / 0.2 / 3.2	**20** Su	03:31 AM / 09:43 AM / 04:12 PM / 10:00 PM	0.1 / 3.5 / 0.2 / 2.9
6 Su	03:27 AM / 09:37 AM / 04:04 PM / 09:54 PM	0.1 / 3.6 / 0.2 / 3.1	**21** M	04:11 AM / 10:24 AM / 04:55 PM / 10:42 PM	0.1 / 3.4 / 0.3 / 2.7
7 M	04:08 AM / 10:21 AM / 04:50 PM / 10:39 PM	0.1 / 3.6 / 0.2 / 3.0	**22** Tu	04:51 AM / 11:05 AM / 05:38 PM / 11:24 PM	0.3 / 3.2 / 0.4 / 2.6
8 Tu	04:53 AM / 11:08 AM / 05:40 PM / 11:28 PM	0.1 / 3.6 / 0.3 / 3.0	**23** W	05:33 AM / 11:48 AM / 06:22 PM	0.4 / 3.1 / 0.6
9 W	05:42 AM / 12:00 PM / 06:34 PM	0.2 / 3.5 / 0.4	**24** Th	12:08 AM / 06:16 AM / 12:33 PM / 07:09 PM	2.5 / 0.6 / 2.9 / 0.7
10 Th	12:22 AM / 06:36 AM / 12:56 PM / 07:32 PM	2.9 / 0.3 / 3.4 / 0.5	**25** F	12:56 AM / 07:04 AM / 01:21 PM / 07:59 PM	2.4 / 0.7 / 2.8 / 0.8
11 F	01:32 AM / 07:38 AM / 01:58 PM / 08:36 PM	2.8 / 0.4 / 3.3 / 0.6	**26** Sa	01:49 AM / 07:57 AM / 02:13 PM / 08:51 PM	2.3 / 0.9 / 2.7 / 0.8
12 Sa	02:29 AM / 08:41 AM / 03:04 PM / 09:41 PM	2.8 / 0.5 / 3.2 / 0.5	**27** Su	02:46 AM / 08:56 AM / 03:07 PM / 09:44 PM	2.3 / 0.9 / 2.6 / 0.8
13 Su	03:39 AM / 09:50 AM / 04:10 PM / 10:44 PM	2.8 / 0.5 / 3.2 / 0.5	**28** M	03:43 AM / 09:56 AM / 04:02 PM / 10:34 PM	2.4 / 0.9 / 2.6 / 0.7
14 M	04:46 AM / 11:05 AM / 05:12 PM / 11:42 PM	3.0 / 0.5 / 3.2 / 0.3	**29** Tu	04:38 AM / 10:54 AM / 04:54 PM / 11:21 PM	2.6 / 0.8 / 2.7 / 0.6
15 Tu	05:47 AM / 12:08 PM / 06:10 PM	3.2 / 0.4 / 3.2	**30** W	05:28 AM / 11:48 AM / 05:43 PM	2.7 / 0.6 / 2.7
			31 Th	12:05 AM / 06:14 AM / 12:38 PM / 06:29 PM	0.4 / 3.0 / 0.5 / 2.8

November

Day	Time	Ht	Day	Time	Ht
1 F	12:48 AM / 06:59 AM / 01:25 PM / 07:15 PM	0.2 / 3.2 / 0.3 / 2.9	**16** Sa	12:42 AM / 06:58 AM / 01:28 PM / 07:13 PM	-0.1 / 3.2 / 0.1 / 2.6
2 Sa	01:31 AM / 07:43 AM / 02:12 PM / 08:00 PM	0.0 / 3.4 / 0.1 / 2.9	**17** Su	01:24 AM / 07:39 AM / 02:11 PM / 07:55 PM	-0.1 / 3.2 / 0.1 / 2.6
3 Su	01:14 AM / 07:28 AM / 01:58 PM / 07:46 PM	-0.1 / 3.5 / 0.0 / 2.9	**18** M	02:04 AM / 08:19 AM / 02:52 PM / 08:36 PM	-0.1 / 3.2 / 0.1 / 2.5
4 M	01:58 AM / 08:14 AM / 02:46 PM / 08:33 PM	-0.2 / 3.6 / -0.1 / 2.9	**19** Tu	02:43 AM / 08:59 AM / 03:32 PM / 09:16 PM	0.0 / 3.1 / 0.1 / 2.4
5 Tu	02:45 AM / 09:02 AM / 03:35 PM / 09:22 PM	-0.3 / 3.7 / -0.1 / 2.9	**20** W	03:22 AM / 09:38 AM / 04:12 PM / 09:57 PM	0.1 / 3.0 / 0.2 / 2.3
6 W	03:34 AM / 09:52 AM / 04:27 PM / 10:15 PM	-0.2 / 3.6 / 0.0 / 2.9	**21** Th	04:02 AM / 10:17 AM / 04:53 PM / 10:39 PM	0.2 / 2.9 / 0.3 / 2.3
7 Th	04:27 AM / 10:45 AM / 05:21 PM / 11:12 PM	-0.1 / 3.5 / 0.0 / 2.8	**22** F	04:44 AM / 10:58 AM / 05:35 PM / 11:23 PM	0.4 / 2.8 / 0.4 / 2.2
8 F	05:25 AM / 11:42 AM / 06:19 PM	0.0 / 3.4 / 0.1	**23** Sa	05:28 AM / 11:41 AM / 06:18 PM	0.5 / 2.7 / 0.4
9 Sa	12:14 AM / 06:28 AM / 12:42 PM / 07:20 PM	2.8 / 0.2 / 3.2 / 0.2	**24** Su	12:11 AM / 06:17 AM / 12:27 PM / 07:04 PM	2.2 / 0.6 / 2.6 / 0.5
10 Su	01:20 AM / 07:36 AM / 01:46 PM / 08:21 PM	2.8 / 0.3 / 3.0 / 0.2	**25** M	01:03 AM / 07:11 AM / 01:16 PM / 07:51 PM	2.2 / 0.7 / 2.5 / 0.4
11 M	02:27 AM / 08:46 AM / 02:50 PM / 09:22 PM	2.8 / 0.4 / 2.9 / 0.1	**26** Tu	01:57 AM / 08:10 AM / 02:08 PM / 08:40 PM	2.3 / 0.7 / 2.4 / 0.4
12 Tu	03:32 AM / 09:54 AM / 03:51 PM / 10:18 PM	2.9 / 0.4 / 2.8 / 0.1	**27** W	02:52 AM / 09:10 AM / 03:02 PM / 09:29 PM	2.4 / 0.6 / 2.4 / 0.3
13 W	04:32 AM / 10:56 AM / 04:48 PM / 11:10 PM	3.0 / 0.3 / 2.8 / 0.0	**28** Th	03:45 AM / 10:08 AM / 03:56 PM / 10:18 PM	2.6 / 0.5 / 2.4 / 0.1
14 Th	05:25 AM / 11:52 AM / 05:40 PM / 11:58 PM	3.1 / 0.2 / 2.7 / -0.1	**29** F	04:36 AM / 11:04 AM / 04:49 PM / 11:07 PM	2.8 / 0.3 / 2.5 / -0.1
15 F	06:13 AM / 12:42 PM / 06:28 PM	3.2 / 0.1 / 2.7	**30** Sa	05:26 AM / 11:56 AM / 05:41 PM / 11:56 PM	3.1 / 0.1 / 2.5 / -0.3

December

Day	Time	Ht	Day	Time	Ht
1 Su	06:16 AM / 12:48 PM / 06:32 PM	3.3 / -0.1 / 2.6	**16** M	01:00 AM / 07:19 AM / 01:52 PM / 07:33 PM	-0.2 / 2.9 / 0.0 / 2.2
2 M	12:45 AM / 07:05 AM / 01:38 PM / 07:23 PM	-0.5 / 3.5 / -0.3 / 2.7	**17** Tu	01:41 AM / 07:58 AM / 02:31 PM / 08:13 PM	-0.2 / 2.9 / 0.0 / 2.2
3 Tu	01:36 AM / 07:55 AM / 02:29 PM / 08:14 PM	-0.6 / 3.6 / -0.4 / 2.8	**18** W	02:20 AM / 08:36 AM / 03:09 PM / 08:53 PM	-0.1 / 2.9 / 0.0 / 2.2
4 W	02:27 AM / 08:45 AM / 03:20 PM / 09:07 PM	-0.6 / 3.6 / -0.4 / 2.8	**19** Th	02:59 AM / 09:13 AM / 03:47 PM / 09:32 PM	-0.1 / 2.8 / 0.0 / 2.2
5 Th	03:20 AM / 09:37 AM / 04:12 PM / 10:02 PM	-0.6 / 3.6 / -0.4 / 2.8	**20** F	03:37 AM / 09:50 AM / 04:24 PM / 10:12 PM	0.0 / 2.8 / 0.0 / 2.2
6 F	04:15 AM / 10:30 AM / 05:05 PM / 11:00 PM	-0.4 / 3.4 / -0.4 / 2.8	**21** Sa	04:17 AM / 10:27 AM / 05:01 PM / 10:52 PM	0.1 / 2.7 / 0.1 / 2.2
7 Sa	05:13 AM / 11:25 AM / 06:00 PM	-0.3 / 3.2 / -0.3	**22** Su	04:58 AM / 11:06 AM / 05:39 PM / 11:35 PM	0.2 / 2.6 / 0.1 / 2.2
8 Su	12:00 AM / 06:15 AM / 12:23 PM / 06:57 PM	2.7 / -0.1 / 3.0 / -0.2	**23** M	05:43 AM / 11:46 AM / 06:19 PM	0.3 / 2.4 / 0.1
9 M	01:03 AM / 07:21 AM / 01:23 PM / 07:56 PM	2.7 / 0.1 / 2.8 / -0.2	**24** Tu	12:22 AM / 06:32 AM / 12:30 PM / 07:02 PM	2.2 / 0.4 / 2.3 / 0.1
10 Tu	02:08 AM / 08:29 AM / 02:24 PM / 08:54 PM	2.7 / 0.2 / 2.6 / -0.1	**25** W	01:12 AM / 07:27 AM / 01:19 PM / 07:49 PM	2.3 / 0.4 / 2.2 / 0.1
11 W	03:11 AM / 09:36 AM / 03:25 PM / 09:50 PM	2.7 / 0.2 / 2.4 / -0.1	**26** Th	02:06 AM / 08:27 AM / 02:14 PM / 08:41 PM	2.4 / 0.4 / 2.2 / 0.0
12 Th	04:10 AM / 10:39 AM / 04:24 PM / 10:43 PM	2.8 / 0.2 / 2.4 / -0.1	**27** F	03:03 AM / 09:29 AM / 03:13 PM / 09:35 PM	2.5 / 0.3 / 2.2 / -0.1
13 F	05:04 AM / 11:35 AM / 05:17 PM / 11:33 PM	2.8 / 0.1 / 2.3 / -0.2	**28** Sa	04:00 AM / 10:31 AM / 04:12 PM / 10:32 PM	2.7 / 0.2 / 2.2 / -0.3
14 Sa	05:53 AM / 12:25 PM / 06:06 PM	2.9 / 0.1 / 2.2	**29** Su	04:57 AM / 11:30 AM / 05:11 PM / 11:28 PM	2.9 / 0.0 / 2.3 / -0.5
15 Su	12:18 AM / 06:38 AM / 01:10 PM / 06:51 PM	-0.2 / 2.9 / 0.0 / 2.2	**30** M	05:52 AM / 12:25 PM / 06:08 PM	3.2 / -0.3 / 2.5
			31 Tu	12:23 AM / 06:45 AM / 01:19 PM / 07:04 PM	-0.7 / 3.3 / -0.4 / 2.6

Tide Table for December 2012 can be found on page 204

Tides: Highs, Lows, Neaps, Springs, Etc.

Tides are caused by the gravitational pull of the sun and the moon on the earth's oceans, and also the centrifugal force which results from the earth's annual circular trek around the sun.

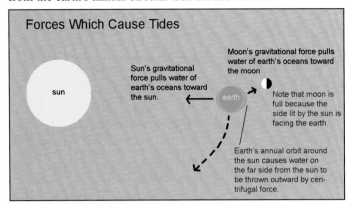

Forces Which Cause Tides

Sun's gravitational force pulls water of earth's oceans toward the sun.

Moon's gravitational force pulls water of earth's oceans toward the moon

Note that moon is full because the side lit by the sun is facing the earth.

Earth's annual orbit around the sun causes water on the far side from the sun to be thrown outward by centrifugal force.

Although the moon is much smaller than the sun, it is much closer to the earth, and its effect on tides is about twice as great as that of the sun.

In Abaco there are generally two high tides and two low tides each day. The difference between them generally varies from about 2.5' to 3.5' (vertically).

This variation is the result of the differing alignment of the sun, the moon, and the earth. When the moon is new (no visible moon) the bodies are lined up and the gravitational force of the sun and moon pull together in a line. Therefore the high tides are higher and the low tides are lower.

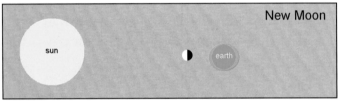

New Moon

When the moon is half, the gravitational forces are at right angles and tend to cancel each other, and tidal fluctuation is not as great. These tides are called **neap tides**.

Half Moon

When the moon is full the moon's gravitation pull supplements the centrifugal force (result of the earth's annual orbit around the sun) and high tides are again higher and low tides are lower than during ncap tides.

Full Moon

When the moon is new or full the tides are described as **spring tides**. Note that this has nothing to do with the season of the year, even though the term is the same. Some persons call these tides moon tides. This is an incorrect and rather confusing way to refer to them because all tides—neaps as well as springs—are caused, in great part, by the moon.

Tide Table - December 2012

Times given are for the Sea of Abaco at Pelican Harbour, but tides throughout Abaco vary by only a few minutes. Heights are in reference to Mean Lower Low Water (MLLW). Times are in Eastern Standard Time for December 2012.

	Time	Ht		Time	Ht		Time	Ht		Time	Ht
1 Sa	03:21 AM 09:37 AM 04:12 PM 09:56 PM	0.1 2.9 0.2 2.2	**9** Su	03:57 AM 10:26 AM 04:10 PM 10:31 PM	2.9 0.1 2.5 -0.3	**17** M	04:57 AM 11:07 AM 05:41 PM 11:41 PM	-0.3 3.1 -0.4 2.7	**25** Tu	06:01 AM 12:35 PM 06:13 PM	2.6 0.2 2
2 Su	04:00 AM 10:15 AM 04:51 PM 10:37 PM	0.2 2.8 0.2 2.2	**10** M	04:54 AM 11:26 AM 05:10 PM 11:27 PM	3.1 -0.1 2.5 -0.5	**18** Tu	05:55 AM 12:01 PM 06:34 PM	-0.1 2.9 -0.3	**26** W	12:22 AM 06:43 AM 01:16 PM 06:55 PM	
3 M	04:41 AM 10:54 AM 05:30 PM 11:21 PM	0.3 2.7 0.3 2.2	**11** Tu	05:50 AM 12:24 AM 06:07 PM	3.4 -0.3 2.6	**19** W	12:40 AM 06:56 AM 12:56 PM 07:28 PM	2.6 0.1 2.6 -0.1	**27** Th	01:03 AM 07:22 AM 01:56 PM 07:36 PM	
4 Tu	05:26 AM 11:36 AM 06:12 PM	0.4 2.7 0.3	**12** W	12:22 AM 06:44 AM 01:19 PM 07:03 PM	-0.7 3.5 -0.4 2.7	**20** Th	01:40 AM 07:59 AM 01:52 PM 08:22 PM	2.5 0.3 2.4 0.0	**28** F	01:42 AM 08:00 AM 02:33 PM 08:15 PM	-0. 2.8 0.0 2.2
5 W	12:09 AM 06:17 AM 12:23 PM 06:58 PM	2.3 0.5 2.6 0.2	**13** Th	01:17 AM 07:38 AM 02:12 PM 07:58 PM	-0.8 3.6 -0.5 2.7	**21** F	02:39 AM 09:02 AM 02:49 PM 09:15 PM	2.5 0.4 2.2 0.0	**29** Sa	02:21 AM 08:37 AM 03:10 PM 08:54 PM	-0.1 2.8 -0.1 2.2
6 Th	01:02 AM 07:15 AM 01:14 PM 07:47 PM	2.4 0.5 2.5 0.2	**14** F	02:11 AM 08:30 AM 03:05 PM 08:53 PM	-0.8 3.6 -0.6 2.8	**22** Sa	03:36 AM 10:04 AM 03:45 PM 10:05 PM	2.5 0.4 2.1 0.0	**30** Su	03:00 AM 09:13 AM 03:46 PM 09:33 PM	-0.1 2.8 -0.1 2.2
7 F	01:59 AM 08:17 AM 02:11 PM 08:40 PM	2.5 0.4 2.4 0.0	**15** Sa	03:06 AM 09:23 AM 03:57 PM 09:48 PM	-0.7 3.5 -0.6 2.8	**23** Su	04:29 AM 11:00 AM 04:39 PM 10:54 PM	2.5 0.3 2.0 0.0	**31** M	03:39 AM 09:50 AM 04:22 PM 10:13 PM	0.0 2.8 -0. 2.3
8 Sa	02:58 AM 09:22 AM 03:10 PM 09:35 PM	2.7 0.3 2.4 -0.1	**16** Su	04:01 AM 10:15 AM 04:49 PM 10:44 PM	-0.6 3.4 -0.5 2.7	**24** M	05:17 AM 11:50 AM 05:27 PM 11:39 PM	2.6 0.3 2.0 0.0			

Determining water depth at times between low and high tides

It should be clear that at half way between low and high tides the water level will be half way between its low and high levels. At other times, if some degree of precision is sought, it is not desirable to use a simple linear progression because water movement is not uniform. Instead, water levels tend to hover at both low tide and high tide, and change in level occurs most rapidly at half tide. The following rule of twelfths can be used to determine water levels fairly accurately.

Time	To Determine Depth	Example*
low tide	from tide table	4'
1 hr. after low	add 1/12 ** (+3")	4' 3"
2 hrs. after low	add 3/12 (+ 9")	4' 9"
3 hrs. after low	add 6/12 (+ 18")	5' 6"
4 hrs. after low	add 9/12 (+ 27")	6' 3"
5 hrs. after low	add 11/12 (+ 33")	6' 9"
6 hrs. after low	add 12/12 (+ 36")	7'

* Example assumes 4' depth at MLW with low water at datum and high water at 3' above datum. Difference in levels is therefore 3' (or 36").

** Add 1/12 of the difference between low tide and high tide (compute this from the tide table).

Index - Selected Abaco Place Names

Index to Advertisers in The Cruising Guide to Abaco: 2013

Ferry and Ship Routes to, from and Within Abaco, Bahamas

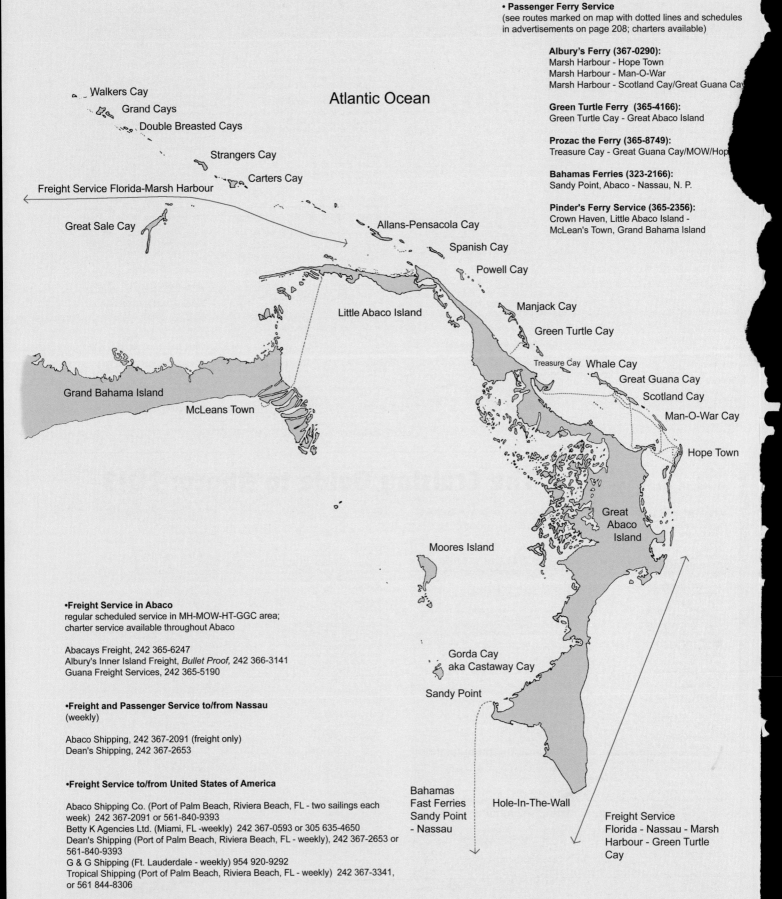

Atlantic Ocean

Walkers Cay

Grand Cays

Double Breasted Cays

Strangers Cay

Carters Cay

Freight Service Florida-Marsh Harbour

Great Sale Cay

Allans-Pensacola Cay

Spanish Cay

Powell Cay

Little Abaco Island

Manjack Cay

Green Turtle Cay

Treasure Cay Whale Cay

Great Guana Cay

Scotland Cay

Grand Bahama Island

McLeans Town

Man-O-War Cay

Hope Town

Great Abaco Island

Moores Island

Gorda Cay
aka Castaway Cay

Sandy Point

Bahamas
Fast Ferries
Sandy Point
- Nassau

Hole-In-The-Wall

Freight Service
Florida - Nassau - Marsh
Harbour - Green Turtle
Cay

• Passenger Ferry Service
(see routes marked on map with dotted lines and schedules
in advertisements on page 208; charters available)

Albury's Ferry (367-0290):
Marsh Harbour - Hope Town
Marsh Harbour - Man-O-War
Marsh Harbour - Scotland Cay/Great Guana Cay

Green Turtle Ferry (365-4166):
Green Turtle Cay - Great Abaco Island

Prozac the Ferry (365-8749):
Treasure Cay - Great Guana Cay/MOW/Hope

Bahamas Ferries (323-2166):
Sandy Point, Abaco - Nassau, N. P.

Pinder's Ferry Service (365-2356):
Crown Haven, Little Abaco Island -
McLean's Town, Grand Bahama Island

• Freight Service in Abaco
regular scheduled service in MH-MOW-HT-GGC area;
charter service available throughout Abaco

Abacays Freight, 242 365-6247
Albury's Inner Island Freight, *Bullet Proof*, 242 366-3141
Guana Freight Services, 242 365-5190

• Freight and Passenger Service to/from Nassau
(weekly)

Abaco Shipping, 242 367-2091 (freight only)
Dean's Shipping, 242 367-2653

• Freight Service to/from United States of America

Abaco Shipping Co. (Port of Palm Beach, Riviera Beach, FL - two sailings each
week) 242 367-2091 or 561-840-9393
Betty K Agencies Ltd. (Miami, FL -weekly) 242 367-0593 or 305 635-4650
Dean's Shipping (Port of Palm Beach, Riviera Beach, FL - weekly), 242 367-2653 or
561-840-9393
G & G Shipping (Ft. Lauderdale - weekly) 954 920-9292
Tropical Shipping (Port of Palm Beach, Riviera Beach, FL - weekly) 242 367-3341,
or 561 844-8306

Freight Service to/from Haiti

about every two weeks from Port of Marsh Harbour

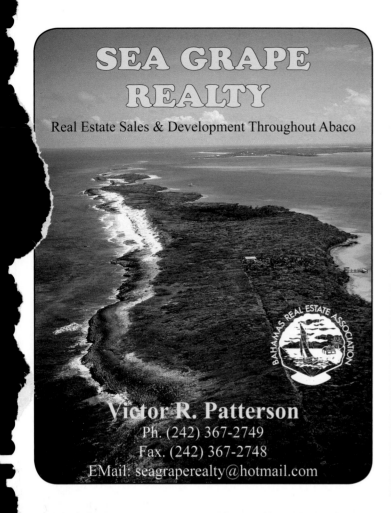

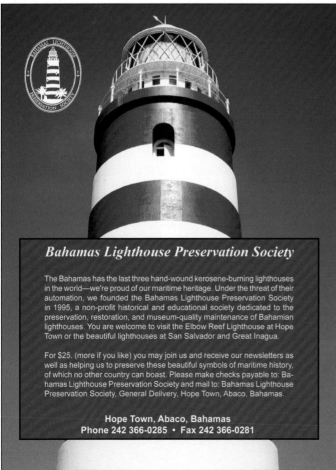
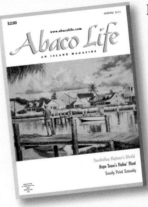

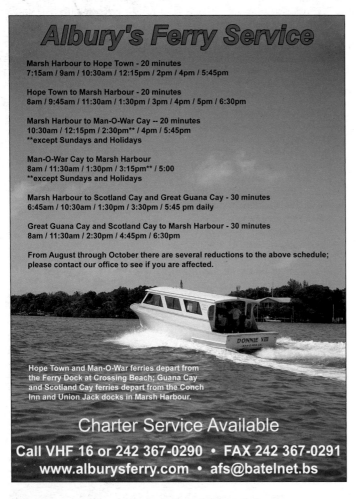
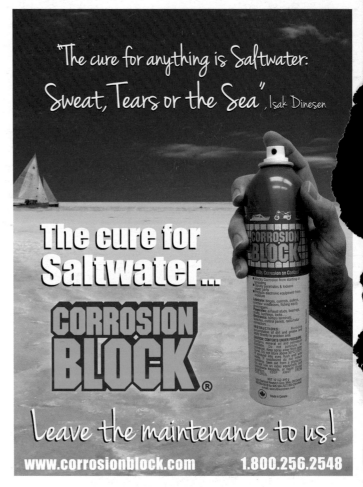

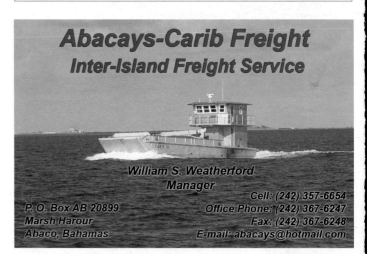